D1313984

An Atlas of International Migration

An Atlas of International Migration

Aaron Segal

Cartography by

Patricia M. Chalk and J. Gordon Shields
The Cartographic Section,
Department of Geography, University of Western Ontario

HANS ZELL PUBLISHERS
London • Melbourne • Munich • New Jersey • 1993

Hans Zell Publishers
is an imprint of Bowker-Saur Ltd, a division of Reed Reference Publishing.
60 Grosvenor Street, London W1X 9DA, United Kingdom.

British Library Cataloguing in Publication Data

Atlas of International Migration
    I. Segal, Aaron   II. Chalk, Patricia M.
    III. Shields, J. Gordon
    304.809

    ISBN 1-873836-30-9

Library of Congress Cataloging-in-Publication Data

Segal, Aaron.
    An atlas of international migration / Aaron Segal : cartography by
Patricia M. Chalk and J. Gordon Shields.
    243 p. 300 cm
        Includes bibliographical references, annotated bibliography, and index.
        Contents: Human migrations -- Voluntary migrations -- Involuntary
migrations -- World's major diasporas -- Global migration characteristics.
        ISBN 1-873836-30-9
        1. Emigration and immigration--Maps .   2. Forced migration--Maps.
    I. Chalk, Patricia M.   II. Shields, J. Gordon.   III. Title.
    G1046.E27S4   1993   <G&M>
    304.8'022'3--dc20   93-19502
                                                                       CIP
                                                                       MAP

Cover design by Robin Caira.
Cover illustration from World Cities Map-National Origin of Immigrants (p. 125).

Printed on acid-free paper.

Printed and bound in Great Britain
by Bookcraft Ltd., Midsomer Norton, nr Bath

CONTENTS

GLOBAL MIGRATION CHARACTERISTICS

REFERENCE SOURCES

ACKNOWLEDGEMENTS

This *Atlas* exists because of the generous assistance of many individuals and institutions. We are particularly indebted to our publisher, Hans Zell, for supporting the original concept, and providing insight, wisdom, and patience. The editors of *Migration World and the Center for Migration Studies* published a first version of several of the maps. Jon Hedderson, then at the University of Texas at El Paso, was instrumental in locating financial support.

Many individuals helped with information and advice. Imogen Forster provided extraordinary library services from her London base. Dominique Tabutin at Louvain University was most generous with African materials and demographic understanding. Christian Girault with the French National Council for Scientific Research in Paris shared his deep knowledge of the Caribbean. Alixa Naff at the Smithsonian Institution made available her outstanding work on Arab-Americans and Lebanese Studies. Kauro Okamoto in Tokyo sent his invaluable work on overseas students. Barbara Harrell-Bond and Felicity Ehrlich of the Refugee Studies Programme at Oxford were invaluable reference sources. Frank Sifuentes provided a gracious ethnic tour of Los Angeles. Elizabeth Cárdenas was our stalwart typesetter. Marian Goslinga provided extraordinary bibliographic services. Barbara Croucher did the proofreading and index. Ed Anderson and Kathy Morse helped with corrections.

Gathering and ordering global international migration data depended on help from many organizations. Our appreciation is extended to the UN Population Division, the UN High Commissioner for Refugees, the UN Development Program, the UN Fund for Population Activities, the World Bank, the US Bureau of the Census, the US Immigration and Naturalization Service, the Bureau of Refugee Programs, US Department of State, the US Committee for Refugees, Population Reference Bureau, Embassy of Sweden in the USA, Centre for Lebanese Studies, and the cities of Amsterdam, London and Toronto.

A special acknowledgement to Sally Segal whose own creative spirit nurtured this work.

We are solely responsible for the contents. It is our objective that this *Atlas* will further the understanding of the role of international migration in human affairs; past, present, and future.

BIOGRAPHICAL NOTES

Author Aaron Segal has conducted research, taught and practised journalism in Africa, the Caribbean, Europe, Latin America, and North America. Professor of Political Science at the University of Texas at El Paso, former editor of *Africa Report*, he is the author of eight books including the *Atlas*. His publications deal with international migration, science and technology policy, regional economic and political integration, and other topics. A Rhodes Scholar with graduate degrees from Oxford and Berkeley he has lectured in several languages at universities in four continents.

Maps and graphs were provided by the Cartographic Section, Department of Geography, Social Science Centre, University of Western Ontario, London, Ontario, Canada. Headed by geographer Patricia Chalk, the Cartographic Section has a reputation for excellence in the provision of a wide range of maps and related services. Design and production credit belongs to Patricia Chalk and Gordon Shields.

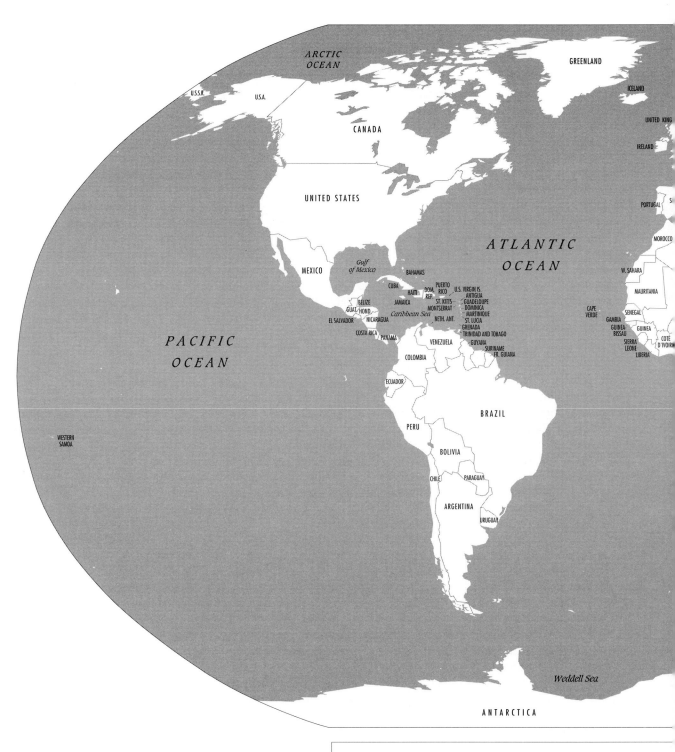

ARCTIC
OCEAN

GREENLAND

ICELAND

UNITED KING

IRELAND

U.S.S.R.

U.S.A.

CANADA

PORTUGAL

UNITED STATES

MOROCCO

ATLANTIC
OCEAN

W. SAHARA

MEXICO

Gulf
of Mexico

BAHAMAS

MAURITANIA

CUBA

PUERTO
RICO

U.S. VIRGIN IS.
ANTIGUA

DOM.
REP.

HAITI

ST. KITTS

GUADELOUPE
DOMINICA

CAPE
VERDE

SENEGAL

BELIZE

JAMAICA

MONTSERRAT

MARTINIQUE

GAMBIA

GUAT.

HOND.

Caribbean Sea

NETH. ANT.

ST. LUCIA

GUINEA-
BISSAU

GUINEA

EL SALVADOR

NICARAGUA

GRENADA

SIERRA

COTE
D'IVOIRE

PACIFIC
OCEAN

COSTA RICA

PANAMA

VENEZUELA

TRINIDAD AND TOBAGO

LEONE

GUYANA

LIBERIA

SURINAME

COLOMBIA

FR. GUIANA

ECUADOR

WESTERN
SAMOA

BRAZIL

PERU

BOLIVIA

CHILE

PARAGUAY

ARGENTINA

URUGUAY

Weddell Sea

ANTARCTICA

WORLD
POLITICAL MAP

SWEDEN
FINLAND
POLAND
CZECH
AUS. HUNG.
YUGO. ROM.
ALB. BUL. Black Sea
GREECE
MALTA
Mediterranean
Sea
CYPRUS SYRIA
LEB.
ISRAEL
JORDAN
LIBYA
EGYPT

SOVIET UNION

Caspian
Sea

TURKEY

IRAQ
KUWAIT
BAHRAIN
QATAR
U.A.E.

IRAN

AFGHANISTAN

PAKISTAN

MONGOLIA

CHINA

N. KOREA
S. KOREA

JAPAN

Sea
of
Okhotsk

Bering
Sea

PACIFIC
OCEAN

SAUDI
ARABIA

OMAN

YEMEN

CHAD
SUDAN

DJIBOUTI

CENTRAL
AFRICAN REPUBLIC

ETHIOPIA

CAMEROON
CONGO
ZAIRE
RWANDA
BURUNDI
UGANDA KENYA

SOMALIA

TANZANIA
MALAWI

ANGOLA

ZAMBIA

NAMIBIA
ZIMBABWE
BOTSWANA

MOZAMBIQUE

SWAZILAND
LESOTHO
SOUTH
AFRICA

COMOROS

MADAGASCAR

MAURITIUS
RÉUNION

INDIA

Arabian
Sea

NEPAL BHU.
BNGL.
BURMA

SRI LANKA

SEYCHELLES

Bay
of Bengal

LAOS

THAILAND
CAMB.
VIETNAM

TAIWAN

HONG KONG

PHILIPPINES

GUAM

MARSHALL IS.

BRUNEI
MALAYSIA
SINGAPORE BORNEO

INDIAN
OCEAN

I N D O N E S I A

PAPUA
NEW GUINEA

SOLOMON IS.

VANUATU

FIJI

NEW
CALEDONIA

AUSTRALIA

NEW
ZEALAND

5000 Kilometres

Robinson Projection

Scale at 0°N/ 0°E

1990

HUMAN MIGRATIONS

INTRODUCTION

This is the first comprehensive *Atlas of International Migration* in any language. Maps and data are global, historical and contemporary, presenting the story of human migrations from their origins in Eastern Africa to the exodus of refugees provoked by the Gulf War in 1991. International migration, whether voluntary immigration, slavery, indentured labour, legal or illegal migrant workers, is delineated. This *Atlas* is intended as a reference volume for anyone interested in international migration, whether in history or at present. It should also be of interest to international and national policymakers, media personnel, and all those concerned with migration matters.

The volume is organized to begin with historical migration from the origins of the human species to AD 1500 when the modern period begins. Voluntary international migration is detailed in a series of maps and texts from each region of the world from AD 1500-1990. This is followed by another series of maps and texts covering global and regional involuntary migration for the same period.

International Migration Policies

International migration produces diaspora communities in many parts of the world. Maps and brief text survey the major contemporary diasporas of the world: Armenians, Cambodians, Chinese, Cubans, Haitians, Jews, Kurds, Laotians, Lebanese, Palestinians, Vietnamese and West Indians.

The impacts of international migration are examined in maps, texts and charts on emigration and immigration policies, sending and receiving countries, international migrant workers, and the global flow of remittances. Four specific types of migration are further considered: global study abroad, freedom of movement in certain regions, international tourism, and the international brain-drain.

The future prospects for international migration are considered in two contexts. The first matches projections for world population and international migration. The second looks at the prognosis for conflicts stemming from future migration.

Voluntary vs. Involuntary Migration

The distinction made between voluntary and involuntary migration is both arbitrary and essential. Individual motives for migration are both multiple and mixed. Individuals can be simultaneously fleeing from perceived persecution and seeking economic or other opportunities in another country. Screening between 'economic migrants' and bonafide refugees/asylum seekers is a foreboding task. This volume deals in aggregates and works with official distinctions while offering its own comments. It records, for instance, Vietnamese boat people in Hong Kong as being classified as 'economic migrants' while textually explaining the circumstances of their departure. Historically we consider migration of convicts and slaves to be involuntary; migration of indentured labour voluntary.

The recognition of boundaries and frontiers is largely a modern phenomenon. The maps display migration movements over time and space while acknowledging that national borders often have a fictive character or are less than fully enforced.

International Migration Data Sources

The data for this *Atlas* come from the United Nations, World Bank, the United States and other national governments, and leading scholars. Where uniform data sets are available from single sources they have been used rather than mixing data from several sources. Data which are approximate or estimated are indicated as such in the text and keys to the maps. Lines on maps do not indicate actual migration routes.

Fully aware of the many gaps and lacunae in the data, the *Atlas* contains a brief annotation of the major works on international migration. This is intended to guide readers and students to the most useful global sources. This is followed by an extensive bibliography.

A world of over 180 independent nation-states poses formidable problems to students and map-makers of international migration. Some governments do not report data. Some data from migrant-sending countries contradict that reported by receiving countries. Some small countries have little data but reputedly high incidences of emigration. Data on illegal, return or circular migration, and students abroad are often problematical. The *Atlas* records data from sending and receiving countries, permits cross-checking, and organizes data over long periods.

The thesis of this *Atlas* is that international migration matters. It explains the peopling of our planet; the diffusion from our common ancestors in Eastern Africa of our species. It helps to account for the exchanges between genetic pools, the spread of epidemics, and the role of plagues in history. The study of international migration is essential to the understanding of multi-ethnic and multi-racial societies. Immigration has made us what we are whether in multi-ethnic Fiji, South Africa, Brazil or the United States of America.

International migration provides the keys to the clarification of the rise and consolidation of the world economy. There is the pivotal role of commercial slavery in the Americas and the Arab world. There is the story of indentured labour in the Caribbean, Southeast Asia, and the building of the railroads in North America.

The flow of labour continues to play its part in the world economy. Remittances from migrant workers were estimated at over $30 billion in 1988. Millions of persons around the world depend on money sent home by relatives abroad. Prospective immigrants seeking legal status commit investment funds in receiving countries. Temporary migrant workers, legal and illegal, from managers and technicians to unskilled labourers, make valuable economic contributions. Students abroad also make an economic contribution. Some remain abroad and become part of a global brain-drain.

International migration is also a significant causal factor in relations between nations, diplomacy, conflict and even wars. Governments insist that control over immigration is fundamental to sovereignty while reluctantly acknowledging that such control requires the cooperation of other governments. International organizations like the United Nations High Commissioner for Refugees have been created to establish and implement a protocol for millions of refugees.

Cross-cultural trade through outpost merchant communities played a key role in the evolution of the world economy. Diaspora communities such as the Chinese and the Lebanese continue the tradition of keeping alive far-flung trading networks.

Historically international migration also facilitated the exchange of innovations and technologies. The most valued and well-treated captured slaves were the craftsmen. Captured Chinese prisoners taught their Mongol captors how to make paper who then transferred their knowledge to the Arabs. Great Britain sought to preserve its being first in the industrial revolution by trying to prevent artisans from emigrating to the American Colonies. While modern communications have transformed the transfer of knowledge, migration still plays a role.

What then is the future of international migration as we approach the twenty-first century? Crudely estimated at totalling annual flows of 25-30 million and stocks of foreign-born estimated at 90 million persons in the early 1990s, is it likely to increase, to decrease, to stabilize, and in what forms? Five scenarios suggest what the future might look like although they are not mutually exclusive.

1. **A Global Talent Hunt.** Receiving countries compete for immigrants who possess scarce and valuable skills and/or financial assets. The global brain-drain becomes an institutionalized method for compensating for low fertility and eroding advanced educational standards in developed countries. Already in the United States a majority of engineering school faculty are immigrants and a near majority of new engineering Ph.Ds go to those foreign born.

2. **Global Freedom of Movement.** As disparities between national standards of living are reduced more countries are willing to permit freedom of movement, travel, residence, and even work to their neighbors. The European Community is the prototype possibly gradually extended to other areas of Europe. Conceivably 10-15 per cent of all human beings may by the twenty-first century, have freedom of movement within a determined geographic region.

3. **Global Temporary Labour.** This is a scenario in which countries with unskilled and semi-skilled labour shortages recruit temporary labour on a global basis. It is an extension of the practise of the oil-exporting states who are already bringing in workers from China, India, South Korea, Sri Lanka and other faraway countries. The belief is that the further a temporary worker is from his home, language, and culture the more likely he will return. It is possible that Japan, with its rapidly ageing population, may recruit temporary workers globally, including Brazilians of Japanese descent.

4. **Regional Preferences.** The alternative to global recruitment of migrant workers is to rely on formal and informal arrangements to import labour from neighbouring countries. This scenario would have the European Community recruiting primarily from Eastern Europe, Turkey, and North Africa; Japan from East Asia; and the United States and Canada from the Caribbean, Central America and Mexico. These regional preferences could be based on formal migrant worker agreements between governments as in the 1970s or even turning a blind eye to enforcement of immigration laws and deportations. The increasing proportion of those over age sixty-five in developed countries combines with fertility close to replacement levels to insure a demand for foreign workers in the service and other labour-intensive sectors. However, the problems associated with temporary migrant workers, especially those from neighbouring countries with greater incentives to stay, are well known. One proposal to avoid importing labour is to organize part-time, low-paid work for the elderly.

5. **International Conflict.** This scenario is based on the demand for emigration in many countries spontaneously exploding and generating a series of international conflicts. The 75,000 Vietnamese boat people seeking asylum in Hong Kong, Japan, Malaysia, the Philippines, Thailand, Singapore, and even South Korea provide a graphic example of just such a situation. These conflicts can take the form of refugees, illegal immigrants, expulsions of migrant workers, and denials of asylum. These conflicts can occur almost anywhere in the world and challenge the limited resources of the international refugee response. Demands to emigrate are already far in excess of permissions to immigrate. Rapidly growing national populations with a concentration of young persons in the age pyramid are the potential combustible for conflict.

The above are scenarios, not predictions. There are no orders of probability. The *Atlas* is designed to enable users to construct their own scenarios.

HUMAN MIGRATIONS:
THE ORIGINS OF MAN TO 1500 YEARS BEFORE THE PRESENT

It took approximately 150,000 years for the human species to migrate from its Eden-like primal habitat in Eastern Africa to all the major continents and islands except Antarctica with its frozen wastes. The peopling of planet earth was an incredible journey undertaken for the most part by small groups of hunter-gatherers on foot encumbered by women and children. Domestication of animals useful for human transport-camels, horses, did not occur until 8,000-10,000 years ago and then only in limited regions. Walking, resting, walking, stopping to hunt, was the way of life for most members of our species.

Migration and Climate

The reasons for incessant migration were primarily in response to traumatic climactic changes. Ice ages, glaciation, desertification, as well as winds and storms made it imperative for humans to move in search of game, shelter and warmth. There was extensive adaptation for difficult climates as evidenced by fashioned tools and uses of animal skins but there was also persistent movement.

Domestication of livestock and rudimentary agriculture combined with hunting and gathering in a few Middle Eastern sites as late as 8,000-10,000 years ago making sedentary village life possible. Irrigation in Central Asia and the Nile and Tigris-Euphrates river valleys began 4500-5000 years ago, thus initiating urban civilizations.

Migration Barriers

Boundaries, territoriality, and tribal and clan rivalries were minor migration factors during this period. Human population density was extremely low, as necessitated by hunter-gatherer societies. Infant mortality, inability to store large quantities of food, and epidemic diseases kept population growth low. Large-scale political authorities did not appear in China, India, Persia, Egypt and elsewhere until several thousand years ago. Migration involved no passports, visas, travel documents and in most instances little use of weapons, to fend off rivals. The peopling of planet earth was a story of indomitable courage, persistence, and risk-taking rather than one of aggression, conquest, and war. It was only after the human species had spread thoughout the earth that borders and defenses appeared.

Instead the barriers to migration were oceans rather than hostile humans. An extended Ice Age made it possible for the Bering Strait to be crossed over ice floes and land and for humans to enter the Americas. The passages from mainland Southeast Asia first to the Indonesian archipelago, and then on to New Guinea, the continent of Australia, New Zealand and the Pacific Islands required thousands of years and the mastery of techniques in navigation and canoe-building. Elsewhere until the modern era only 500 years ago the oceans were formidable barriers to migration, much more effective than political controls.

African Origins

The story began nearly two million years ago in the dry, open plains of Eastern Africa. It is here that Homus Erectus learned to make fire, and possibly in response to falling world temperatures to follow other mammals to Europe and Asia.

Homo Sapiens, our direct ancestors, appeared about 200,000 years ago and within 100,000 years had migrated to most parts of Africa. They were attracted by the temperate climates of Southern Africa and by a brief Saharan interval of abundant game and water. They were also drawn into the Nile Valley and a corridor to the Middle East. Possibly by 100,000 years ago Neanderthal peoples were established in Europe and Western Asia. However, they became extinct, as did Homus Erectus earlier, handicapped perhaps by not having fully developed speech.

Early Diffusions

Archaeological research at the Middle Eastern sites of Qafzeh and Skhul disagrees as to whether these are late Neanderthal sites, 50,000 years ago, or Homo Sapien migrants from Africa. Since there is no documented record of seafaring in the Mediterranean prior to 8,000 years ago the Middle East was almost certainly first peopled by land migrants.

Although there are proponents of an independent human evolution, possibly in China 40,000 years ago, the dominant view is that Asia was peopled by waves of migrants originating in Africa. 20,000 years ago dry land joined the Southeast Asian mainland to Sumatra, Borneo, the Philippines and Malaya. Mainland Southeast Asia may have been colonized about 75,000 years ago.

The dramatic first human seafaring across ocean waters took place between Southeast Asia and New Guinea and Australia. Dates and technologies are controversial but one estimate places this migration as at least 40,000 years ago.

A prolonged Ice Age in Europe from 30,000 to 10,000 years ago prompted the remarkable adaptation of the Cro-Magnons. Relying on reindeer hunting and reindeer derived tools, the Cro-Magnon spread throughout Europe from about 40,000 years ago. One of their legacies is the cave paintings at Lascaux and Altamira in France and Spain.

After the extinction of the Neanderthals it was not until 36,000 years ago that the Central Russian Plains were re-colonized. The settlers were Homo Sapiens, probably moving east from Central Europe after mastering techniques for hunting and slaughtering mammoth and bison.

There is evidence for the presence of Homus Erectus in China between 700,000 and 200,000 years ago but not of its evolution. Instead migrant Homo Sapiens' sites date from 36,000 to 40,000 years ago with the first possible appearance of seafarers from mainland China in Japan about 30,000 years ago. Northeast Asia and Siberia were first settled 14,000-12,000 years ago by peoples whose dental features (sundadonts) match those of the first migrants to the Americas.

The Americas

An ice-free shelf mostly joined Alaska and the Siberias. Debate rages as to when the first humans traversed that shelf and began to move south across the Americas. While archaeologists dispute dates of crossing and sites in North and South America the most widely held view is that the Americas were uninhabited until 15,000 years ago. Discoveries in Chile, Venezuela, Brazil and the USA Western plains argue for an earlier crossing from Siberia and arrivals in South America. The opponents maintain that the 11,000-11,500 years ago sites of the Clovis big-game hunting peoples in the American West represent the oldest verified human presence.

Our post-glacial age, known as the halocene, began about 12,000 years ago. It has made possible the transfer of plants and cultigens and the organization of complex societies 6,000-8,000 years ago in different parts of the world (Indus Valley, Southeast Asia, Europe, Central America). It was preceded 8,000-10,000 years ago in parts of the Middle East by the domestication of livestock and agriculture although hunting and gathering continued alongside for extended periods.

Polynesian Seafarers

Long-distance seafaring began in island Melanesia about 6,000 years ago and was then transferred to Polynesia. South Pacific sailors reached Easter Island 1500 years ago, Hawaii 1400 years ago, and New Zealand between 1000 and 800 years ago.

Current Research

The story of how our species, Homo Sapiens, spread over most of the planet from our origins in Eastern Africa is continuously being researched, revised, and debated. The broad outlines are widely accepted but the specifics are subject to new discoveries and interpretations. New technologies are improving on radio-carbon dating to establish chronologies. New finds are constantly adding information. Yet the fundamental role of migration is established from a single region of Africa. All our ancestors in a very real sense are Africans.

Source: Brian M. Fagan, *The Journey From Eden, The Peopling of Our World,* London: Thames and Hudson, 1990.

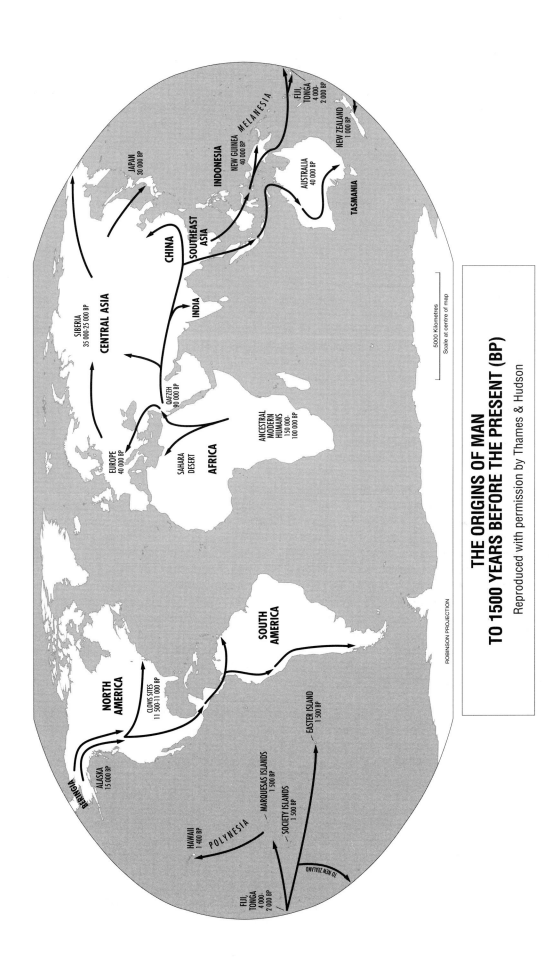

**THE ORIGINS OF MAN
TO 1500 YEARS BEFORE THE PRESENT (BP)**

Reproduced with permission by Thames & Hudson

ROBINSON PROJECTION

5000 Kilometres

Scale at centre of map

SIBERIA
35 000-25 000 BP

CENTRAL ASIA

JAPAN
30 000 BP

CHINA

**SOUTHEAST
ASIA**

INDONESIA

NEW GUINEA
40 000 BP

MELANESIA

FIJI,
TONGA
4 000-
2 000 BP

AUSTRALIA
40 000 BP

NEW ZEALAND
1 000 BP

TASMANIA

INDIA

QAFZEH
90 000 BP

EUROPE
40 000 BP

SAHARA
DESERT

AFRICA

ANCESTRAL
MODERN
HUMANS
150 000-
100 000 BP

**NORTH
AMERICA**

CLOVIS SITES
11 500-11 000 BP

BERINGIA

ALASKA
15 000 BP

**SOUTH
AMERICA**

EASTER ISLAND
1 500 BP

HAWAII
1 400 BP

POLYNESIA

MARQUESAS ISLANDS
1 500 BP

SOCIETY ISLANDS
1 500 BP

FIJI,
TONGA
4 000-
2 000 BP

TO NEW ZEALAND

MAJOR MIGRATIONS: 2000 BC - AD 1500

The rise of urban, agriculturally-based civilizations about 5000 years ago changed the very nature of migration. While small bands of hunter-gatherers and agriculturalists continued to march steadily towards more arable land and greener pastures, for the first time organized societies were capable of moving thousands of people, whether for purposes of war or settlement. Instead of a few miles a day the introduction of horses, donkeys, and in a few regions camels and elephants greatly extended human mobility. Travel over water remained limited by the exigencies of winds and sail and mostly hugged to shorelines, except for the extraordinary ocean voyages of the Polynesians.

State-Organized Migrations

Spontaneous migration continued but was increasingly superseded by new state-organized forms. The dominant motive was conquest, pillage, and tribute. Seldom did these massed armies and their camp-followers lead to permanent settlement. Thus the Mongol Empire swept out of Central Asian steppes from AD 1100-1400 to wreak destruction on what is today Iran, Iraq, Central Russia and parts of China and India. Yet it left behind no new cities or towns, no colonization, and a legacy almost entirely of destruction. Other historic invasions such as those of the Vandals and other Northern Tribes against the dying Roman Empire AD 400-650 were also bereft of migration effects. Even the seven Crusades (1096-1274) to retake the Holy Lands left far more destruction and disorder in their wake than lasting migrations.

Religious Conversions

Conquest in the name of religious conversion was far more conducive to migration. Each of the worlds' universal religions (Buddhism, Christianity, Judaism, Islam and Hinduism) sent missionaries, preached to the unconverted, and established communities of new and old converted. Migration, conversion, intermarriage and settlement became a closely related process.

The extraordinary expansion of Islam was marked by this combination of conquest, conversion, some religious accommodation with non-believers, migration, intermarriage and settlement. It ceased to be effective for the Arabs by about AD 1280 but using a more subtle administrative approach it enabled the Islamicized Ottoman Turks to build a long-lasting Empire.

Migration and Slavery

Conquest also created commercial slavery as prisoners of war could be bought and sold and transported over long distances. Already Athens in the fifth century BC was depopulating its captured cities, selling their captives as slaves, and replacing them with Greek colonists. A fortunate few Greek slaves were acquired by Roman families as tutors for their households. However, throughout the ancient world captured slaves were transported to the mines, to public works projects, and to agricultural labour. Commercial slavery was a big business among the Romans, Egyptians, Arabs and others capable of moving thousands of prisoners of war to distant centres.

Forced migration was not confined to slaves. The Hebrews were expelled from Jerusalem at the time of the Babylonian conquest in 586 BC and were later to experience a series of expulsions. Perhaps the most traumatic was that from Spain in 1492 when the Catholic rulers, under pressure from the Inquisition, expelled 200,000 Jews and Muslims.

Migration Seeking Sanctuary

One alternative for heretical religious communities in periods of religious intolerance and persecution was to seek a safe haven or sanctuary. The Jewish Diaspora between 600 BC and AD 1500 spread over much of the Middle East and Europe in search of safety. Muslim Shiite communities after the fall of the Fatimid Empire in Egypt (969-1171) sought refuge in predominantly Shiite Persia, while the heretical Druze created their stronghold in the Lebanese Shouf mountains. The Ismaili sect first found a sanctuary in thirteenth century Persia and then in the sixteenth century joined brethren in Bombay.

Religious interest could also produce intellectual migrations. During the AD fourth century monks from India brought Buddhism to China. One response was a flow of Chinese Buddhist scholars to India. Similarly the Mongol Empire hosted scholars and travelers from Christian Europe in what was an extraordinarily cosmopolitan capital. The Islamic world was noted for its great intellectual travelers who were welcomed in spite of political rivalries.

What was strikingly new was colonization; the deliberate, state-organized movement of peoples for political purposes. The Greek city-states were probably the first to practise it beginning in the ninth century BC. Established cities provided funds, logistics, and prospective settlers. The colonists were sources of trade, cultural exchange, and security. The Roman Republic also colonized to extend its influence throughout Italy and its environs. At first it promised to enfranchise local people as citizens of Rome and to free slaves it conquered. Soon though it turned to administrative controls to extract tributes and taxes. The Chinese also resorted to colonization as invaders depopulated the Northwest. Settlers were sent deep into Southern China where there was unused arable land. Colonization often proved cost-effective as it enabled the expansion of political control, taxes and trade without providing military garrisons.

Early Immigration Policies

Alongside colonization there were the first immigration policies. Rome under the Empire and the Republic used the granting of citizenship and other privileges to cultivate loyalty from non-Romans. It was a device to be later practised by the Ottoman Empire and others. Religious minorities like the Jews avidly sought citizenship under whatever authority they lived under as a means of protection.

Ancient Egypt may have been the first state to have a policy of selective immigration. A nineteenth century BC document refers to an Egyptian border post in Nubia turning back Bedouin fleeing a famine. A system of fortresses and archers prevented unauthorized Nubians from going downstream. However, the Sinai border posts were open at various times to Bedouin and to the Hebrews.

Permanent Migration Effects

Our map depicts major migrations during this period which have left a permanent mark on history. It is often not possible to know when these migrations began and ended. Estimates of population involved are seldom available or reliable. However, the numbers are likely to be in the thousands and in some instances hundreds of thousands. The distances traveled, except for the Polynesians, were in the hundreds of miles but they required prodigies of organization benefiting from the invention of alphabets and writing. A few migrations (Aryans, Ottomans, Normans) resulted in the creation of new empires while others contributed to over-extend Imperial rule (Aztecs, Romans).

Other Migrations

Many other migrations occurred during this period. Bantu-speakers moved across Central Africa through Southern Africa in a centuries-long march of warriors, peasants, and herdsmen. First the Arawak and then the Carib tribesmen paddled island by island north from Lake Orinoco to populate the Caribbean Islands. The Assyrians followed the Sumerians and other peoples into the Tigris-Euphrates but were unable to assimilate the indigenous inhabitants. Instead it oppressed them and paid the price in frequent revolts. One of the earliest seafaring migrant peoples were the Philistines who sired the sea-going Phoenicians and Carthaginians only to succumb to Rome.

European Invaders

Europe played host to waves of invaders, some of whom became migrants. The Magyars established themselves in Hungary in the AD eighth century; the Bulgarians did the same a century later. The Berbers, under the influence of Islam, swept out of the Rif Mountains of Morocco in AD 1200 to seize the Arab Caliphate of Cordoba, the glory of the Islamic world. But they lost it 250 years later to the advancing armies of Christian Spain.

Migration was one of the many factors that shaped history over this extended period of time. It was an important instrument of state formation and state expansion. It brought slavery into the embryonic world economy-centered on the Mediterranean. It proved a powerful vehicle for the spread of ideas and technological innovations, especially religious beliefs. Men no longer lived isolated in their own societies. Whether through slaves, captured artisans, raiding armies, missionaries or merchant-travelers, the outside world was beginning to implode.

MAJOR MIGRATIONS
Explanation
(2000 BC to AD 1500)

(Dates are approximate estimates. Geographic names are given in comtemporary rather than earlier designations; e.g. Iraq rather than Mesopotamia.)

Major Migrations with Approximate Dates and Destinations

1. Arabs: AD 640-1250 Mecca and Medina to Syria, Iraq, Palestine, Egypt, North Africa, Iran, Cyprus and Spain. Expansion through conquest, religious conversion, intermarriage, settlement, and slavery.

2. Aryans: 2000-1700 BC Invaders from Northwest use conquest, slavery and settlement to bring Indo-European languages (Sanskrit), slavery and caste system to Northern India.

3. Aztecs: Conquest and migration south from Northern Mexico. Mexico City founded in AD 1325; captured by Cortes in 1519.

4. Central Asian Muslims: AD 1200-1500; 1530-1700 (Mughal Empire). Invasions establish Sultanates in Northern India (Bahmani, Bengal). Followed later by Mughal Empire of Central Asian Turkish origins. Reliance on conquest, migration, settlement, religious conversion to Islam and religious accommodation with Hindu aristocrats.

5. Chinese: AD 300-900 Planned migrations and colonization (Hunan, Kiangsi, Kwangtung) in response to depopulation of Northwest by invaders. Large-scale emigration abroad from Southeastern China begins in sixteenth century.

6. Greeks: 950 B.C. to 800 BC Colonies founded by Greek city-states throughout the Eastern Mediterranean and in Italy. Athens in fifth century BC conquers towns, sells off inhabitants as slaves, and colonizes. Colonies as vehicles for culture and trade.

7. Hausa: AD 1300-1800 Islamicized Africans migrate from Western Sudan to establish through conquest, religious conversion, and slavery Sultanates in what is now Northern Nigeria and Lake Chad area.

8. Incas: AD 1300-1533 The last of several thousand years of Andean civilizations. Migrations, settlements and conquest governed by the capital at Cuzco captured by Pizzaro in 1530.

9. Mayas: AD 600-1200 Migration north from present Honduras, Guatemala, and Belize to Yucatan through conquest by city-states, slavery, and intermarriage. Decline due to civil wars; other factors.

10. Normans: AD 900-1100 A branch of the Viking invaders from Scandinavia. Conquer and settle Normandy in present Northwest France and then invade England in 1066. Conquest, settlement, intermarriage.

11. Ottoman Turks: One of several Central Asian tribes, the Ottomans migrate and settle Anatolia AD 100-1300 Conquest, migration, settlement, and religious conversion to Islam combine with administration by religious communities to extend the Empire to the Balkans, Egypt, Syria, North Africa, Cyprus and Hungary. Constantinople captured in 1453; becomes Istanbul.

12. Polynesian: Polynesian and Melanesian groups migrate in long-distance voyages in outrigger canoes to settle New Zealand AD 1000; Hawaii AD 1400. Easter Island AD 1500 and other South Pacific settlements. Distantly related voyagers, possibly from Indonesia, first settle the island of Madagascar off the African coast in the AD fifth century, introducing yams and bananas.

13. Romans: 140 BC to AD 640 Initial establishment of colonies throughout Italy, the Eastern Mediterranean and North Africa by enfranchising locals and slaves as Roman citizens. Colonies become provinces by 75 BC; subject to Roman taxes and tributes. Commercial slavery a big business under the Empire.

14. Slavs: Starting from a homeland stretching north of the Carpathian mountains from the Elbe to the Vistula rivers the Slav-speaking tribes migrated in three directions: AD 600-900 a) Southern Slavs invaded the Balkans, established a Christian Bulgarian Kingdom, and were then conquered by the Ottomans. b) Western Slavs migrated to present Bohemia and Poland. c) Eastern Slavs settle Central Russia and trade with the Vikings.

15. Swahilis: AD 1100-1400 Migrations by sea from Oman, Bahrain, and Persia and by land from inland Africa establish Indian Ocean trading ports on the East African coast: Mombasa, Malindi, Kilwa, Mogadishu. These serve as the basis for commercial slavery.

Sources: John A. Garraty, Peter Gay (eds.) *The Columbia History of the World,* New York: Harper and Row, 1985
Historical Atlas of the World, New York: Barnes and Noble, 1981.

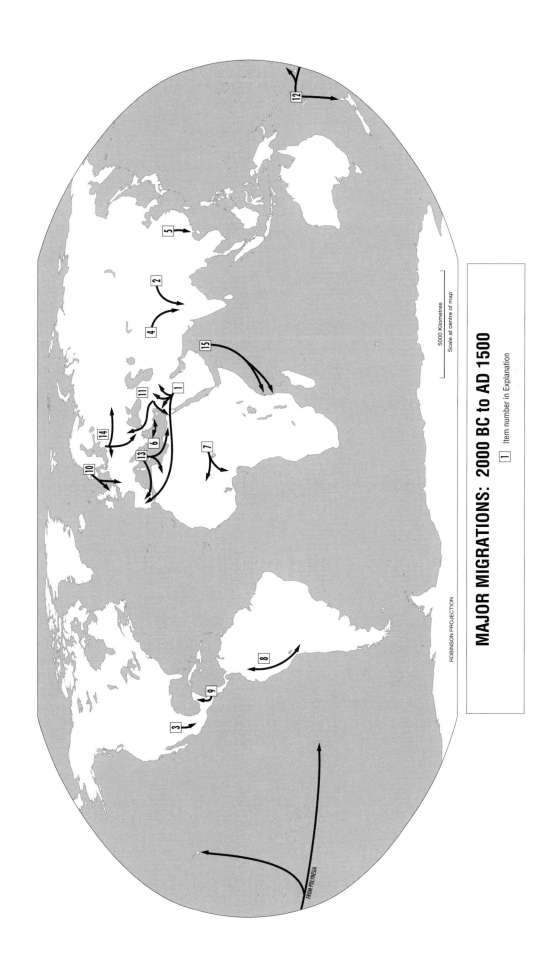

ROBINSON PROJECTION

5000 Kilometres

Scale at centre of map

MAJOR MIGRATIONS: 2000 BC to AD 1500

1 Item number in Explanation

FROM POLYNESIA

VOLUNTARY MIGRATIONS

GLOBAL VOLUNTARY MIGRATIONS
Explanation
(1500-1814)

Voluntary / Involuntary

The distinction between voluntary and involuntary international migration cannot be hard and fast given the multiple factors involved in migration decisions. The emphasis is on absence of physical coercion while recognizing that many other forms of coercion exist. No distinction is made between emigrants who are regarded in receiving societies as illegal or legal except for the problems in counting the illegals. Even harder to count are those who return to the sending society or recycle or those who re-emigrate to third countries.

Because national boundaries are subject to frequent change, international migration is defined as a migration from one political jurisdiction to another, even within an empire, e.g., Indians from British India to Fiji. Similarly national numbers of emigrants are disaggregated when possible to indicate their internal ethnic/racial composition, e.g. Jews as a percentage of Russian emigrants.

Indentured labourers are classified as voluntary although often they were subject to various forms of coercion, e.g. Chinese to Cuba.

Voluntary Migration Movements Shown on the Map
Sending Countries

1. Spain to Caribbean, Central and South America and Mexico, 437,000 for 1506-1650.
2. Portugal to Brazil, 70,000 by 1650.
3. United Kingdom, including Ireland and Scotland to North America, 1.0 million by 1815.
4. United Kingdom to Caribbean, 100,000 with extensive re-emigration to North America and return to England.
5. France to Quebec, 10,000 mostly arrive before 1700.
6. Netherlands to settlements in New York, Capetown, and Indonesia.
7. Chinese to Taiwan (Formosa), colonization begins in seventeenth century.
8. Inter-African, there were four major migration movements leading to state formation: a) Sudan to West African Savannah; b) Nilotics to East Africa; c) Sotho-Tswana-Nguni within Southern Africa; d) Lunda and Luba to Central Africa.

Sail and Colonial Settlement

Improvements in navigation, shipbuilding, cartography and provisions made mass migration across oceans possible. The principal routes were Western Europe to North, South, and Central America and the Caribbean. Much emigration occurred in response to colonial settlement. Although reliable numbers are scarce, the total number of voluntary migrants was substantially less than the slaves, indentured laborers, convicts, and refugees. Few figures for return or re-emigration exist.

Sources: C. McEvedy and R. Jones, *Atlas of World Population History*, New York: Penguin, 1978.
M. Mörner, *Adventures and Proletarians, The Story of Migrants in Latin America*, Pittsburgh: University of Pittsburgh Press, 1985.

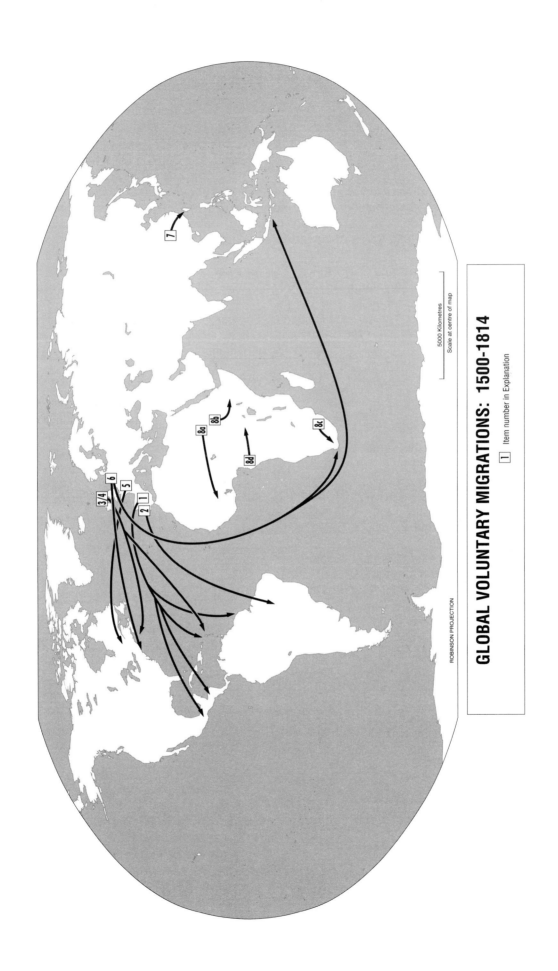

ROBINSON PROJECTION

GLOBAL VOLUNTARY MIGRATIONS: 1500-1814

5000 Kilometres
Scale at centre of map

1 Item number in Explanation

GLOBAL VOLUNTARY MIGRATIONS
Explanation
(1815-1914)

Voluntary Migration Movements Shown on the Map
Sending Countries

1. Japan to United States including Hawaii, 150,000; Japan to Peru, emigration scheme fails 1898-1907; Japan to Brazil, begins in 1908; Japan to Asia 6 million.
2. China to Southeast Asia, 12.0 million. Includes Taiwan (1.3 million); Indo-China (300,000); Singapore (begins in 1825), Malaya, Burma, Indonesia, Thailand and United States (550,000). Indentured labor to Cuba, Guyana, Trinidad, Peru, South Africa (1902-1910); 100,000 repatriated.
3. India to South Asia and East and South Africa, 1.5 million. Includes Fiji (60,000), South Africa, East Africa, Ceylon (Sri Lanka), Mauritius and Burma. Indentured labor to Guyana, Trinidad and Réunion. Estimated 4.25 million to Malaya 1786-1957: two-thirds return.
4. Poland (not independent until 1920). Emigrants from Polish areas in Austro-Hungarian and Russian Empires including Jews and Ukrainians to Canada and United States, 2.6 million; Germany, 600,000; Argentina and Brazil, 200,000.
5. Italy to United States and Canada, 5.0 million; Argentina, 2.4 million; Brazil, 1.3 million; Austria, Switzerland and Germany.
6. United Kingdom (including 4.1 million from Ireland) to United States, 11.0 million; Canada, 2.55 million; Australia and New Zealand, 2.0 million; South Africa, 850,000.
7. Mexico to United States and Canada, 300,000.
8. Inter-African, neighboring territories to South Africa after 1869 discovery of diamonds and gold in 1886.
9. Germany to United States and Canada, 5.0 million; Argentina and Brazil, 300,000.
10. Portugal to Brazil, 1.4 million.
11. Spain to Argentina, 1.2 million; Brazil, 600,000; Cuba, 200,000; Uruguay and North Africa.
12. France to Algeria, 650,000; Morocco, 200,000; Tunisia, 200,000; United States, 500,000.
13. Scandinavia to United States and Canada, 2.7 million. Includes Sweden (1.25 million), Norway (850,000), Denmark (350,000), Finland (250,000). Estimated high return migration rates.
14. Russia to Siberia, 6.0 million between 1880-1914 after railway completion; Caucasus and Central Asia, 4.0 million; United States and Canada, 2.2 million primarily Poles, Jews and Ukrainians from Western-Russia; Argentina and Brazil, 300,000.
15. Austro-Hungarian Empire to United States and Canada, 3.2 million; Germany, France, Argentina, Brazil, Chile, 5.2 million. Includes Czechs (2.0 million), Croats (500,000), Hungarians (1.0 million), Slovenes (400,000), Serbs, Poles, Jews and others. Estimated 2.0 million Jews from all destinations to North America.

Steamships and European Exodus

This was the maximum period of voluntary international migration in recorded history. It was characterized by five streams of intercontinental migration: 1) about 60 million persons from Europe and elsewhere went to the Americas, Oceania, and South and East Africa between 1815 and 1914; 2) an estimated 10 million persons voluntarily migrated from Russia to Siberia and Central Asia; 3) one million persons migrated from Southern Europe to North Africa; 4) about 12 million Chinese and 6 million Japanese left their homelands for Eastern and Southern Asia; 5) 1.5 million persons emigrated from India to Southeastern Asia and South and East Africa. These figures do not include estimates of return or re-emigration.

Sources: M. Gilbert, *Atlas of Russian History*, New York: Dorset, 1985.

R. Hughes, *The Fatal Shore, The Epic of Australia's Founding*, New York: Knopf, 1986.

CNRS, *Les Migrations Internationales De La Fin Du XVIII Siècle á Nos Jours*, Paris: CNRS, 1980.

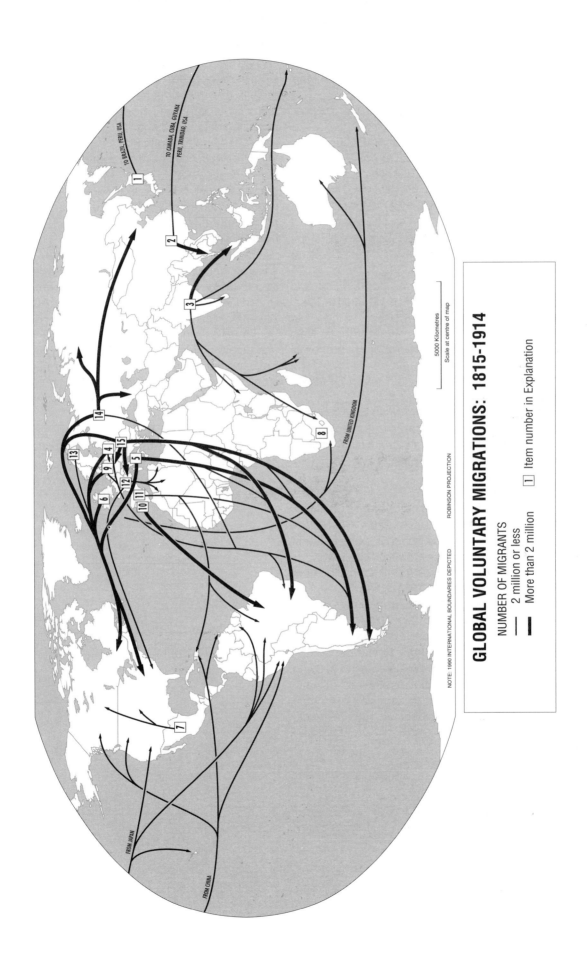

GLOBAL VOLUNTARY MIGRATIONS: 1815-1914

NOTE: 1990 INTERNATIONAL BOUNDARIES DEPICTED   ROBINSON PROJECTION

5000 Kilometres

Scale at centre of map

NUMBER OF MIGRANTS

— 2 million or less

— More than 2 million

1 Item number in Explanation

TO BRAZIL, PERU, USA

TO CANADA, CUBA, GUYANA
PERU, TRINIDAD, USA

FROM UNITED KINGDOM

FROM JAPAN

FROM CHINA

GLOBAL VOLUNTARY MIGRATIONS
Explanation
(1919-1939)

Voluntary Migration Movements Shown on the Map
Sending Countries

1. Japan to Brazil, 200,000; Manchuria, 819,000; China, 200,000.
2. China to French Indochina (Vietnam), 3.0 million; Thailand, 3.0 million; Malaya, 2.3 million; Indonesia, 1.4 million (includes Chinese born abroad).
3. India to Burma, East Africa, Fiji, Malaya, Mauritius, South Africa and Ceylon (Sri Lanka), estimated at 1.5 million by 1940 including persons born abroad.
4. Poland to United States, Canada, France, Argentina and Brazil, estimated net migration 1919-1937 of 1.5 million including Jews.
5. Italy to Argentina, Brazil, Libya, North Africa and United States. Mussolini restricts emigration in 1927. Net return emigration.
6. United Kingdom to Canada, South Africa, New Zealand and United States. Net return migration of 500,000 for the period.
7. Mexico to the United States. Net return migration after repatriations of the 1930s.
8. Inter-African, migrant labour movements occur between French colonies and between British colonies on a small scale. South Africa recruits migrant mine labor from neighbouring territories.

Receiving Countries

9. Australia, immigration declines from 313,000 from 1921-1930 to 33,200 from 1931-1940.
10. Brazil, immigration declines from 65,000 per year in 1920-1930 to 26,000 per year from 1931-1940.
11. Canada, immigration declines from 1.23 million from 1920-1930 to 158,000 from 1931-1940.
12. Argentina, immigration declines from 900,000 from 1921-1930 to 300,000 from 1931-1940.
13. United States, immigration declines from 1.9 million from 1921-1930 to 528,000 from 1931-1940.
14. France, 3.7 million foreigners registered in 1926 and 2.2 million in 1936 plus 500,000 naturalized citizens.
15. North Africa (Algeria, Morocco, Tunisia), estimated 1.5 million Europeans resident in 1939 (French, Italians, Spaniards).

Depression, Contraction, Repatriation

In spite of improvements in commercial aviation, ocean shipping, and ground transport international voluntary migration decreased sharply between World Wars I and II. In 1924 the United States adopted a restrictive immigration policy and other countries followed suit. The Great Depression of the 1930s resulted in a drastic decline in world trade, mass unemployment in many countries, and the forced/voluntary repatriation of millions of migrants (Mexicans from the United States, Italians from Argentina, etc.)

During this period the patterns of pre-World War I emigration continued, but at much lower levels as receiving countries closed their doors. Europeans emigrated to the United States, Canada, South Africa, Australia, New Zealand, Argentina and Brazil; Chinese and Japanese to Southeast Asia, and Indians went to other British colonies. The rise to power of the Nazis in 1932 provoked a new wave of European migrants, mostly refugees. Most receiving countries, including Palestine, a British mandate since 1919, held to their restrictive policies.

Sources: M. Reinhard, A. Armengaud and J. Dupaquier, *Histoire Generale de la Population Mondiale*, 3rd ed., Paris: CNED, 1968.
CNRS, *Les Migrations Internationales De La Fin Du XVIII Siècle á Nos Jours*, Paris: CNRS, 1980.

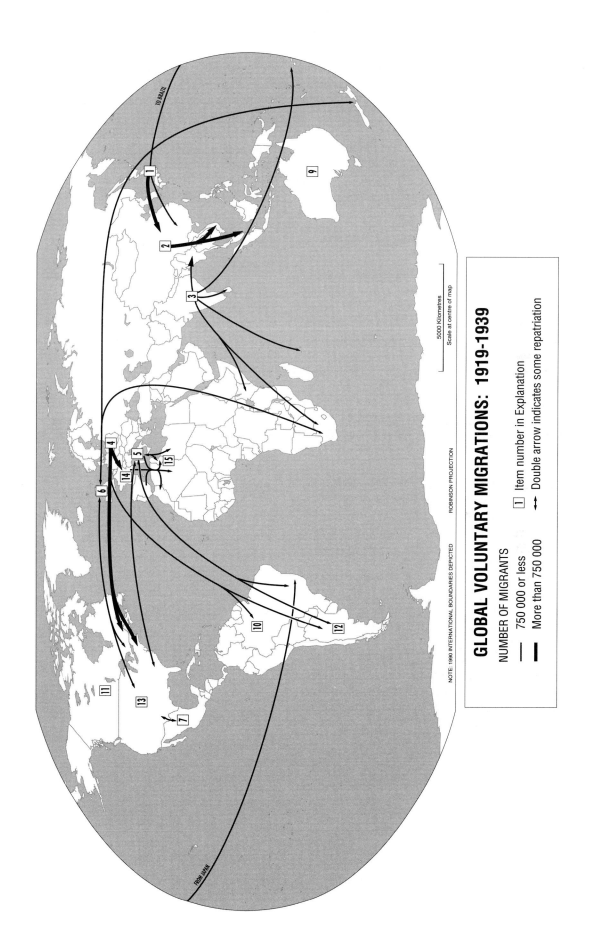

GLOBAL VOLUNTARY MIGRATIONS: 1919-1939

NOTE: 1990 INTERNATIONAL BOUNDARIES DEPICTED   ROBINSON PROJECTION

5000 Kilometres

Scale at centre of map

NUMBER OF MIGRANTS

— 750 000 or less

— More than 750 000

1 Item number in Explanation

↔ Double arrow indicates some repatriation

TO BRAZIL

FROM JAPAN

GLOBAL VOLUNTARY MIGRATIONS
Explanation
(1945-1980)

Voluntary Migration Movements Shown on the Map
Sending Countries

1. Mexico to United States, 4.5 million. Estimate includes legal and illegal emigrants and 1942-1964 *bracero* program of legal temporary workers.
2. Central America to United States, 1.0 million. Estimate includes legal and illegal immigrants from Guatemala, El Salvador, Honduras, Costa Rica, Nicaragua, Panama and Belize.
3. Caribbean to United States, 3 million (includes 1 million Puerto Ricans who are US citizens); Dominican Republic to United States, 800,000; Haiti to United States, 600,000; West Indies (Jamaica, Trinidad, Guyana, Barbados and smaller islands) to United States, 600,000. West Indies to Canada, 200,000; Haiti to Canada, 100,000. West Indies to United Kingdom prior to 1962 immigration act, 300,000. Suriname to Netherlands, 150,000. French Antilles to France, 200,000 (as French citizens).
4. Colombia to Venezuela, 900,000; United States, 400,000.
5. Uruguay to Argentina, 500,000. Does not include Bolivia, Chile and Paraguay to Argentina.
6. Ireland to United Kingdom, United States, Canada and Australia. Does not include Northern Ireland emigration.
7. Yugoslavia to Europe, 900,000. Includes to West Germany, Austria, France, Switzerland and Sweden.
8. Poland to Western Europe, 100,000 per year since 1981. Includes to West Germany and France.
9. Turkey to Western Europe, 1.9 million. Includes to West Germany and Belgium.
10. North Africa to Western Europe, 1.1 million. Includes Algeria to France, Morocco to France and Spain, Tunisia to France and Italy.
11. Jordan to Saudi Arabia, Kuwait and Persian Gulf states 500,000.
12. West Africa to Western Europe, 300,000.
13. West Africa to Côte d'Ivoire, 1 million, principally from Burkina Faso (ex-Upper Volta) and Guinea.
14. West Africa to Nigeria, 2.0 million, principally from Ghana, Niger, subject to two official expulsions since 1970.
15. Southern Africa to South Africa, 1.5 million, principally from Botswana, Lesotho, Swaziland and Mozambique. Includes recruited mineworkers and others.
16. India to United Kingdom prior to 1962 (includes Pakistanis), 600,000; United States and Canada, 400,000; Persian Gulf, 300,000.
17. Philippines to United States, 600,000; Persian Gulf and Saudi Arabia, 800,000 (migrant workers).

Jets, Guestworkers, Brain Drain

This period is characterized by the rapid movement of labour in response to perceived economic opportunities. Much of the movement is from developing to developed countries and includes so-called "guestworkers", brain-drains, and illegal immigrants. The major post-1945 receiving societies are the United States, Canada, Australia, the European Community (EC), Israel for Jews, Sweden, Norway, Saudi Arabia, the Persian Gulf states, and Libya. Sending societies include the Caribbean, much of Latin America, North Africa and others with voluntary migration a way of life for many small countries. Global trends favor controlled movements of temporary workers and entry for immigrants restricted to those highly skilled and/or family reunification.

Sources: B. Levine, (ed.), *Caribbean Exodus,* New York: Praeger, 1987.

Open University, *Third World Atlas,* Philadelphia: Milton Keynes, Open University Press, 1983.

G. Therborn, "Migration and Western Europe: The Old World Turning New", *Science,* 237:1183-1188, Sept. 4, 1987.

US Department of State, Bureau of Public Affairs, *Atlas of United States Foreign Relations*, Washington, DC, June 1983.

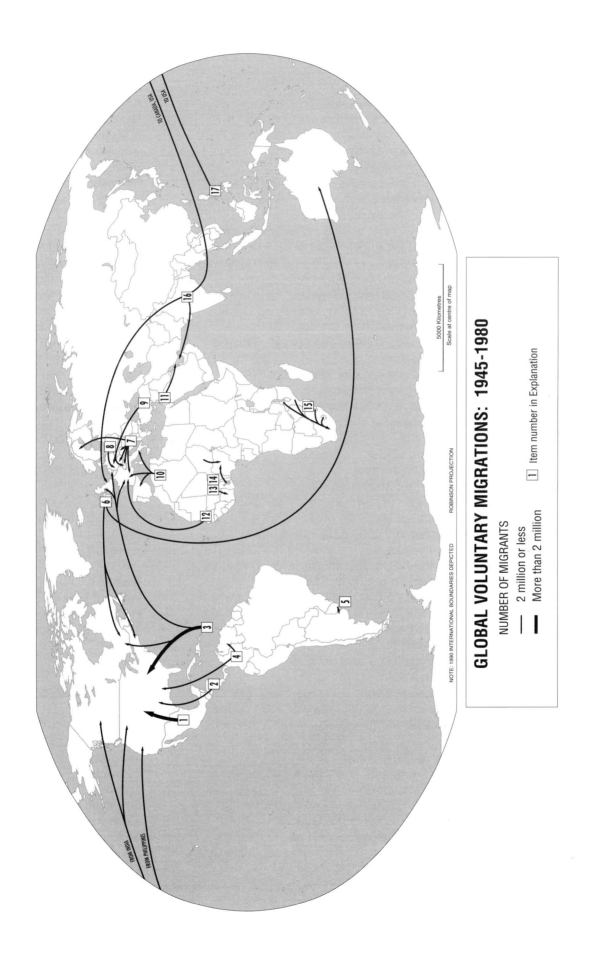

GLOBAL VOLUNTARY MIGRATIONS: 1945-1980

NOTE: 1990 INTERNATIONAL BOUNDARIES DEPICTED   ROBINSON PROJECTION

5000 Kilometres

Scale at centre of map

NUMBER OF MIGRANTS

—— 2 million or less

━━ More than 2 million

[1] Item number in Explanation

GLOBAL VOLUNTARY MIGRATION: SENDING COUNTRIES
Explanation
(Estimates for 1990)

Sending Countries
REGION - AFRICA (Estimates for 1985)

1. Algeria — Estimated 400,000 legal and illegal workers in France, Belgium
2. Benin — Exports middle-level manpower to francophone Africa
3. Botswana — 60,000 farm and mineworkers to South Africa
4. Burkina Faso — 900,000 farm workers to Côte d'Ivoire
5. Cape Verde — Emigration to the USA, Portugal, Guinea-Bissau
6. Ghana — Brain-drain to North America, Europe, Côte d'Ivoire, Nigeria
7. Guinea — Estimated 250,000 farm workers to Ivory Coast, Senegal
8. Guinea-Bissau — Estimated 25,000 farm workers to Senegambia
9. Lesotho — Estimated 140,000 in South Africa; farm and mineworkers
10. Morocco — Estimated 400,000 legal and illegal workers in France, Spain, Belgium
11. Mozambique — Estimated 75,000 in South Africa; farm workers
12. Nigeria — Estimated 25,000 high-level manpower in USA, United Kingdom, Middle East
13. Rwanda — Estimated 200,000 in Uganda as farm labour
14. Senegal — Estimated 200,000 migrant workers in France, Italy, Spain
15. Somalia — Estimated 50,000 in Saudi Arabia/Gulf; brain-drain
16. Sudan — Estimated 500,000 in Saudi Arabia/Gulf; brain-drain
17. Swaziland — Estimated 60,000 farm workers in South Africa
18. Tunisia — Estimated 200,000 in France; 100,000 in Italy; 50,000 in Libya; unskilled

REGION - ASIA/PACIFIC

19. Bangladesh — 250,000-300,000 to Saudi Arabia/Gulf; unskilled
20. China — Less than 100,000 construction and other workers to Gulf; 1 million to USA (includes Hong Kong and Taiwan)
21. Fiji — 2,000/year as emigrants to Australia, Canada, New Zealand; mostly businessmen and professionals of Indian origin
22. Hong Kong — Professionals and businessmen emigrate to Singapore, Australia, Canada, United Kingdom, USA, New Zealand, francophone Africa
23. India — 800,000 to 1.0 million unskilled workers to Gulf on contracts; 600,000 to USA
24. Indonesia — Estimated 350,000 illegal in Malaysia; less than 100,000 contract labour in Gulf
25. Malaysia — Estimated 80,000 contract labour in Singapore
26. Pacific Islands — Guam and American Samoa to USA, Hawaii, Papua Guinea, Cook and other islands to Australia, New Zealand, French Polynesian Islands to France
27. Pakistan — 850,000-1.1 million to Saudi Arabia/Gulf; pre-1990 90,000 to Kuwait; 81,000 to USA
28. Philippines — 700,000-800,000 to Saudi Arabia/Gulf; estimated 1 million in Malaysia; 20,000 legal in Singapore, 50,000 in Hong Kong; 50,000 in Japan, 900,000 in USA legal and illegal. Many skilled
29. South Korea — 800,000 immigrants in USA; 1.7 million temporary workers on overseas construction projects 1963-1990
30. Sri Lanka — 200,000-300,000 to Saudi Arabia/Gulf on contracts
31. Thailand — Border-crossing illegal migrants in Malaysia; 110,000 to USA
32. Vietnam — 190,000 contract workers to Eastern Europe, ex-USSR pre-1989

REGION - CARIBBEAN/CENTRAL AMERICA/MEXICO/ NORTH AMERICA

33. Barbados — Estimated 50,000 to United Kingdom before 1963; 100,000 to Canada/USA
34. Belize — Estimated 50,000 to USA; skilled
35. Canada — Estimated 750,000 emigrants, retirees, temporary workers; to USA, etc.
36. Costa Rica — Estimated 50,000 to USA; immigrants and illegals
37. Dominican Republic — 800,000 legal/illegal to USA; 50,000 to Puerto Rico
38. El Salvador — Estimated 800,000 to USA; migrant workers/illegals

23

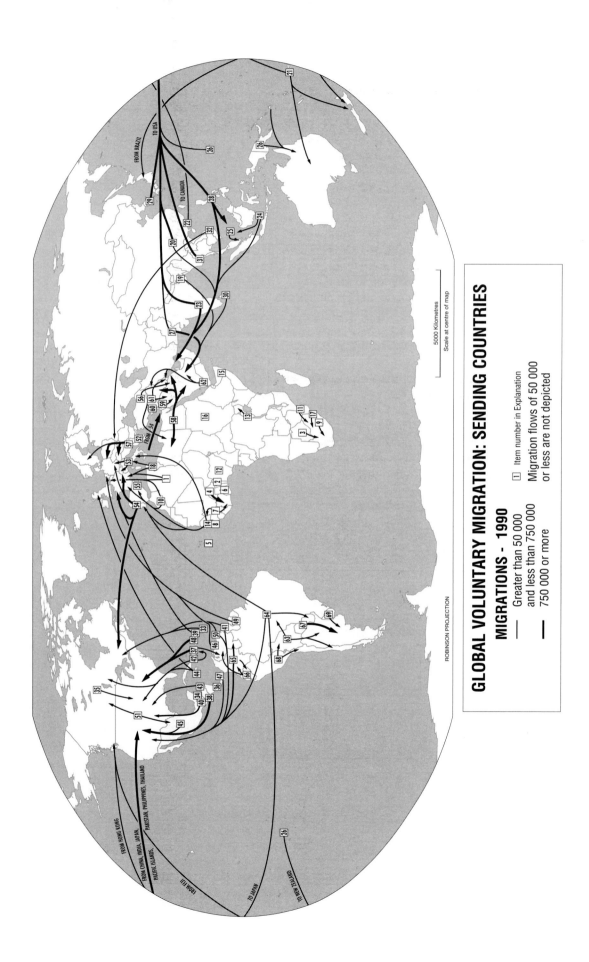

GLOBAL VOLUNTARY MIGRATION: SENDING COUNTRIES

MIGRATIONS - 1990

Greater than 50 000
and less than 750 000

750 000 or more

1 Item number in Explanation

Migration flows of 50 000
or less are not depicted

5000 Kilometres

Scale at centre of map

ROBINSON PROJECTION

39. French Antilles, French Guiana 400,000 to metropolitan France

40. Guatemala Estimated 200,000 migrant workers/illegals; to USA

41. Guyana 200,000 immigration to Canada/USA; mainly East Indians

42. Haiti Estimated 600,000 immigrants and illegals to USA; 100,000 to Canada; 25,000 illegal to Bahamas; 500,000 to Dominican Republic; 50,000 in French Antilles, French Guiana; unskilled brain-drain

43. Honduras Estimated 100,000 migrant workers to USA

44. Jamaica 200,000 to United Kingdom pre-1963; 400,000 to USA; 125,000 to Canada; immigrants

45. Mexico 1.2 million/year to USA; legal and undocumented, 4.3 million

46. Netherlands Antilles 50,000 to Netherlands as citizens

47. Panama 100,000 to USA; mostly immigrants

48. Puerto Rico Net emigration to continental USA of 1.5 million; citizens

49. Suriname 150,000 to Netherlands after 1975 as immigrants

50. Trinidad and Tobago 100,000 to Canada as immigrants; 120,000 to USA

51. USA 1990 USA census records 922,000 US citizens overseas; mainly military, dependants, retirees, businessmen; estimated nearly half of non-military in Canada and Mexico

REGION - EUROPE

52. Greece Sends workers, 80 per cent to West Germany from 1950-1980; most return and current emigration is circular in EC

53. Italy 150,000 migrant workers/year to West Germany, Switzerland, and others declines to less than 15,000 by end of 1970s. Middle-level manpower to Switzerland, Austria, Germany

54. Portugal Over 2 million workers 1960-1980 to France, West Germany, Switzerland, USA, Middle East. Many remain abroad but emigration declines in 1980s

55. Spain Migrant workers to Germany, Switzerland, and others declines from 130,000/year in 1971 to 9,000 in 1986

56. Turkey Estimated 100,000 on contract in Saudi Arabia/Gulf; 900,000 legal and illegal in Europe; mostly Germany

57. Yugoslavia Nearly 1 million in Germany, Austria, Sweden

REGION - THE MIDDLE EAST

58. Egypt 2.9 million to Saudi Arabia, Gulf, Iraq, Libya before the Gulf War

59. Jordan 400,000 to Saudi Arabia / Gulf; many skilled. Includes Palestinians on Jordanian passports

60. Lebanon Emigrants to France, West Africa, USA, others

61. Syria 200,000 to Libya, Saudi Arabia, Kuwait on contract

62. Yemen 500,000 to Saudi Arabia expelled during Gulf War; 200,000 to Iraq, Kuwait

REGION - SOUTH AMERICA

63. Bolivia 700,000 to Argentina, mostly farm workers; 100,000 in Brazil; 125,000 in Chile

64. Brazil 335,000 squatters to rural Paraguay; 630,000 skilled workers to Japan (Japanese-Brazilians), Portugal, USA

65. Colombia Estimated 800,000 legal and illegal in Venezuela; 100,000 Ecuador; 400,000 USA

66. Dominican Republic 15,000 middle-level manpower in Venezuela; 800,000 to USA

67. Ecuador Estimated 80,000 in Colombia and Venezuela, USA 150,000

68. Paraguay Estimated 800,000 in Argentina; farm labour, urban services

69. Peru Estimated 100,000 in Chile; 35,000 in Bolivia, USA 150,000

70. Uruguay Estimated 200,000 legal and illegal in Argentina; skilled

Sources: US Bureau of the Census, *1990 Census Reports*, Washington, DC.
UN Population Division, *World Migrant Populations: The Foreign-born*, New York: United Nations, 1990.

GLOBAL VOLUNTARY MIGRATION: RECEIVING COUNTRIES
Explanation
(Estimates for 1990)

Receiving Countries
REGION - AFRICA

1. Cameroon	Estimated 250,000 farm workers from Chad, Central African Republic
2. Côte d'Ivoire	Estimated 2 million agricultural and service workers, traders from Burkina Faso, Mali, Ghana, Niger, Guinea
3. Europe	Algerians, Moroccans, Malians, Tunisians, Turks, Senegalese, Nigerians and others in Belgium, France, Italy, United Kingdom, Spain, others
4. Gabon	Estimated 300,000 from Cameroon, Equatorial Guinea, etc.
5. The Gambia	Estimated 50,000 farm labour from Guinea, Guinea-Bissau
6. Nigeria	Estimated 1 million from Chad, Niger, Ghana, Togo, Benin. Estimated 2.5 million at time of 1983 mass expulsion. Skilled/ unskilled
7. Senegal	Estimated 350,000 from Guinea; 50,000 from Mauritania expelled in 1990; mostly petty traders
8. South Africa	Estimated 500,000; recruited mineworkers, legal and illegal farm workers; Botswana, Swaziland, Mozambique, Lesotho
9. Zaïre	Estimated 600,000 from Burundi, Rwanda, Congo, Central African Republic, Tanzania; farm labour; squatters

REGION - ASIA/PACIFIC

10. Australia	125,000 immigrants per year; skilled, one-third from Asia
11. Hong Kong	Estimated 58,000 mostly from Philippines
12. Japan	Estimated 250,000-300,000 from Philippines, Malaysia, Sri Lanka, others. Includes foreign students, trainees, legal and illegal workers
13. Malaysia	Estimated less than 100,000 legal and 400,000-1 million illegal workers from Indonesia, Philippines, Thailand; mostly rural labour
14. New Zealand	Approximately 25,000 legal immigrants/year; nearly half from Asia and Pacific Islands
15. Singapore	Estimated 150,000; half from Malaysia. Strict recruiting

REGION - CARIBBEAN/CENTRAL AMERICA/NORTH AMERICA

16. Canada	100,000 immigrants from Haiti; 125,000 from Jamaica; 100,000 from Guyana, other West Indies
17. Dominican Republic	500,000 migrant workers from Haiti; some recruited
18. Trinidad and Tobago	Estimated 50,000 migrants from Eastern Caribbean
19. USA	800,000 legal and illegal from Dominican Republic; 600,000 legal and illegal from Haiti; 600,000 from West Indies. Legal and illegal migration from El Salvador, Guatemala, Brazil, Colombia, Jamaica, Argentina, Nicaragua, and other regional and extra-regional immigration. Mexico estimated at 1.2 million legal and illegal migrants/year to USA

REGION - EUROPE

20. Austria	Estimated 250,000 legal and illegal; Yugoslavia, Eastern Europe
21. Belgium	900,000 workers from Morocco, Turkey, other EC
22. Denmark	80,000 migrant workers including other EC
23. France	1.5 million migrant workers including 400,000 from other EC; estimated 500,000 illegal workers; Algeria, Morocco, Tunisia, sub-Saharan Africa
24. Germany	1.5 million migrant workers from Turkey, Italy, Poland, Spain and others. 350,000 ethnic German immigrants from East Europe
25. Italy	Estimated 1.2 million illegal migrants from Tunisia, West Africa, etc.
26. Luxembourg	100,000 legal migrants from Italy, Spain, other EC
27. Netherlands	800,000 migrant workers from Turkey, Yugoslavia, other EC

28. Spain	Estimated 300,000 illegal workers from Morocco, Senegal, etc.
29. Sweden	250,000 migrant workers from Finland, Yugoslavia
30. Switzerland	800,000 migrant workers from Italy, Spain, Yugoslavia, others
31. United Kingdom	800,000 workers from Italy, Spain, other EC; immigrants and migrants from Nigeria, Ghana, India, Pakistan, etc.
Note:	Greece, Italy and Spain after two decades of rapid economic growth have changed from historic exporters of labour to attracting mostly illegal migrant workers.

REGION - MIDDLE EAST

32. Bahrain	70,000 on contract from Pakistan, India, others
33. Iraq	400,000 from Egypt, Jordan, others prior to Gulf War
34. Israel	185,000 from ex-USSR in 1990; 18,000 from Ethiopia in 1991
35. Jordan	100,000 unskilled from Egypt before Gulf War
36. Kuwait	600,000 prior to Gulf War; Egypt, Jordan, others
37. Libya	500,000 from Tunisia, Egypt, Pakistan, others; many skilled
38. Oman	200,000 from India, Pakistan, others
39. Qatar	90,000 from Pakistan, India, other Asian
40. Saudi Arabia	1.4 million from Yemen, Egypt, Jordan, Sudan, Somalia, Lebanon, Oman, Pakistan, India, Bangladesh, Sri Lanka, Philippines

REGION - SOUTH AMERICA

41. Argentina	Estimated 2 million from Bolivia, Paraguay, Uruguay, others
42. Paraguay	350,000 farmers and workers from Brazil in Eastern Region
43. Venezuela	Estimated 800,000 legal and illegal Colombians; middle level and professional manpower from Argentina, Chile, Dominican Republic, others

Sources: Applicable to receiving and sending countries.
European Community, *Employment in Europe*, Brussels, 1989.
United Nations, *World Survey of Foreign-Born*, New York, 1990.
U.S. Bureau of the Census, *1990 Census Estimates of Foreign-Born*.

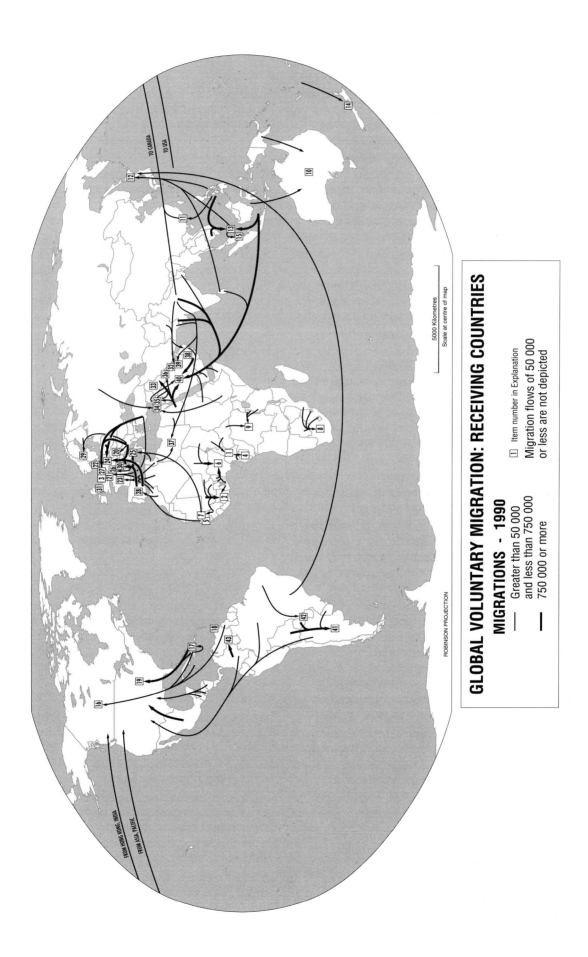

GLOBAL VOLUNTARY MIGRATION: RECEIVING COUNTRIES
MIGRATIONS - 1990

ROBINSON PROJECTION

5000 Kilometres
Scale at centre of map

— Greater than 50 000
and less than 750 000

— 750 000 or more

☐ Item number in Explanation

Migration flows of 50 000
or less are not depicted

VOLUNTARY MIGRATION: AFRICA
Explanation
(Estimates for 1985)

Receiving Countries

1. Cameroon	250,000 estimated. Mostly agricultural workers from Chad, Central African Republic, Nigeria
2. Côte d'Ivoire	Estimated 2 million from agriculture and service workers and traders from Burkina Faso, Mali, Guinea, Ghana, Niger
3. Europe	Algerians, Moroccans, Tunisians, Senegalese, Nigerians and others in Belgium, France, Italy, United Kingdom, Spain, others. Estimated 1.2 million; sub-Saharan Africa 200,000
4. Gabon	Estimated 300,000 from Cameroon, Equatorial Guinea, Congo, Benin, Senegal, Mali. Strict immigration controls not enforced
5. The Gambia	Agricultural labour from Guinea and Guinea-Bissau 50,000
6. Nigeria	Estimated 1 million from Chad, Niger, Ghana, Togo, Benin, Burkina Faso. 2.5 million estimated in 1983 at time of mass expulsions; mostly unskilled workers but also pre-1983 teachers, mechanics, etc.
7. Senegal	Estimated 350,000 from Guinea; 50,000 Mauritanians, mostly petty traders, expelled in 1990
8. South Africa	Estimated 500,000, includes recruited mineworkers from Botswana, Lesotho, and Swaziland and legal and illegal farm workers from same countries and Mozambique
9. Zaïre	Estimated 600,000 from Burundi, Rwanda, Congo, Central African Republic, Tanzania. Legal and illegal farm labour, rural squatters

Sending Countries (does not include refugees)

10. Algeria	Estimated 400,000 unskilled and semi-skilled workers; Belgium, France
11. Benin	Historically provides middle-manpower to West Africa
12. Botswana	60,000 to South Africa; mineworkers, farm labour
13. Burkina Faso	900,000 mostly farm labour to Côte d'Ivoire; part seasonal
14. Cape Verde	Historic emigration to USA, Guinea-Bissau, Portugal, Angola. Family reunification emigration continues
15. Central African Republic	200,000 seasonal farm labour to Cameroon
16. Egypt	Estimated 2.9 million migrant workers to Gulf States, Libya. Mostly unskilled workers but includes teachers, technicians
17. Ghana	Brain-drain to Europe, North America. Skilled workers to Côte d'Ivoire, Nigeria
18. Guinea-Bissau	Estimated 25,000 farm labourers to Senegambia
19. Guinea	Estimated 250,000 to Côte d'Ivoire, Senegal; semi-skilled
20. Lesotho	Estimated 140,000 in South Africa; $274 million remittances
21. Mali	200,000 to Senegal, France
22. Morocco	Estimated 400,000 in France, Spain, Belgium. Urban workers
23. Mozambique	Estimated 75,000 legal and illegal farm workers in South Africa. Recruited mine workers, illegals repatriated 1986
24. Nigeria	Estimated high-level manpower; USA, United Kingdom, Middle East 25,000
25. Rwanda	Estimated 200,000 in Uganda from historic emigration of farm workers. Most arrive before 1970 and settle
26. Senegal	Estimated 200,000 migrant workers, France, Italy, Spain
27. Somalia	Estimated 50,000 in Saudi Arabia / Gulf. Brain-drain
28. Sudan	Estimated 500,000 in Saudi Arabia/ Gulf. Brain-drain
29. Swaziland	Estimated 60,000 farm and service workers in South Africa
30. Tunisia	Estimated 200,000 in France and Italy; 50,000 in Libya

Note: Data on international migration in Africa are extremely unreliable. Many countries have not had a recent census and census data are unavailable for other countries. The foreign-born are often not counted or undercounted, especially if illegal. Estimates are based on combinations of census data and projections. Includes legal and illegal temporary migrants, permanent immigration

Sources: Sharon Stanton Russell, Karen Jacobsen, William Deane Stanley, *International Migration and Development in Sub-Saharan Africa*, World Bank Discussion Papers, Number 102, 2. Vols.,Washington, DC: World Bank, 1990.
Sergio Ricca, *International Migration in Africa, Legal and Administrative Aspects*, Geneva.: International Labour Office, 1989.

RECEIVING COUNTRIES

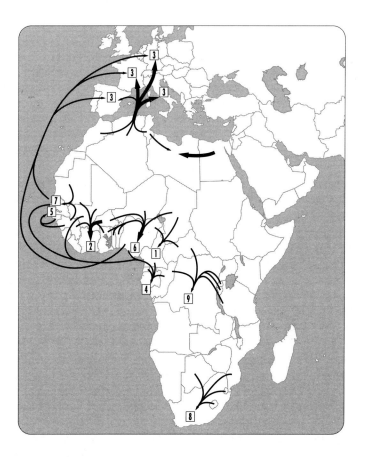

SENDING COUNTRIES

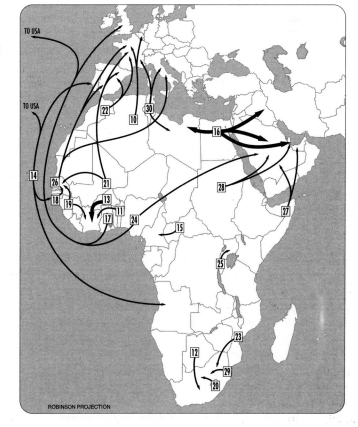

**VOLUNTARY MIGRATION:
AFRICA - 1985**

NUMBER OF MIGRANTS

—— 750 000 or less

━━ More than 750 000

[1] Item number in Explanation

3000 Kilometres

Scale at centre of map

NOTE: 1990 INTERNATIONAL BOUNDARIES DEPICTED

ROBINSON PROJECTION

VOLUNTARY MIGRATION: AFRICA 1985

International voluntary migration has deep roots in Africa. Throughout the pre-colonial period there were prolonged movements of ethnic groups over time and space. The peopling of Africa by Bantu, Nilotic and other linguistic groups was a story of migrations in search of arable land, water, and pasturage.

Colonial Migration Patterns

During the colonial period in many parts of Africa plantation and mine labour was recruited across boundaries. Combinations of monetary incentives, coercions and head taxes were often relied on to induce these migrations. While they generally occurred within particular colonial regimes, e.g. British, French, Portuguese colonies, often they crossed these frontiers. Togolese migrated for work to the Gold Coast, Africans living in French Cameroon and British Cameroon crossed a border to seek work, and Rwanda peasants and herdsmen left a Belgian territory to seek work and cattle in British Uganda. South Africa deliberately recruited contract labour for its mines and farms from neighbouring British and Portuguese colonies. Wage-seekers, often leaving their families behind, regularly migrated in pursuit of cash employment. Both under colonialism and after, the movement of persons in search of employment was, in much of Africa, more important than the movement of goods and services between colonies and states.

Post-Independence Migration

Independence has made it harder for Africans to migrate internationally. Governments have imposed residence and work permits in Nigeria (1983), Zaïre (1969), Ghana (1969) and other countries have expelled hundreds of thousands of foreign workers in response to nationalist pressures. Regional cooperation agreements in West Africa (ECOWAS) and in Central Africa (UDEAC) have provided for freedom of movement and residence although not employment. They have been blatantly ignored as governments do not hesitate to discriminate in favour of their own nationals. Fear of migrant workers being carriers of AIDS disease has added to the pretence used by governments to deny work to foreigners.

What is remarkable is the extent to which international voluntary migration continues in spite of the many barriers and obstacles. While there is minimal permanent legal immigration to which most governments are hostile, legal and illegal migrants are quick to respond to opportunities to earn cash. A majority are still engaged in seasonal agricultural labour, whether from Burkina Faso in the Côte d'Ivoire, Guineans helping with Senegambian groundnut harvests, and Chadian and Central African farmworkers in Cameroon. South Africa has significantly cut back on the recruitment of foreign mine labour but migrants from Botswana, Lesotho and Swaziland are still working on South African farms.

Importance of Remittances

Remittances from African international migrant workers provide subsistence, consumption and limited investments for dependants at home. Fertility tends to be lower among migrants due to absent males. Given opportunities international migrants are also active in petty trade and other informal sector activities. The money sent home helps to cover massive formal trade deficits in countries such as Senegal, Botswana, Cape Verde and Lesotho. Studies of Senegalese and other workers in France indicate that they save and send home one-third or more of their earnings.

High-Level Manpower

Since independence there has been a stepped-up movement of high-level manpower within Africa. However, many countries prefer to recruit non-African expatriates on brief contracts rather than hire an African from another country who might be tempted to stay. The majority of high-level African manpower 'mal-distributed' in "reverse transfers of technology" is employed in Western Europe, North America, and the Middle East. The term "brain-drain" is frowned upon officially but countries such as the Sudan, Somalia, Gambia and Ghana have experienced a significant loss of high-level manpower. Whether as African universities increase their enrolments and promotions skilled-manpower short countries will turn to those with excess supply remains to be seen.

Voluntary international migration in Africa has been directed, since independence, at the handful of countries whose economies have grown, at least intermittently (Cameroon, Nigeria, Côte d'Ivoire). Frontier controls, work permits, and expulsions have slowed down but not stopped these migrations, especially where borders are costly to patrol. Colonial-style contractual recruitment is being replaced by spontaneous migration. Should African economies begin to recover Africans will respond by moving across borders to find work.

VOLUNTARY MIGRATION:
ASIA/PACIFIC 1990

The Asia/Pacific region is moving to the forefront of global voluntary migration. This is primarily in response to the rapidly growing economies of the Newly Industrializing Countries (Hong Kong, Taiwan, Singapore, South Korea), and a second tier of export-industrializers (Malaysia, Thailand, Indonesia). The growth of export manufacturing is resulting in shortages of unskilled and some skilled labour. At the same time Saudi Arabia and the Gulf States have been recruiting annually 3 to 3.5 million Asian workers for their needs. Even Japan with its passionate commitment to the maintenance of ethnic and cultural homogeneity is experiencing a shortage of unskilled labour for jobs shunned by Japanese.

Immigration to Australia and New Zealand

Legal immigration within the region is almost entirely confined to Australia and New Zealand. Each has moved away from its historic white settler immigration colonies to accept educated immigrants from Asia and the Pacific Islands in limited numbers. The Chinese takeover of Hong Kong in 1997 is expected to precipitate a permanent emigration to Canada, the USA, the United Kingdom, and within the region to Australia, New Zealand and Singapore. While most emigrants from Hong Kong are wealthy businessmen or highly educated persons, their relocation within the region is important to commercial ties.

Historical Precedents

The movement of migrant labour, legal and illegal, from poor to rich societies within the region has few precedents. Emigrant Chinese beginning in the sixteenth century established themselves throughout Southeast Asia and gradually some built commercial empires. However, lack of arable land, ethnic conflicts, and slow-growth economies ruled out mass migration until the 1970s. Instead, the British and French relied on indentured labour from India in Fiji, New Caledonia and other colonial outposts. Wage and other differentials were not sufficient to produce spontaneous mass migration. Japanese colonialism brought Koreans to Japan as forced labourers prior to World War II but mostly used indigenous forced labour in Formosa and Manchuria.

The future of voluntary migration in the region is uncertain. The recruiting of unskilled workers from India, Pakistan, and other states to the Gulf depends on world oil prices, Middle Eastern politics, investment decisions, and availability of other contract labour supplies. During the 1980s it yielded an estimated $10 billion a year to Asian sending states and was vital to the foreign exchange earnings of Bangladesh. Its continuance is widely considered as desirable although probably at lower levels of recruitment.

Regional employment in manufacturing for export is moving away from Japan, South Korea and Taiwan to less labour costly locales such as Malaysia and Thailand. These economic transformations are resulting in new demands for low-paid, service workers in Japan as well as factory unskilled workers elsewhere. Japan resists recruiting labour on a large-scale and is committed, with its ageing population, to automating services to reduce overseas dependence. South Korea and Taiwan are reluctantly confronting an upward wage drift which is hurting their exports, and creating some labour shortages. Meanwhile the opportunities for urban wage employment are generating shortages of rural labour in Malaysia and elsewhere, partly filled by Indonesian migrants.

Legally or illegally the prospects are good for a pronounced expansion of migrant labour within the region. Unfortunately legal status, protection of workers, health benefits, and other measures to assist migrants are woefully lacking except in tightly controlled Singapore. Governments are accustomed to allowing private employers broad powers and are relatively indifferent to the situation of migrant workers. The rapid growth in wage differentials provides the incentive for migration and the willingness to accept for some time grim working conditions. Efforts by the International Labour Organisation and other agencies to protect migrant workers have had little impact to date in the region.

The number and nature of receiving countries is likely to expand with domestic and world economic growth. South Korea and Taiwan are likely to accept reluctantly some migrant labour to restrain rapidly rising wages. Japan with the world's second largest economy and impressive growth rates could potentially employ several million migrant workers. Its official opposition may be overcome by demand pressures from sending countries and bottlenecks due to labour shortages.

Two sending countries are scarcely represented in the present lists. Vietnam, with high fertility and an economy decades behind its neighbours, is capable of exporting millions of unskilled workers. Whether the 75,000 or more annual Vietnamese boat-people are "economic migrants" or "refugees", they represent the potential for mass migration. Vietnam also has the cheapest labour in the region and is striving to attract export industries. It has not sent workers to the Middle East but it did provide thousands to Eastern Europe before 1989.

China, with its population estimated at 1.2 billion, one-fifth of the human race, could supply most of the labour needs of the entire region. But the Chinese, known for their propensity to stay and entrepreneurial skills, are not welcome except for an educated few in Singapore. Chinese workers on engineering projects in the Gulf and West and East Africa have returned. However, Chinese participation in emerging voluntary migration within the region is likely to be strictly limited and controlled.

Culture, language, and nationalism also limit the movement of high-level manpower. Countries such as Afghanistan and Burma are experiencing acute brain-drains, often outside of the region. The rapidly growing economies have invested heavily in human resources and claim few shortages at those levels. South Korea,

VOLUNTARY MIGRATION: ASIA/PACIFIC
Explanation
(Estimates for 1990)

Receiving Countries

1. Australia	Approximately 125,000/year; one-third from Asia; foreign-born in 1986 at 20.8 per cent of population
2. Hong Kong	58,000; mostly from Philippines as migrant workers
3. Japan	Estimated 250,000-350,000 including legal and undocumented, foreign students, mail-order brides from Philippines, Sri Lanka, Japanese-Brazilians
4. Malaysia	Estimated less than 100,000 legal; 400,000-1 million undocumented plantation workers from Philippines, Indonesia, Thailand. Some replace Malays employed in Singapore
5. New Zealand	Approximately 25,000 per year; nearly half from Asia and Pacific Islands. Foreign-born in 1981 at 14.6 per cent
6. Singapore	Estimated 150,000; half from Malaysia; unskilled. Incentives for educated immigrants from Hong Kong.
7. USA	Immigrants from Asia/Pacific increase 2 million 1980-1990: China, Taiwan, Philippines, India, Japan, South Korea, Vietnam

Sending Countries

8. Bangladesh	250,000-300,000 Saudi Arabia and Gulf; unskilled
9. China	Less than 100,000 construction workers to Gulf; estimated 1 million to USA, Canada, and Australia includes Taiwan, Hong Kong
10. Fiji	Approximately 2,000 per year to Australia, Canada, New Zealand mostly businessmen and professionals of Indian origin
11. Hong Kong	500,000 per year since 1990 or more to Canada, USA, United Kingdom, etc.
12. India	800,000-1 million unskilled workers to Gulf; 600,000 to USA as skilled
13. Indonesia	Estimated 350,000 undocumented rural labour-Malaysia
14. Malaysia	Estimated 180,000 legal to Singapore
15. New Zealand	Net emigration to Australia, 100,000

16. Pacific Islands, Guam, American Samoa	150,000 to USA
17. Papua New Guinea, Cook other Pacific Islands	2,000 estimated per year to Australia, New Zealand
18. Pakistan	850,000-1 million to Saudi Arabia, Gulf; 81,000 to USA
19. Philippines	700,000-800,000 to Saudi Arabia, Gulf; 900,000 to USA; 1 million to Malaysia; 200,000 to Singapore; 50,000 to Hong Kong; 50,000 to Japan
20. South Korea	800,000 to USA; 500,000 residents in Japan since World War II. 1.7 million migrant workers in Middle East earn $16 billion 1963-1990
21. Sri Lanka	200,000-300,000 to Saudi Arabia, Gulf
22. Thailand	Border-crossing migrant workers to Malaysia; 110,000 to USA

Note: Citizens of American Samoa and Guam have US citizenship. Citizens of French Polynesia and New Caledonia are French citizens. Cook and other Pacific Islanders have freedom of movement to New Zealand.

Sources: Reginald T. Appleyard, "International Migration in Asia and the Pacific", in R. Appleyard, (ed.), *International Migration Today*, Volume I: Trends and Prospects, pp. 89-167, Paris: UNESCO, 1988.
Freda Hawkins, *Critical Years in Immigration, Australia and Canada*, Toronto: McGill University Press, 1989.
Philip L. Martin, "Labor Migration in Asia", *International Migration Review*, Vol. 25, Spring 1991, pp. 176-193.
US Bureau of the Census, *We, the Asian and Pacific Islander Americans*, Washington, DC, 1990.

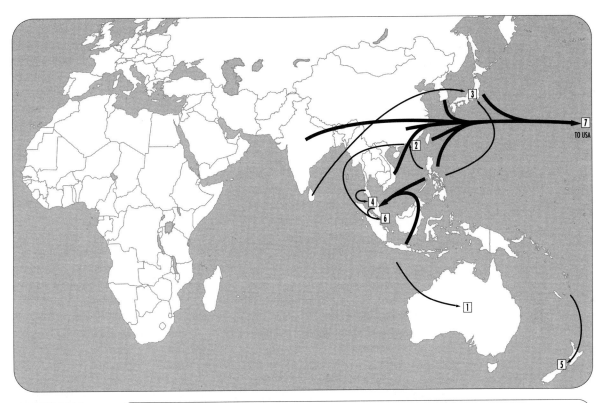

RECEIVING COUNTRIES

SENDING COUNTRIES

VOLUNTARY MIGRATION: ASIA/PACIFIC - 1990

1 Item number in Explanation

NUMBER OF MIGRANTS

— 750 000 or less

━ More than 750 000

5000 Kilometres
Scale at centre of map

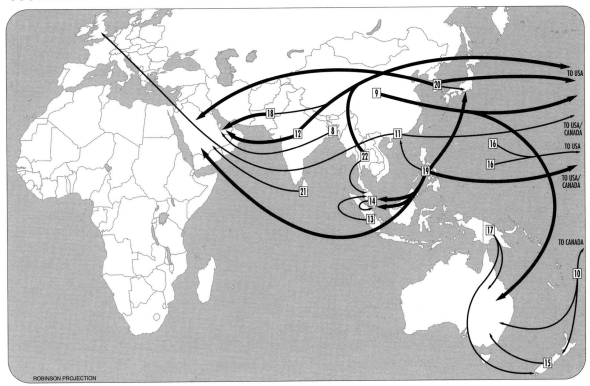

ROBINSON PROJECTION

Singapore and Taiwan have been remarkably successful at the use of economic and cultural incentives to lure back engineers and other professionals from abroad. Export drives headed by overseas educated professionals starting small companies have been highly effective. The brain-drain is regarded by several governments as a problem to be resolved at national rather than international levels.

Asia/Pacific appears as the region of the world most capable of expanding and sustaining voluntary migration. The need is to protect workers and to ensure decent working conditions.

VOLUNTARY MIGRATION: CARIBBEAN/CENTRAL AMERICA/NORTH AMERICA 1990

Historically Central America has not been known for emigration while the Caribbean has. During the 1980s both regions became massive exporters of emigrants and migrant workers, and even refugees, primarily to the USA. Net emigration accounts for 5-10 per cent of nearly every Caribbean society and for comparable proportions in El Salvador, Guatemala and Nicaragua.

Central American Emigration

The five Central American countries and Panama experienced modest immigration throughout the colonial period. These were mestizo societies except for Costa Rica with its small farmers of European descent. Natural increase produced most population growth. A handful of Lebanese, European, and other immigrants in the late nineteenth century played an important role in the expansion of export crops and the development of commerce. West Indians recruited to work on the Panama Canal emigrated north to add to the distinctive multi-racial character of the sparsely populated Caribbean coast. Those who remained in Panama or the Canal Zone often intermarried with Panamanians of African descent.

Although the trail of Central American migrants north through Mexico seeking work in the USA began in the 1960s it became a flood in the 1970s and after. Mexican authorities, sometimes extracting bribes, allowed Guatemalans, Salvadoreans, Hondurans and others to ride buses across Mexico to the US border. Building on embryonic networks of relatives and friends migrants were able to enter the USA illegally and proceed to Houston, Washington, Los Angeles and other cities where work was available. Whether their expectations were for temporary or permanent stays deteriorating economic conditions and violence at home impeded their return. The 1986 US amnesty law, with its requirements of proof of stay and work, assisted more long-staying Mexicans than Central Americans.

Central American Internal Strife

Civil war in Guatemala, El Salvador and Nicaragua has generated refugees in neighbouring countries, the USA, and Canada. Honduras sought external assistances from the UNHCR and other agencies to cope with Salvadorean and Nicaraguan refugees. Costa Rica experienced an influx of wealthy and middle-class Nicaraguans, many with friends and relatives, as well as border crossers fleeing violence. The USA supporting the Contra forces, accepted Nicaraguans as refugees while turning down most Salvadorean asylum requests. Guatemalan Indians fled across the Mexican border from army raids and predation.

Negotiated peace settlements and democratic elections resulted in some repatriation of refugees to Guatemala and to Nicaragua. The imposing burden on Honduras and Costa Rica was reduced. Many Guatemalans opted to remain in Mexico and were removed from the immediate border region and encouraged to integrate. The prolonged negotiations failed to produce a definitive settlement to the Salvadorean civil war but some refugees opted to return home from refugee camps in Honduras.

Refugees and/or Migrants

The reduction in the Central American refugee crisis has not lessened voluntary emigration. Stricken economies, landlessness, social networks abroad, rising expectations, and population pressures contribute to a steady trek of young men and women north. Costa Rica, with its higher standard of living and reviving economy, generates more emigrants than migrant workers. Immigrant visa seekers in the other countries are out-numbered by those who try illegal entry to the USA. Democratically elected governments have been able to do little to stem the outflows.

Central America also has its share of environmental refugees. Deforestation, earthquakes, and other natural and man-made disasters have afflicted each country. Their impact is primarily in terms of internally displaced persons but they also produce cross-border refugees.

Demographically Central America is exporting annually perhaps 500,000 persons, mostly as illegal workers to the USA. Remittances are listed as unknown by World Bank sources but unofficially they may be one-third or more of export earnings in El Salvador, and over 10 per cent in Guatemala and Honduras. The Nicaraguan middle-class communities in Costa Rica, Miami and Los Angeles are also important sources of dollars. Emigration, legal or illegal, has become a way of life in Central America although future outlets are problematical.

Caribbean Emigration History

Emigration has been a way of life in the Caribbean for more than a century. Shortly after slave emancipation in the British West Indies in 1832 boat-loads of freed slaves from Barbados went to Guyana and to Trinidad in search of land. The introduction into the Caribbean of indentured labourers from India, China and the Madeiras was partly in response to the emigration of ex-slaves rejecting plantation labour.

Following 350 years of importation into the Caribbean of African slaves and Indian indentured labourers has been a century of emigration to North America, Western Europe, Venezuela, and within the region. Since 1945 the net emigration outside the region and from nearly each island is the highest proportionately in the entire world. Caribbean diaspora communities have been established in London, Paris, Amsterdam, New York, Toronto and Miami.

Except for Cuban refugees since 1959 and Surinamese refugees to French Guiana, Caribbean emigration has been voluntary and largely spontaneous. Controversy continues over US decisions to repatriate Haitians as "economic migrants" rather than refugees. Most Caribbean emigrants, though, arrive as legal immigrants or else overstay tourist or other visas.

VOLUNTARY MIGRATION:
CARIBBEAN/CENTRAL AMERICA/NORTH AMERICA
Explanation
(Estimates for 1990)

Receiving Countries

1. Canada	100,000 immigrants from Haiti; 125,000 from Jamaica; 100,000 immigrants from Guyana, other West Indies
2. Dominican Republic	500,000 migrant workers from Haiti
3. Mexico	400,000 mostly retirees, USA
4. Trinidad and Tobago	Estimated 50,000 migrants from Eastern Caribbean
5. USA	800,000 legal and illegal from Dominican Republic; 600,000 legal and illegal from Haiti; 600,000 from all West Indies; Estimated 1.4 million legal and illegal from El Salvador, Guatemala, Nicaragua, Belize, other Central America. Estimated 1.2 million/year legal and illegal from Mexico

Sending Countries
Central America

6. Belize	Estimated 50,000 to USA; Los Angeles, New Orleans, Miami
7. Costa Rica	Estimated 50,000 to US; migrant workers/illegals
8. El Salvador	Estimated 800,000 to USA, migrant workers, illegals
9. Guatemala	Estimated 200,000 to USA
10. Honduras	Estimated 100,000 to USA
11. Panama	100,000 immigrants

Sending Countries
Caribbean

12. Barbados	Estimated 50,000 immigrants to United Kingdom pre-1963; 100,000 immigrants to Canada, USA
13. Dominican Republic	800,000 legal/illegal migrants to USA; 50,000 to Puerto Rico
14. French Antilles:	French Guiana 400,000 to metropolitan France; citizens
15. Guyana	200,000 immigration to Canada/ USA; mainly East Indians
16. Haiti	Estimated 600,000 immigrants and illegals to USA; 100,000 to Canada; 25,000 in Bahamas; 500,000 migrants to Dominican Republic; 50,000 in French Antilles; French Guiana
17. Jamaica	200,000 to United Kingdom pre-1963; 400,000 to USA; 125,000 to Canada as immigrants
18. Netherlands Antilles	50,000 to Netherlands; citizens
19. Puerto Rico	Net immigrants to continental USA of 1.5 million citizens
20. Suriname	150,000 as immigrants to Netherlands after 1975
21. Trinidad and Tobago	100,000 to Canada as immigrants; 120,000 to USA

Sending Countries
North America

22. Canada	750,000 emigrants mostly to USA
23. Mexico	Estimated 1.2 million/year legal and undocumented to USA
24. USA	Estimated 922,000 overseas in Canada, Europe, Mexico, etc.

Sources: Barry B. Levine, (ed.) *The Caribbean Exodus*, New York: Praeger, 1987.
James M. Malloy, Eduardo A. Gamarra, (eds.), *Latin America and Caribbean Contemporary Record*, Vol. VII, 1987-88, New York: Holmes and Meier, 1989.
Georges Vernez and David Ronfeldt, "The Current Situation in Mexican Immigration," *Science*, 8 March 1991, pp. 1189-1193.

**RECEIVING
COUNTRIES**

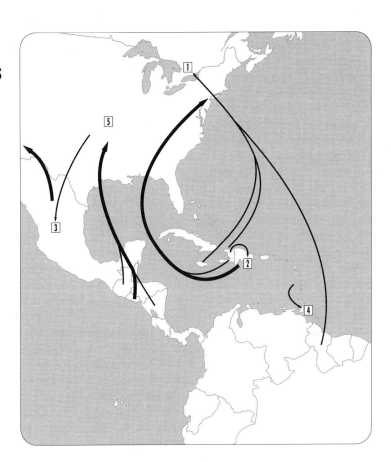

**SENDING
COUNTRIES**

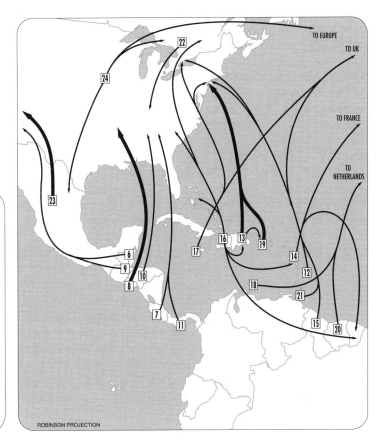

**VOLUNTARY MIGRATION:
CARIBBEAN/
CENTRAL AMERICA/
NORTH AMERICA
1990**

NUMBER OF MIGRANTS

⎯⎯ 750 000 or less

━━━ More than 750 000

1 Item number in Explanation

2000 Kilometres

Scale at centre of map

Caribbean Inter-Island Migration

Inter-island migration has been based primarily on economic opportunities. Cuba, during its sugar boom of the 1920s recruited Haitian and Jamaican labour for its estates who were then repatriated during the Great Depression. An estimated 150,000 West Indians, mainly from Barbados and Jamaica, were recruited to work on the Panama Canal from 1880-1914. After World War II British transport authorities recruited workers from Barbados and other islands.

Most inter-island migration, though, has been spontaneous in response to economic growth poles generating paying jobs. The Trinidad and Tobago, Aruba and Curacao petroleum industries drew workers from the Eastern Caribbean from 1940-1980. The construction industry in French Guiana with its space rocket base attracts Haitians, Surinamese and others. The US Virgin Islands with their tourism and services have been a magnet for smaller island job-seekers. Migration within the Caribbean, legal and illegal, represents less than five per cent of the regional labour force but its mobility is pronounced.

Caribbean Colonial Migrations

Extra-regional emigration has only recently become an important factor. Although many Caribbean residents were subjects of a metropolitan colonial state and enjoyed freedom of movement, high transport costs were a formidable barrier until the introduction of cheap air fares. Puerto Ricans have been US citizens since 1917 but only began moving to New York in large numbers in 1947. West Indian emigration to Britain responded to recruiting, jobs, and low-cost transport between 1946 and 1963 when immigration laws were changed. The massive movements from the French Antilles and French Guiana to metropolitan France began during the 1960s.

Caribbean Overseas Migrants

Approximately five million Caribbean residents currently enjoy free migration to their respective metropoles. Data collection on these movements is difficult and less than reliable. An estimated 400,000 persons from the Caribbean live in metropolitan France although some go back and forth. About 50,000 persons from the Netherlands Antilles have moved to the Netherlands where they hold concurrent citizenship; a legal status no longer valid for Surinamese. More than 1.5 million persons born in Puerto Rico and the US Virgin Islands live in the continental USA. Freedom of movement to metropoles has resulted in extensive emigration, some return migration, but not massive exodus.

West Indian emigration to the USA and Canada dates to the turn of the twentieth century. West Indian intellectuals played an important role in the Harlem Renaissance of the 1920s and in Black American cultural life in general. Marcus Garvey from Jamaica led a Black Nationalist movement in the USA during the 1920s until he was imprisoned and then deported. West Indians played a similar role in Afro-Canadian society.

Migration Switch to USA, Canada

In the 1960s it was the closing of the British immigration door that prompted a renewed West Indian emigration shift towards Canada and the USA. Many educated professionals and technicians came legally while illegal entrants also increased. West Indians in Toronto, Montreal, New York and Miami proved to be high achievers and investors in education for their offspring. Family reunification proved a useful instrument in fostering further immigration, especially as first-comers acquired citizenship. Emigration was also sensitive to minority status within the Caribbean as East Indians from Guyana and Trinidad flocked to Canada.

Emigration from the Dominican Republic and Haiti has also been spontaneous and adaptive. Dominicans have often used Puerto Rico as a transit-point for New York; some losing their lives in small boats in the treacherous Mona Straits. Haitians, especially professionals, had begun to emigrate prior to the Duvalier regime coming to power in 1957. However, 30 years of a tyrannical family dynasty turned emigration into survival for many. Haiti experienced both one of the most crippling brain-drains in the world and an outflow of peasants fleeing famine, drought, and repression. Since the Duvaliers were overthrown in 1986 there has been some slight repatriation but Haiti continues to generate hundreds of thousands of spontaneous migrants, including sugar estate workers in the Dominican Republic.

The Cuban Situation

Cuban emigration since 1959 has been one of refugees to the USA. However, between 1880 and 1920 Cuba attracted more than 200,000 Spanish immigrants, including the father of Fidel Castro. Between 1919 and 1939 it was also a modest haven for Jews from Eastern Europe, some Lebanese, and other immigrants. Historically Cubans emigrated to the US voluntarily in modest numbers before 1959, helping to establish the cigar industry in Tampa, Florida.

The future of migration in a post-Castro Cuba is a matter of speculation. Legal emigration to the USA based on family reunification, under present rules cannot possibly contain the numbers of Cubans wanting to leave. Spontaneous migration to request asylum is unacceptable on a large scale to many Americans. Like Eastern Europeans since 1989 Cubans may have to settle for freedom to travel and forego emigration.

Migration and Caribbean Fertility

Massive, spontaneous emigration over more than 40 years has contributed to the reduction of fertility in the Caribbean and to the completion of the demographic transition in many countries except Haiti. The persistence of unemployment, underemployment, and young populations generates frustrations fed by media images and relatives' accounts of life overseas. Provided that Canada and the USA continue their global open-door immigration policies, many Caribbean islanders can realistically hope to emigrate. This accentuates the existing brain-drains, especially of nurses and technicians, but does continue the flow of remittances.

The evolving relations between Caribbean islands and their prospering North American diaspora communities are being carried into island politics, economics and culture. Emigration has become a way of life in many islands. Its continuance depends on the involvement of the diasporas and particularly those generations born abroad.

Mexican emigration to the USA is more than a century old. It has consisted both of migrant workers seeking rural and urban employment and individuals and families in search of new homes. Mexican legal immigrants to the USA numbered 405,172 in 1989; 37.1 per cent of all immigrants to the USA in that year. Another 2.3 million Mexicans took advantage of the 1986 USA amnesty legislation to apply for a changed status.

The numbers of Mexicans who illegally enter the USA can only be estimated on the basis of deportations. It is estimated to be several times greater than the number of legal immigrants. Increasingly, both the legals and the undocumented are coming to stay, to establish households, and to acquire legal status if possible. A working estimate would be approximately 1.2 million Mexicans a year entering the USA, primarily as job-seekers, with California being by far the destination of choice.

The Mexico-USA Free Trade Agreement currently being negotiated will also include Canada. It will not explicitly refer to free movement of persons at USA insistence. Some observers believe that it will generate increased new manufacturing employment in Mexico and reduce the incentives to emigrate. Mexico's 2 per cent population growth rate and population under the age of twenty generates large annual increases in the labour force. Emigration to the USA is becoming a way of life for many Mexican young people rather than a short-term means of earning dollars.

VOLUNTARY MIGRATION: EUROPE
Explanation
(Estimates for 1986)

Receiving Countries

1. Austria — Estimated 250,000 legal and illegal; Yugoslavia, Eastern Europe; foreign-born 4 per cent of total population

2. Belgium — Estimated 900,000 Morocco, Turkey, other EC 2 million foreign-born 9 per cent of total population

3. Denmark — 80,000 foreign residents; 50,000 migrant workers; mostly EC

4. France — Estimated 1.5 million legal and illegal migrant workers; Algeria, Morocco, Tunisia, Italy, Portugal, sub-Saharan Africa; foreign-born 11.1 per cent of 1981 total population

5. Germany — Estimated 1.5 million legal and illegal from Turkey, Italy, Poland, Spain; 4.5 million foreign residents; 3 million EC 1983 census and foreign-born 7.4 per cent of total population

6. Greece — Less than 100,000 migrant workers; 100,000 foreign residents

7. Italy — Estimated 1.2 million legal and illegal migrant workers; Tunisia, Morocco, Algeria, sub-Saharan Africa, others. Foreign-born 2 per cent of 1981 population

8. Luxembourg — 100,000 or 25 per cent of total population; mostly EC

9. Netherlands — 800,000 legal and illegal; Morocco, Turkey, Suriname, etc. 3.8 per cent of 1986 population

10. Spain — Estimated 300,000 legal and illegal; Morocco, Senegal

11. Sweden — Estimated 250,000 Finland, Yugoslavia, others. Estimated foreign-born 4.7 per cent of 1986 population. Refugee resettlement

12. Switzerland — 800,000 legal and illegal; Italy, Spain, Yugoslavia, others foreign-born at 16.7 per cent of 1980 population

13. United Kingdom — 800,000 migrant workers from Italy, Spain, other EC. Foreign-born at 6.3 per cent of total population in 1981. India, Pakistan, Bangladesh, Nigeria, Ghana, West Indies

Sending Countries

Greece, Spain, Italy, Portugal, Ireland continue to send small numbers of migrant workers to EC member states and to Switzerland. However, the principal sources of legal and illegal migrants are Algeria, Morocco, Tunisia, Turkey and Yugoslavia.

Sources: W.R. Böhning, *Studies in International Migration*, New York: St. Martin's, 1984.
European Community, *Employment in Europe*, Brussels, 1989.
W.A. Shadid, "The Integration of Muslim Minorities in the Netherlands," *International Migration Review*, Vol. XVI, No. 2, pp. 355-74.

**RECEIVING
COUNTRIES**

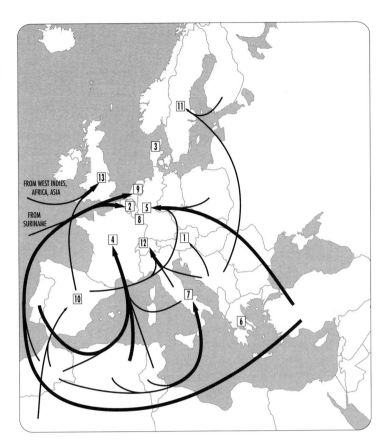

FROM WEST INDIES,
AFRICA, ASIA

FROM
SURINAME

**SENDING
COUNTRIES**

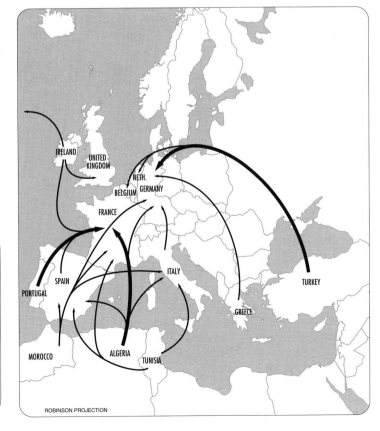

IRELAND

UNITED
KINGDOM

NETH.
BELGIUM GERMANY

FRANCE

SPAIN
PORTUGAL

ITALY

TURKEY

GREECE

MOROCCO
ALGERIA
TUNISIA

**VOLUNTARY MIGRATION:
EUROPE - 1986**

NUMBER OF MIGRANTS

——— 750 000 or less

━━━ More than 750 000

1 Item number in Explanation

|___1000 Kilometres___|
Scale at centre of map

NOTE: 1990 INTERNATIONAL BOUNDARIES DEPICTED

ROBINSON PROJECTION

VOLUNTARY MIGRATION:
EUROPE 1986

Europe since the sixteenth century has been the continent of emigration. Over four centuries more than 60 million Europeans peopled the Americas, Australia, South Africa, New Zealand, North Africa and other parts of the globe. While rates of return were often high it was the European exodus that changed the nature of the world. Individual countries participated to different degrees in that exodus but all experienced net emigration over extended periods of time. Countries with ample arable land and a gradual demographic transition like France and Switzerland had relatively less emigration. Countries of severe land pressure. multi-ethnic minorities, and high fertility were the principal senders, especially Germany and the Austro-Hungarian Empire.

European Historic Migration
Voluntary migration within Europe during this period was circumscribed. Oppressed minorities such as Jews, Poles, and Armenians were able to obtain limited asylum in France, Germany, Belgium, the Netherlands and the United Kingdom prior to 1914. Migration for employment and land occurred within the Russian and Austro-Hungarian Empires, sometimes as part of imperial expansion and settlement. However, only a handful of European businessmen, bankers and craftsmen were able to move freely across national boundaries in the eighteenth and nineteenth centuries. There was more freedom of movement for students, scholars and artists taking advantage of cosmopolitan traditions persisting from Catholic Church dominated medieval Europe.

Colonialism and Emigration
Colonialism made it possible for certain elites to travel freely to and from the metropoles. Spanish Americans of wealth and standing needed no visas to travel to colonial Spain nor did Brazilians to Portugal. The British, French and Dutch empires also facilitated a limited overseas travel to the home country. Wealthy planters in the British West Indies and other colonies often lived in England while occasionally visiting their estates.

There was little, though, in European experience to prepare for the emergence in the 1950s of voluntary migration on a mass scale. It was a push-pull response to the rapid economic expansion following World Way II and the appearance of shortages of unskilled labour. Britain was the first to open its doors and recruit West Indians between 1946 and 1963. France attracted workers from Algeria, Morocco, Tunisia and some of its Black African colonies. West Germany and Austria turned to Yugoslavia, Turkey, Spain, Greece and Italy for factory hands for their booming industries. Most Northern European countries became, by the mid 1960s, major importers of migrant workers. The lack of contact with communist controlled Eastern Europe meant that the Southern Mediterranean and North Africa were the principal sources.

Guestworkers in Europe
Most legal migrant workers were formally recruited for specified periods of time. Western European trade unions insisted on contracts guaranteeing humane treatment and eventual repatriation. However, many workers were able to stay, legally or illegally, and to reunite their families. Problems of education and integration for migrant worker children born in receiving countries arose in country after country. As citizens these children could not be repatriated and could, when of age, petition for their parents.

The slow-down of economic growth, and the emergence of domestic unemployment, partly triggered by the 1973-74 oil crises, put an end to voluntary migration. However, a Conservative Party government in Britain in 1963 had already ended easy migration from the West Indies and the rest of the Commonwealth. Concerned over rising racial tensions and the problems of integrating a new generation of "Black Britons", the 1963 British Immigration Act flatly rejected both migrant workers and permanent immigration. Within a decade most Western European countries had adopted closed door immigration policies and begun to phase out migrant worker schemes.

Repatriation of Guestworkers
The persistence of high unemployment rates and slow growth in many countries during the 1970-90 period gave emphasis to repatriating so-called "guestworkers." Credit, monetary and other incentives were tried in France, West Germany and other countries to induce workers to return voluntarily. These were most effective with Italians, Spaniards and Portuguese in Germany and Northern Europe. The expansion of economic opportunities at home combined with incentives to produce large-scale voluntary repatriation. Italy and Spain, after centuries of emigration, had become by 1990 the receivers of illegal migration from North Africa and elsewhere. However, a new, smaller exodus of better-educated migrant workers from Italy and Spain emigrated to Germany and Switzerland.

Voluntary repatriation has proved much more difficult with migrant workers from Turkey, Yugoslavia and North Africa where fewer opportunities exist. Governments have terminated recruitment from these and other countries. Family reunification has been allowed generally on a case by case basis as well as naturalization. Western European countries have become *de facto* multi-ethnic as communities formed of migrant workers and their dependants. Integration is the official policy in most countries while migrants and their offspring often demand recognition of home languages and cultures. These issues have become highly sensitive in France with its North African populations, and Germany with a Turkish-German group. Switzerland continues to deny strictly access to citizenship and to encourage repatriation and rotation.

Return of Global Settlers

The colonial legacy also presented migration problems. At the time of independence in 1975, 150,000 Surinamese, or one-third of the population, opted for Dutch citizenship and residence in the Netherlands. Their integration has proved difficult. Britain reluctantly accepted 30,000 Asians expelled from its ex-colony in Uganda in 1971 and is expected to take 50,000 persons from Hong Kong before 1997. An estimated 400,000 persons from the French overseas departments of Guadeloupe and Martinique have taken advantage of their French citizenship to move to the metropole. These ex-colonial commitments vary in nature from country to country.

Future of European Migration

The future of extra-regional migration in Europe is in doubt. Faced with high fertility, extremely young populations, and massive unemployment and underemployment, Algeria, Morocco and Tunisia would like to resume legal temporary worker schemes. Turkey as a candidate for membership in the European Community has renounced this objective. Like Portugal and Greece it would prefer massive EC investments to create jobs at home. Meanwhile in 1990 more than 600,000 persons from around the world requested asylum in European countries; an indicator of demands for employment.

Economic decline and political liberalization is resulting in a rush of work-seekers from Eastern Europe and even the ex-Soviet Union. Germany has accepted about 350,000 ethnic Germans but refuses to return to guestworkers or ethnic strangers. Austria has allowed Czechs, Hungarians, and Poles to visit without visas while also rejecting foreign workers. Nowhere in Western Europe plagued by unemployment, especially among the young, is there any interest in guestworkers.

European Community Immigration Policies

The EC by the 1957 Treaty of Rome is committed to freedom of movement, residence and employment for its citizens. Remaining barriers are to be removed at the end of 1992 when these rights are extended to Spain and Portugal.

Reality is another matter. About 250,000 people regularly cross borders to work in Europe; half from France to Switzerland. Cross-border migration after 1992 within the EC should be free of most formalities. (Cross-border migration between Ireland and the United Kingdom is already free but there is little movement.)

Wage and other differentials within EC countries have not generated large-scale migrations. Less than 2 million EC nationals are estimated to be working in another EC country compared to more than 2 million non-EC migrant workers. Germany, France and the United Kingdom host the most EC and non-EC workers. Austria and Sweden as high-income candidates for EC membership are unlikely to change this picture.

European Community Freedom of Movement

Freedom of movement within the EC is of considerable benefit to students, researchers and professionals seeking experiences in another country. The removal of multiple licensing and other requirements should make it easier for physicians, accountants, lawyers and others to move about Western Europe. The EC has initiated scholarships under Project Erasmus to encourage students to study in other countries. Already businessmen working in the EC enjoy *de facto* freedom of movement.

It is unlikely that European countries will return to formal migrant worker schemes. Yet they need to respond to urgent demands from Eastern Europe and North Africa for employment and foreign exchange earnings. Mobility within the EC may not be sufficient to provide needed labour if higher rates of growth are achieved. Ageing populations may also need to import labour for services. It is conceivable that Western Europe will again become a major importer of labour in the future, perhaps from Eastern Europe.

VOLUNTARY MIGRATION: MIDDLE EAST
Explanation
(Estimates for 1990 pre Gulf War)

Receiving Countries

1. Bahrain	70,000 contract workers from Pakistan, India, etc. Foreign-born in 1981 estimated at 32 per cent of total population
2. Iraq	400,000 from Egypt, Jordan, etc. prior to Gulf War
3. Israel	185,000 in 1990 from ex-Soviet Union; professionals and skilled; 18,000 Ethiopian Jews in 1990 airlift
4. Jordan	100,000 unskilled Egyptians replace Jordanian emigrants pre-1990 war
5. Kuwait	600,000 Egypt, Jordan, Palestine, Asians; 80 per cent of population pre-1990 war
6. Libya	500,000 from Tunisia, Egypt, Pakistan, etc. Mostly unskilled with some professionals and technicians
7. Oman	200,000 from India, Pakistan, etc.
8. Qatar	90,000 Pakistan, India, other Asian
9. Saudi Arabia	1.4 million Egypt, Jordan, Sudan, Somalia, Oman, Pakistan, India, Bangladesh, Sri Lanka, Philippines. 500,000 Yemenis expelled 1990

Sending Countries

10. Algeria	400,000 legal and undocumented to France, Belgium; unskilled
11. Bangladesh	250,000 to Saudi Arabia, Gulf; unskilled
12. Egypt	2.9 million in Saudi Arabia, Iraq, Gulf, Libya; mostly unskilled
13. India	800,000-1 million Saudi Arabia, Gulf, unskilled and semi-skilled
14. Indonesia	100,000 Saudi Arabia; construction and service workers
15. Jordan	400,000 Saudi Arabia, Kuwait, Gulf (includes Palestinians with Jordanian passports)
16. Lebanon	Emigrants to France, West Africa, USA, etc.
17. Morocco	400,000 France, Belgium, Spain, mostly unskilled
18. Pakistan	850,000-1.1 million Saudi Arabia, Gulf; mostly unskilled
19. Philippines	700,000-800,000 Saudi Arabia, Gulf, Kuwait; service workers, maids
20. Somalia	50,000 Saudi Arabia
21. Sudan	500,000 Saudi Arabia, Gulf; unskilled to professionals
22. Syria	200,000 Libya, Saudi Arabia, Kuwait
23. Thailand	100,000 Saudi Arabia, Gulf; construction/service
24. Tunisia	200,000 Italy, France; 50,000 to Libya; mostly unskilled
25. Yemen	500,000 to Saudi Arabia expelled during Gulf War; 200,000 to Iraq, Kuwait. North and South Yemen unite as single state in 1989. Mostly unskilled migrants

Note: Migrants are mostly adult males without dependants.

Sources: J.S. Birks, C. Sinclair, *Arab Manpower: The Crisis of Development*, London: Croom Helm, 1980. Philip L. Martin, "Labor Migration in Asia", *International Migration Review*, Vol. 25, Spring 1991, pp. 176-193.

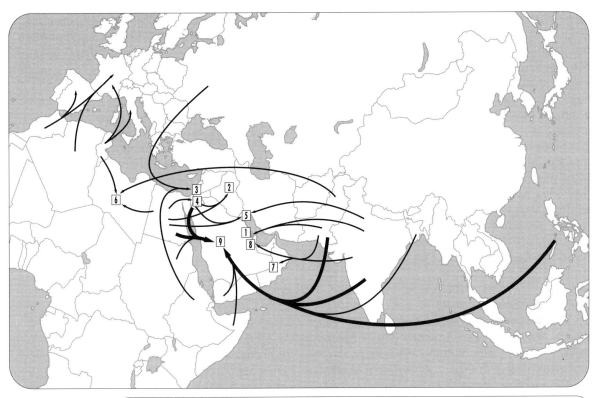

RECEIVING COUNTRIES

SENDING COUNTRIES

VOLUNTARY MIGRATION: MIDDLE EAST - 1990

1 Item number in Explanation

3000 Kilometres
Scale at centre of map

NUMBER OF MIGRANTS
750 000 or less
More than 750 000

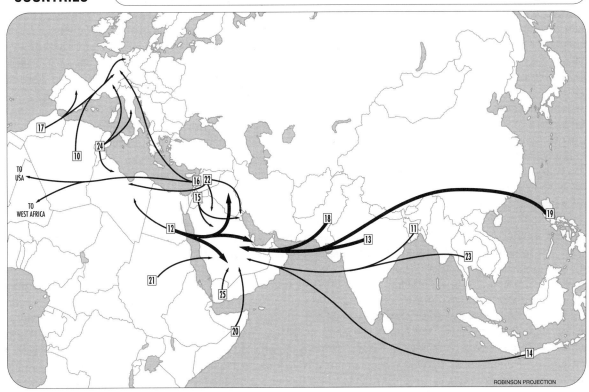

ROBINSON PROJECTION

VOLUNTARY MIGRATION: MIDDLE EAST 1990

Voluntary migration on a massive scale is a recent phenomenon in the Middle East. While distinguished travelers such as Ibn Battuta and Ibn-Khaldun roamed freely over much of the Islamic world during the thirteenth and fourteenth centuries, most Arabs and Muslims lived and died within sight of their birth places. During five centuries of Ottoman Empire rule migration was discouraged as much by lack of economic development as by bureaucracies. It was only in the last declining phase of the Empire from 1880-1914 that an estimated 300,000 Syrians and Lebanese emigrated to North and South America, the Jewish Zionist emigration to Palestine began, and restive Armenians discussed having a land of their own. Known as "Turks", the mostly Christian emigrants to the New World founded important diaspora communities in Argentina, Brazil, Chile, Canada, the USA and throughout the Caribbean.

Colonial Middle East Migration
Modern voluntary migration was initiated under French colonial rule. Nearly 1 million Arab and Berber-speaking Algerians took advantage of French citizenship to seek work in metropolitan France. Among these migrant workers the seeds of Algerian nationalism were planted. Lesser numbers of Moroccan and Tunisian workers and students resided in colonial France.

The impetus for mass migration began with the expansion of oil production in Saudi Arabia and the Gulf States in the 1950s. Initially unskilled and skilled workers were recruited from Egypt, the two Yemens, and other Arab states whose wage levels and economies were distinctly inferior. High-level manpower was drawn regionally also from Egypt with its surplus of university graduates, among Jordanians and Palestinians, and from the Sudan with its reputation for qualified professionals.

Oil Industry Migration
Several factors promoted this new and unprecedented flow. All the major oil-exporters except Algeria and Iraq had small and low density populations and acute shortages of skilled labour. As their revenues increased from petroleum they mounted major economic and social projects which required labour imports. Egypt and other densely populated countries were mired in economic stagnation combined with high fertility. The initial flows of high-level manpower became a flood-tide of several millions each year of the unskilled, mostly young men, finding work in construction and services.

Remittances soon became more important than Inter-Arab trade which never amounted to more than 10 per cent of the regions' total trade. Millions of dependants lived off these remittances, especially in Egypt, Yemen and among the Palestinians. Governments taxed the remittances in various ways in order partly to offset chronic balance of payments deficits.

Historian Albert Hourani maintains that by the end of the 1970s there were about 3 million Arab migrants with half in Saudi Arabia and the rest in Kuwait, the Gulf States and Libya. Even Iraq, with its large and cosmopolitan domestic population, began to import Egyptian workers. Egypt provided perhaps one-third of all migrants; Yemen another third, and the rest from Jordan/Palestine, Syria, Lebanon, Tunisia and Morocco.

Migration and Middle East Investment
The slump in oil revenues and prices during much of the 1980s did not disrupt the flow. Saudi Arabia and Kuwait used their overseas investments partly to finance major projects. However, there was a pronounced shift in the recruitment of workers to Pakistan, India, Bangladesh, the Philippines, Sri Lanka and other Asian states. This reflected both expanding labour demands that could not be met within the Arab world, and a desire to ensure that foreign workers would not be motivated to stay. Already by 1980 Asian migrant workers were nearly 60 per cent of the total. No distinction was made between Muslims and non-Muslims as Chinese, South Koreans and others were brought in to realize construction projects.

Effects of Remittances
Detailed analysis of the impacts of these remittances at the micro and macro levels indicates their expenditure for consumption and investment. Egypt and Yemen in particular remained highly dependent on remittances for foreign exchange.

Each of the receiving countries insisted on the exclusion of dependants in most instances, reliance on recruiting firms and fixed term contracts, and *de facto* segregation between migrant workers and host societies. These arrangements were not always strictly enforced, especially for Egyptians and other Arabic-speakers but rigid laws barred citizenship and overstays. The incidence of illegal migration is not known but it is generally regarded to be low. Instead of acquiring a sense of freedom of movement within the Arab world, migrants were objects of labour.

Middle East Brain-Drains
The voluntary exodus has produced a pronounced brain-drain within the region due to superior wages and working conditions in the rich countries. The Sudan has lost a majority of its educated professionals, especially physicians, and Somalia, Egypt and Jordan have also been severely impacted. The rich countries have invested substantially in education, including study abroad, but they remain high-manpower deficient given their massive projects. A kind of Arab labour market in professionals has emerged although confined to limited contracts.

The fragility of these flows was evidenced during the 1990-91 Gulf War including the pre-war period. More than 1 million migrant workers were evacuated from Iraq and the other countries creating a brief refugee situation. Saudi Arabia expelled 500,000 Yemenis long-resident in their country on the grounds that their government favoured Iraq. An estimated 170,000 Palestinians fled Kuwait before and after the war. Economic activity largely ground to a halt in the Gulf due to the loss of workers and remittances.

As the war ended governments pledged to reduce their dependence on imported labour. However, Saudi Arabia began to replace Yemenis with Egyptians. Kuwait resumed its recruiting and Iraq resigned itself to rebuilding with its own resources.

Maghreb Migration Patterns

The three Maghreb states have participated in the flow of labour to the Gulf only marginally. Tunisia has provided unskilled and some skilled labour to Libya only to experience two expulsions for political reasons.

The Maghreb has instead concentrated on legal and illegal migration to France, Belgium, Italy and Spain. Although the European Community responded to the 1973 oil crisis and a decade of unemployment and economic stagnation by terminating overseas migrant worker recruitment many North Africans managed to stay on. As EC economic growth resumed Italy and Spain became prime targets for North African clandestine migration. Several million legal and illegal workers from North Africa, mostly unskilled, were employed in Western Europe in the 1980s.

How lasting is this massive export of labour within and outside the region? It reflects the demography of sending societies with rapidly growing youthful populations. It corresponds to the low fertility, ageing, services intensive societies of Western Europe. The disadvantages are those of family separation, dependence on remittances, lack of protection for migrant workers, and the risks of political disruptions The tensions involved in poor Arabs working in menial jobs in Europe and the Gulf must also be considered. Essentially, voluntary migration has become a form of redistribution of income through employment. It is not a substitute for economic development but it has become so for many.

VOLUNTARY MIGRATION: SOUTH AMERICA
Explanation
(Estimates for 1990)

Includes permanent immigration, legal and illegal migration

Receiving Countries

1. Argentina	Estimated 2 million; Bolivia sends 700,000 farm labour and urban unskilled workers; Paraguay 800,000 farm workers, construction; Chile 300,000 rural workers; Uruguay 200,000 urban skilled; post-World War II immigration of Syrians, Lebanese, Germans, etc. 1946-55
2. Europe	Brain-drains from Argentina, Brazil, etc.
3. Paraguay	Estimated legal and illegal 350,000 Brazilians. Mostly squatters and soya bean farmers in sparsely populated Eastern Paraguay
4. USA	Estimated 500,000 from Argentina, Brazil, Colombia, others
5. Venezuela	Estimated 800,000 legal and illegal Colombians in urban services, farm work; 15,000 middle-level manpower from Dominican Republic 1946-1955: legal middle-level manpower from Italy, Portugal, Spain, etc.

Other temporary legal and illegal migrations on a small scale occur between most South American countries. There are also modest flows of students and researchers.

Sending Countries

6. Argentina	Estimated 500,000 skilled to USA, Western Europe
7. Bolivia	700,000 to Argentina, mostly rural labour in neighbouring provinces; 100,000 to Brazil; 125,000 to Chile
8. Brazil	Estimated 630,000 to Japan, Western Europe, USA; 335,000 rural squatters to Paraguay
9. Colombia	Estimated 800,000 illegal and legal in Venezuela; urban services; estimated 100,000 in Ecuador; 400,000 USA
10. Dominican Republic	Estimated legal 15,000 middle-level manpower to Venezuela
11. Ecuador	Estimated 80,000 in Colombia and Venezuela; semi-skilled, 150,000 to USA
12. Paraguay	Estimated 800,000 in Argentina, rural and urban unskilled; estimated 70,000 in Brazil in border areas
13. Peru	Estimated 100,000 in Chile, skilled and semi-skilled; 35,000 Bolivia, 150,000 to USA
14. Uruguay	Estimated 200,000 legal and illegal in Argentina; professionals and skilled

Note: Due to undercounting of illegal migrants, lack of recent census data, and frequency of border-crossing data are often not reliable. Projections are based on most recent data.

Sources: Sergio Díaz-Briquets, *International Migration in the Americas*, New York: Center for Migration Studies, 1983.

Mary M. Kritz, *Migraciones Internacionales en Las Américas*, Caracas: CEPAM, 1980.

Nicolás Sánchez-Albornoz, *The Population of Latin America, A History*, Berkeley: University of California Press, 1974.

RECEIVING COUNTRIES

TO USA [4]

FROM ITALY, PORTUGAL, SPAIN

PRE - 1955

[2] TO EUROPE

[5]

FROM GERMANY, SYRIA, LEBANON

[3]

[1]

PRE - 1955

SENDING COUNTRIES

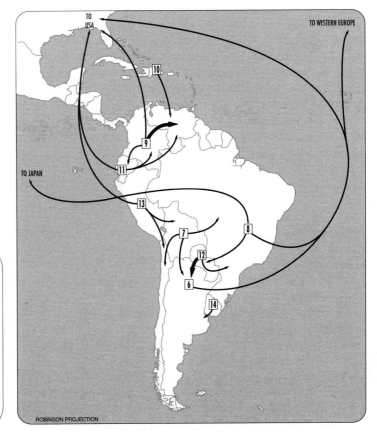

TO USA

TO WESTERN EUROPE

[10]

TO JAPAN

[9]

[11]

[13]

[8]

[7]

[12]

[6]

[14]

ROBINSON PROJECTION

VOLUNTARY MIGRATION: SOUTH AMERICA - 1990

NUMBER OF MIGRANTS

—— 750 000 or less

━━ More than 750 000

[1] Item number in Explanation

2000 Kilometres
Scale at centre of map

VOLUNTARY MIGRATION: SOUTH AMERICA (Estimates for 1990)

Voluntary immigration, regional and extra-regional, has played a declining role since the 1950s. In spite of a history of massive nineteenth century immigration in Argentina and Brazil these and other countries have ceased to be attractive to outsiders. Legal and illegal intra-regional migration has been frustrated by high rates of unemployment and underemployment and periodic economic recessions. Intra-regional migration accounts for less than 5 per cent of the total labour force of South America and is concentrated in the urban centres of Caracas and Buenos Aires and a few zones of seasonal agricultural harvest.

Historic South American Patterns

For a decade after World War II there was significant European and Middle-Eastern immigration to Argentina, Chile, Venezuela and Brazil. Many of these immigrants returned although significant new communities of persons of Lebanese descent remained in Argentina and Brazil. However, since the mid-1950s the recovery of European economies, a tightening of South American immigration rules, and local intermarriage has kept extra-regional legal immigration to a minimum. An important factor has been the high growth rate of the Spanish economy, long the source of impoverished immigrants to South America.

Ostensibly there should be extensive legal and illegal migration. Cultures and languages are similar, especially in border areas where multiple crossings are frequent. The opportunities for assimilation of migrants are considerable. Except for a few traditional rivalries (Bolivia-Paraguay, Chile-Bolivia, Ecuador-Peru) ethnic and other prejudices are not strong. There is a modest but long-standing movement of students, researchers, and professionals between the countries, especially to Argentina, Venezuela, and Chile with their well-regarded academic centres. Although national and sub-national accents and dialects are readily identifiable there are fewer cultural and linguistic barriers to migration in South America than in any other part of the world for Spanish-speakers.

Prospects for Migration

The problem is why there is so little international migration in the Americas when it is so relatively easy? The answer lies in the nature of the economic and other disparities between countries and regions. Where these disparities are significant major migrations do occur (Bolivia, Paraguay and Uruguay towards Argentina; Colombia to Venezuela). Elsewhere, as among the Andean countries, or Brazil and its neighbours, standards of living are sufficiently close to discourage mass migration. Enforcement of stricter immigration laws and work and residence permits serves with pervasive unemployment to discourage high-risk international migration.

Migration Pull Factors: South America

Argentina and Venezuela have per capita incomes two to three times greater than the principal sending countries. (Uruguayan emigration to Argentina is mostly middle-class and an exception). Elsewhere the pull factor is weak as economic disparities between countries are less wide. However, there is extensive and often unrecorded illegal border-crossing for purposes of smuggling, seasonal farm labour, etc. Where economic disparities are widening, as between rapidly growing Chile and declining Peru, clandestine migration is on a sharp rise.

South America is one of the few regions of the world where extensive unused arable land exists. This has prompted spontaneous emigration from several countries into the Amazon Basin which borders six nations. This has accelerated deforestation and other ecological dangers while facilitating smuggling, drug-trafficking, and related acts in a region with little governmental control. The peopling of the Amazon has been facilitated by government investments in roads and other infrastructure but it is basically spontaneous. Most of the migration is on the Brazilian side but all of the Amazon border areas are experiencing rapid demographic growth. Extensive cross-border movements are likely to continue.

What are the prospects for future international migration in the Americas? Immigration from outside is unlikely unless governments greatly increase their willingness to accept refugees. Experiences in Brazil and to a lesser extent in Paraguay and Peru prior to 1940 with Chinese and Japanese immigrants, many of whom returned, are not conducive to mass acceptance of Indochinese refugees. Governments are convinced that population scarcity is not a problem.

Responsiveness to Migration Factors

Migrants within South America move swiftly in response to perceived economic opportunities and growth poles. A continent which is now 70 per cent urbanized does not generate large numbers of unskilled jobs for outsiders. Persistent rates of unemployment, underemployment and low prevailing wages are not incentives to international migration. Democratically-elected governments may be less likely to allow migrant workers to compete for jobs.

South American Regional Cooperation

The several proposals and schemes for regional economic cooperation in South America have not provided for free movement of labour. The current five-nation Andean Pact, and the four-nation proposed Southern Cone Common Market are strictly confined to free movement of goods and services, not people. However, there is potential for legislation which could facilitate the movement of professionals and technicians across national boundaries; a movement which is already taking place to a limited extent. Argentina and Brazil are experiencing an acute brain-drain to Europe and to North America which might at least be alleviated by selective regional high-manpower migration. Already the two governments have agreed on the establishment of a joint nuclear research centre and other facilities.

The potential and the reality of international migration in South America are far apart. Theoretically there are major gains from freer movement of high and middle-level manpower. In reality these are the posts where politically nationalism in the public and private sectors is most opposed to hiring foreigners who might stay. However, these objections are changing. Movement of unskilled labour has been deterred by a decade of economic recession in most countries and lack of economic opportunities. A revival of sustained economic growth could reduce the gap between theory and practice.

INVOLUNTARY
MIGRATIONS

WORLD INVOLUNTARY MIGRATION
Explanation
(1500-1900)

Involuntary Migration Movements Shown on Map
1.   West Africa to North America,500,000.
2.   West Africa to Mexico and Central America,500,000.
3.   West and Central Africa to the Caribbean,4 million.
4.   West Africa to Northern South America,750,000.
5.   West and Central Africa to Brazil,3.6 million.
6.   West and Central Africa to southern South America, 250,000.
7.   West Africa to Western Europe, 150,000.
8.   West Africa to Southern Europe, 150,000.
9.   Northeast Africa to the Middle East,250,000.
10.   Northeast Africa to the Arabian Peninsula,2.5 million.
11.   East and Central Africa to the Arabian Peninsula, 500,000.
12.   East and Central Africa to the Persian Gulf,400,000.
13.   United Kingdom to Australia, 156,000.

Sources: Philip D. Curtin, *The Atlantic Slave Trade, A Census,* Madison: University of Wisconsin Press, 1969, p.258
Colin McEvedy, Richard Jones, *Atlas of World Population History*, New York: Penguin,1978, p.215-17
Paul E. Lovejoy, *Transformations of Slavery, A History of Slavery in Africa*, London: Cambridge University Press,1983

World Involuntary Migration
1500-1900
The African Slave Trade to North and South America, the Caribbean, Europe, the Middle East, and the Persian Gulf dominated international involuntary migration from 1500 until 1900 when it was both legally abolished and largely, although not entirely, suppressed. An estimated 9-11 million Africans were taken as slaves to the Americas and Europe during this period and an estimated 4.3 million to the Middle East and the Persian Gulf. The extent and duration of this intercontinental involuntary migration was far greater than the many involuntary migrations within and between societies on any single continent. The Age of Sail and improvements in navigation made it possible to move large numbers of persons against their will over long distances. Other forced migrations included Jews and Moors expelled from Spain in 1492 and from Portugal in 1650, Protestant Hugenots expelled from France from 1580-1600, and exiles due to the French Revolution 1791-1798.

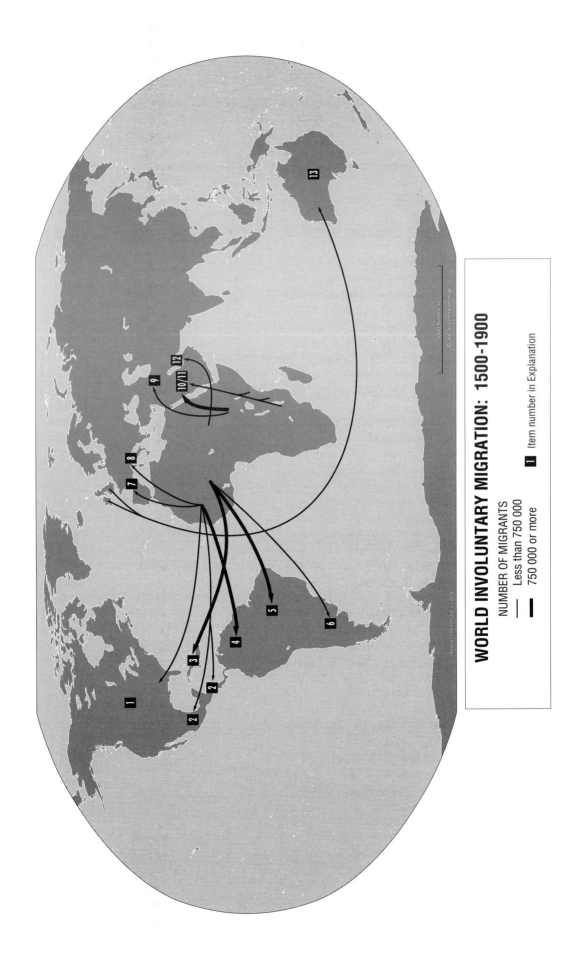

WORLD INVOLUNTARY MIGRATION: 1500-1900

NUMBER OF MIGRANTS
— Less than 750 000
▬ 750 000 or more

1 Item number in Explanation

ROBINSON PROJECTION

5000 Kilometres
Scale at centre of map

WORLD INVOLUNTARY MIGRATION
Explanation
(1900-1980)

Sending Countries

Involuntary Migration Movements Shown on the Map

1. El Salvador, Guatemala, and Nicaragua to the USA and Mexico,1970 to 1980, 500,000
2. Cubans to the USA 1960 to 1980, 900,000
3. Germans from Poland to Germany, 1918-1925 and 1944-47, 6.7 million
4. Russians and others from the ex-Soviet Union to Europe, 1918-1922, 1.15 million
5. Poles and others from the ex-Soviet Union to Europe, 1918-1925, 2 million
6. Reich Germans from the ex-Soviet Zone to the US and British Zones of Occupation, Germany, 1945-46, 4 million; ethnic Germans from Czechoslovakia to Germany and Austria, 1945-46, 4 million; ethnic Czechs and Slovaks from inner Czechoslovakia to former German Sudetenland,1946-47,1.8 million
7. Jews from Germany and elsewhere in Europe to extermination camps in Poland, 1940-44, 5 million
8. Hungarians to Austria and re-emigration after 1956 uprising, 250,000
9. Spaniards to France and re-emigration to Mexico and elsewhere during the Spanish Civil War,1936-1939, 250,000
10. Greeks to Greece from Turkey, 1922-1923,1.2 million
11. Armenians expelled from Turkey to Russia and elsewhere,1913-1922, 500,000
12. Palestinians to Middle East in aftermath of 1948 War of Israeli Independence, 700,000
13. Eritreans and others from Ethiopia to Somalia and Dijibouti, 1975 to the present, 700,000
14. African refugees to neighboring states from Burundi, Chad, Equatorial Guinea, Ethiopia, Rwanda, Sudan, Uganda, Western Sahara (SADR) and others to Algeria, Botswana, Cameroon, Kenya, Nigeria, Tanzania and others, 1960 to 1980, 5 million. Several states, Mozambique, South Africa, Uganda, Zimbabwe, have at different times received or generated refugees
15. Afghanistan to Pakistan and Iran after the Soviet invasion, 1979 to the present, 3.2 million
16. India to Pakistan refugee exchanges during 1947 Partition, 15 million
17. Bangladesh and Pakistan exchanges in 1972 war of secession, 2 million
18. Vietnamese, Laotians, and Cambodians to Thailand, Malaysia, Hong Kong, Singapore, and Indonesia for re-emigration to the USA, France, China, Canada, Australia and elsewhere, 1975 to the present as aftermath of Vietnam War, 1.5 million
19. South Koreans from North to South Korea during and after Korean War, 1950-54, 5 million

Sources: Charles Tilley, "Migration in Modern European History". In *Human Migration*. Edited by Ruth S. Adams and William McNeil, Bloomington: Indiana University Press, 1977, pp.61 -82

G. Beijer, "Modem Patterns of International Migration Movements". In *Migrations*. Edited by J.A. Jackson, London: Cambridge University Press, 1984, pp.18-22

US Department of State, *Atlas of US External Relations*, Washington, DC: 1984. Refugee Migration Settlement since 1945.

World Involuntary Migration
1900-1980

The map figures refer to all forms of involuntary migration across national boundaries during this period, primarily refugees. The tentative and approximate total for the last four decades of the twentieth century is nearly 70 million persons who have involuntarily left one country for another whether during times of war or lesser conflicts. The total number of international refugees since 1900 probably exceeds the total of involuntary international migrants in all previous recorded human history. The causes include World Wars I and II and a series of national or regional conflicts which have uprooted people across international boundaries on a scale never previously known.

Refugee resettlement in third countries is problematical. Between 1914 and 1945 there were few overseas takers for the millions fleeing war and fascism. At the end of World War II Argentina, Australia, Canada, New Zealand and the USA opened their doors to millions of European displaced persons. Since then refugee resettlement abroad on a large-scale has been available mainly to Cubans, Czechs, Hungarians and Vietnamese fleeing communist regimes.

57

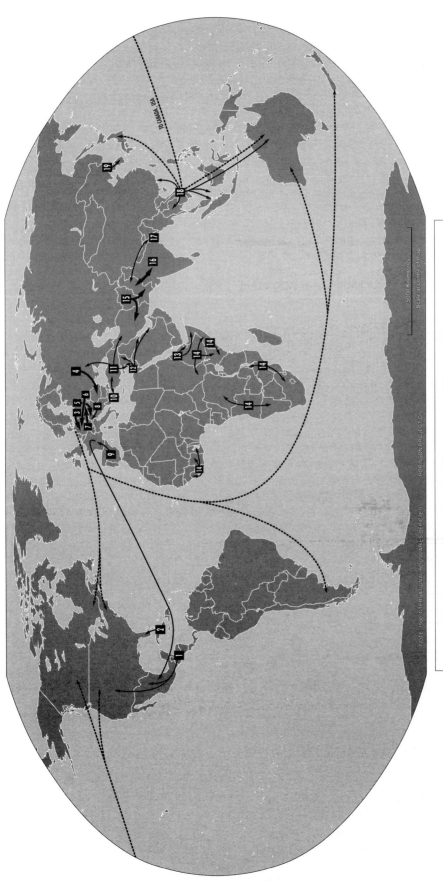

WORLD INVOLUNTARY MIGRATION: 1900-1980

NUMBER OF MIGRANTS

— 2 million or less

▌ Greater than 2 million

■ Item number in Explanation

- - - - Refugee resettlement

↔ Double arrow indicates some repatriation

5000 Kilometres
Scale at centre of map

NOTE: 1990 INTERNATIONAL BOUNDARIES DEPICTED   ROBINSON PROJECTION

WORLD INVOLUNTARY MIGRATION: SENDING COUNTRIES
Explanation
(Estimates for 1990)

REGION - AFRICA

1. Angola — A post-independence civil war has sent refugees to neighbouring Zaïre, Namibia, and other countries: 1975-present

2. Burundi — Persistent conflicts between the governing minority Tutsi and the majority Hutu generate refugees: 1965-present

3. Chad — Series of civil wars and foreign interventions send refugees to neighbouring countries: 1975-present

4. Ethiopia — Secessionist civil wars and internal strife generate refugees. Ethiopia accepts refugees from Sudanese civil war: 1974-present

5. Liberia — Civil war directed against a military government leads to outpouring of refugees to Guinea, Côte d'Ivoire, Sierra Leone: 1989-present

6. Mozambique — Post-independence civil war results in massive exodus to Malawi, South Africa, Zimbabwe: 1975-present

7. Mauritania — Refuge for Mauritanians expelled from Senegal in 1990 ethnic violence. Expels Senegalese living in Mauritania

8. Namibia — Independence movement (SWAPO) wins 1989 election after decades in exile: large-scale return, 1960-1989

9. Rwanda — Hutu majority expels Tutsis to Uganda, Zaïre, Tanzania. Tutsi re-invasion from Uganda fails in 1990: 1964-present

10. Senegal — Accepts nationals expelled from Mauritania in 1990. Expels Mauritanians resident in Senegal: 1990-present

11. Somalia — Refugees from 1977 military defeat vs. Ethiopia: refugees from civil war which overthrew Barre government: 1991

REGION - ASIA/PACIFIC

12. Afghanistan — Civil war and Soviet military intervention sends more than 6 million Afghans to Pakistan and Iran for refuge: 1979-present. Soviets withdraw but war continues; limited repatriation

13. Burma (Myanmar) — Continuing repression of minorities, students and others generates refugees to Thai, Bangladesh border areas: 1980-present

14. Cambodia — Civil war, Vietnamese occupation, Khmer Rouge massacres generate more than 800,000 refugees, mostly in Thailand: 1979-present

15. Laos — Estimated 350,000 emigrants mainly in Thailand, USA

16. Sri Lanka — Spontaneous migration to India and return: civil war 1988

17. Vietnam — Mass exodus in 1979 following end of Vietnam war. Exodus due to political repression and economic plight: 1980-present. Spontaneous emigration via small boats to neighbouring countries.

China accepts 252,000 ethnic Chinese from Vietnam 1978-1982: resettlement to USA (includes 13,000 Amerasians), Canada, Australia, France, etc. Estimated 1.5 million refugees since 1979

REGION- CARIBBEAN/CENTRAL AMERICA

18. Cuba — Limited legal emigration to USA; others flee or defect.

19. El Salvador — Civil war drives Salvadoreans into exile in Guatemala, Honduras, Nicaragua. Some return as war winds down: 1979-present

20. Guatemala — Indians flee into Mexico from army raids: 1983-1986. Some return with Guatemalan elected government, others in camps.

21. Haiti — Boat-people interdicted and repatriated since 1982 by US Coast Guard. US courts limit asylum to Haitians

22. Nicaragua — Refugees in Costa Rica and Honduras due to civil war. Some repatriation after 1989 election

REGION - EUROPE

23. Albania — Spontaneous exodus in 1990-1991 to Greece and Italy; forced repatriation except for ethnic Greeks

24. Bulgaria — Ethnic Turks expelled and encouraged to leave, 1989; some allowed to return 1990.

25. Poland — Estimated 800,000 to 1 million emigration since 1980 including 250,000 ethnic Germans. Few qualify as refugees

26. Romania — Expels some ethnic Hungarians in 1989; allows most Jews to emigrate to Israel; 17,000 ethnic Germans leave

27. Soviet Union — Ethnic Germans, Jews, ethnic Greeks allowed to leave (1989-1991); some Armenians, dissidents allowed to leave

REGION - MIDDLE EAST

28. Iran — Political exiles and others since 1979 Islamic Revolution

29. Iraq — Kurdish, Shiite and other minorities fleeing violence: 1980-present

30. Palestinians — Expelled from Kuwait and other countries before and after Gulf War due to pro-Iraq views: 1990-present

REGION - SOUTH AMERICA

31. Chile — Over 100,000 political exiles after the 1973 military coup. Many return after 1989 elections: 1973-1989

32. Suriname — Ethnic conflicts, insurgency, and military repressions force Maroons into neighbouring French Guiana: 1985-present

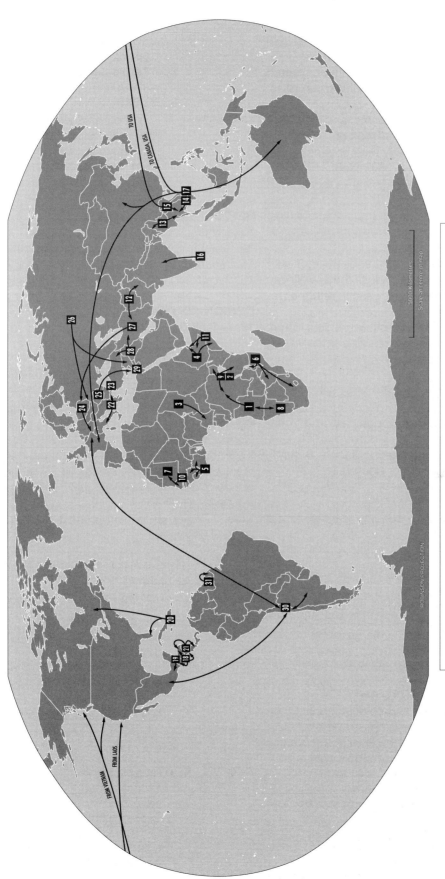

WORLD INVOLUNTARY MIGRATION: SENDING COUNTRIES MIGRATIONS - 1990

■ Item number in Explanation

↔ Double arrow indicates some repatriation

5000 Kilometres

Scale at centre of map

ROBINSON PROJECTION

TO USA

TO CANADA, USA

FROM VIETNAM

FROM LAOS

WORLD INVOLUNTARY MIGRATION: RECEIVING COUNTRIES
Explanation
(Estimates for 1990)

REGION-AFRICA

1. Côte d'Ivoire — Receives Liberian refugees from 1990-1991 civil war

2. Djibouti — This miniscule port city harbours Ethiopian, Somali civil war refugees: 1977-present

3. Malawi — Massive influx of Mozambican refugees stretches resources. Refugees constitute nearly ten per cent of total population: 1975-present

4. Sierra Leone — Accepts refugees from Liberian civil war: 1991

5. South Africa — Accepts return of South African exiles. Limited asylum for Mozambican civil war refugees

6. Tanzania — Refugees from Burundi, Rwanda, and Mozambique. One of the few African governments to allow refugee resettlement

7. Zambia — Houses refugees from Angola, Zaïre, and Mozambique while encouraging their repatriation. Namibians return 1989

8. Zimbabwe — Refugees from Mozambique's civil war. During Zimbabwe's War for Independence, Mozambique helped its refugees

Others — Kenya, Cameroon, Gabon, Burundi, Rwanda, Zaïre, Uganda

First Asylum Countries
Most African receiving countries except Tanzania

REGION-ASIA/PACIFIC
First Asylum Only
Hong Kong, Indonesia, Malaysia, Philippines, Singapore, Thailand, Iran, Pakistan
Refugee Resettlement Countries
Australia, New Zealand

REGION-CARIBBEAN/CENTRAL AMERICA

9. Belize — Accepts Salvadorean refugees for resettlement.

10. Costa Rica — Offers temporary asylum to refugees from Salvadorean and Nicaraguan civil wars: 1979-present

11. Honduras — Accepts Salvadorean refugees in 1980s in spite of 1968 Honduras-El Salvador War; Nicaraguan Contra forces and refugees pre-1989

REGION-EUROPE

19. First Asylum   Austria, Greece, and Spain

Asylum — France, United Kingdom, Norway, Sweden, Switzerland, Denmark, and the Netherlands. These and other European countries granted 65,000 persons resettlement or asylum in 1989.

12. Turkey — Accepted ethnic Turk refugees from Bulgaria in 1989 but encouraged their repatriation. Accepted a limited number of temporary asylum Kurdish refugees from Iraq in 1991

REGION-MIDDLE EAST

13. Jordan — Accepts Palestinians
14. Israel — Accepts Jews for resettlement
15. Lebanon — Repatriation as civil war declines
16. Syria — Limited number of Palestinians

REGION-SOUTH AMERICA

17. Argentina — Returns to democracy in 1983; offers asylum to Chileans, etc.

18. French Guiana
Refugees from Suriname

19. Countries Offering to Resettle Refugees

Australia, Austria, Canada, Denmark, Finland, France, Germany, Japan, Netherlands, Norway, Spain, Sweden, Switzerland, United Kingdom. During 1989 the USA resettled or granted asylum to 106,250 persons: the rest of the world to 105,373 (Canada 35,000, Australia 11,663)

Note: Regional sections contain further details and refugee estimates.

Sources: US Committee for Refugees, *World Refugee Survey*, Washington, DC, 1990.
UNHCR *Map of World Refugee Populations*, Geneva, 1991.

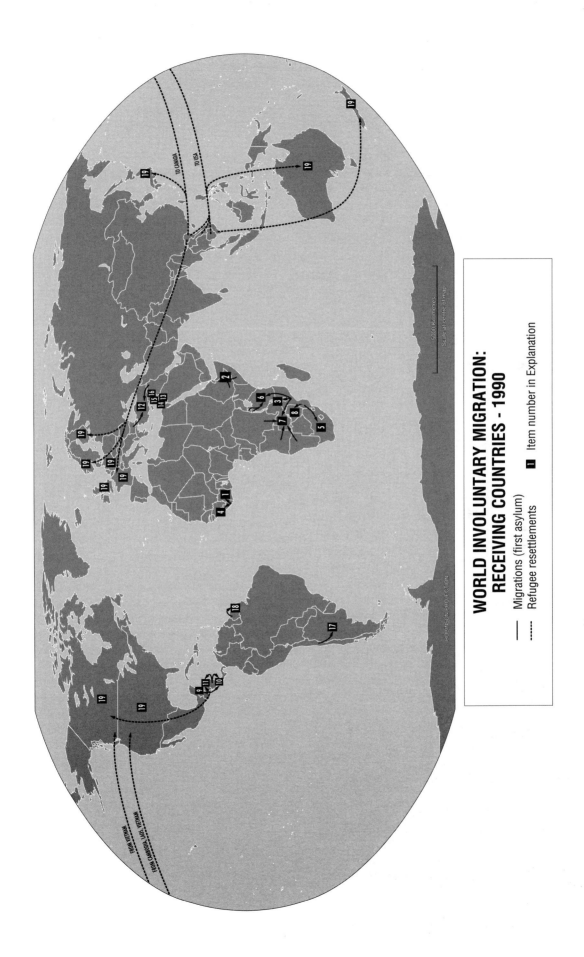

WORLD INVOLUNTARY MIGRATION: RECEIVING COUNTRIES - 1990

— Migrations (first asylum)

---- Refugee resettlements

■ Item number in Explanation

TO CANADA

TO USA

FROM VIETNAM

FROM CAMBODIA, LAOS, VIETNAM

5000 Kilometres
Scale at centre of map

ROBINSON PROJECTION

WORLD INVOLUNTARY MIGRATION 1980-1990

The world refugee crisis is a test of international compassion. At the end of 1989 there were an estimated 15.2 million refugees in the world, up from 8 million in 1980. The map shows more than thirty countries generating refugees during this period. The potential for internal violence and/or inter-state conflict generating even more refugees exists in dozens of other countries. The prospect of refugees spilling out of China, India or the ex-Soviet Union has to be taken seriously.

Nature of Refugee Situations

The map and data indicate that few refugee situations are resolved quickly. Many involve prolonged conflicts, wars of attrition in which mostly refugee women and children are trapped for years in camps. While diplomacy can solve disputes and permit refugees to return, as in Namibia or Nicaragua, this too requires many years rather than months.

Refugees and Democracy

Can the diffusion of democratically elected regimes reduce the incidence of refugees? It has done so in South America and apparently in Central America but the verdict is not yet in. Democratic governments can break down, especially in multi-ethnic societies, thus generating new violence and refugee crises. Majority rule in a democracy can and sometimes does trample on the rights of ethnic minorities. Democracy promises more than authoritarian regimes to alleviate the tensions that breed refugee crises but it is no panacea. Where the tensions involve demands for autonomy or even secession as in the Soviet Union, majority rule can make things worse. What matters is that most consent-based governments are less likely to deliberately foment refugee crises.

Mounting Refugee Crises

Meanwhile, as the absolute numbers of refugees mounts, there are disturbing signs of donor fatigue and declining compassion. Government contributions to the five official refugee organizations (UNHCR, International Red Cross, UN Border Relief Operation, UNRWA, and the International Organization for Migration) totalled nearly $1.1 billion in 1989. This is less than $70 per refugee. The USA provided about 22 per cent: Japan contributed $146 million or 12 per cent; Germany $77.8 million or 7 per cent. It is Australia, Canada, Denmark, Norway and Sweden whose generous contributions proportionately far exceed the size of their economies, that are keeping the system going. The rapidly-growing newly industrializing countries (South Korea, Singapore, etc.) do not contribute at all nor do most of the oil-exporting states. Granted in many receiving countries there are often national committees and private organizations which support refugee services. Still, the organizations cannot lurch from crisis to crisis without broader-based financial support. This means in particular Germany, obsessed with unification and assimilating ethnic Germans from Eastern Europe,

and Japan determined not to accept refugees in its homogeneous society. A larger financial effort by these two economic giants and by the European Community is essential to meet present and future challenges.

Internally Displaced Persons

The biggest gap in coverage continues to be the millions of internally displaced persons. One of the lessons of the Gulf War is that assisting refugees and helping the internally displaced go together. Repatriation can only occur when the safety of those who have stayed behind is guaranteed.

Similarly, the need to work with long-term refugees is urgent. A wide variety of literacy, community development, agricultural, vocational, and other donor programs have been attempted with some success. Strapped for funds the UNHCR and its associates are unable to improve the human resources of most refugees. Perhaps some kind of endowment might enable the refugee organizations to escape the dilemma of annual funding when they must respond to unpredictable crises and demands.

Meeting Refugee Needs

Ultimately the global network to assist refugees needs to be extended and deepened. While a globally-televised rock concert can reach hundreds of millions and raise considerable funds there is often little follow-up. Many private refugee relief organizations are marginal in their societies as are government refugee commissions. Compassion needs to be converted into lasting political support. Otherwise the world will have more and more refugees and fewer resources to help.

INVOLUNTARY MIGRATION: AFRICA 1990

The African refugee crisis is steadily worsening. The total number of refugees at the end of 1989 was estimated at 4.227 million, up from 4.01 million in 1988. The number of refugees has been doubling every decade since the era of political independence in the 1960s. Currently thirty-three of fifty-two independent African states are hosting refugees: eleven countries are both hosting and generating refugees.

Causes of African Refugee Crises

The main causes are prolonged internal civil wars in multi-ethnic societies. Most refugees in Africa are rural dwellers who have fled violence across a nearby border, often where they have kinsmen or relatives. The number of internally displaced persons from these civil wars who cannot access a safe border is much greater than the number of refugees. Providing external assistance to these internally displaced in combat zones is a hazardous and frustrating task.

Government Responses to Refugee Needs

Most African governments have been extremely generous in providing temporary asylum to refugees. Permanent resettlement has been less forthcoming due to scarcities of arable land and other resources. Donor agencies have had to be careful that their refugee projects did not favor newcomers over nationals. The prevailing assumption has been that political violence would eventually end and that refugees would be able to return. However, conflict has continued in Angola, Mozambique, Ethiopia, Somalia, and the Sudan for more than a decade, stranding millions of refugees. With resettlement rejected and return too dangerous, the refugee camps have become a way of life, financed by donors and resented by hosts. There is no alternative to political settlements which provide a minimum of security for ethnic minorities.

INVOLUNTARY MIGRATION: AFRICA
Explanation
(Estimates for 1990)

Receiving/Sending Countries

1. Angola — 9,700 from Zaïre partly integrated. Return of refugees to Namibia, and to South Africa
2. Benin — 800 from Chad. Some are returning
3. Botswana — 740 from several countries. Some returning to Namibia, South Africa, Zimbabwe
4. Burkina Faso — 360 refugees from Chad and Ghana. Illegal Burkina Faso migrants return from the Côte d'Ivoire and Ghana
5. Burundi — 80,000 from Rwanda and 20,000 from Zaïre. Partly integrated
6. Cameroon — 3,700 from Chad and 400 from other countries. Some Chadians are returning
7. Central African Republic — 1,720 (1,600 from Chad). Some returning
8. Congo — 2,300 from Chad and 3,370 total. Some Chadians returning
9. Côte d'Ivoire — 530 from several countries. Accepts Vietnamese. 1989-1990 civil war refugees from Liberia, 120,000. Does not include illegal migrant workers from Burkina Faso, Mali, etc.
10. Dijibouti — 27,500 from Somalia and 1,450 from Ethiopia
11. Ethiopia — Refugees to Dijibouti, Kenya, Somalia, Sudan, estimated 750,000
12. Gabon — 800 from several countries including Angola
13. Ghana — 80 from all countries well-integrated
14. Kenya — 12,450 (6,200 from Ethiopia, 3,000 from Uganda; 2,000 from Rwanda). 200,000 Ethiopia, Somalia, 1991. Some forced repatriations of Somalis and Ugandans
15. Lesotho — 30 from all countries. Lesotho exiles abroad
16. Liberia — Estimated 250,000 refugees from civil war in Guinea, Côte d'Ivoire, Sierra Leone
17. Malawi — 823,000 from Mozambique. About ten per cent of population
18. Mali — 1,500 from Mauritania. Some return
19. Mauritania — 20,000 from 1990 conflict with Senegal, expels Senegalese
20. Mozambique — 350 from several countries. Refugees in Malawi, Zimbabwe, South Africa
21. Namibia — 30,000 from Angola/Zambia return from exile
22. Nigeria — 2,150 from several countries; subject to expulsion
23. Rwanda — 23,500 from Burundi. Invasion in 1990 by Rwanda exiles based in Uganda
24. Senegal — 48,000 from Mauritania after 1990 conflict; 5,000 from Guinea-Bissau
25. Sierra Leone — 20,000 in 1990-1991 from Liberian civil war
26. Somalia — 350,000 Ethiopian refugees, mostly from Ogaden Region. Somali refugees in Djibouti, Sudan, Kenya from Somali civil war
27. South Africa — 250,000 refugees from Mozambique. Estimated 40,000 South African exiles return in 1989-1990
28. Sudan — 22,000 refugees from Chad; 697,500 from Ethiopia, 25,000 from Uganda, 5,000 from Zaïre. Millions of internally displaced persons from civil war
29. Swaziland — 6,500 refugees from South Africa; 18,300 from Mozambique. Does not include illegal migrants
30. Tanzania — 55,000 from Burundi partly settled; 16,000 from Zaïre, 22,300 from Rwanda, 72,000 from Mozambique
31. Togo — 400 from Ghana and other countries
32. Uganda — 74,400 from Rwanda, 54,500 from Sudan; 1,750 from other countries
33. Zaïre — 310,000 from Angola partly integrated; 12,000 from Rwanda; 4,000 from Uganda: 13,300 from Burundi: 1,800 from other countries
34. Zambia — 97,000 from Angola; 9,000 from Zaïre; 1,900 from Namibia; 3,000 from South Africa; Mozambique, 21,500: other countries 2,600. Some Namibians and South Africans returning
35. Zimbabwe — 68,000 from Mozambique: 300 from South Africa

Source: US Department of State, Bureau for Refugee Programs, *World Refugee Report,* Washington, DC, September 1990.

B. Harrell-Bond, *Imposing Aid*, Oxford: Oxford University Press, 1986.

Other Receiving Countries not shown on map: Algeria from Mali and Western Sahara; Egypt from Somalia; Benin, Central African Republic, and Congo from Chad.

RECEIVING COUNTRIES

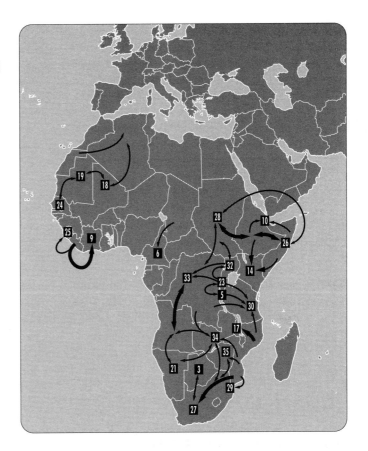

SENDING COUNTRIES

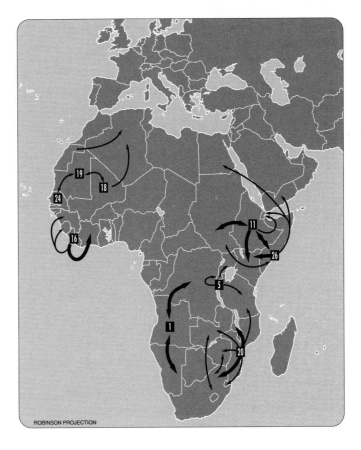

INVOLUNTARY MIGRATION: AFRICA - 1990

NUMBER OF MIGRANTS

— 100 000 or less

━ More than 100 000

↔ Double arrow indicates some repatriation

■1 Item number in Explanation

3000 Kilometres

Scale at centre of map

ROBINSON PROJECTION

INVOLUNTARY MIGRATION: ASIA/PACIFIC
Explanation
(Estimates for 1990)

Receiving Countries

1. Australia — 11,663 refugees in 1989; half from Indochina. Settles over 450,000 refugees since 1946 from all over the world
2. Canada — Approximately 15,000 refugees from Indochina in 1989
3. Hong Kong — 56,000 Vietnamese in camps; 7,000 granted first asylum
4. Japan — Temporary asylum for 2,110 Vietnamese refugees
5. India — 800,000 from Sri Lanka (Tamils); 65,000 from Bangladesh (Chittagong Hills); 20,000 from Afghanistan; 1,300 from Burma, Iran, others
6. Indonesia — 7,342 Vietnamese granted temporary asylum
7. Malaysia — 20,500 Vietnamese granted temporary asylum; 90,000 from Philippines (Mindanao conflict); accepts Muslims from Burma, Cambodia
8. New Zealand — 800 resettled in 1989 from all countries including Indochina
9. Pakistan — 3.78 million from Afghanistan; 1,600 from Iran; 2,000 from Iraq
10. Philippines — 9,600 from Vietnam for temporary asylum: 16,800 from Indochina for orderly departure to third countries
11. Singapore — 320 mostly ethnic Chinese from Vietnam
12. Thailand — 13,600 from Vietnam; 333,200 from Cambodia; 68,700 from Laos; 27,500 from Burma not granted refugee status
13. USA — 41,000 Vietnamese refugees admitted in 1990; 615,000 since 1975

Sending Countries

14. Afghanistan — 3.78 million to Pakistan; 2.35 million to Iran
15. Burma (Myanmar) — 25,000 ethnic minorities and 2,500 students to Thailand, Bangladesh
16. Cambodia — Estimated 800,000 refugees in Thailand, along border, and internally displaced. 150,000 to USA: others to Canada, Australia
17. Laos — 70,000 in Thailand, mostly hill tribes: 170,000 to USA, others
18. Philippines — 90,000 to Malaysia from Mindanao separatist conflict
19. Sri Lanka — 135,000 to India (Tamils); 43,000 return
20. Vietnam — 56,000 boat-people to Hong Kong; 9,587 to Philippines; 20,475 to Malaysia: 7,342 to Indonesia; 13,754 to Thailand: 615,000 to USA since 1975: receives 20,000 Cambodian refugees

Sources: US Department of State, Bureau for Refugee Programs, *World Refugees Report*, Washington, DC, September 1990.
US Committee for Refugees, *World Refugee Survey 1991*, Washington, DC, 1991.

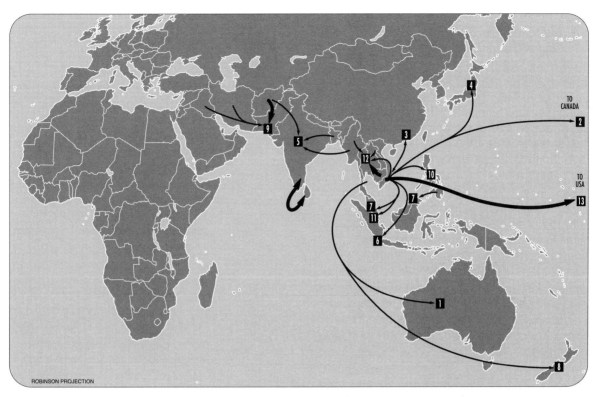

RECEIVING COUNTRIES

SENDING COUNTRIES

INVOLUNTARY MIGRATION: ASIA/PACIFIC - 1990

▪ Item number in Explanation

↔ Double arrow indicates some repatriation

5000 Kilometres
Scale at centre of map

NUMBER OF MIGRANTS

— 100 000 or less
━ More than 100 000

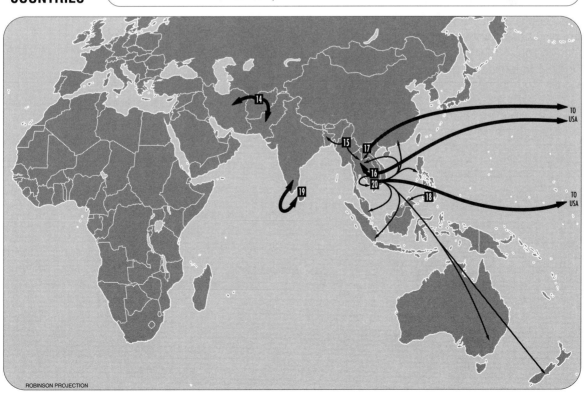

INVOLUNTARY MIGRATION:
ASIA/PACIFIC 1990

Wars past and present continue to generate refugees in the Asia/Pacific region. Seventy-five thousand Vietnamese fled their country in 1989. Coping in a twenty-one year old civil war hundreds of thousands of Cambodians sought refuge in Thailand as did many Laotians. Burma's intermittent conflict with certain of its ethnic minorities generated refugees, as did the long-standing Christian-Muslim separatist struggle in the Philippine island of Mindanao. The total number of refugees in East Asia was calculated at 664,400 at the end of 1989 compared to 623,400 at the end of 1988. This did not include 3.78 million Afghans clustered on the Pakistan border waiting for a protracted war to end in order to return safely.

Pacific Rim Economic Gains
Impressive economic gains in many of the countries of the region made the costs of refugees more bearable but not yet acceptable. Indonesia, Malaysia, Hong Kong, Thailand and Singapore insisted on granting only temporary asylum and kept refugees mostly confined in camps. Thailand, with security problems on its borders and several hundred thousand actual and potential refugees, particularly resisted the idea of internal resettlement. Various multilateral plans for reducing the exodus from Vietnam and accelerating third country settlement of refugees in camps all need more money and political support.

Vietnamese Forced Repatriation
The use of forced repatriation to deter or to slow the Vietnamese exodus was opposed by the USA, the UNHCR, and other donors. It was practised on a small-scale in Hong Kong, Malaysia and Indonesia although not yet in the open seas way that the USA turns back Haitian boat people. Less authoritarian governments and sharing in the region's economic growth could stem the flow of refugees. Meanwhile there was a pronounced reluctance to let the refugees in.

INVOLUNTARY MIGRATION: CARIBBEAN/CENTRAL AMERICA/NORTH AMERICA 1990

The Caribbean and Central American refugee situations remained distinct in the 1990s although there were signs of possible convergence. The common denominator was the USA as the principal extra-regional destination.

Caribbean Involuntary Emigration

Caribbean emigration has few refugees or expulsions. USA authorities have consistently denied Haitians refugee or asylum status although this is being contested in the courts. The 1991 military coup in Haiti prompted a new exodus of boat-people. The possibility exists for a massive Cuban refugee exodus but quietly Havana and Washington, DC are working to avert such a crisis through a modest legal emigration program based on family reunification and political dissenters.

Violence in the Caribbean has not been accompanied by refugee crises, partly because of ocean distances. The coup and USA military intervention in Grenada in 1983, the hostage-taking in Trinidad and Tobago in 1990 and other events had more impact on emigration than generating refugees. Yet the internal tensions are such in several countries such as Haiti that widespread violence could occur.

Central American Civil Wars

Central America during the 1980s experienced full-scale civil wars in El Salvador and Nicaragua and a minor insurgency in Guatemala. Geographic, cultural, and familial proximity led hundreds of thousand of persons to seek refuge in a neighbouring country. External donor intervention coordinated by the UNHCR was needed to avoid chaos. Host countries were overwhelmed by refugee demands on already scarce resources. Moreover, concentrated refugees represented threats to both domestic security and to civil conflicts spilling over borders. It took dramatic intervention by Central American leaders to initiate peace settlements and the eventual repatriation of many refugees.

Central American Refugee Crisis

At the same time as Central America experienced its first internal refugee crisis, hundreds of thousands of Guatemalans, Salvadoreans, and Nicaraguans sought refuge in the USA. Only the Nicaraguans professing opposition to the Sandinista regime received generous USA asylum. Other Central Americans transited Mexico to enter the USA illegally. Most asylum requests were denied by USA authorities although some are being re-heard as a result of court decisions.

Central American Economic Pressures

Whether as 'economic migrants' or refugees many Central Americans are likely to continue to flee deplorable economic, social, and political conditions. The fact that they traverse Mexico suggests that their primary interest is employment in the USA. While 3,800 Salvadoreans and 42,300 Guatemalans were listed in 1989 as refugees in Mexico, more than ten times as many Central Americans sought to enter the USA in the same year (Guatemalans in Mexico were mostly border-area Indians fleeing rural violence). Thus the likelihood for the 1990s, if Central America can curb its civil wars, is for mass emigration north to grow as the number of refugees declines.

INVOLUNTARY MIGRATION: CARIBBEAN/CENTRAL AMERICA/ NORTH AMERICA
Explanation
(Estimates for 1990)

Receiving Countries

1. Belize   3,400 refugees from El Salvador some of whom may become rural settlers. 1,360 refugees from Guatemala
2. Canada   Accepts limited numbers of Salvadoreans denied asylum in USA
3. Costa Rica   36,500 refugees from Nicaraguan civil war. Many return. 6,300 Salvadorean refugees and 3,000 from other countries. Costa Rica is a major asylum centre
4. Dominican Republic 450 exiles and refugees from Haiti including several prominent political and military figures
5. Guatemala   3,400 Nicaraguan and 2,250 Salvadoreans fleeing civil wars: expected to repatriate
6. Honduras   23,300 Nicaraguans including remnants of Contra civil war forces; 10,300 Salvadoreans fleeing rural combat zones. Honduras anxious to repatriate refugees
7. Mexico   46,000 refugees from Guatemala in border area. Settlement and voluntary repatriation
8. Nicaragua   7,000 Salvadoreans mostly associated with civil war insurgents. Some repatriation with political settlement
9. USA   Refugee status for Cubans, some Nicaraguans prior to 1989, denied to others

Sending Countries

10. Cuba   Orderly departure for qualified to USA but increasing numbers escape across open seas
11. El Salvador   Estimated 28,000 refugees in Guatemala, Honduras and Nicaragua. Some voluntary repatriation after political settlement of war
12. Guatemala   Estimated 220,000-300,000 undocumented in United States, Mexico: many deported. Guatemalan refugees settling in Mexico
13. Haiti   Boat-people denied asylum in Bahamas, Cuba, USA Some repatriation
14. Nicaragua   Voluntary repatriation from Honduras, Costa Rica since 1989

Sources: US Department of State, Bureau for Refugee Programs, *World Refugee Report*, Washington, DC, September 1990.
US Committee for Refugees, *World Refugee Survey 1991*, Washington, DC, 1991.

RECEIVING
COUNTRIES

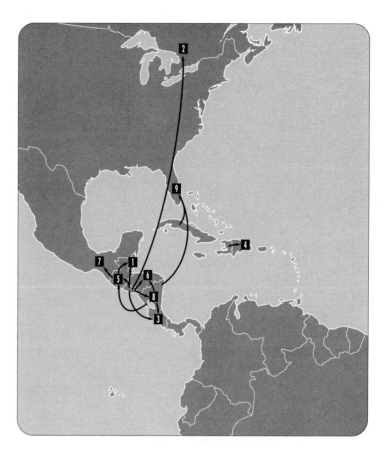

SENDING
COUNTRIES

INVOLUNTARY MIGRATION:
CARIBBEAN/
CENTRAL AMERICA/
NORTH AMERICA
1990

NUMBER OF MIGRANTS

—— 100 000 or less
—— More than 100 000

←→ Double arrow indicates some repatriation

■ Item number in Explanation

2000 Kilometres
Scale at centre of map

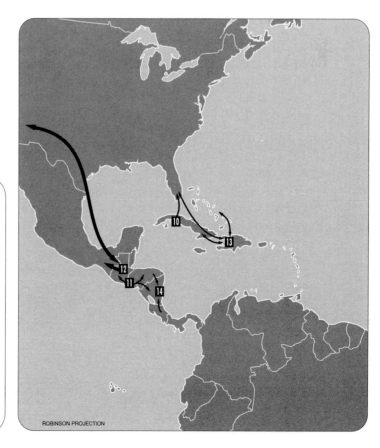

ROBINSON PROJECTION

INVOLUNTARY MIGRATION: EUROPE
Explanation
(Estimates for 1990)

Receiving Countries
Map Estimates for 1989 - Persons Seeking Asylum

1. Austria — 13,546 from Eastern Europe. Since the fall of neighbouring communist regimes Austria has tightened up on asylum granting while removing visa requirements for travel

2. Belgium — 8,200 asylum requests from diverse countries with few concessions

3. Denmark — Received 4,668 asylum requests in 1988; granted 2,196

4. France — 61,372 asylum requests in 1989. Tightening of asylum procedure in response to flood of requests from many countries. Preference for Indochinese refugee resettlement

5. Germany — Accepts 377,600 ethnic Germans from Eastern Europe, the Soviet Union. Most asylum requests rejected

6. Greece — 12,762 requests in 1989; 7,766 from Poland; 2,490 from Ethiopia. Known as an easy provider of asylum for those seeking to re-emigrate

7. Hungary — 26,500 Hungarian-speakers from the Transylvania border region of Romania. Hungary discourages a mass exodus

8. Italy — 1,393 requests in 1989 from many countries. Faced with growing hostility to illegal immigrants Italy has been restrictive on asylum. Albanians rejected, forced repatriation

9. Netherlands — 13,898 requests from all countries in 1989 and 2,755 persons granted asylum or resettled. An active refugee support network of private organizations makes the Netherlands a significant receiving country. However, the social tensions of Surinamese immigration and foreign migrant workers are changing some Dutch attitudes

10. Norway — 4,443 requests in 1989 and 7,450 persons resettled including Vietnamese, Chileans and Iranians. One of the world's most generous receiving countries with the advantage of full employment and a buoyant economy

11. Spain — 24,844 requests from nationals of many countries in 1989; 3,677 concessions. Tendency to grant asylum readily to persons likely to re-emigrate, e.g. Poles, Cubans

12. Sweden — 28,970 requests in 1989; 23,961 concessions. Sweden attracts asylum requests from all over the world and has been exceptionally generous, especially to Chileans, Yugoslavs, Ethiopians, Iranians, Lebanese and others

13. Switzerland — 23,193 requests in 1989, primarily from Turkey, Sri Lanka, Lebanon, and Yugoslavia; only 821 concessions. The Swiss maintain a strict policy on granting asylum while contributing generously to the UNHCR and the International Red Cross

14. Turkey — Accepted 241,014 Turkish-speaking refugees from Bulgaria in 1989 and 31,688 refugees from Iraq in the same year, plus an estimated 250,000 Kurds from Iraq after the 1991 Gulf War. Turkey is hard-pressed to find the resources, even with external donor aid, for its refugee population. It is anxious about the effects of the refugees on its domestic politics and its relations with its neighbours. Its main concerns are for Turkish-speaking minorities in Bulgaria, Greece and the ex-Soviet Union

15. United Kingdom — 15,537 requests in 1989 and 1,587 concessions. Britain combines tight immigration laws with a tough policy on asylum and resettlement. It is a generous contributor relatively to world refugee organizations.

Sending Countries

16. Albania — Refused asylum in Italy after 1989; ethnic Greeks to Greece

17. Bulgaria — Ethnic Turks expelled to Turkey in 1989; many return

18. Poland — Ethnic Germans to Germany, thousands of asylum-seekers to Western Europe

19. Romania — Ethnic Germans, Jews and some Hungarians emigrate; many asylum-seekers

20. ex-Soviet Union — Ethnic Germans, Greeks, Jews emigrate; other asylum-seekers

Source: US Department of State, Bureau for Refugee Programs, World Refu*gee Report*, Washington, DC, September 1990.

UNHCR *Annual Report on Status of Refugees*, Geneva, 1990.

Figures refer to Persons Seeking Asylum in Europe Calendar Year 1989, and Refugees Resettled and Persons Granted Asylum, Calendar Year 1989.

73

RECEIVING COUNTRIES

SENDING COUNTRIES

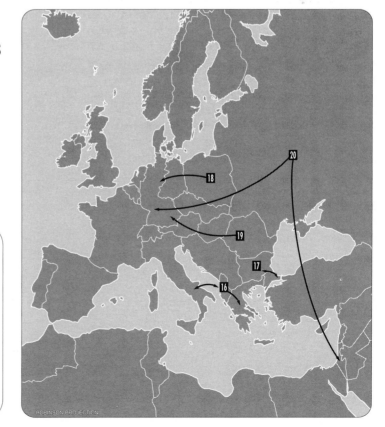

**INVOLUNTARY MIGRATION:
EUROPE - 1990**

NUMBER OF MIGRANTS

— 100 000 or less
━ More than 100 000

↔ Double arrow indicates some repatriation

■ Item number in Explanation

1000 Kilometres
Scale at centre of map

INVOLUNTARY MIGRATION: EUROPE 1990

Involuntary migration will be quite different in Europe in the 1990s from the previous decade. While the hordes of political asylum-seekers from many countries will continue, they are less likely to win their demands. The European Community (EC) intends to put in place in all twelve of its members by the end of 1992 a uniform draft convention on political asylum and a system for implementation. The objective is to have asylum-seekers evaluated at their first entry into the EC and that decision to be binding. The goal is to convince governments such as Greece and Spain, which have been relatively quick to grant asylum, to adopt uniform standards. Refugee support organizations are apprehensive that the EC system will screen out genuine asylum seekers.

Eastern Europe and Russian Uncertainties

Meanwhile there is considerable uncertainty over the new situations in Eastern Europe and the ex-Soviet Union. No longer eligible for asylum, these nationalities are for the first time being allowed by their own governments to emigrate and to travel in the West. A trickle of asylum-seekers may become a mass of job-hunters turning to asylum. Berlin and Vienna since 1989 have been inundated by all sorts of travelers from the East. Another concern is the revival of mass refugees from the resurgence of ethnic violence. A taste was provided in 1989 with the exodus of the Turkish minority from Bulgaria although many later returned. The desperate efforts of 20,000 or more Albanians to enter Greece and Italy in 1991 showed how decades of denial of emigration could combine with ethnicity to provoke a crisis. The disintegration of Yugoslavia, the plight of the Hungarian minority in Romania, hostility in France and elsewhere toward foreign migrant workers, were all reminders that Europe was not immune to inter-ethnic violence breeding refugee situations.

European Political Organizations

Political leadership through the EC, the Council of Europe, and the European Conference on Security and Cooperation, and other organizations was sensitive to old problems and to new threats. Refugees and asylum-seekers are on the agenda. The break-up of Yugoslavia in 1991-92 resulted in an estimated 1.2 million internally displaced persons; the worst refugee crisis in Europe since the end of World War II.

INVOLUNTARY MIGRATION: MIDDLE EAST 1990

The Middle East continues to be the worlds' most volatile region for generating refugees and displaced persons. The Gulf War resulted in an estimated 2.5 million migrant workers fleeing or being expelled from the region. There was not only the loss of much needed remittances by their dependants but also many scenes of distress as they struggled to leave.

Gulf War Refugee Effects

The war and its aftermath generated a new wave of refugees; Kurds fleeing Iraqi violence to Iran, Turkey and the borders; Shiites from Southern Iraq fleeing Iraqi military repression to Iran and seven refugee camps in Saudi Arabia. An estimated 170,000 Palestinians long resident in Kuwait also fled or were expelled. Gulf governments pledged to replace pro-Iraqi migrant workers with Egyptians, Syrians, and others. At the outbreak of the war Saudi Arabia expelled an estimated 500,000 Yemeni workers on the grounds that their government was pro- Iraq.

Palestinian Refugees

Thus the war added a million or more refugees to a region already overburdened. It worsened the plight of the 1.5 million Palestinians receiving UN aid in camps in Lebanon, the West Bank, the Gaza Strip and Jordan. The only glimmer of hope was for a UN mediated referendum in the Western Sahara to end that fifteen-year-old war, and permit some refugees to return. Arab/Israeli peace talks, begun in 1991, could change the status of Palestinians without ending their refugee conditions.

Israel further implemented its law of return refugee policy for all Jews anywhere. A spectacular airlift brought the last 18,000 Falasha Jews to Israel from Ethiopia. Relaxation of ex-Soviet Union emigration laws enabled an estimated 185,000 Soviet Jews to emigrate to Israel in 1990 with the prospect of even larger numbers in coming years, if suitable employment is available.

Middle East Refugee Policies

Old and new conflicts threatened to exacerbate persistent refugee crises in the region. Resettlement outside the region remains a very limited option. Refugee policy in the region has long been reduced to keeping people alive without hope.

It remains to be seen whether multilateral military action to compel the Iraqi government to respect the rights of internal displaced persons, and to allow the return of some refugees represents a new precedent. Certainly it is much more than any UN peace-keeping force can do. It is also a powerful breach of sovereignty; albeit that of a defeated, aggressor state.

INVOLUNTARY MIGRATION: MIDDLE EAST
Explanation
(Estimates for 1990)

Receiving/Sending Country

1. Algeria — 100,000 from Western Sahara; 9,000 from Mali, some return; 4,000 from Niger, some return; 4,000 Palestinians partly integrated

2. Egypt — 6,000 from Somalia; 70,000-100,000 estimated Palestinians, partly integrated; 1,600 from other countries

3. Gaza Strip — 474,000 UN registered Palestinian refugees

4. Iran — Estimated 2.35 million Afghan refugees in 1988; estimated 70,000 Iraqi Shiite refugees after 1990 Gulf War. Estimated 250,000 Iraqi Kurdish refugees after 1990 Gulf War. Estimated 300,000-500,000 Iranian exiles and refugees in France, USA, Germany, etc. since 1979

5. Iraq — Estimated 30,000 Iranian refugees at end of 1989. Most return

6. Israel — Accepts 185,000 mostly Soviet and East European Jews in 1990, 18,000 Falasha Jews airlifted from Ethiopia in 1991

7. Jordan — 908,000 Palestinians estimated at end of 1989 (UN registered). During and after Gulf War Palestinians expelled from Kuwait and other countries return to Jordan. 190,000

8. Kuwait — 170,000 Palestinians leave during and after Gulf War

9. Lebanon — 295,000 UN registered Palestinians. Lebanese internal displaced persons due to civil war; exiles in France, USA, etc.

10. Morocco — 800 refugees from all countries

11. Saudi Arabia — Not considered as refugees; includes 160,000 from Ethiopia; 1,000 from Somalia; 30,000 from Afghanistan; 10,000 from Yemen; 70,000 Palestinians. Legal resident status

12. Syria — 275,000 UN registered Palestinian refugees

13. Tunisia — 2,000-3,000 Palestinians not considered refugees

14. Turkey — 325,000 ethnic Turks from Bulgaria in 1989; 100,000 return; Iraqi Kurds from 1988 attacks and post-Gulf War 1991: 150,000 Turkish asylum-seekers in Western Europe

15. West Bank — 402,000 UN registered refugees

16. Yemen — 700 Somalis and 2,200 Ethiopians, mostly Eritreans; no legal refugee status

Sources: US Department of State, Bureau for Refugee Programs, *World Refugee Report*, Washington, DC, September 1990.

Other Sending Countries: Afghanistan to Iran, Saudi Arabia; Ethiopia to Israel, Saudi Arabia, Yemen; Somalia to Egypt, Saudi Arabia, Yemen; Sudan to Saudi Arabia; many as migrant workers not recognised as refugees.

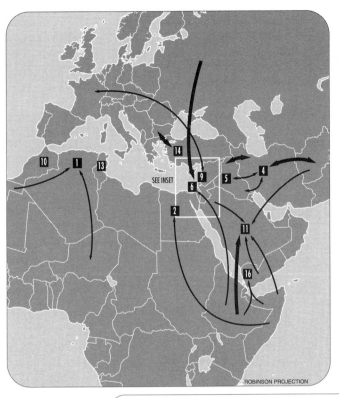

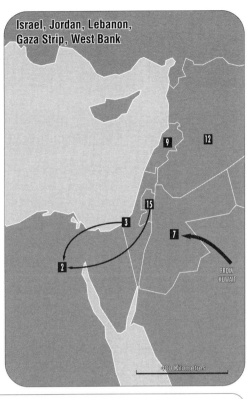

Israel, Jordan, Lebanon,
Gaza Strip, West Bank

SEE INSET

ROBINSON PROJECTION

300 Kilometres

RECEIVING COUNTRIES

SENDING COUNTRIES

INVOLUNTARY MIGRATION: MIDDLE EAST - 1990

NUMBER OF MIGRANTS
— 100 000 or less
— More than 100 000

↔ Double arrow indicates some repatriation
█ Item number in Explanation

3000 Kilometres
Scale at centre of map

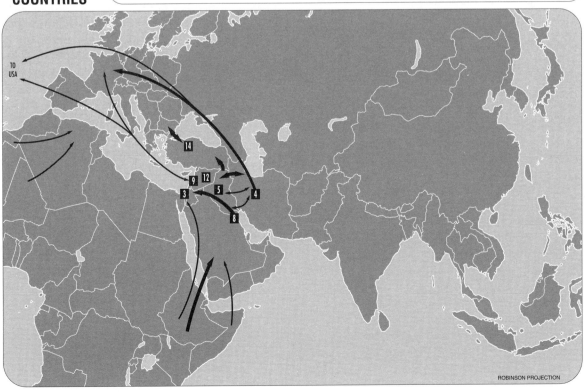

TO USA

ROBINSON PROJECTION

INVOLUNTARY MIGRATION: SOUTH AMERICA
Explanation
(Estimates for 1990)

1. Argentina — Accepts 1,720 refugees from Indochina, some of whom seek to re-emigrate. 9,900 Chilean refugees many of whom are expected to return to democratic Chile

2. French Guiana — 7,000 refugees from the guerrilla war in neighbouring Suriname. Mostly women and children related to the guerrilla forces

3. Chile — Estimated 200,000 exiles after 1973 coup and military regime to Argentina, Mexico, Venezuela, Canada and Western Europe. Some repatriate with 1990 return to democracy.

4. Brazil — Several thousand exiles mostly to Western Europe during 1964-1986 military regime. Some return post-1986.

Sources: US Department of State, Bureau for Refugee Programs, *World Refugee Report*, Washington, DC, September 1990.

INVOLUNTARY MIGRATION: SOUTH AMERICA 1980-1990

The advent of civilian elected regimes during the 1980s in Argentina, Brazil, Chile, Uruguay and Paraguay dramatically transformed the South American refugee situation. Thousands of exiled Chileans since the 1973 military coup returned from Europe and from Colombia, Argentina, Ecuador and Mexico. Previously smaller numbers of exiles had returned to Argentina and Brazil.

In spite of a decade of economic stagnation and recession there were no major expulsions of legal and illegal foreign workers in South America. Although pressured by widespread unemployment and demands by organized labour, elected Argentine and Venezuelan governments resisted deportations. A military coup and subsequent elected government in Paraguay also resisted demands to expel the several hundred thousand Brazilians occupying land in the Eastern region.

Only the record of civil war and repression in multi-ethnic Suriname marred the decline in the number of refugees. Yet the situation was highly unstable. A prolonged insurgency, economic distress and the outbreak of a cholera epidemic was propelling Peruvians to seek to leave as their neighbours closed their doors. Colombia's continued minor insurgencies and drug wars also led to emigration as an escape.

Whether elected governments can cope with economic decline and popular expectations remains to be seen. Whether the breakdown of democracies will again lead to authoritarian regimes and to refugees remains a possibility. Involuntary migration in South America is in hiatus rather than over.

INVOLUNTARY MIGRATION: SOUTH AMERICA - 1990

NUMBER OF MIGRANTS

— Less than 10 000
— 10 000 - 200 000

2000 Kilometres
Scale at centre of map

⟷ Double arrow indicates some repatriation

1 Item number in Explanation

WORLD'S
MAJOR
DIASPORAS

THE WORLD'S MAJOR DIASPORAS

The word diaspora comes from the Ancient Greeks who were the first to deliberately establish colonies of their Greek-speakers overseas. It has come to refer to communities of persons living more or less permanently outside their homelands while retaining ties of solidarity. These ties can be religious as in the case of Jews, Greeks, Armenians and others. Often there are bonds of language and/or religion as for Haitians with Creole and Kurds with Kurdish. There are bonds of a shared sense of history, symbols, foods, festive occasions, intermarriage, music and other integrative activities.

History of Diaspora Communities

Some diaspora communities have spread due to voluntary migration; others primarily as a result of war and violence. Some, like the Jews and Armenians, maintain world wide religious and secular organizations with explicit political goals. Others like the Chinese are organized more in terms of clan and home village networks. Relations with home governments may be distant or even hostile (Vietnamese, Cambodians, Laotians) or close if complex (Jews and Israel).

Organized diaspora communities have played an important role in maintaining and sustaining political nationalism. Diaspora support for the creation of an independent state has been instrumental on several occasions (Poland, Israel). Other diaspora have kept alive the desire for an independent state or at least an autonomous region in spite of decades of frustration (Kurds, Palestinians, Armenians).

There are literally thousands of diaspora communities in the world; almost everywhere there are clusters and networks of immigrants and refugees. Participation may decline among the generations born abroad, especially if there is extensive integration into the host society. However, where homeland ties, connections, culture, and language are valued, especially if new immigrants continue to arrive, then the sense of belonging to a diaspora often persists. Language is an important but not controlling variable, especially where religion is also a factor.

The Politics of Diasporas

These maps delineate major diaspora groups chosen because of their political importance. Each group is represented in an organized manner in at least one country outside its homeland; some, like the Armenians, Jews and Palestinians in many countries. As mentioned some diaspora communities are tightly organized around religious and/or political structures; others are informal occasional get-togethers. Some reside in ethnic neighborhoods and operate economic mutual support efforts; others born abroad are more residentially and economically integrated with their host societies. Historian Philip Curtin has analyzed the importance of cross-cultural trade and ethnic merchant outposts in the rise of early capitalism. Chinese and Lebanese diaspora merchants continue to be adept at functioning as outpost merchant traders, whether in West Africa for the Lebanese or Indonesia for the Chinese.

Religious-Based Diasporas

Religiously-based diaspora communities have often survived over centuries as tolerated minorities in a sometimes hostile environment. This has led to a search for their own homeland (Jews, Armenians) or societies which pledge to guarantee their status and separateness. This has resulted in such twentieth century voluntary migrations as Mennonite communities to Belize and to Paraguay. Others have emigrated for economic reasons while bringing their religious practices with them, e.g. Ismailis, Sikhs, and Chaldean Christians to the USA and Canada.

Diasporas are dynamic or they do not survive. They are also in process of formation and re-formation. New members arrive from the homeland; some elders may retire there. Persons of East Indian origin from Guyana or Trinidad in Canada relate to their homelands, not to the India of their great-grandparents. Often one diaspora community will take the initiative in establishing another in a third country, e.g. Chinese, Lebanese. These family-based multinational business networks start small and often remain so, although not always. Diasporas have lives of their own, separate from their homelands.

Source: Philip Curtin, *Cross Cultural Trade in World History*, London: Cambridge University Press, 1984. S. Thernstrom, *Encyclopedia of American Ethnic Groups*, Cambridge, MA.: Harvard Belknap Press, 1981.

CUBAN DIASPORA

Cuban emigration to the United States began in the 1880s with the recruitment of workers for cigar factories in Tampa, Florida. However, Cuba was a land of net immigration prior to the 1959 Revolution. More than 200,000 Spaniards were drawn to Cuba during the sugar boom years, especially 1915-1925. Another 300,000 Haitians and 50,000 West Indians were recruited to work on the sugar estates during the same period although many were repatriated during the 1930s depression years. Another 25,000 indentured labourers from the Canton region of China were recruited during the 1880s to replace emancipated slaves on the plantations. Eventually they moved into urban service businesses and occupations and virtually left Cuba en masse for the United States after 1959. Similarly, a community of Eastern European Jews, who found refuge in Cuba during the interwar years, also mostly emigrated after the Revolution.

Cuban-US Emigration
Cuban emigration since 1959 is almost entirely directed at the United States, sometimes using third countries as transit points. Moreover, 90 per cent of Cuban emigrés resettled in the Miami, Florida metropolitan area in spite of initial efforts to relocate them elsewhere. Thus the Cuban diaspora, now to a considerable extent citizens of the United States, represents the most cohesive diaspora community in the world in close proximity to its homeland. Yet the seventy miles of open water between Florida and Cuba, USA trade sanctions, and barriers on both sides to communications and travel have separated Cubans and Cuban-Americans.

Cuban Emigration
Emigration from Cuba has taken place in four distinct periods. Between 1959 and 1962 emigration was allowed, if discouraged, and approximately 300,000 persons left; primarily urban, middle-income, and well-educated. Between 1967 and 1973 another 400,000 left under an officially sponsored airlift which screened out those of military draft age and professionals. The ending of the airlift built up emigration pressures to the point that a spontaneous movement in 1980 resulted in 125,000 Cubans leaving by way of the designated port of Mariel in small boats. Since 1987 a Cuban-USA bilateral agreement enables a maximum of 20,000 persons annually to enter the United States legally on the basis of family reunification. Meanwhile, small numbers of Cubans continue to risk perilous waters to escape to the USA where they seek asylum.

Cubans in Miami
The Cuban diaspora community with its offspring born in the USA has achieved impressive social and economic mobility. It has helped to convert Miami into the financial and transport hub of the Caribbean. Prosperous in USA society, many Cuban-Americans remain passionately involved in the politics of change in Cuba.

The future of this diaspora is uncertain. The isolation of the Castro regime in Cuba will certainly come to an end. It is unlikely that the stricken Cuban economy can support many returnees from Miami unless they are willing to invest. Pressures within Cuba to emigrate are enormous after more than thirty years of communism, material shortages, and awareness of the life-styles of relatives in Miami. American official and public opinion hostility to another wave of spontaneous emigration like the 1980 Mariel boat-people remains high. Nor is the Cuban-American community well prepared to accept another wave of immigrants without extensive federal help. The most likely prospect, then, is for a Miami-based diaspora which provides multiple assistance to a Cuban population which eventually obtains the freedom to emigrate but not a destination.

HAITIAN DIASPORA

Haiti became the first independent Black Republic in the world in 1804, after a ten-year revolutionary war against France that devastated its slave economy and society. Throughout the nineteenth century there was little net emigration from a subsistence economy and an isolated and despotic polity.

Haitian Historical Emigration
Massive Haitian emigration began in the 1920s under the benevolent eye of the United States Occupation Forces. However, the Great Depression of the 1930s resulted in the repatriation of most of the 300,000 Haitian sugar cane workers in Cuba. A further tragic blow occurred in 1937 when the Dominican Republic President, Rafael Trujillo, ordered the military massacre of an estimated 20,000 Haitians found on the Dominican Republic side of the border.

Emigration of professionals and technicians was a response to the terror and economic decline brought about by the father and son Duvalier family dynasty (1957-1986). Several thousand qualified Haitians found work in francophone Africa while others headed for Montreal, Canada, New York City, New York, and Miami, Florida. They were followed by legal and illegal migrants to the Bahamas Islands, Canada, the Dominican Republic, and the USA drawn from all sectors and regions of Haiti. During the 1970s famine and political oppression prompted mass emigration of Haitian boat-people headed in fragile vessels for Florida. A 1982 agreement between Haiti and the USA allows the United States Coast Guard to intercept at sea these vessels and to repatriate their passengers. A military coup in 1991 prompted a resurgence of Haitian boat-people seeking asylum in the USA.

Desperate economic conditions in a land eroded and deforested, drive Haitians to seek employment in the Dominican Republic, in spite of deplorable working conditions. Emigration has become a way of life for many Haitians, remittances a condition of survival for others. Meanwhile the Haitian diaspora spread over four countries is a source of political and cultural activity, strong ties to the homeland, and determined economic drives.

CARIBBEAN DIASPORAS
Cubans/Haitians/West Indians
Explanation

Sending Countries

1. Cuba - 900,000 to USA since 1959. Ninety per cent regrouped in Miami. Others to Puerto Rico, Spain

2a. Haiti - 600,000 to USA, legal and illegal. (New York, Miami)

2b. 100,000 to Canada (Montreal)

2c. 500,000 to Dominican Republic (unskilled)

2d. 25,000 illegal to Bahamas

Others: Lesser numbers to French Antilles, French Guiana, boat-people repatriated en route to USA; not shown on map, repatriated by Cuba

3a. West Indies (Barbados, Jamaica, Trinidad and Tobago, other islands) - 400,000 to United Kingdom prior to 1963

3b. 225,000 to Canada (Toronto)

3c. 600,000 to USA (New York, Miami)

Others: Lesser numbers from Leeward Islands to US Virgins; Windward Islands to Trinidad and Tobago; not shown on map

Sources: Alejandro Portes and Robert L. Bach, *Latin Journey: Cuban and Mexican Immigrants in the United States*, Berkeley: University of California Press, 1984.

Felix Roberto Masud-Pilato, *With Open Arms, Cuban Migration to the U.S.*, New Jersey: Rowman, 1988.

Brian Weinstein and Aaron Segal, *Haiti The Failure of Politics*, New York: Praeger, 1992.

Raymond T. Smith, *Kinship and Class in the West Indies*. London: Cambridge University Press, 1988.

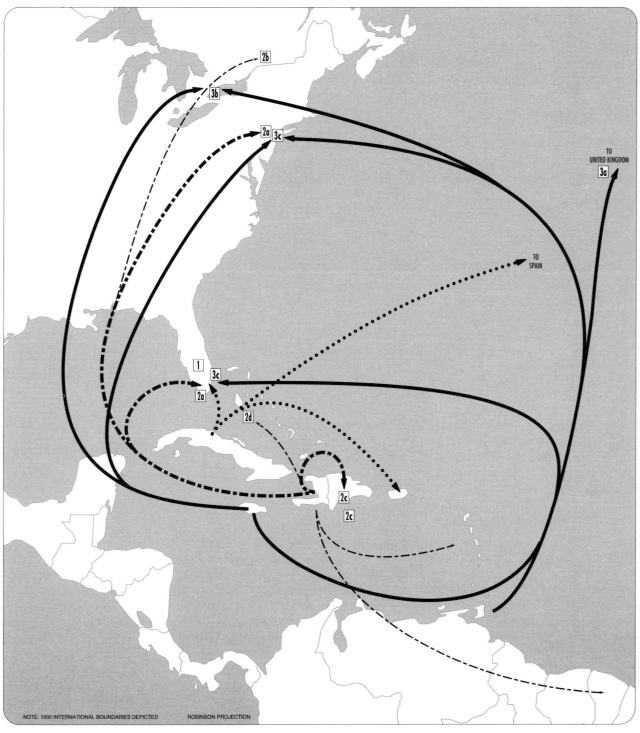

NOTE: 1990 INTERNATIONAL BOUNDARIES DEPICTED   ROBINSON PROJECTION

CARIBBEAN DIASPORAS: CUBANS / HAITIANS / WEST INDIANS

CUBANS	HAITIANS	WEST INDIANS	
1	2	3	
– · –	– · –	——	100 000 or less
•••••	■ ■ ■	——	More than 100 000

1 Item number in Explanation

1000 Kilometres
Scale at centre of map

WEST INDIAN DIASPORA

West Indians began to emigrate internationally soon after Great Britain abolished slavery in 1832. Ex-slaves from Barbados and smaller Eastern Caribbean islands emigrated by boat to Guyana and to Trinidad and Tobago in the 1840s in search of unused arable land. Slave labour was replaced by indentured workers from India and the Madeira Islands in Trinidad and Guyana between 1840 and 1880. This did little to stem the demands to emigrate, primarily in search of wage employment. An estimated 150,000 West Indians were recruited between 1880 and 1914 to work on the Panama Canal. Some remained in the Canal Zone or migrated up the Caribbean coast to Nicaragua and Costa Rica. Others returned to the West Indies.

West Indian Historical Emigration

The next major emigration wave was to the USA, primarily between 1915 and 1930. West Indian intellectuals played an important role in the Harlem Renaissance. Black nationalist leader Marcus Garvey from Jamaica served a prison sentence and was then deported but his message appealed to many West Indian immigrants and to black Americans. West Indians during this period also found work on the sugar estates of the Dominican Republic and Cuba.

The end of World War II, a labour shortage in England, and freedom of movement brought 400,000 West Indians to England between 1946 and 1963. This mass movement was halted by the strict British Immigration Act that made even family reunification difficult. Most West Indians remained in Great Britain, acquired citizenship, and reduced their home ties. Their offspring, known as 'black Britons' resettled in certain neighbourhoods of London, Birmingham and Liverpool. Educational achievement, earnings and social mobility of black Britons has not matched those of their white peers.

West Indians to Canada/USA

Denied access to Great Britain since 1963 West Indians turned in large numbers to Canada and to the USA, legally and illegally. An estimated 225,000 live in Canada, principally in Toronto. It is a population with a significant proportion of professionals, technicians and small businessmen who have both acquired Canadian citizenship and retained close ties to home islands. Canada, with its skills-based immigration requirements, has particularly attracted persons of Indian origin from Guyana and Trinidad; the descendants of nineteenth century indentured labourers.

The flow of West Indians to the USA has steadily increased since 1963 as well as the 1966 United States Immigration Act which first assigned Jamaica, Barbados and other islands an annual quota. New York City, New York, and Miami, Florida are the major West Indian centres but there are also active diaspora communities in Los Angeles, California, Washington, DC, Boston, Massachusetts and other cities. Historically and since 1963 West Indian immigrants in the USA have significantly exceeded black Americans in their economic and educational achievement levels, as well as being above American norms. This diaspora of approximately 600,000 contributes a disproportionate share of elected officials, professionals and civic leaders.

West Indian Homeland Ties

West Indians generally emigrate with a strong sense of identity to their home island and little sense of regional solidarity. It is in London, New York City and Toronto that many acquire a sense of being 'West Indian' through shared experiences, neighbourhoods, mutual assistance organizations, and perceptions imposed by their hosts.

More than a century of mass emigration has structured West Indian family life and kinship ties. Immigrants frequently enhance their earning power by sending children home to be raised by grandparents. Like other Caribbean emigrants families that are separated devise many methods for sustaining contacts. Adaptation to emigration as a permanent condition is one of the most impressive features of the West Indian diaspora.

CHINESE DIASPORA
Explanation
Population in 1982
World - 26,092,000

Asia - 23,631,231

1. Burma - 700,000. Net emigration due to economic recession
2. Cambodia - 50,000. Figures for 1983. Net emigration due to war
3. Hong Kong - 5,313,200. Figures for 1983. Re-emigration to Canada, Singapore, United Kingdom, Australia, etc. prior to transfer of Hong Kong to China in 1997
4. India - 110,000. Traders and small businessmen near Burma border
5. Indonesia - 6,150,000. Large businesses, industries, regional trade
6. Iran - 300
7. Japan - 54,607. Includes students, illegal workers, academics, etc.
8. South Korea - 46,192. Figures for 1980, unskilled workers
9. Laos - 10,000. Figures for 1983, traders and merchants
10. Malaysia - 4,100,000. Urban trade and industry
11. Pakistan - 3,600
12. Philippines - 1,036,000. Business, industry, professions. Some intermarriage
13. Ryukyu Islands - 2,400. Japanese outer islands
14. Saudi Arabia - 45,000. Migrant workers in construction, etc.
15. Singapore - 1,856,211. Figures for 1983. Population is 75 per cent Chinese who dominate business, industry, government, professions
16. Sri Lanka - 3,000
17. Thailand - 4,800,000. Figures for 1980. Chinese active in business, industry, professions. Some intermarriage
18. Turkey - 36,000. Traders, businessmen. Includes some Chinese Muslims
19. Vietnam - 700,000. Figures for 1983. Estimated 250,000 emigrate to China after 1975. Once prosperous urban business community.

Americas - 1,663,075

20. United States - 910,843. Large communities in New York, San Francisco. Economic and educational achievement well above US norm; continued immigration from China, Hong Kong, Taiwan
21. Canada - 325,000. Large communities in Vancouver and Toronto. Extensive immigration from Hong Kong. Business and professions.
22. Argentina - 2,000. Small business, Buenos Aires
23. Bolivia - 2,000. Small business in cities
24. Brazil - 65,000. Small business concentrated in Rio de Janeiro and Sao Paulo
25. Chile - 2,000. Urban small business
26. Colombia - 5,600. Urban small business
27. Costa Rica - 6,000. Small business in San Jose, etc.
28. Cuba - 7,000. Net emigration of 18,000 to Miami since the 1959 Cuban Revolution
29. Dominican Republic - 5,500. Extensive intermarriage
30. Ecuador - 12,800. Small business in the major cities
31. El Salvador - 500
32. Guatemala - 13,400. Small business in urban and rural areas
33. Haiti - 150
34. Honduras - 1,000. Small business in cities
35. Jamaica - 20,000. Active in business, professions; some intermarriage
36. Mexico - 20,000. Small business in Mexico City; US-Mexico border cities
37. Nicaragua - 800. Emigration after Sandinistas take power in 1979 due to decline of private sector
38. Panama - 33,000. Business, trade, industry, services, intermarriage
39. Peru - 52,000. Descendants of nineteenth century indentured labourers. Extensive intermarriage; small business in cities
40. Trinidad and Tobago - 4,000. Business, professions, intermarriage
41. Uruguay - 250
42. Venezuela - 14,000. Urban business and services

Europe - 550,826

43. Austria - 4,500
44. Belgium - 4,000. Urban small business
45. Denmark - 2,000
46. France - 210,000. Includes Chinese from Vietnam, Cambodia, Laos. Urban small business, professions; intermarriage
47. Germany - 20,000. Urban small business
48. Greece - 200
49. Italy - 3,500
50. Luxembourg - 680
51. Netherlands - 60,000. Includes Chinese from Indonesia, Suriname. Professions, urban small business
52. Norway - 600. Figures for 1983
53. Portugal - 2,500. Includes Chinese from Angola, Mozambique, Macao
54. Spain - 3,500
55. Sweden - 5,000
56. Switzerland - 3,200. Urban small businesses
57. United Kingdom - 230,000. Concentrated in London, Liverpool, Manchester. Small business,

professions; intermarriage, immigration from Hong Kong on special visas prior to 1997 for 50,000

Oceania

58. Australia - 122,700. Major centres in Sydney, Melbourne, Brisbane. Small businesses, professions, students; immigration from Hong Kong
59. Fiji - 4,600. Figures are for 1980. Small businessmen
60. New Zealand - 20,000. Centres in Auckland and Wellington. Small business, professions
61. Western Samoa - 1,100. Figures for 1983

Africa

62. Egypt - 20
63. Madagascar - 13,600. Wholesale and retail trade
64. Mauritius - 34,100. Wholesale and retail trade, professions; intermarriage
65. Réunion - 13,400. Urban small business
66. South Africa - 11,000. Figures for 1983. Centres in Johannesburg, Durban. Urban merchants, professions
67. Zimbabwe - 200

Note: The definition used includes all persons with any Chinese ancestry. Immigrants and persons born abroad are included.

Sources: Lynn Pan, *Sons of the Yellow Emperor: A History of the Chinese Diaspora*, Boston: Little Brown, 1990.
Dudley Poston, Jr., Mei-Yu Yu, "The Distribution of Overseas Chinese in the Contemporary World," *International Migration Review*, Vol. 21, Fall 1990, pp.480-508.

CHINESE DIASPORA

The Chinese diaspora is the largest and most widely distributed of all the world's diasporas. Defined as all persons of Chinese ancestry it was estimated in the early 1980s to include between 26.8 million and 27.5 million persons in more than 130 countries, perhaps 30 million in the 1990s. Benevolent societies, friendship associations, cultural centres, familial burial groups, secret societies, and other networks relate many overseas Chinese to their ancestral villages in China. Since the end of the Cultural Revolution and the re-opening of travel many overseas Chinese have visited China and/or Taiwan.

Chinese Historical Emigration

Constituting about one-fifth of the human race, emigration has played a minor role in Chinese history. During the period 3,000 to 1800 years ago there was some mostly spontaneous emigration south into Southeast Asia. However, it was not until the early AD sixteenth century under the Ching dynasty that periods of state-sponsored colonization were initiated over ocean water. These were sporadic and often ineffectual.

During the nineteenth century the recruitment of Chinese labour for public works projects began at the initiative of Britain, the USA, France and other powers. Indentured labour, mostly from the villages near Canton in the south was recruited for railroad construction in the USA and Canada, to replace slaves on the sugar estates of Cuba, Guyana and other Caribbean islands, and as clerks, miners, labourers and petty traders in Southeast Asia. Although harshly treated and often repatriated many Chinese coolies remained abroad. Due to the overwhelmingly male composition of those who stayed there was extensive miscegenation and intermarriage in many distant lands. Others sent home for brides.

Chinese family structure proved adaptive to the organization of small immigrant businesses; restaurants, laundries, shops, and other service enterprises. Where education and economic opportunities existed, as in Canada and the USA the first generation born abroad moved swiftly into the professions while continuing to help with family enterprises. Confucian values demonstrably served emigrant enterprises based on family sweat equity. Some immigrant entrepreneurs in Southeast Asia built vast trade, manufacturing and shipping empires.

Similarly among the overseas Chinese fertility and infant mortality have declined rapidly in response to material achievement. Assimilation and intermarriage have been extensive in certain diaspora communities. Chinese in the USA and Canada prefer to call themselves Chinese Americans or Chinese Canadians rather than overseas Chinese. Sensitive to anti-Chinese immigration laws during the nineteenth century in many countries, diaspora Chinese tend to acquire local citizenship where possible. Both Taiwan and Beijing have renounced dual nationality and reduced their efforts to cultivate the diaspora.

The overseas Chinese are a demographic majority only in Hong Kong, Macao and Singapore. Elsewhere they are minorities relying on educational investment and business skills to protect themselves rather than political activism. Divided internally by religion (Buddhist, Christian, Confucian, Muslim), language (Mandarin, Cantonese, various dialects), and by ties to home villages, Pan-China sentiment has not been a major factor. What persists over generations is generally a pride in being Chinese, some knowledge of language, cuisine, Confucian values instilled in early childhood, family structure and other shared characteristics. Residentially, immigrants and offspring are often clustered in Chinatowns (Bangkok, San Francisco, Vancouver) which reinforce ethnic identity.

Overseas Chinese in Southeast Asia

Ninety per cent of overseas Chinese live in Southeast Asia; nearly 5 million in Hong Kong which reverts from

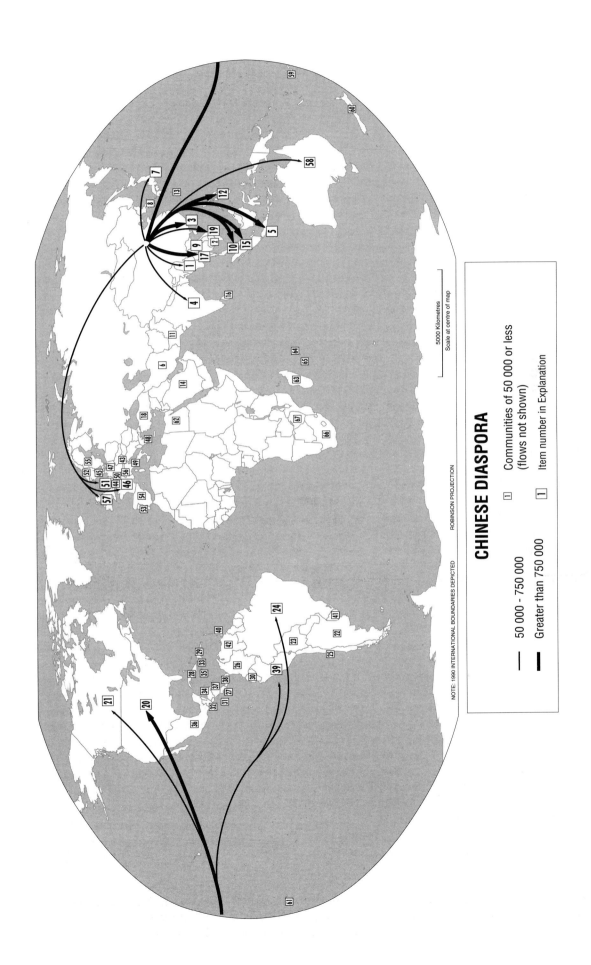

CHINESE DIASPORA

NOTE: 1990 INTERNATIONAL BOUNDARIES DEPICTED

ROBINSON PROJECTION

5000 Kilometres

Scale at centre of map

— 50 000 - 750 000

▬ Greater than 750 000

⊡ Communities of 50 000 or less (flows not shown)

1 Item number in Explanation

British to Chinese rule in 1997. Here governments tightly control immigration and most population growth is from natural increase. Prosperity generates resentment and social tensions with majority communities. Chinese in Southeast Asia have proved particularly adept at export industrialization based on shipping, banking and commercial family ties. Family firms have become multinational corporations without opening up employment or ownership to non-Chinese.

The Hong Kong and Singapore economic successes are based on the export of manufactured goods and services. Chinese businessmen have demonstrated that they can compete in regional and world economies. Like the Lebanese the Chinese have converted the diaspora into a trading instrument.

The smaller diaspora in Africa, Europe, the Middle East and the Americas have had different experiences. Investment in education has been the vehicle of social mobility from family firms to broader opportunities. However, many overseas Chinese remain the owner-managers of small family enterprises that barely provide for their immediate kin.

Except for Hong Kong, where there is a pre-1997 exodus to Australia, Canada, Singapore and the USA, there is little prospect for further Chinese emigration. This fascinating diaspora which cherishes its sense of being Chinese is more and more on its own.

LAOTIAN DIASPORA

Since 1975 when a communist regime came to power after years of civil strife and involvement in the Vietnam War, 350,000 Laotians have left the country, nearly 10 per cent of the total population. Most fled to refugee camps along the extensive Thai border where 70,000 remained at the end of 1989. During that year 3,358 entered the camps; the lowest total ever, and 1,698 were voluntarily repatriated.

Sandwiched between the larger and more populous states of Cambodia, Thailand and Vietnam, the Laotians trace their history back to the medieval kingdom of Chiengmai, and earlier. Deeply divided between the lowland Lao and the highland Lao their survival as a people and a society has been based on their isolation. Independence came as a result of the 1954 and 1962 Indochina peace settlements but it did not bring about internal reconciliation.

Laotians Overseas

The Laotian diaspora consists of refugees in the camps and those resettled overseas (nearly 149,000 in the USA and smaller numbers in Canada, Western Europe, and Australia). The highland Lao (Hmong), a distinct and oppressed minority in Laos, have sought resettlement in groups while the lowland Lao have been more willing to return, especially as there has been some economic improvement. The USA accepted 89 per cent of the 12,227 Laotians resettled in 1989; another 55,000 highland Lao and 15,000 lowlanders remained in the camps at the end of 1989.

The highland Lao have experienced severe cultural shock in the transition from their mountain villages to the refugee camps to urban centres in the USA. Few in the camps are willing to return to Laos and other countries are not interested in resettling them.

Sources: USA Department of State, Bureau for Refugee Programs, *World Refugee Report*, Washington, DC, September 1990.
Arthur Domnen, *Laos, Keystone of Indochina*, Boulder: Westview, 1985.
Martin Stuart-Fox, *Laos Politics, Economics and Society*, Boulder: L. Rienner, 1986.

VIETNAMESE DIASPORA

As a direct consequence of the Vietnam War approximately 1.5 million Vietnamese, mostly refugees, are now living in more than 20 countries around the world. A global diaspora has been created in less than 15 years. Another 76,000 Vietnamese illegally left the country, mostly in small boats, to seek asylum in 1989. A multilateral program enabled still another 30,072 to emigrate legally as refugees in the same year. These staggering totals represent 2 per cent of the total population of a country with a similar annual population growth rate.

Vietnamese Historical Migration

When Ho Chih Minh, later to become Vietnam's communist and nationalist leader, went to Paris as a student after World War I, he found there a diverse Vietnamese community. However, Paris remained the only diaspora centre until the refugee explosion.

Vietnamese diaspora communities overseas are generally into their second generation, struggling with the problems of assimilation and integration in host societies. Many Vietnamese in the USA have relocated to southern California, Arlington, Virginia and other ethnic communities. While highly motivated parents and children have done extremely well in competitive educational systems there have also been many instances of Vietnamese gangs and anti-social behavior. Lacking a consensual organizational and common religious structure, diaspora communities have relied often on local efforts to preserve culture and language. Since the Vietnamese government itself has sought to eradicate some cultural and religious elements the diaspora has had to rely on its own resources.

Vietnamese Exodus Continues

The future of the older refugee diaspora communities is complicated by the continuing exodus from Vietnam. Unlike the earlier waves of urban civil servants, military, businessmen and others who had supported the losing South Vietnamese side in the prolonged war, the "boat-people" are quite different. They come predominantly from the north, are rural fishermen and farmers, and have no history of political dissent. Their status as "economic migrants" is contradicted by the risks they run in leaving from arrest to pirates to being denied asylum. The orderly departure program is directed at cleaning up the legacy of the War; helping the Amerasian children of US fathers, and ex-political detainees to leave, as well as reuniting families. Given cooperation from the Vietnamese government which is opening its once closed economy, about 40,000 persons a year may be able to emigrate legally. This is only a minute portion of the demand in a country still subject to political repression and one of the lowest standards of living in the region.

Diaspora - Vietnam Relations

The relations between the diaspora and Vietnam are in rapid transformation. Limited travel and other exchanges with the diaspora serve to increase the pressures within Vietnam for political and economic openings. The impressive human resources of the diaspora represent an opportunity for backward Vietnam to overcome two decades of isolation. Political unification of a once divided country is a fact now accepted by much of the diaspora. While repatriation is unlikely for many strong bonds of culture and family survive.

Source: USA Department of State, Bureau for Refugee Programs, *World Refugee Report*, Washington, DC, September 1990.
Stanley Karnow, *Vietnam, A History*, New York: Penguin, 1991.

INDOCHINESE DIASPORA
Cambodians/Laotians/Vietnamese
Explanation
(Estimates for end of 1989)

Sending Countries
Cambodia

1a. Cambodians (Kampucheans) - 17,000 in UN refugee camps in Thailand

1b. Cambodians - 270,000 in camps run by military factions on Thai border. Repatriation depends on political settlement; others displaced in Thailand

1c. Cambodians - 20,000 displaced in Vietnam

1d. Cambodians - 220,000 resettled in USA (approximately 45,000 in Long Beach, California)

Others: Cambodians - approximately 15,000 resettled in Australia, Canada, France and other European countries

Laos

2a. Laotians - 70,000 in refugee camps in Thailand

2b. 149,000 resettled in USA (90,000 Hmong)

2c. Lesser numbers resettled in Canada, Australia

Vietnam

3a. Vietnamese - 56,000 interned in Hong Kong as economic migrants

3b. 7,300 in Indonesia awaiting third country resettlement

3c. Vietnamese - 110 in Japan as asylum-seekers

3d. Vietnamese - 230 in South Korea as economic migrants

3e. Vietnamese - 9,630 asylum-seekers in Philippines and 16,300 awaiting orderly departure to third country resettlement

3f. Singapore - 320 Vietnamese classified as economic migrants

3g. Vietnamese - 170 in Taiwan as economic migrants

3h. Vietnamese - 13,600 in Thailand as asylum-seekers

3i. Vietnamese - USA approximately 615,000 resettled since 1975 under various programs; 22,000 in 1989. Includes 13,621 Amerasians (US father; Vietnamese mother); 9,000 ex-political detainees

3j. Vietnamese - Australia approximately 4,000 resettled

3k. Canada - 12,000 Vietnamese resettled

3l. Germany - approximately 10,000 Vietnamese

3m. Vietnamese - 80,000 in France includes pre and post-1954 immigrants and refugees

3n. Vietnamese - Eastern Europe estimated 60,000 contract migrant workers stranded after 1989 political changes. Some seek asylum

Others - Lesser numbers resettled in Sweden, Norway, Finland, Denmark, New Zealand and other countries (not shown on map)

Sources: US Department of State, Bureau for Refugee Programs, *World Refugee Report*, Washington, DC, September 1990.
US Committee for Refugees, *World Survey*, Washington, DC, 1991.

CAMBODIAN (KAMPUCHEAN) DIASPORA

The Cambodian refugee exodus is among the most tragic of the twentieth century. Victims of Japanese occupation during World War II, French colonialism, the Vietnam War including the 1970-71 US bombing and invasion, Vietnamese invasion and occupation in 1978, the genocidal Pol Pot regime which massacred its own people, and two decades of civil war, the Cambodians have survived by fleeing. Only Thailand, a hostile kingdom for many centuries, has provided some kind of sanctuary.

Cambodian Refugee Plight

Shocked by the slaughter within Cambodia and the hundreds of thousands of refugees with their tales of horror several countries have responded with resettlement programs. The US has accepted about 220,000 Cambodian refugees, many of whom have regrouped in the Long Beach, California area in conflict with Hispanic neighbours. Smaller refugee diaspora communities have been formed elsewhere.

Although negotiations for a political settlement continue, and the Vietnamese have largely withdrawn, safe repatriation of refugees is not yet in sight. Thailand tolerates their presence in a sensitive border area so long as the fighting is kept at a distance. Resettlement continues for a fortunate few overseas but the donors are anxious to set repatriation in motion. The prospects of repatriation depend on a political settlement enforced by UN peace-keeping.

Sources: US Department of State, Bureau for Refugees Programs, *World Refugee Report*, Washington, DC, September 1990.
Elizabeth Becker, *When the War is Over, The Voices of the Cambodian Revolution*, New York: Simon and Schuster, 1985.
Michael Vickery, *Kampuchean Politics, Economics and Society*, Boulder: L. Rienner, 1986.
David W. Harney, (ed.) *Refugees as Immigrants, Cambodians, Laotians, and Vietnamese in America*, New Jersey: Rowman & Littlefield, 1988.

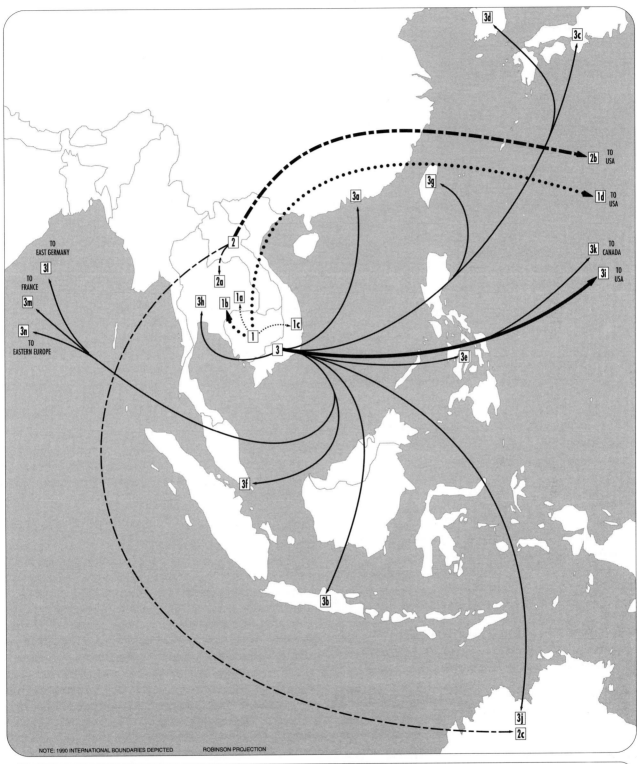

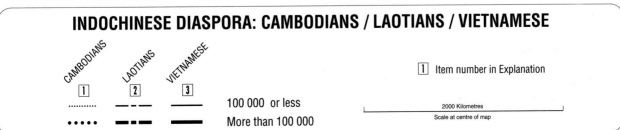

INDOCHINESE DIASPORA: CAMBODIANS / LAOTIANS / VIETNAMESE

CAMBODIANS LAOTIANS VIETNAMESE

1 2 3

1 Item number in Explanation

.... ── ── ── ─── 100 000 or less

••••• ━━ ━━ ━━ ━━━ More than 100 000

2000 Kilometres
Scale at centre of map

MIDDLE EAST DIASPORAS
Armenians/Kurds
Explanation
(Estimates for 1990)

Receiving Countries
Armenians

1a.   Armenians - Republic of Armenia. Estimated three million; 90 per cent Armenians. Declares independence in 1991

1b.   Armenians - Estimated 185,000 concentrated in Nagorno-Karabakh and Nakhichevan enclaves in Azerbaijan. Estimated 75 per cent of Armenians repatriate to Armenia after 1988 and later violence. Azerbaijan declared independent in 1991

1c.   Other ex-Soviet Union, estimated 800,000 including Russian Republic and elsewhere

1d.   Armenians - 500,000-600,000 in USA; concentrated in California, Massachusetts

1e.   Armenians - 100,000 in Canada with 25,000 in Montreal

1f.   Armenians - 200,000 in France concentrated in Marseilles

1g.   Armenians - 250,000 in Syria and Lebanon; mostly Beirut, Damascus; 30,000 emigrate to USA from Lebanon since 1975

1h.   Armenians - 200,000 in Iran, mostly Teheran

1i.   Armenians - Estimated 40,000 in Iraq; Catholics and Orthodox

Others: Armenians - Cyprus, China, Hong Kong, United Kingdom (10,000 mostly Manchester), Ethiopia (two churches), India (Calcutta), Singapore, Australia (13,000), Romania down from 50,000 to 5,000; Bulgaria down to 25,000, not shown on map

Note: Armenian diaspora communities both pre and post-date the 1915 massacres in Turkey. Most Armenians have acquired national citizenships. Figures do not distinguish between places of birth.

Sources: David M. Lang, *Armenians in Exile*, London: Unwin, 1989.
Robert Mirak, "Armenians," in Stephan Thernstrom, ed., *Harvard Encyclopedia of American Ethnic Groups*, Cambridge, MA: Harvard Belknap Press, 1981, pp.136-149.
Christopher J. Walker, *Armenia, The Survival of a Nation*, New York; St. Martin's, 1990, 2nd. ed.

Kurds

2a.   Kurds - Estimates of 8-10 million in Eastern Turkey. Turkish census does not record Kurdish-speakers. Post-Gulf War approximately 250,000 Iraqi Kurds receive temporary asylum in Turkey or on the Iraq-Turkey border. At end of 1989 31,000 Iraqi Kurds in Turkish refugee camps

2b.   Syria - Estimated 900,000 Kurds but no reliable data

2c.   Ex-Soviet Union - Estimated 300,000 Kurds in the region of Kurdistan along the Turkish border

2d.   Kurds - Estimated 1.5 to 2 million in Northwest Iran but figures are not reliable. 250,000 or more receive temporary asylum at end of Gulf War. Kurds move readily between Iran and Iraq

2e.   Kurds - Estimated 1.5 to 4 million in Iraq prior to Gulf War and 1988 attacks by Iraqi military. Estimated 1.2 million internal displaced persons after failed uprising at end of Gulf War

2f.   USA - 12,000 Kurds

2g.   Kurdish communities in Germany and Sweden for migrant workers; 335 Kurdish refugees resettle in France

Note: Estimates for the total number of Kurds in 1990 vary from 7 to 20 million. Reliable figures are not available and national governments have been reluctant to enumerate Kurds. Even using high estimates Kurds are no more than 10-20 per cent of the total population of the countries where they live.

Sources: John Keegan, Andrew Wheatcroft, *Zones of Conflict: An Atlas of Future Wars*, New York: Simon and Schuster, 1985.
Clyde Haberman, "The Kurds: In Flight Once Again," *New York Times Sunday Magazine*, May 5, 1991, pp.32-37, 52-54.
Stephen Pelletier, *The Kurds, An Unstable Element on the Gulf*, Boulder: Westview, 1984.
David McDowell, *The Kurds*, London: Minority Rights Group, 1989.

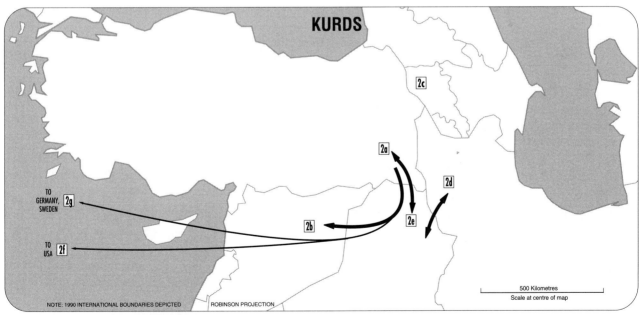

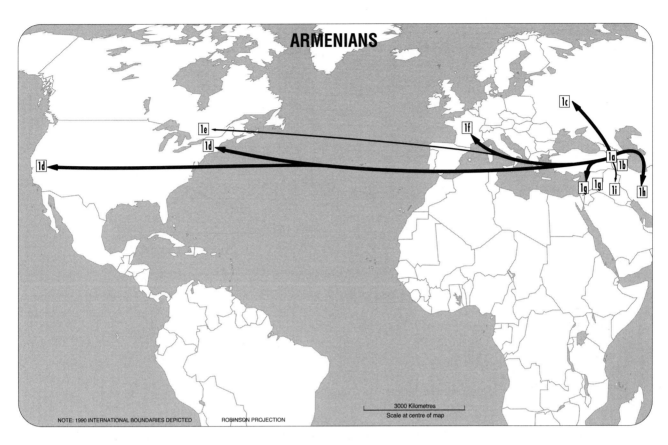

MIDDLE EAST DIASPORAS: ARMENIANS / KURDS

— 100 000 or less

— More than 100 000

←→ Double arrow indicates some repatriation

1 Item number in Explanation

ARMENIAN DIASPORA

Armenians scattered around the world are held together by bonds of shared language, religion, history, culture, and most of all common grievance. After five centuries as a Christian minority in the Ottoman Empire the Armenians of Anatolia were massacred and deported by Turkish nationalist forces in 1915-1916. The survivors took refuge in Lebanon, Syria, Egypt, France, the United States and other countries. The memory of these events and the failure to punish those responsible has provided Armenians throughout the diaspora with a common cause in spite of their frequent factional differences.

Armenian Historic Migrations

The Armenian historic homeland, the plains and hills near Mt. Ararat in the Transcaucasus, had recorded settlements dating back to 1400 BC. Armenian conversion to Christianity is dated somewhere between AD 286 and 314, making the Armenian Apostolic Church with its own clergy, liturgy, and independence one of the world's oldest Christian sects. The invention of a script for written Armenian in AD 404 made a religious and secular literature possible which is still familiar to most Armenians.

A series of medieval Armenian kingdoms waxed and waned in size and prosperity. Overrun by Arab, Mongol and Persian invaders, Armenia survived mostly through alliances with the Byzantine Empire, Crusaders and other Christian forces. Armenian merchants and traders established extensive networks and made themselves useful to Persian, Russian and Ottoman rulers. Already in the sixteenth century there was a prosperous Armenian merchant community in Mughal India. One of its members financed the first printing press in Armenia in 1771.

Armenian Western Contacts

Caught between the expanding Russian and Ottoman Empires, and the declining Persian dynasties, educated Armenians often served as vehicles for the introduction of western ideas and goods. Most Armenians, though, were peasants living harsh and oppressed lives on the Anatolian plains. The impetus for change came from the arrival of American Protestant missionaries in the 1820s, introduction of western education for boys and girls, and further contacts with the western world, and Russian nationalist and revolutionary ideas.

Perhaps 1500 Armenians had emigrated to the USA by the late 1880s and comparable numbers to Western Europe. Outbreaks of violence by Turkish authorities and Tartar (Azerbaijani) Muslims, prompted an Armenian exodus with over 50,000 arriving in the USA by 1914. Accused of plotting against the Turkish nationalist successors to the fallen Ottoman Empire, Armenians were singled out in 1915-1916. The survivors of the killings, forced marches and deportations fled to Lebanon and Syria from Cilicia, to Egypt, Iran, Russian Armenia, Europe and North America. Turkish refugees expelled from Western Thrace by Greek forces were moved to Anatolia to replace the murdered Armenians.

The Armenian Holocaust

Observers at the time estimated that there were between 1.5 million and 2.0 million Armenians living in the Ottoman Empire. About 250,000 escaped to Russia, and another 150,000 elsewhere. The number killed, nearly half women and children, is believed to be over one million. Thus virtually every member of the Armenian diaspora has a family experience of these events.

In spite of extensive western sympathy and relief aid, and the World War I defeat of Turkey, Armenians were not able to convert their tragedy into a viable independent state. Their dream of a homeland from the Black Sea to the Mediterranean became little more than a forlorn, unrecognized shriveled Armenian Republic between 1918 and 1920. Caught between rising Turkish nationalism led by Mustapha Kemal and Soviet Russia, Armenian leaders reluctantly agreed to become a Soviet Republic in 1921. Between 1920 and 1924 another 30,000 Armenians emigrated to the USA, and thousands of others to the Middle East and Western Europe.

All Armenian diaspora communities continue to be deeply scarred by this tragic history. Political movements have been divided between those accepting a homeland within the Soviet Union and those espousing anti-communism. Some Armenian militants have carried out terrorist acts against Turkish officials abroad. Since the decline of Soviet communism there has been a shift away from anti-Turkish attitudes to concern over the plight of Armenian minorities outside the Armenian Republic.

The Scattered Diaspora

Out of an estimated 6 million Armenians in the world, 3 million live in Armenia. Another 1 million live elsewhere in the ex-Soviet Union including 185,000 in the enclave of Nagorno-Karabakh surrounded by an Azerbaijani majority. About 500,000 live in the USA, primarily in California and Massachusetts and another 25,000 in Montreal. There are smaller Armenian communities in Iran, Lebanon, Syria, France, Ethiopia, Argentina and elsewhere. Strong family ties encourage reunification, primarily out of the Middle East, especially Lebanon, towards France and the USA. Following World War II groups of Armenians repatriated to the Soviet Union but were quickly disillusioned and tried to re-emigrate.

Hopes for an Independent Diaspora

The 1915 massacres, loss of Turkish Armenia, and the indifference of the western powers (the US Senate rejected a League of Nations mandate for Armenia in 1920) have convinced some that an independent state is not feasible. The Armenians have a term, *ëspiurk*, for their dispersion. The diaspora majority are prosperous, well-integrated citizens of their new lands. Recent diaspora attention has centered on earthquake relief for Soviet Armenia, and the outbreaks of inter-ethnic violence affecting Armenian minorities in Azerbaijan. Reports indicate that 180,000 of the 400,000 Armenians in Azerbaijan fled in 1988-89 as did 150,000 Azeri living in Armenia. As many as 100,000 of the 200,000 Armenians living in the multi-ethnic oil city of Baku also fled. Armenia is becoming more and more dependent on the diaspora for remittances, financial aid, and political lobbying. Meanwhile there has been a significant exodus of Armenians from the ex-Soviet Union whose emigration is sponsored by relatives abroad.

Armenian Diaspora Institutions
The diaspora is solidly anchored by a number of organizations. The Armenian Apostolic Church, and the smaller Armenian Catholic and Protestant congregations play religious and social roles. The Armenian General Benevolent Union founded in Cairo in 1906, and the Armenian Relief Society founded in 1910, carry out a wide range of benevolent activities. They helped 30,000 Armenians from a community of 160,000 in Lebanon to emigrate. There is also an active political, literary, and cultural life.

The Armenian diaspora is slowly relocating its members in Western Europe and the USA away from the ex-Soviet Union and the Middle East. About 2,000 well-educated, mostly young Armenians emigrate to the USA every year. This is a mature, well-organized ethnic-religious diaspora re-examining its relation with its homeland. The establishment of an independent Armenian Republic in 1991 presents the diaspora with its foremost challenge.

geographic core of this proposed Kurdistan includes the Iraqi oil cities of Mosul and Kirkuk, and substantial chunks of Northwestern Iran and Eastern Turkey, all areas in which there is a Kurdish majority.

The Divided Kurdish Diaspora
Denied its demands in 1921, Kurds were split between Iraq, Iran and Turkey with smaller minorities in Syria and the Soviet Union. Periodic uprisings in 1925, 1932, 1961 and 1970 have been unsuccessful as was that of 1991. Previous promises of autonomy by Iraqi leaders have not been implemented.

The Kurdish diaspora has its political parties but its force still comes from tribal and religious leadership. The small diasporas in the west provide little lobbying or financial support. Kurdish guerrillas have sought arms and money by playing off Iran against Iraq; the Soviet Union against the USA. Neither guns nor diplomacy has helped the Kurds whose cause has little sympathy in the Arab world or the west. Split between three intensely nationalist regimes the Kurds appear to be condemned to continue as a diaspora without a homeland.

KURDISH DIASPORA

As the coalition forces inflicted a crushing defeat on Iraqi President Sadam Hussein, the Iraqi Kurdish minority took to arms in support of its historic demand for autonomy. The Iraqi military turned to rout the Kurdish insurgents and over a million Kurds fled to the mountains and the Iranian and Turkish frontiers. While the world watched in horror, relief and repatriation efforts were mobilized to induce them to leave the barren mountains and to return to their homes with safeguards against Iraqi reprisals.

Kurdish History
Who are the Kurds? Their history is traced back to 2500 BC when they migrated into the region with other Indo-European peoples. Their language spoken in three major dialects is close to that of Parsi. Proverbial mountain people, warriors and shepherds, the Kurds have defended their valleys against Christian Assyrians and Armenians, and particularly against Arabs. Bitterly divided into multiple tribes and clans, they have never been able to form and to sustain a state of their own. Religiously they are Sunni Muslims; culturally they are Kurds historically adverse to being Arabicized or Turkicized.

The Ottoman Empire used the Kurds for centuries to guard its frontiers, especially with Iran. When the Ottoman Empire disintegrated the Kurds, in 1919-1921, made a bid for a state or autonomous region of their own. The

JEWISH DIASPORA
Explanation
(Estimates for 1984)

Receiving Countries

1. USA - 5.72 million including many non-religious
2. Canada - 330,000, primarily from Eastern Europe; recent Sephardic migrations
3. France - 670,000. Older Ashkenazi community and majority Sephardic Jews immigrating from North Africa
4. United Kingdom - 360,000 dates back to eighteenth century plus immigration
5. Argentina - 250,000 primarily from Eastern Europe
6. Brazil - 130,000 primarily from Eastern Europe
7. Hungary - 75,000 Ashkenazi and Sephardic
8. Mexico - 40,000 primarily from Eastern Europe; some Sephardics
9. Uruguay - 44,000 primarily from Eastern Europe
10. Venezuela - 17,000 Ashkenazi and Sephardic communities
11. Australia - 70,000 primarily from Eastern Europe
12. South Africa - 105,000 primarily from Eastern Europe; extensive emigration to Israel
13. India - 7,000, dates back over one thousand years; extensive emigration to Israel
14. Ethiopia - 18,000. Falasha Jews cut-off historically from other Jewish communities. Most emigrate to Israel 1980-1991
15. Iran - 35,000. Extensive emigration to Israel and elsewhere; post-1970
16. Italy - 35,000. Sephardic community dates back many centuries
17. Turkey - 21,000. Sephardic community dates to fifteenth century
18. Syria - 4,000. Sephardic prevented from legally emigrating
19. Morocco - 17,000. Sephardic, emigration to France, Canada, Israel
20. Soviet Union - 1.76 million. Legal emigration to Israel since 1989; previous limited emigration to USA, Germany
21. Romania - 30,000 extensive emigration to Israel
22. Switzerland - 21,000 from Germany, Eastern Europe
23. Netherlands - 28,000 dates back to expulsion from Spain and earlier
24. Belgium - 41,000, primarily from Eastern Europe
25. Germany - 42,000 includes post-World War II returnees
26. Spain - 13,000 mostly Sephardic

Others - There are smaller Jewish communities in many other countries including New Zealand, Costa Rica, Peru, Colombia, Ecuador, Tunisia, Egypt and Hong Kong (not shown on map)

Sources: Howard M. Sachar, *Diaspora An Inquiry into the Contemporary Jewish World*, New York: Harper and Row, 1985.
Max L. Margolis and Alexander Marx, *A History of the Jewish People*, New York: Atheneum, 1973.

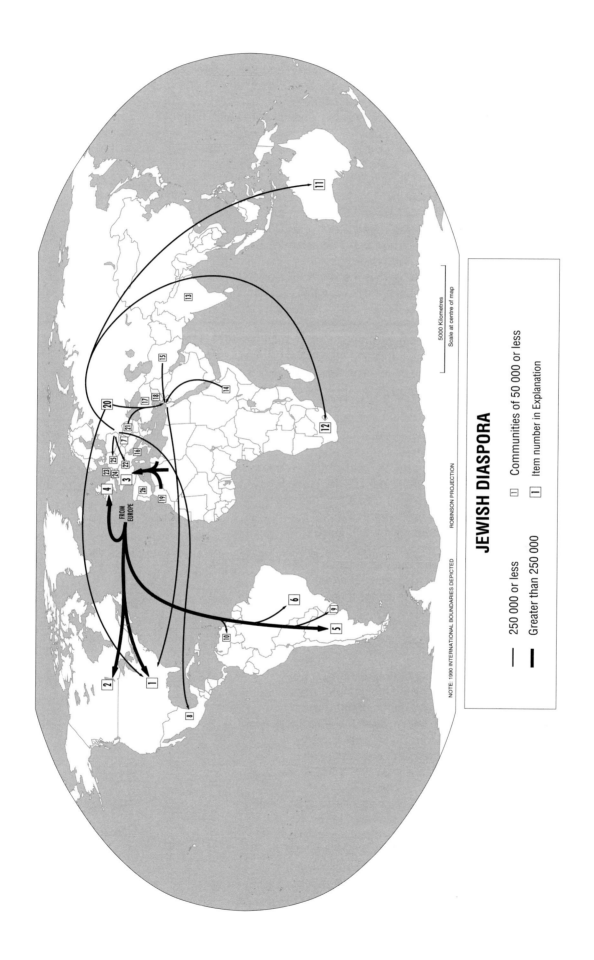

JEWISH DIASPORA

NOTE: 1990 INTERNATIONAL BOUNDARIES DEPICTED   ROBINSON PROJECTION

5000 Kilometres
Scale at centre of map

| | 250 000 or less | ⊡ | Communities of 50 000 or less |
| | Greater than 250 000 | 1 | Item number in Explanation |

JEWISH DIASPORA

Jews represent the world's oldest and most widespread diaspora. It began in 586 BC with the capture of Jerusalem and their expulsion to Babylon. Much of Jewish history consists of expulsions, forced migrations, and deliberate movements to evade persecution. It is a history of diaspora par excellence in which at no time prior to the independence of Israel did a majority of Jews live in the Holy Land. Currently 3.7 million Israeli Jews are outnumbered by an estimated 9 million others living in 70 or more countries.

Historically it has been religion that has bound the diaspora communities. The divisions between Sephardic Jews living in the Middle East, North Africa and the Mediterranean shores and Ashkenazi Jews from Russia, Eastern and Central Europe were not those of religious belief or doctrine. Each retained Hebrew as the liturgical language while speaking the tongues of the lands where they lived. Each retained the belief in the holiness of Jerusalem and Israel although the Zionist expression of political nationalism appeared first among the Ashkenazi. Multi-ethnic and even multi-racial as Judaism spread to India and Ethiopia, the diaspora for many centuries lived in isolated, religious communities organized to survive persecution.

Pre-1948 Migrations to Israel
The establishment of Israel in 1948 was preceded by several earlier mass emigrations which fundamentally altered Jewish life and thought. Russian and East European Jews moved from the late eighteenth century on to Central and Western Europe, and then later to the Americas. Sephardic Jews moved in lesser numbers to Western Europe in response to French and Italian colonial conquests. These contacts with industrial, secular societies had a profound impact on those who left and those who stayed behind, thus the response across much of the diaspora to the launching of the Zionist initiative for Israel in the late nineteenth century.

Post-1948 Migrations
The idea of a diaspora regaining its homeland was not new but its practical realisation was another matter. What made Israel a reality before and after 1948 was the planned emigration of diaspora communities from Morocco to India; the European survivors of the Holocaust to Argentine Jews. It was the creation of a multi-ethnic, multi-racial society from the dreamers, discontented, and survivors of the diaspora.

The problems of teaching Hebrew as a common language to these immigrants from many lands; to reconciling the education advantages of the Ashkenazi with the demographic majority of the Sephardim; and not least to balance religion and secularism in a new, militarised society had to be met. Immigrants had to be quickly transformed into Israelis with universal military service for both sexes one method to promote new loyalties.

These developments brought great changes within the diaspora. Most Jews living in Arab states left, legally or not, whether for Israel, France or Canada. Nearly 1200 years of Muslim-Jewish coexistence was abruptly ended. The once flourishing diaspora communities of Cairo, Baghdad, Damascus and Tunis shrank to handfuls of elderly unable or unwilling to leave.

The Jewish Diaspora and Israel
The western diaspora became the political and financial support of Israel, especially in the USA but also in France, Canada, South Africa and elsewhere. Religious and non-religious diaspora joined to support the existence of Israel while frequently differing over specific policies. While Israeli-diaspora relations can be sticky, especially in the USA, the diaspora commitment is firm. The memory of the 6 million Jews killed in World War II is a strong bond.

Meanwhile Jewish survivors of the Holocaust in the Soviet Union and Eastern Europe fared badly under Communist rule. Religious practise was discouraged and anti-semitism at times encouraged. Once allowed, Jews emigrated from these countries in droves, especially from Romania. Committed to accept all Jews from anywhere, the Law of Return, Israel is hard-pressed to absorb another wave of emigrants from the ex-Soviet Union, Eastern Europe and even Ethiopia. Once again it will turn to the wealthy diaspora for financial and political support.

The relationship with Israel has supplemented religion for much of the diaspora. The idea that all diaspora Jews would return to Israel has been replaced by the reality that some will return from lands where they are threatened, while others contribute to help them to return.

LEBANESE DIASPORA

Multi-ethnic and multi-religious Lebanon has produced one of the world's most remarkable diasporas. During more than a century Lebanese have emigrated to the four corners of the world while frequently maintaining close ties with their homeland. Remittances, village and sect associations and ties, retirement, investments, marriages and other devices have been used to retain contact. These ties have been retained in spite of a 1975-90 civil war that has devastated Lebanon economically and morally and often disrupted communications with the diaspora. Hundreds of thousands of Lebanese fled the fighting by moving to Cyprus, France and other Mediterranean countries, generally as visitors rather than refugees.

Lebanese Historical Emigration
Lebanese emigration was initiated at the end of its five centuries under Ottoman Empire rule. Between 1880 and 1914 Maronite Christians and a few Sunni Muslims left Lebanese villages for North and South America. Carrying Ottoman passports they were often known as "Turks" although in fact they were leaving both the economic stagnation and the political repression of Ottoman Turk rule.

The first wave of emigrants were 90 per cent Christians (Maronites, Greek Orthodox, Catholics) and mostly adult males. Working first as peddlers and petty traders their talents for savings and entrepreneurship led many from retail into wholesale trade and eventually to create small industries. Economic success in Argentina, Brazil, the Caribbean, the USA and other countries brought prosperity to home villages and often Lebanese brides overseas. Benevolent associations were established to further link emigrants and home-stayers. Knowledge and use of Arabic quickly declined but Church and religion bulwarked the diaspora.

Lebanese Emigration Waves
Between 1914 and 1950 Lebanese emigration slowed due to weakening overseas economies. However, some Lebanese, as French subjects, moved to West Africa where they soon expanded businesses to neighbouring British colonies.

Independent from France at the end of World War II, Lebanon encouraged emigration and diaspora contacts. Beirut as a centre of financial and trading services both benefited from diaspora investments and cultivated business interests. For the first time other Lebanese communities such as the Druze, Sunni and Shiites began to send large numbers of young men abroad. Australia, Canada and West Africa became favoured destinations for those hoping to make their fortunes and to return.

The Diaspora and the Lebanese Civil War
The prolonged civil war and the breakdown of religious and ethnic tolerance in Lebanon deeply distressed the diaspora. Since most diaspora communities, except in West Africa, are predominantly Maronite, they were quick to take sides. A significant brain-drain of professionals and technicians occurred, primarily to France. The sense of pride in being Lebanese was replaced for many by a sense of humiliation and shame.

Whether the Syrian military presence and the painstakingly negotiated political settlement can restore Lebanon to some form of peace is uncertain. Beirut for many years has ceased to be the destination of diaspora investments or business deals. The diaspora has learned to survive economically without the homeland. Intermarriage has increased naturalizations and identification with new homelands. Younger Lebanese born in the USA are prone to call themselves Arab-Americans rather than Lebanese-Americans. The diaspora have distanced themselves to some extent from the internecine warfare of the mother country.

The diaspora no longer needs the protection of an impotent Lebanon. It has constructed national and some multi-national businesses with impressive economic scope. Ties to Lebanon have become fraternal, sympathetic, and affective without the commercial nexus that once mattered. Lebanese shopkeepers in distant lands still carry the familiar homeland products such as olive oil but more from nostalgia than profit. Perhaps another resumption of mass emigration will be needed to reunite the Lebanese at home and abroad.

LEBANESE DIASPORA
Explanation

Receiving Countries
Estimates for 1990 include emigrants, migrants, residents abroad

1. France - 800,000 includes persons with dual nationality
2. Brazil - 200,000 includes naturalized Brazilians; emigrants since 1945
3. West Africa - 200,000 in Nigeria, Sierra Leone, Côte d'Ivoire, Ghana, Zaïre and others. Many with dual nationality
4. Argentina - Estimated 200,000 immigrants
5. Australia - Estimated 100,000 immigrants
6. Canada - 100,000 immigrants
7. Gulf States/Saudi Arabia - Estimated 200,000 includes some Palestinians
8. USA - Estimated 400,000 since 1945. Immigrants, 300,000 pre-1914

Others - Chile, Colombia, Venezuela and other South American states, Cyprus, Caribbean; estimated 100,000 in Dominican Republic, Haiti, French Antilles, Trinidad and Tobago and others (not shown on map)

Note: Lebanon permits dual nationality but some receiving countries do not. Descendants of pre-1914 emigrants are generally citizens of host countries as are many immigrants since 1945. Figures do not include extensive return or cyclical migration and some repatriation since 1989 peace settlement.

Sources: A. Hourani, N. Shahady, eds., *The Lebanese and the World, A Century of Emigration*, New York: St. Martin's Press, 1991.
Alixa Naff, "Arabs" in Stephan Thernstrom, ed. *Harvard Encyclopedia of American Ethnic Groups*, Cambridge, MA: Harvard Belknap Press, 1981, pp.128-136.
A.Hourani, *Syria and Lebanon*, London: Oxford University Press, 1968.

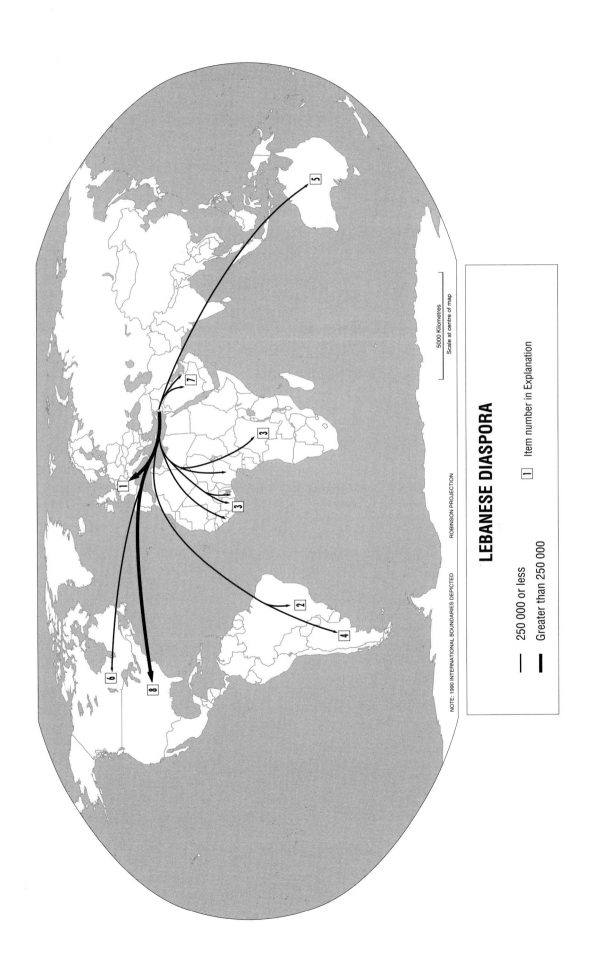

LEBANESE DIASPORA

NOTE: 1990 INTERNATIONAL BOUNDARIES DEPICTED

ROBINSON PROJECTION

5000 Kilometres
Scale at centre of map

—— 250 000 or less

— Greater than 250 000

1 Item number in Explanation

PALESTINIAN DIASPORA
Explanation
(Estimates for 1989-1990)

Receiving Countries

1.   Israel - 700,000 Israeli Arabs/Palestinians. Descendants of those who did not leave during the 1948 Arab-Israeli War

2.   Gaza Strip - 474,000 registered with UNRWA (UN Reliefs and Works Agency for Palestinian Refugees in the Near East). Under Israeli occupation since 1967 war. Gaza population 700,000

3.   West Bank - 402,000 registered with UNRWA. Total population of the West Bank estimated at 1.1 million including 80,000 Israeli settlers. Under Israeli military occupation since 1967

4.   Jordan - 908,000 registered with UNRWA. Estimated 50-60 per cent of Jordanian population of 3.9 million of Palestinian origin

5.   Lebanon - 295,000 registered with UNRWA; approximately 100,000 others including some with Lebanese citizenship

6.   Syria - 275,000 registered with UNRWA. Approximately 25,000 others

7.   Egypt - Estimated 70,000-100,000. No refugee camps; integrated partly into Egyptian society

8.   Algeria - 4,000 integrated into Algerian society

9.   Tunisia - 2,000-3,000 partly integrated into Tunisian society

10.   Saudi Arabia - 70,000 on migrant worker status

11.   Kuwait - Estimated 300,000 migrant workers prior to the Gulf War. Approximately 150,000-170,000 return to Jordan.

12.   United Arab Emirates, Bahrain, Qatar, Oman - Estimated 150,000 before the Gulf War. Most remain

13.   USA - Estimated 150,000 include those who entered on Jordanian, Lebanese and other passports and as resettled refugees

Others - Palestinian communities in Greece, Cyprus, Argentina, Brazil and other countries. Estimated 150,000. Total Palestinian population estimated 5.5 million (not shown on map)

Note: Reliable figures are hard to come by due to limited access by Palestinians to Jordanian and other passports. At the end of 1989 there were over 2 million registered refugees. Due to political opposition from several quarters refugee resettlement for Palestinians has been terminated.

Sources: US Department of State, Bureau for Refugee Programs, *World Refugee Report*, Washington, DC, September 1990.
Albert Hourani, *A History of the Arab People*, Cambridge, MA: Harvard Belknap Press, 1991.

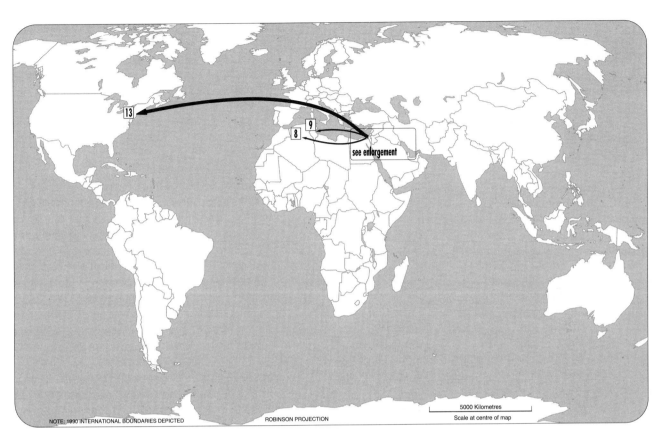

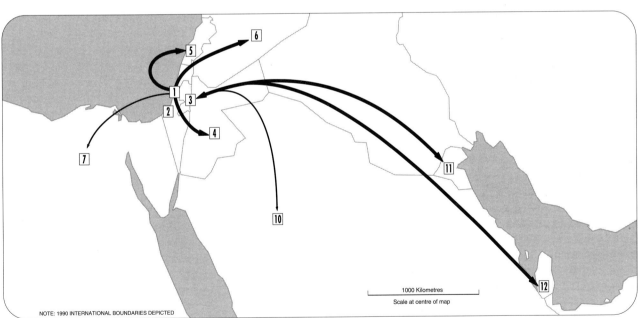

PALESTINIAN DIASPORA

— 100 000 or less

— More than 100 000

→← Double arrow indicates some repatriation

1 Item number in Explanation

PALESTINIAN DIASPORA

The Palestinian diaspora is the result of the clash over the same land between the Jewish diaspora and a people with a centuries old title. Converted to Islam and to Arabic in the eighth century the Palestinians had survived two centuries of Christian Crusaders, and 500 years of Ottoman Turkish rule. When Jewish diaspora settlement began in the 1880s the Palestinians were still living under clan and religious rule with an embryonic sense of national identity.

During the 1948 war of independence Arab armies were defeated by Israeli forces with the Palestinians on the sidelines. Two-thirds fled, many prodded by the Israeli military to leave. UNRWA was created in 1948 to deal with a refugee situation which has persisted to this day. Arab states supported Palestinian demands for repatriation and the destruction of Israel and rejected resettlement. Only Jordan, overwhelmed by refugees, was willing to give full citizenship to some Palestinians.

Palestinian Historic Emigration
Between 1948 and the 1967 war some Palestinians were able to emigrate to the USA, South America and other parts of the world. However, the 1967 war put an end to overseas resettlement and added the inhabitants of the Gaza Strip, the West Bank, and East Jerusalem to the number of Palestinians under Israeli occupation.

Faced with a bleak and indefinite existence in the refugee camps many Palestinians took advantage of the economic oil boom in Saudi Arabia, Kuwait, Iraq and the Gulf. Their advanced education and skills made them well-paid migrant workers. Although many became long-term residents and established businesses, like all the other foreign migrant workers, they were not eligible for citizenship. During the 1980s an estimated 500,000 Jordanians and Palestinians were employed in the Gulf States. Communities of resident Palestinians often including dependants sprang up. Another estimated 100,000 Palestinians living in the Gaza Strip and the West Bank commute to work in Israel.

Palestinian Diaspora Tactics
Once convinced that the Arab states would not win for them the return of Israel the diaspora militants adopted their own tactics. The Palestine National Council was created in the 1960s as an elected umbrella organization over a fractious Palestinian Liberation Organization (PLO) and several smaller armed groups. A politicized diaspora was expected to provide financial support for the cause of Palestinian nationalism.

Militancy clashed with the interests of diaspora host countries. The PLO and the Jordanian army fought a bloody battle in 1970 which resulted in the PLO armed units moving to Lebanon. Their presence accelerated a civil war and was used by the Israeli army to rationalize its 1982 invasion. Eventually the PLO headquarters were re-located in Tunisia, a country far from the front-lines and with a small Palestinian community.

Political initiatives shifted in 1988 from the PLO to the inhabitants of the Gaza Strip and the West Bank (Israel had annexed East Jerusalem and placed it under direct rule). Strikes, mass demonstrations, stone-throwing and other tactics made it clear the Palestinians opposed Israeli occupation but did little to change the situation. Hence it was not surprising that totally frustrated Palestinians throughout the diaspora rallied to the cause of Iraq and Saddam Hussein during the Gulf War. Unable to defeat the Israelis on the battlefield or the streets the Palestinians reverted to the idea of an Arab saviour, as they had regarded Egyptian President Gamel Abdel Nasser before 1967.

Palestinian Refugee Options
The options are stark for this diaspora. One is continued subjugation to Israeli occupation with the Israelis increasing the numbers of Jewish settlers in the West Bank. A second option is to accept some form of local rule in the occupied territories hoping that it will lead to autonomy and eventual independence. The third option of inflicting a military defeat on the Israelis appears to be beyond Palestinian and combined Arab resources. The fourth option is individual rather than collective. It involves seeking migrant work in the Gulf, attempting to emigrate outside the region, requesting Jordanian citizenship if available.

Ironically the Palestinian diaspora is the best educated and resourceful people in the Arab world. It has learned to adapt and to take advantage of its precarious diaspora existence.

GLOBAL MIGRATION CHARACTERISTICS

GLOBAL MIGRATION: SENDING COUNTRIES
(Estimates for 1990)
Includes all types of international migration: voluntary, Involuntary

Sending Countries

Africa

1. Algeria — Estimated 400,000 legal and illegal workers in Belgium, France
2. Angola — 9,700 refugees to Zaïre
3. Benin — Middle-level manpower to francophone West Africa
4. Botswana — 60,000 mineworkers to South Africa
5. Burkina Faso — 900,000 farm workers to Côte d'Ivoire
6. Burundi — 100,000 refugees from Rwanda and Zaïre
7. Cape Verde — Emigration to Portugal, USA, Guinea-Bissau
8. Egypt — Estimated 2.9 million in Gulf States and Saudi Arabia, Libya
9. Ethiopia — 385,000 refugees from Sudan; 335,000 from Somalia. 1,450 Ethiopian refugees in Djibouti; estimated 200,000 refugees, mostly from Eritrea in Sudan
10. Ghana — Brain-drain to United Kingdom, USA, Canada, Nigeria, Côte d'Ivoire
11. Guinea-Bissau — Estimated 25,000 farm workers to Senegal, Gambia
12. Guinea — Refugees to Senegal
13. Lesotho — Exiles abroad, labourers to South Africa estimated 140,000
14. Liberia — Estimated 250,000 refugees to Côte d'Ivoire, Guinea, Sierra Leone
15. Mauritania — 48,000 refugees to Senegal
16. Morocco — 400,000 workers to France, Spain, Belgium
17. Mozambique — Estimated 1.3 million in Malawi, Zambia, Zimbabwe, Swaziland, South Africa as refugees; 75,000 workers in South Africa
18. Nigeria — Estimated 25,800 high-level manpower to North America, United Kingdom, Middle East
19. Rwanda — 74,400 farm labourers partly integrated in Uganda
20. Senegal — Estimated 200,000 in France, Italy, Spain; unskilled to professionals
21. Somalia — Estimated 500,000 refugees in Djibouti, Ethiopia, Sudan, Kenya; estimated 50,000 migrant workers in Saudi Arabia/Gulf
22. Sudan — Estimated 500,000 migrant workers in Saudi Arabia/Gulf; 385,000 refugees in Ethiopia; 55,000 in Uganda
23. Swaziland — 60,000 mine and farm workers in South Africa
24. Tunisia — Estimated 300,000 in France and Italy; 50,000 in Libya. Mostly unskilled workers

Asia/Pacific

25. Bangladesh — 250,000-300,000 migrant workers to Saudi Arabia/Gulf, Bangladesh
26. Burma — Estimated 27,000 unrecognized refugees in Thailand
27. Cambodia — Estimated 800,000 refugees to Thailand, USA, Canada, Europe
28. China — Less than 1 million (Taiwan, Hong Kong, China); construction and other workers to Gulf
29. Fiji — Estimated 2,000 emigrants per year to Australia, Canada, etc.
30. Hong Kong — Emigrants to Australia, Canada, Singapore, United Kingdom
31. India — 800,000-1 million migrant workers to Saudi Arabia/Gulf, 600,000 to USA
32. Indonesia — Estimated 350,000 farm workers to Malaysia
33. Japan — Estimated 620,000 overseas, businessmen, students
34. Laos — Estimated 70,000 refugees in Thailand, USA 170,000, others
35. Malaysia — 80,000 migrant workers in Singapore
36. Pacific Islands — Guam and American Samoa to USA as citizens; 150,000 French Polynesia, New Caledonia to France as citizens; Papua New Guinea, Cook Islands and others to Australia and New Zealand as immigrants
37. Pakistan — 850,000-1.1 million to Saudi Arabia/Gulf States; 81,000 to USA
38. Philippines — 700,000-800,000 to Saudi Arabia/Gulf States; 900,000 to USA as immigrants; estimated 15,000 to Hong Kong, Japan, Singapore as migrants
39. South Korea — 800,000 to USA as immigrants; 800,000 resident in Japan; 1.7 million temporary migrant workers estimated 1963-1990 on overseas construction projects
40. Sri Lanka — Approximately 800,000 to India as unrecognized refugees
41. Vietnam — 56,000 non-recognized refugees in Hong Kong; nearly 10,000 refugees in Philippines; 20,000 in Malaysia; 7,000 in Indonesia; 13,500 in Thailand; 1.2 million resettled since 1975 in USA, Canada, Australia, other. USA 615,000

Europe

42. Bulgaria — 250,000 ethnic Turks as refugees to Turkey
43. Turkey — Estimated 100,000 in Saudi Arabia/Gulf. Estimated 900,000 in EC countries, mostly Germany

INVOLUNTARY MIGRATION

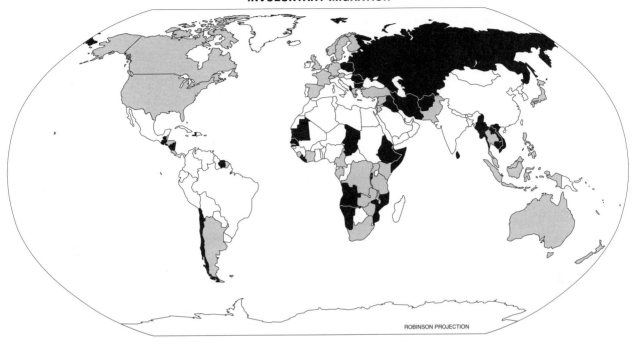

VOLUNTARY MIGRATION

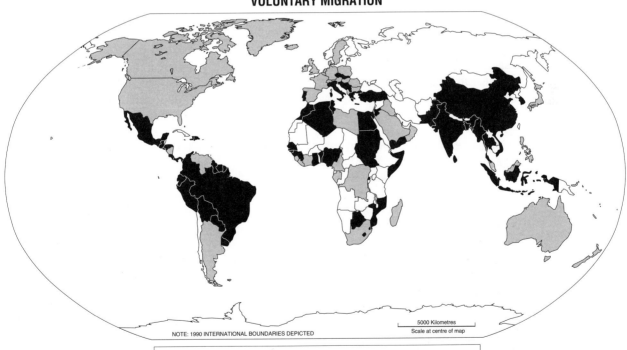

NOTE: 1990 INTERNATIONAL BOUNDARIES DEPICTED

5000 Kilometres
Scale at centre of map

GLOBAL TOTAL INTERNATIONAL MIGRATION: INVOLUNTARY/VOLUNTARY MIGRATIONS

PRIMARY MIGRATION TYPE BY COUNTRY

Sending Receiving

44. European Community

Estimated 2 million working in 1986 outside their own country within the EC. Principally Greece, Italy and Spain to Germany, Portugal to France. Also to Switzerland

Middle East

45. Afghanistan   3.8 million refugees to Pakistan, Iran

46. Iran   300,000-500,000 exiles in Europe, North America since 1979 Revolution

47. Jordan   400,000 to Saudi Arabia/Gulf

48. Lebanon   Non-recognized refugees, migrants, and immigrants to France, Cyprus, USA, Canada, West Africa, Australia, others. Estimated at over 1.5 million

49. Syria   200,000 to Libya, Saudi Arabia, Kuwait

50. Yemen (united in single state in 1989)

700,000 to Saudi Arabia/Gulf, Iraq

North America

51. Canada   750,000 to Western Europe, North America as professional and skilled workers.

52. Mexico   2.5 million to USA, two-thirds undocumented

53. USA   Estimated 900,000 resident overseas in 1990 Census. Includes military

South America

54. Argentina   Estimated 500,000 to Western Europe, North America as professional and skilled workers

55. Bolivia   700,000 to Argentina; mostly farm workers

56. Brazil   Estimated 600,000 to Western Europe (Portugal), Japan, and North America as skilled workers, professionals

57. Colombia   Estimated 800,000 to Venezuela as migrant workers, 400,000 to USA; legal, undocumented

58. Ecuador   Estimated 80,000 in Colombia and Venezuela as migrants; USA 150,000

59. Paraguay   Estimated 800,000 in Argentina as migrants

60. Peru   Estimated 100,000 in Chile as migrants; USA 150,000

61. Uruguay   Estimated 200,000 in Argentina as skilled migrant workers

Caribbean/Central America

62. Barbados   Estimated 50,000 to United Kingdom pre-1963; estimated 100,000 to USA and Canada as immigrants, migrant workers (Canada)

63. Belize   Estimated 50,000 to Canada, USA as emigrants

64. Costa Rica   Estimated 50,000 to USA as emigrants

65. Cuba   900,000 to USA as refugees since 1959 Revolution; 125,000 spontaneous migrants in 1979

66. Dominican Republic

800,000 legal and illegal migrants and immigrants to USA

67. El Salvador   Estimated 800,000 to USA since 1979 civil war began; mostly as unrecognized refugees. Refugees to Honduras, Guatemala

68. Guadeloupe and Martinique

Estimated 400,000 in metropolitan France

69. Guatemala   Estimated 200,000 as migrants

70. Honduras   Estimated 100,000 to USA as migrants

71. Guyana   200,000 emigrants to Canada, USA

72. Haiti   600,000 estimated immigrants and migrants to USA; 100,000 to Canada; 25,000 illegals in Bahamas; 500,000 migrants in Dominican Republic; 50,000 in French Guiana

73. Jamaica   200,000 to United Kingdom pre-1963; 400,000 immigrants and migrants in the USA; 125,000 in Canada

74. Nicaragua   Estimated 250,000 to USA, Honduras, Costa Rica as refugees since 1979 civil war

75. Panama   Estimated 100,000 including residents of Canal Zone to USA

76. Puerto Rico   Freedom of movement to continental USA as citizens. Net emigration of 1.5 million since 1946

77. Suriname   150,000 to Netherlands after independence in 1975; 7,000 as refugees to French Guiana

78. Trinidad and Tobago

100,000 to Canada (mostly East Indians); 120,000 to USA

79. Sending Countries with populations less than one million not listed above due to lack of data; Comoros, Western Samoa, St. Vincent, St. Lucia, Dominica, Grenada, St. Kitts, Marshalls, Reunion

Sources: See previous maps for Voluntary Migration and Involuntary Migration

OECD, *The Future of Migration*, Paris, 1987.

UNDP, *Human Development Report 1990,* New York: Oxford University Press, 1990.

GLOBAL MIGRATION: RECEIVING COUNTRIES
(Estimates for 1990)
Includes all types of international migration: voluntary, Involuntary

Receiving Countries

North America

1. Canada	125,000/year including refugees, legal, undocumented
2. Mexico	45,000 refugees from Guatemala
3. USA	Approximately 2 million/year including immigrants, refugees and undocumented; 1980-90 Asia 2 million (India 600,000; Vietnam 615,000 Laos 170,000; Cambodia 149,000; Pakistan 81,000)

Caribbean/Central America

4. Bahamas	25,000 undocumented from Haiti
5. Belize	3,400 refugees from El Salvador; 1,360 from Guatemala
6. Costa Rica	36,500 refugees from Nicaragua; 6,300 from El Salvador; 3,000 from other countries. Some return
7. Dominican Republic	Estimated 500,000 from Haiti legal and undocumented
8. Trinidad and Tobago	Estimated 50,000 undocumented from Eastern Caribbean islands

South America

9. Argentina	12,000 refugees from Chile and Indo-China; estimated 2.0 million legal and undocumented from Bolivia, Paraguay, Uruguay
10. French Guiana	7,000 refugees from Suriname; 20,000 legal and undocumented workers from Brazil, Colombia, Haiti
11. Paraguay	Estimated 350,000 legal and undocumented from Brazil. Squatters
12. Venezuela	Estimated 800,000-1 million legal and undocumented from Colombia, Ecuador, others

Europe

13. Austria	Estimated 250,000 refugees and migrants; Eastern Europe
14. Belgium	Estimated 900,000; workers from Morocco, Algeria, Turkey
15. Denmark	3,000 refugees from Indochina
16. France	Estimated 1.5 million legal and undocumented workers from Algeria, Morocco, Tunisia, black Africa; refugees from Indochina
17. Germany	377,000 ethnic Germans from Eastern Europe, USSR; estimated 1.5 million migrant workers from Turkey, Yugoslavia, Poland, others.
18. Hungary	26,500 ethnic Hungarians from Romania
19. Italy	Estimated 1.2 million legal and undocumented workers from Tunisia, Senegal, Morocco, others
20. Luxembourg	60,000 legal workers from Spain, Italy, other EC
21. Netherlands	Estimated 190,000 Surinamese; 400,000 Morocco, Turkey, others
22. Norway	8,000 refugees from Indochina
23. Portugal	Estimated 250,000 returnees from former African colonies, Brazil
24. Spain	Estimated 300,000 legal and undocumented; Morocco, Algeria, Senegal, Latin America
25. Sweden	Over 20,000 refugees from Indo-China, Chile; legal migrants
26. Switzerland	Estimated 1 million legal and illegal migrant workers from Italy, Spain, Yugoslavia, others
27. Turkey	Estimated 150,000 ethnic Turkish refugees from Bulgaria
28. United Kingdom	Estimated 600,000 post-1963 immigrants and legal migrants from India, Pakistan, Nigeria, Hong Kong, West Indies, others

Africa

29. Côte d'Ivoire	Estimated 2 million legal and illegal migrants from Burkina Faso, Mali, Niger, Guinea, Ghana
30. Djibouti	Estimated 27,000 refugees from Somalia
31. Ethiopia	Estimated 385,000 refugees from Sudan and 335,000 from Somalia
32. Gabon	Estimated 300,000 from Cameroon, Congo, Benin, Senegal, Mali, Equatorial Guinea
33. Gambia	Estimated 50,000 migrant labour from Guinea, Guinea-Bissau
34. Kenya	Estimated 20,000 refugees from Ethiopia, Somalia, Uganda
35. Nigeria	Estimated 1 million from Chad, Ghana, Niger, Benin, Togo, Burkina Faso; illegal workers
36. Senegal	Estimated 350,000 from Guinea (migrant labour). Senegalese expelled from Mauritania accepted; expels Mauritanians
37. Sierra Leone	20,000 refugees from Liberia
38. Somalia	350,000 refugees from Ethiopia
39. South Africa	250,000 refugees from Mozambique; estimated 500,000 legal and illegal migrants from Botswana, Lesotho, Swaziland, Mozambique

40. Sudan	Estimated 700,000 refugees from Ethiopia, Chad, Uganda
41. Swaziland	Estimated 25,000 refugees from Mozambique and South Africa
42. Tanzania	Estimated 250,000 refugees from Mozambique, Burundi, Rwanda
43. Uganda	Estimated 125,000 refugees from Rwanda, Sudan, others
44. Zaïre	Estimated 600,000 legal and illegal migrants from Burundi, Rwanda, Congo, Tanzania, Central African Republic. Estimated 350,000 refugees from Angola, Burundi, Rwanda, Uganda, others
45. Zambia	Estimated 140,000 refugees from Angola, Zaïre, South Africa, Mozambique, others
46. Zimbabwe	Estimated 170,000 refugees from Mozambique

Asia/Pacific

47. Australia	12,000 refugees/year---100,000 legal immigrants from Asia, Europe, others
48. Hong Kong	56,000 Vietnamese seek first-country asylum; estimated 75,000 legal and 20,000 illegal migrants from Philippines, others
49. Japan	250,000-350,000 includes illegal migrants from Bangladesh, Philippines, Pakistan, China, Thailand; 81,000 legal migrant workers (Brazil); 65,000 foreign students and trainees
50. India	Estimated 175,000 refugees from Bangladesh, Afghanistan, Burma, Sri Lanka, others
51. Indonesia	7,342 refugees/year/25,000 legal immigrants/year
52. Malaysia	20,500 refugees from Vietnam and 90,000 from Mindanao in first asylum; estimated 400,000 to 800,000 illegal migrants from Indonesia, Philippines
53. New Zealand	Accepts 800 refugees/year/25,000 legal immigrants/year
54. Pakistan	3.8 million refugees from Afghanistan
55. Philippines	About 25,000 refugees from Indochina for first asylum
56. Singapore	150,000 legal migrants from Malaysia, Thailand, Philippines; recruits immigrants from Hong Kong
57. Thailand	Estimated 450,000 refugees from Burma, Cambodia, Laos, Thailand, Vietnam

Middle East

58. Bahrain	Estimated 70,000 from India, Pakistan, others. Legal migrants
59. Iran	Estimated 2.35 million Afghan refugees; 325,000 Iraqi refugees

60. Iraq	Estimated 300,000 prior to Gulf War; legal migrants from Egypt, others
61. Israel	18,000 Ethiopia Jews in 1991 airlift; 185,000 Soviet Jews in 1990
62. Jordan	980,000 Palestinian refugees registered with UN
63. Kuwait	Estimated 400,000 before Gulf War; Palestinians, India, Pakistan, Bangladesh, Sri Lanka, etc. Legal migrants
64. Lebanon	295,000 UN registered, Palestinian refugees
65. Libya	Estimated 600,000 from Tunisia, Egypt, Pakistan, India, etc. Legal
66. Oman	Estimated 150,000 from Pakistan, India, other Asia. Legal migrants
67. Qatar	Estimated 50,000 Pakistan, India, others. Legal migrants
68. Saudi Arabia	1.2 million legal migrants from Yemen, Egypt, Jordan, Sudan, Somalia, Pakistan, India, Syria, Lebanon, others
69. Syria	275,000 UN registered, Palestinian refugees
70. United Arab Emirates	Over 400,000 legal migrants from Pakistan, India, Egypt, Yemen, Oman, others

Source: Previous maps and texts and Reginald Appleyard, ed. *International Migration Today*, Volume I: Trends and Prospects, Paris: UNESCO, 1988.

Susan J. Lapham, The Foreign Born Population in the United States: 1990, Washington, DC: *U.S. Bureau of the Census,* 1992.

United Nations Population Division, *World Migrant Population*: The Foreign-born, New York: UN, 1990.

GLOBAL MIGRATION: SENDING COUNTRIES

At the end of the twentieth century the disequilibrium between migrant sending and receiving countries had attained unprecedented proportions. More countries in every region of the world were generating emigrants, migrant workers, and refugees than there were receiving countries. Unlike the period 1500-1914 when there were vast empty lands and recruiting efforts for settlers, the world is running out of desirable physical space and political willingness to receive migrants.

A world divided into more than 180 sovereign states of an enormous diversity of sizes and population is not yet a world divided into 180 air-tight boxes for purposes of movement of labour. However, demands to emigrate for life or for temporary work or for refugee resettlement are now far in excess of offers of entry. Receiving countries continue to enact and intermittently to enforce a wide range of measures intended to restrict and to curtail migration.

Pressures to Emigrate

What is driving the actual and potential emigrants? One factor is population pressure due to the momentum of young age distributions, early marriage, and fertility of three or more children per woman of child-bearing age. The UN estimates South countries at 67 per cent of world population in 1950, 75 per cent in 1980, and 84 per cent in 2025. Age distributions of 50 per cent under age 20 in many developing countries mean massive annual entries of men and women in saturated labour markets. Access to information about living standards in developed countries, contacts with friends and relatives abroad, and rising expectations from mass communications compel more and more better educated city-dwellers to risk emigration.

Demand in receiving countries is a major factor. Emigrants often rely on social networks of ethnic kin to find jobs and job niches. These are increasingly low-paid, urban service jobs disparaged by nationals at prevailing wages. Others find work in contracting-out manufacturing, and low-wage production work threatened by offshore lower labour costs. Rural agricultural labour also continues to draw migrants in Côte d'Ivoire, Malaysia and other countries. Wage differentials, the chance of savings, and remittances, and the lack of opportunities at home all contribute to generating millions of prospective emigrants.

Is it possible to admit migrant workers legally without their insisting on staying? The Gulf States do so through strict enforcement and denial of entry to dependants. Switching a majority of recruiting from the Arab World to the Asian states has also deterred motives to stay. Sending countries have been willing to enter into these arrangements so strong is their desire for foreign exchange.

The desire for foreign exchange is also reflected in the bizarre worlds of international brides and adoptions.

Japan allows the immigration of mail-order brides, mostly for older men, from the Philippines and Sri Lanka. An estimated 15,000 infants and young children are adopted annually from 24 countries with one-third coming from Romania. American couples adopted 3,000 Romanian children in 1990 alone. These forms of international migration are entirely subject to national regulations at the sending and receiving ends.

Geography of Voluntary Migration

Sending voluntary migrants is more than a North-South affair. Most voluntary migration occurs within a region between developing countries, e.g. Bolivia-Argentina, Indonesia-Malaysia. Extra-regional migration represents probably less than 25 per cent of the global total. It is wage differentials within a region and employment opportunities that generate most temporary international migration.

Nor does population size correlate with emigration. China, India, and Indonesia, three of the world's largest countries in terms of population, are senders. So are more than 20 countries with populations less than one million whose dependence on remittances is pronounced. However, only in the smaller countries does emigration have a significant effect on fertility, mostly by removing men and some women. The population effects of mass emigration in large countries such as Algeria, Yugoslavia, and Turkey have been primarily through increased labour force participation of women and delayed marriage. A country whose population grows at 2-3 per cent a year will replace its emigrants with new-borns in a year or two.

Characteristics of Sending Countries

Analysis of sending countries confirms that most migration is regional. More than 50 countries regularly generate voluntary migrants, the majority spontaneous, to their richer neighbours. Few governments are willing or able to recruit for emigration although the Philippines has registered more than 3 million potential emigrants including many nurses, doctors and other professionals.

The prevalence of regional over global migrant labour markets results in a proliferation of sending countries. No country has more than 10 per cent of the estimated global total for voluntary migration. Instead senders dominate regional markets with Mexico in the USA, Egypt in the Arab World; or there are multiple sub-regional senders, e.g. West Africa, Southeast Asia.

Changing Migrant Compositions

What is changing, with the shift from rural to urban employment in many receiving countries, is the social composition of migrants. Historically rural migrant labour has been overwhelmingly adult male with little or no formal education and concentrated in the ages 15-35. Haitian cane-cutters in the Dominican Republic and Burkina Faso seasonal farm workers in Côte d'Ivoire continue to match this profile.

Increasingly emigration is matching the niche economic needs of receiving countries. These may be for English-speaking maids (Hong Kong, Canada), or furniture workers (USA, Singapore). Niche employment, often based on word-of-mouth information from family and friends, attracts urban better educated, slightly older (20-40) men and women. Sending countries such as India and the Philippines which educate in English surplus technical manpower are well-placed to respond to these employment opportunities. Rich countries with ageing populations are likely to look increasingly to certain sending countries to meet specific job needs, mostly in the service sectors.

Migration Effects on Sending Countries

The pros and cons to sending countries of migrant worker emigration have been extensively debated. The pros centre on remittances, foreign exchange earnings, skills and experiences acquired abroad, reduction of domestic unemployment and small-scale investments by migrants. The negatives include family separations, dependence on vulnerable remittances, loss of skilled workers, excess consumption due to remittances, and the welfare costs of those who remain behind. Evaluating costs and benefits to emigrants, their families, local communities, and sending societies is complex. W.R. Böhning has proposed that receiving countries pay a 1 per cent of earnings transfer tax to sending country governments above remittances. This would be in addition to the $30 billion in 1988 the World Bank estimates was transferred to sending countries by way of remittances.

Emigration for most sending countries is a way of buying time. It is not a substitute for increasing exports, or generating domestic employment. It is, though, for many small countries such as Cape Verde, the Eastern Caribbean islands, and some Pacific islands a way of life. These have become remittance societies with one-third or more of adult males abroad, money transfers the better part of the gross domestic product, and the old and the very young left behind. Tourism, small-scale agriculture, crafts, offshore banking and other activities earn less than exporting workers.

Dwindling Global Labour Markets

Big and small sending countries cannot rely on overseas labour markets expanding for migrant workers. The world economy for goods and services, estimated at 2.5 trillion dollars in 1990, does not exist for labour. Most labour markets are nationally regulated and accessible only marginally to outsiders, whether legal or illegal migrants or professional man-power. Remittances are only a miniscule portion of world trade; less than 5 per cent. Moving goods and services is infinitely easier than moving people. Not even a rapid and sustained expansion of the world economy will significantly reduce the multiple barriers to the movement of labour. Sending countries are left with the frustrations of negotiating from a position of weakness accords to export labour to receiving countries.

Potential for Refugee Situations

The situation of refugees is totally different. They are the victims of internal and interstate conflicts and it is difficult to predict their extent or number. During the 1980s more than half the world total of refugees came from Afghanistan, Ethiopia, Somalia, Sudan, Mozambique and Vietnam. Prolonged wars of attrition drove civilian populations into exile where they remained supported in part by global charity. The geography of war results in the Sudan, Ethiopia, Somalia, and Vietnam both sending and receiving refugees from different border areas. Overburdened neighbours such as Malaysia and Thailand provided first asylum for more people than they could manage.

The potential for future refugee situations is global. Ethnic strife and/or civil war could erupt in Algeria, Mexico, the ex-Soviet Union, Romania or many other countries. No region of the world is free from the prospect. The global diffusion of weapons insures that civilians will be threatened.

While a limited number of refugees may continue to be resettled in third or neighbouring countries, for most the only option is repatriation. This has happened in Namiba, South Africa, Uganda and other countries with minimal violence. The working-out of repatriation may require stronger international guarantees against retaliation, as in Iraq. The UNHCR and other refugee relief organizations need more effective global capabilities. Refugee crises can and do occur in every region of the world from Central America to Southeast Asia.

Environmental refugees are the victims of natural disasters such as drought, famine, flood, and cyclones. These are often worsened by war and violence. An estimated ten million or more persons are internally displaced persons or border refugees from primarily environmental causes.

The prospect of global warming and massive climactic changes in the next century raises the spectre of environmental refugees on a massive scale. Those likely to be most threatened are living in the densely populated coastal lowlands of countries such as Bangladesh. The puny international resources available for assisting political refugees at the end of the twentieth century will prove totally inadequate if global climate change occurs.

GLOBAL MIGRATION: RECEIVING COUNTRIES 1990

Estimating the annual flow of international migration is a difficult and complex exercise. Distinctions between refugees, asylum-seekers and economic migrants are blurring. Reporting of illegal migrants is problematical at best and often used for political purposes. Sorting out those who enter as tourists and overstay visas from illegal and legal migrants is a complex task. Record-keeping is uneven and reporting to the UN or other authorities often lags. Keeping track of international migration flows-refugees, immigrants, asylum-seekers, legal and illegal migrants, has become a major task for national and international authorities. Most of the burden falls on receiving countries who are most likely to be concerned about the consequences.

Global Migration Flows

During the 1980s the total global flow of migration ran at an approximate 25-30 million a year. Depending on political events and natural disasters 3-4 million a year consisted of refugees, usually finding sanctuary in neighbouring countries. Whether in Afghanistan, Mozambique or Ethiopia several million more persons a year were internally displaced. Permanent legal immigration was directed at a limited number of countries, principally Canada, the USA, Australia and New Zealand. Its flow during the 1980s was about 2 million persons a year, not including those who returned. The European Community states, Japan and much of the rest of the world erected high barriers to legal immigration which was little more than a trickle. A few countries, such as Norway, Sweden and the Netherlands, were more open to the resettlement of refugees from their first country asylums than in accepting voluntary immigrants.

International Migration Growth

The growth in international migration came primarily from legal and illegal migrant workers. The six Gulf States including Saudi Arabia were the principal destinations. However, even Japan increased its use of migrant labour while EC legal obstacles were replaced in part by increased clandestine migration. The vast majority of asylum-seekers in Western Europe and North America were evaluated as economic migrants. This is another indication of the number of persons seeking temporary employment which is all that being granted asylum confers in many countries. The heated-up economies of Southeast Asia-Singapore, Malaysia, Thailand, also began to rely on their neighbours for migrant workers.

Amnesty laws were enacted in the USA, Australia, France and other countries to legalize the status of some illegal migrants. Amnesty appeared to have a limited deterrent effect on future illegal entries. The EC states remained adamantly opposed to a renewed resort to legal contract labour; the principal recruiting device relied on in the Gulf States. Although the Gulf States are able to recruit labour without their dependants and without mas-

sive overstays other receiving countries reject their methods.

Total Stocks of International Migrants

The total stocks of international migrants can be partly identified through census data on foreign-born persons, immigration figures, and other techniques. It has been estimated at approximately 85 million persons in 1987 although this probably includes some double-counting and less than uniform data. Like the flows the stocks are growing primarily through legal and illegal migrant workers, estimated at 25-30 million in 1984, rather than refugees or immigrants. These are the categories for which data are the least reliable. Return migration and repatriation of refugees and asylum-seekers complicates any estimates of migrant stocks.

The future prospects for access to receiving countries are mixed. Fifteen countries continue to accept refugees from their first countries of asylum but only a total of 105,373 in 1989. Most of the world's 15 million plus refugees face the choice of repatriation or remaining in camps in ever more reluctant countries of first asylum. Resettlement in a third country is an option for only refugee special cases such as the Amerasians.

Prospects for Legal Immigration

Permanent legal immigration through national quotas or other formulas is effectively restricted to Canada, the USA, and Australia although there are exceptions in other countries. Nineteenth century receiving countries such as Argentina and Brazil have abandoned pro-immigration policies and there are no other takers in sight. Germany and Israel practise selective ethnic/religious immigration. Singapore has indicated its willingness to accept certain ethnic Chinese from Hong Kong but the limits to ethnic immigration confine it to a few countries. Instead there is a tendency in Australia, Canada and the USA to increase immigration quotas for certain professions irrespective of nationality.

Projections for International Migration

Projections depend, then, on the state of the world economy and demands for trans-national temporary workers. The prospects are sober. As the world moves towards regional economic trading blocs the movement of workers from outside those zones becomes more difficult. A Canada-Mexico-USA Free Trade Agreement will exclude free movement of persons. However, it is likely to increase directly and indirectly the Central American/Caribbean/Mexican flow of mostly illegal labour north. The intention is to accelerate Mexican exports and employment at home but it will also serve to raise expectations and expand social networks to help migrant workers. Japan is officially opposed to the use of migrant workers in its homogeneous society, and is instead relying on automation. However, several hundred thousand legal and illegal migrant workers from East Asia have found work in Japan. The European Community, with Germany as its economic centre, is struggling to provide jobs for former East German workers and several hundred thousand immigrant ethnic Germans from Eastern Europe. Like other EC states it is encouraging resident migrant workers from Turkey and other countries to repatriate. Meanwhile liberal asylum laws attracted hundreds of thousands of asylum-seekers from many countries.

The prognosis is for older receiving countries to try to stabilize their migrant in-flows. Newly industrializing countries such as South Korea and Singapore will try to minimize use of foreign workers through increased productivity. Meanwhile the demand for employment and foreign exchange earnings is sweeping Eastern Europe, penetrating the ex-Soviet Union, and is pervasive elsewhere. Those seeking to migrate, internationally, legally and illegally, are likely to far outnumber the opportunities for employment in a limited number of receiving countries. Some will find work in underground economies and informal sectors; some will be employed as contract labour, mostly in the Gulf; and others will live with their frustrations.

DONOR CONTRIBUTIONS TO THE MAJOR INTERNATIONAL REFUGEE ORGANIZATIONS 1990
(in US dollars)
Receiving Countries

I - UN High Commissioner for Refugees (UNHCR)

Governments and Intergovernmental Organizations	Amount	% of Total Contributions
1. United States	$112,485 million	19.8
2. European Community	64,904	11.4
3. Sweden	57,766	10.2
4. Japan	51,024	9.0
5. Norway	40,039	7.0
6. United Kingdom	35,441	6.2
7. Germany	35,904	6.1
8. Finland	29,952	5.3
9. Netherlands	26,468	4.7
10. Denmark	25,858	4.6
11. Canada	21,986	3.9
12. Switzerland	21,160	3.7
13. France	16,312	2.9
14. Italy	9.613	1.7
15. Australia	5,310	0.9
16. Saudi Arabia	3,570	0.6
17. Spain	1,736	0.3
18. Belgium	1,139	0.2
19. India	796	0.1
20. New Zealand	399	0.1
21. Kuwait	398	0.1
22. Luxembourg	322	0.1
23. Others	1,899	0.3
24. United Nations System	922	0.2
25. Non-governmental Organizations	3,726	0.7
Grand Total	$568,140	100

II - Total for four Refugee Organizations - 1990

1. United Nations Relief and Works Agency (UNWRA) - $268.8 million
2. United Nations Border Relief Operation (UNBRO) - $29.9 million
3. International Committee of the Red Cross (ICRC) - $240.1 million
4. International Organization for Migration (IOM) - $94.4 million

1990 Total for Five Organizations including UNHCR - $1.2 billion
Donor Percentages: United States 20%; European Community 15%; Japan 7%; Germany 6%; Norway 5%; Sweden 8%; Canada 4%; Finland 5%; Others 30%.

INTERNATIONAL MIGRATION: POPULATION TRENDS AND PROJECTIONS

International migration and world population marched closely in step from the fifteenth to the nineteenth centuries. Voluntary and involuntary migration represented a minute proportion of total world population and population increase. The rapid expansion of world migration beginning about 1500 was consistent with the slowly rising curve of world population. Similarly the takeoff of international migration in the nineteenth century was a response to the rise in world population.

Population and Migration Trends

The population explosion of the twentieth century, due primarily to declining infant mortality, has not been matched by a corresponding growth in international migration. Instead during the 1919-1939 period migration actually fell as the Great Depression reduced employment and incentives. A world population increasing at slightly over 2 per cent annually has completely outstripped international migration.

Population projections by the UN, the World Bank, and other sources have planet earth arriving at a stationary population late in the twenty-first century; much earlier for many countries. There is no equilibrium for international migration. The implications for migration of a stationary world population well over 10 billion have yet to be examined. Possibly a world of such high and widely diffused population densities would have little room for migration, even with zero population growth.

International Migration Projections

Projecting international migration is not easy. Refugees constitute one-third or more of annual flows in some years. Numbers of undocumented migrants are believed to be on the increase but many are missed by censuses. International migration correlates closely with the performance of the world economy which in turn is subject to many variables.

International migration is projected to decline as a proportion of world population. Using several rates of projection migration trails behind world population and labour force increases. Nor does migration affect world fertility even if emigrants themselves reduce their fertility as is often the case. The relevance of migration is to international economics and politics rather than to world population.

International migration has had a fundamental impact on the historical demography of many countries from Argentina to the USA. Among the world's poorest countries many continue to have international migration accounting for 10 per cent or more of their current populations (Ethiopia, Sudan, Mozambique, Somalia, Malawi). These impacts mostly result from refugee crises which require massive external assistance. International migration as a percentage of total population is for most countries a manageable factor and an asset for some in the form of remittances. The absence of unsettled new lands means that international migration has lost its historic role of settlement. It has become for most countries sending or receiving a modest, incremental factor in increasing or slowing population increase. It has become much more important for its ability to add a multi-ethnic dimension to a society even if the absolute numbers involved are low. International migration retains its ability to change the social composition of societies without transforming their demography.

Sources: Colin McEvedy, Richard Jones, *Atlas of World Population History*, New York: Penquin, 1978.
World Bank, *World Development Report*, 1990, Washington, DC: World Bank, 1990.
United Nations Population Division, *World Migrant Population: The Foreign-Born*, New York: UN 1989.

WORLD MIGRATION TRENDS
TOTAL NUMBER OF FOREIGN-BORN IN ALL COUNTRIES

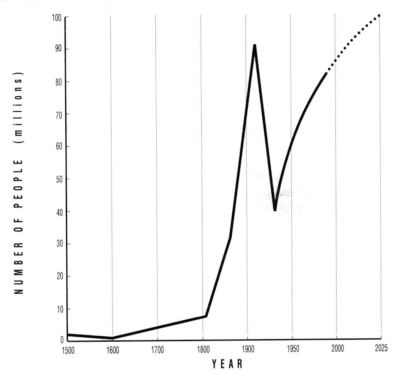

MIGRANTS FROM DEVELOPING COUNTRIES
PERCENTAGE OF TOTAL MIGRATION

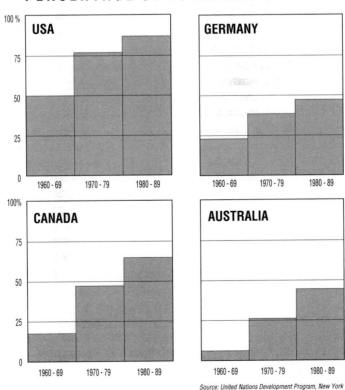

Source: United Nations Development Program, New York

INTERNATIONAL TOURISM: SENDING AND RECEIVING COUNTRIES

International tourism dwarfs international migration in volume and expenditures. The World Tourism Organization (WTO) with headquarters in Switzerland estimates that in 1987 there were 360 million visitors for purposes of pleasure to countries other than their own. Obviously there was some double-counting and including of commercial travelers. However, tourism accounts for two-thirds to three-quarters of all world travel by volume. One study concludes that tourism in 1987 had $2 trillion in sales and 6.3 per cent of the global work-force. At approximately 10 per cent of the world economy it is expected to grow at 4.2 per cent during the 1990s.

Characteristics of International Tourism
As the map indicates international tourism is overwhelmingly concentrated in certain sending and receiving countries and destinations. It is dominated by flows between North America and Europe, within Europe, and from Japan to North America and Europe. Nationals of Germany, Great Britain, Japan, France and the USA account for more than 50 per cent of total international travel expenditure; up to 80 per cent of all international travel by volume is made by nationals of 20 countries. At the same time domestic tourist expenditures are estimated to be seven times greater than international; suggesting that the market is far from being saturated.

The leading countries in international tourist arrivals (France, Spain and Italy) are also major sources of travelers. The availability of discount air fares, package tours, longer and more frequent holidays, and increased discretionary income has consolidated the era of mass tourism. Spain is the prime example of a country which has used tourism to modernize and to diversify its economy and society. Other countries, from Mexico to Thailand, are attempting to emulate the Spanish example.

Benefits of International Tourism
The pros and cons of various kinds of international tourism for developing countries have been extensively discussed. The disadvantages include the volatile nature of the tourist industry, the rapid growth of cruise ships whose on-shore expenditures are minimal, the contrasts between the luxury life-styles of visitors and local values, environmental and cultural damage and other factors. The advantages consist in labor-intensive employment, foreign exchange earnings, infrastructure modernization, and comparative advantage of scenic resources. The debate rages over how much tourist revenue over time leaks out of the local economy for imported goods as opposed to being spent at home.

International Tourism and Development
Development strategies based heavily on international tourism have been adopted throughout the Caribbean including Cuba, much of the Mediterranean on both shores but not Algeria nor Libya, among the South Pacific islands, and in Thailand, Singapore, Mexico, Senegal and Kenya. Although developing country destinations accounted for less than 20 per cent of global totals in 1990, several, such as Thailand, Singapore and Nepal have been increasing extremely rapidly. International tourism in 1984 provided more than 10 per cent of the gross national product of sixteen developing countries including the Bahamas, Barbados, Jamaica, the Gambia, Cyprus, Singapore and Malta.

Migration and Tourism
The causal relations between international tourism and international migration are complex and not easily determined. Some major countries of emigration like the Philippines, Lebanon and Poland are minor tourist destinations. Major tourist sending and receiving countries such as France, Spain and Italy are net receivers of immigrants, legal and illegal. Densely populated small island states in the Caribbean and the Indian Ocean are net exporters of people as well as major tourist receivers.

The simplest relationship is that international tourism tends to increase frequency and volume of flights as well as discount and charter rates. This facilitates emigration even if host governments attempt to restrict travel on these carriers. A related effect is that international tourism tends to make it easier for host country nationals to obtain visas and to travel abroad. The overstay of a legal tourist visa is the most frequent and least risky form of illegal immigration; whether of Irish nationals to the USA or Algerians to France.

International Tourism and Ethnic Migration
International tourism with its multiple service sector investments and jobs also promotes international migration. It encourages the ethnic communities and networks in several countries that facilitate migration. One example is provided by Thai, Indian and Pakistani restaurants in Europe and North America. International tourism serves to diffuse demand for products and services that can be provided by ethnic networks. Yet international tourism is in most cases a marginal factor in the flows of international migration. It is absent in refugee situations.

Does international tourism serve to deter voluntary international migration? Does it generate sufficient employment at all levels of remuneration to keep nationals at home? The evidence from the Caribbean, the Mediterranean and the Indian Ocean suggests that its effects on motives to migrate are mixed. Exposure to the consumption levels, life-styles and languages of visitors certainly raises expectations and in some instances desires to emigrate. The prospect of managerial and skilled and semi-skilled positions in the tourist industry at home does inhibit some from emigrating. The issue is whether, as in Spain, the tourist industry leads to broad-based economic growth and employment or merely to a seasonal enclave. Tourism alone cannot provide a non-coercive barrier to widespread desires to emigrate.

121

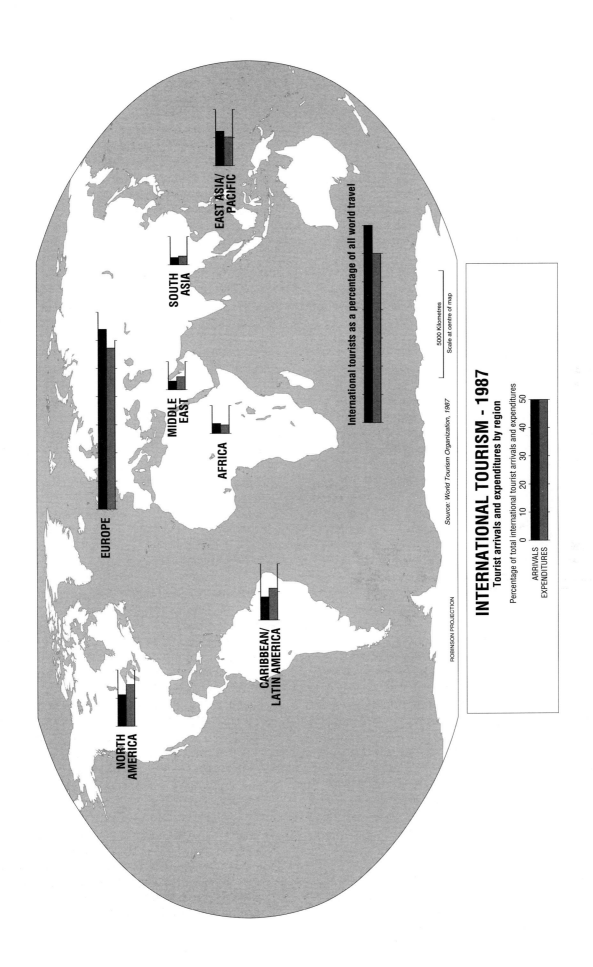

ROBINSON PROJECTION

Source: *World Tourism Organization, 1987*

5000 Kilometres
Scale at centre of map

INTERNATIONAL TOURISM - 1987
Tourist arrivals and expenditures by region

Percentage of total international tourist arrivals and expenditures

ARRIVALS
EXPENDITURES

0   10   20   30   40   50

Tourism and Freedom to Travel

As Eastern European and ex-Soviet citizens discover the joys and frustrations of international travel beyond the no longer Iron Curtain, the right to travel re-emerges as an unqualified human good. Germany dropped visas in 1991 for visitors from Czechoslovakia and Poland as Austria has done for Hungarians. However, most members of the human species, whatever their nationality, cannot travel for pleasure freely without visas and other documents. Made comfortable by a host of nineteenth and twentieth century inventions (rail, auto, plane, ship, medicine) mass travel for pleasure in the twenty-first century will remain the prerogative of a relatively privileged few.

Sources: G. Caves, *Le Tourisme International: Mirage Ou Strategie D'Avenir?* Paris: Hatier, 1989.
"World Travel and Tourism: A Survey", *The Economist, London:* March 23, 1991, pp. 58-68.

WORLD CITIES: AMSTERDAM, LONDON, LOS ANGELES, NEW YORK CITY, PARIS, SYDNEY, TORONTO

Certain cities are particularly conducive to international migration. Generally they are ports active in world trade, financial and services centres, with diversified economies capable of absorbing unskilled and professional labour. Politically they are tolerant, open, growing, with housing and commercial areas for ethnic communities. Intellectually they have major academic and research institutions drawing talent globally as well as entertainment and sports complexes.

Characteristics of World Cities
The characteristics of a world city in this definition include a high proportion of foreign-born residents (5-10 per cent), immigrants from two or more of the world's major regions, and the existence of multiple organized ethnic communities as reflected in churches, mosques, temples, restaurants, cultural centres and other facilities. World cities are multi-ethnic and multi-religious although they may be dominated by a single group.

Most of the UN list of the world's largest urban areas in 1990 have some of the characteristics noted above. However, only a few combine all the characteristics. For instance Tokyo and Osaka, Kobe have resident Korean and other foreign communities but their absolute numbers are small and many members are transient. Buenos Aires has a high-proportion of foreign-born but its earlier generations of Italian, Spanish and Syrian-Lebanese immigrants have been replaced by naturalized and assimilated offspring. Lagos has a population estimated at 7.2 million for 1990 with a low proportion of foreign-born. Its multi-ethnicity comes from the mix of Nigerian ethnic and religious groups. Nowhere in Africa, Asia, the Middle East or Latin America is there yet a complete world city, although there are several potential candidates. Four decades of strict controls over internal and international migration has precluded ex-Soviet, Eastern European, and Chinese urban areas from becoming world cities. This is changing and Moscow before 1913 and Shanghai before 1948 were hosts to important communities of international migrants.

Criteria for World Cities
The world cities selected are all In North America and Western Europe plus Sydney, Australia. This reflects the prevalence of open immigration policies at the national level or the legacy of having been the capital of a global empire. Other cities which have had this status in the past and are on the road to regaining it are Berlin and Vienna. Each has resumed its historic role as a crossroads for immigration from Eastern Europe and the ex-Soviet Union. Each attracts immigrants from the Mediterranean, the Middle East and other regions.

World Cities and Immigrants
World cities must cope with multi-ethnic and religious tensions, multiple languages, educational systems that both respect cultural pluralism and integrate new arrivals, and the politics of what has been called in New York City "Beyond the Melting Pot." Only rapid economic transformation can generate the jobs and fiscal revenues to incorporate immigrants and allow for their differences. Where economies stagnate as in Buenos Aires unemployment threatens the process. World cities thrive on the expansion of services, and integration into the world economy, often at the expense of manufacturing jobs. Increasingly they attract better-educated and qualified immigrants as well as unskilled men and women for low-paying jobs. As the children of the immigrants take advantage of educational opportunities, many achieve some degree of social mobility. Another generation of unskilled immigrants may then be needed, through legal and illegal entry. The history of Chinese diaspora communities in several world cities illustrates this process (New York, Paris).

The world cities themselves are quite different.

1) Amsterdam with an urban population of 1.81 million is the smallest. Its multi-ethnic and religious character stems partly from immigrants from the ex-Empire; Indonesia, Moluccas, Suriname and the Netherlands Antilles, as well as migrant workers from Morocco, Turkey, Tunisia, Yugoslavia and elsewhere. Nearly half its foreign-born residents are Muslims. Cultural pluralism, religious tolerance, and political diversity characterize this world city and port which thrives as a world financial and services centre.

2) London is both a political and financial capital with a services-intensive economy, and an urban area population of 11.6 million. Host in the late nineteenth century to Eastern European refugees, it now houses Indians, Pakistanis, Africans, West Indians, Europeans and many others. Strict immigration laws in effect since 1963 have kept numbers stable and encouraged naturalization. London, like other world cities, is struggling to integrate the children of its foreign-born, and to generate employment matching their rising expectations. London must remain a world city to prosper economically which means attracting American, Japanese and other high-level manpower.

3) Los Angeles is well on its way to becoming a world city, with a sprawling urban area of 10.5 million. A rapid influx of legal and undocumented immigrants from Mexico, Central America, South Korea, several Pacific islands, Iran and other countries is changing its schools, neighbourhoods and character. The pull of the powerful Pacific Rim economies is generating the diverse employment needed. Sheer size and resources make Los Angeles the major Pacific Ocean world city, well ahead of San Francisco, Seattle and Vancouver. Yet the 1992 riots revealed the extent of its multi-ethnic tensions.

4) New York City is the largest and most ethnically diverse of all the world cities, with an urban area of 15.7 million. Once the first home for millions of European immigrants, an estimated 25 per cent of its current popu-

WORLD CITIES
Explanation
National Origin of Immigrants (Estimates for 1990)

1. Amsterdam   Indonesia, Morocco, Netherlands Antilles, Suriname, Turkey, Yugoslavia, others

2. London   Ghana, Hong Kong, India, Nigeria, Pakistan, South Africa, West Indies, others

3. Los Angeles   American Samoa, El Salvador, Guam, Guatemala, Japan, Mexico, Nicaragua, South Korea, others

4. New York City   China, Colombia, Dominican Republic, Haiti, India, Jamaica, Mexico, Pakistan, Philippines, Puerto Rico, ex-USSR, others

5. Paris   Algeria, French Antilles, Lebanon, Morocco, Senegal, Tunisia, Vietnam, others

6. Sydney   Fiji, Greece, Hong Kong, Indonesia, Italy, New Zealand, Papua New Guinea, United Kingdom, Vietnam, Yugoslavia, others

7. Toronto   Czechoslovakia, Hong Kong, India, Italy, Pakistan, Portugal, Vietnam, West Indies, others

Source: UN Department for International Economic and Social Affairs, *The Prospects of World Urbanization*, New York: United Nations, 1989.
Saskia Sassen, *The Global City, New York, London, Tokyo*, Princeton: Princeton University Press, 1991.

125

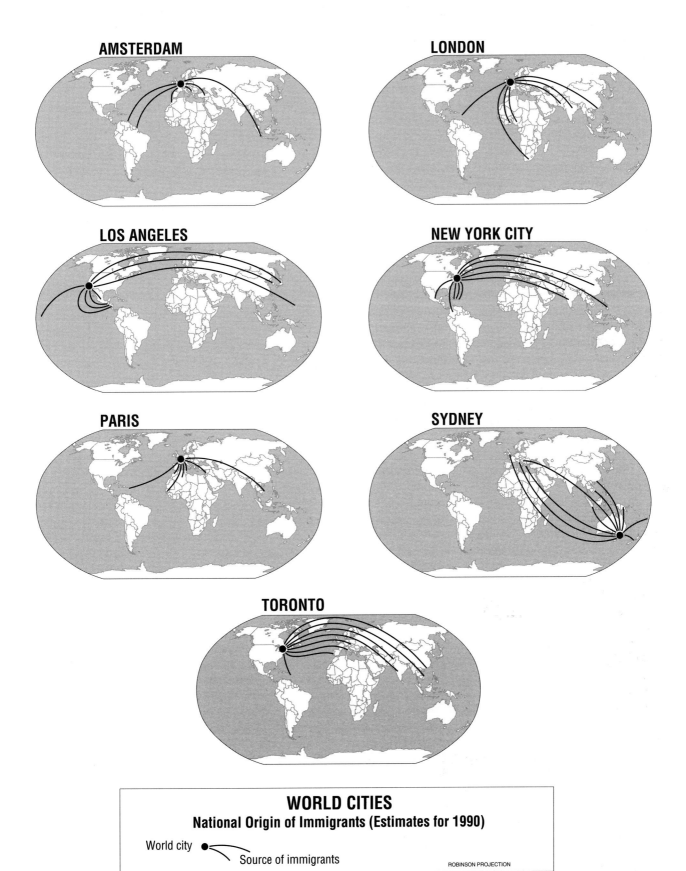

WORLD CITIES
National Origin of Immigrants (Estimates for 1990)

World city ● Source of immigrants

ROBINSON PROJECTION

lation comes from the Caribbean and Latin America. Nearly every sending country in the world is represented in New York including India, Bangladesh, Pakistan, Turkey, Nigeria, and dozens of others. The loss of manufacturing jobs means that the latest generation of immigrants finds work in finance, services, or an active underground economy. The presence of ethnic neighbourhoods, religious centres, commercial activites, and politics contributes to the global nature of this city built by immigrants. The problems of education, housing, employment, integration and pluralism are daunting if already confronted by earlier immigrants.

5) Paris is a multi-ethnic city of 6.5 million in the urban area based on the legacy of empire and its cultural, financial and other attractions. Its Algerian, African, Moroccan, Tunisian, Vietnamese, Antillean, Lebanese and other ethnic groups are partly drawn by ex-colonial ties. Its streets are cleaned by crews of workers recruited from Senegal and Mali. Its cultural and educational institutions attract students from around the world. Its business and finance increasingly recruit staff from other European Community countries. French expenditures on the export of language and culture serve as magnets to draw foreigners. The French commitment to assimilation of resident foreigners is causing problems with North Africans and others. Historically France and Paris in particular have accepted and then assimilated foreign minorities (Poles, Jews, Armenians). Paris is a world city with a dominant culture and language in a way that no other world city operates.

6) Sydney with an estimated urban area population of 3.8 million in 1990 is the fastest growing of the world cities. A generous Australian open-door immigration policy since 1945 has attracted to Sydney Italians, Greeks, Yugoslavs, Hungarians, Vietnamese, Chinese and many other nationalities. Its port, commercial hustle, and cosmopolitan character has made it the most multi-ethnic of all Australian cities. Its predominantly British and Irish immigrant stock has been replaced first by southern Europeans and increasingly by Asians. It has been the most willing of all world cities to accept and resettle refugees and this policy has paid-off handsomely. Like Los Angeles, the multi-ethnic composition of Sydney is in constant flux adding to its economic expansion.

7) Toronto is another world city built largely by immigrants with a current population of 3.3 million. Canada's open immigration policies brought Italians, West Indians, Czechs, Chinese and many other nationalities. A foreign-born population close to 25 per cent, strong ethnic definition of neighbourhoods and support groups, and a national policy of cultural pluralism make Toronto the target of many immigrants to Canada. The natural resources based economy has added finance, services and manufacturing to absorb the newcomers. Although there are the usual problems of integration and diversity, immigrant children in the schools, and political conflicts, Toronto is the world city most comfortable with its multi-ethnicity.

Other cities such as Miami, Montreal, São Paulo, Rio de Janeiro, Johannesburg and Singapore may become world cities. Participation in the world economy necessitates opening space to foreigners, whether as permanent or temporary residents. The world cities of the next century may be those which do best at making strangers feel at home.

EMIGRANTS AS A PERCENTAGE OF SENDING COUNTRY POPULATION

Nearly one-third of the world's 200 independent states and dependent territories are senders of voluntary and involuntary emigrants. Yet their participation in those flows and the impact on sending societies varies enormously. This map illustrates some of those differences.

Characteristics of Emigrant Sending Countries

Countries where emigrants abroad are 10 per cent or more of the total population are either caught in a prolonged refugee crisis like Afghanistan and El Salvador or countries with small populations and special relationships with receiving countries (French Antilles, American Samoa). The exceptions are Haiti and Somalia which combine refugee and other emigration to several countries.

The impact on a country of having 10 per cent or more of its population abroad is immense. Whether these are refugees or migrant workers, whether remittances are being sent, makes a difference. However, the strains on family and social structure, especially if a dependent population remains, are heavy.

The sending countries with 6-9 per cent of total population abroad include generations of refugees or migrants. The common denominator is that high-levels of emigration have become a sustained collective activity. Its disruption would result in serious political and economic problems although these are not remittance societies as such. Emigration has become an important means of coping with a perceived hostile external environment.

Sending countries with 1-5 per cent of their total populations abroad mostly have large populations with a few exceptions (Fiji, Jordan). Emigrants are an insignificant part of the labour force and their remittances, while important to families and to foreign exchange deficits, are a minor factor in the national economy. The loss of emigration and remittances would hurt but not cripple most of these countries.

Former Sending Countries

Worth noting is that Greece, Italy, Spain, South Korea, Portugal and Turkey have, within two decades, gone from exporting 5-10 percent or more of their populations to much lower levels. Remittances in each instance have contributed to domestic investments, employment generation, and large-scale repatriation. The experience of these countries indicates that emigration for employment can contribute to domestic economic development. However, in sending countries such as Burkina Faso and Lesotho, with lengthy histories of migrant workers, emigration has had more negative experiences. The relationships between emigration, and its impacts on sending societies need further unraveling.

Colonial Migration Ties

Some emigration is the product of colonial and ex-colonial legacies. Large-scale movement to France and the USA from Caribbean and Pacific dependencies results from grants of citizenship, preferential air fares, and job opportunities. The difference can be clearly seen in former British colonies where no rights to British citizenship exist and emigration is at a lower level and directed to other receiving countries. Freedom of movement between countries can generate its own flows, especially where wage and opportunity disparities are wide.

Receiving countries like Germany, Japan, the USA and the United Kingdom are also senders. However, their citizens abroad are likely to be temporary businessmen, technicians, students and some retirees. Although the data are limited there is no indication that the total numbers involved are anywhere near 1 per cent of total populations.

EMIGRANTS AS A PERCENTAGE OF SENDING COUNTRY POPULATIONS
(Estimates for 1990)
Includes emigration of all kinds (emigrants, migrants, illegal)

Codes on map for each sending country according to percentage of total population.
a) More than 10 per cent of total; b) 6-9 per cent of total; c) 1-5 per cent of total; d) Less than 1 per cent of total

A. Sending countries with emigrants as 10 per cent or more of total population:
Afghanistan, Belize, Bolivia, Burkina Faso, Cambodia, Cape Verde, Chad, Eastern Caribbean (Dominica, Grenada, St. Kitts, St. Vincent, St. Lucia, Antigua), El Salvador, French Antilles, Guyana, Haiti, Jamaica, Laos, Lesotho, Liberia, Mozambique, Netherlands Antilles, Nicaragua, Pacific Islands (Solomon, Western Samoa, American Samoa, Guam, Marshall), Paraguay, Puerto Rico, Somalia, Suriname, Trinidad and Tobago

B. Sending countries with emigrants as 6-9 per cent of total population:
Angola, Botswana, Burundi, Cuba, Dominican Republic, Guinea, Ireland, Lebanon, Sudan, Uruguay, ex-Yugoslavia

C. Sending countries with emigrants as 1-5 per cent of total population:
Albania, Algeria, Bulgaria, Colombia, Egypt, Ethiopia, Fiji, Guatemala, Guinea-Bissau, Jordan, Iran, Mauritania, Mexico, Morocco, Netherlands Antilles, Pakistan, Panama, Philippines, Poland, Romania, Rwanda, South Korea, Sri Lanka, Syria, Turkey, Tunisia, Vietnam

D. Sending countries with emigrants less than 1 per cent of total population:
Bangladesh, Burma, Canada, Chile, China, Costa Rica, Ecuador, France, Ghana, Greece, Honduras, Hong Kong, India, Indonesia, Italy, Malaysia, Peru, Portugal, Spain, Thailand, ex-USSR, USA, others

Sources: World Bank, *World Development Report 1990,* Washington, DC, 1990.
US Department of State, Bureau for Refugee Programs, *World Refugee Report,* Washington, DC, September 1990.
UN, *World Population Trends and Policies 1989 Monitoring Report,* New York: UN 1990.

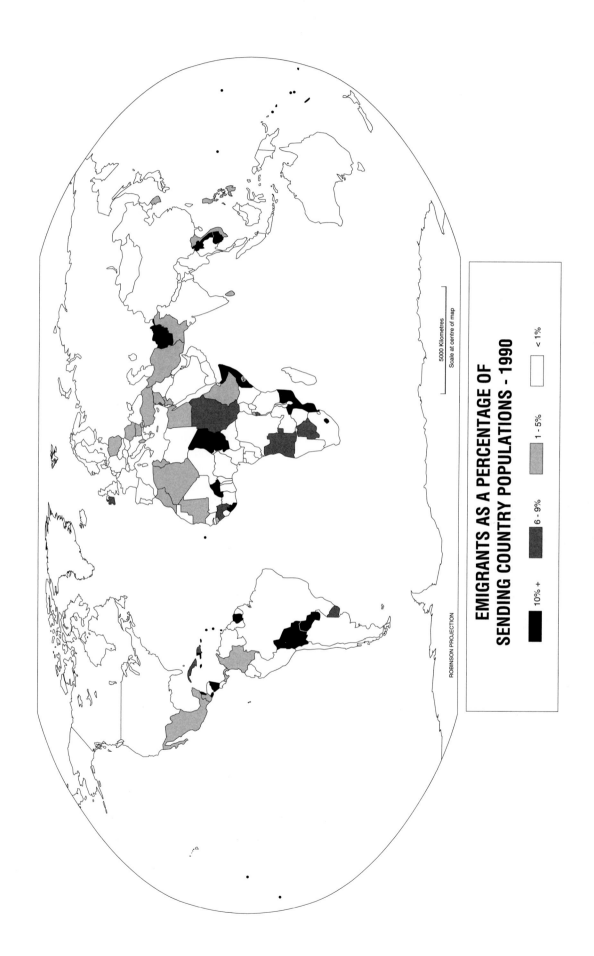

5000 Kilometres

Scale at centre of map

ROBINSON PROJECTION

EMIGRANTS AS A PERCENTAGE OF
SENDING COUNTRY POPULATIONS - 1990

10% +

6 - 9%

1 - 5%

< 1%

IMMIGRANTS AS A PERCENTAGE OF RECEIVING COUNTRY POPULATIONS
Estimates for 1990 include all forms of immigration
(immigrants, migrant workers, undocumented migrants)

A. Countries with immigrants 10 per cent or more of total population:
Antigua, Australia, Bahamas, Bahrain, Brunei, Canada, Côte d'Ivoire, France, French Guiana, Gabon, Gambia, Grenada, Guadaloupe, Guam, Hong Kong, Israel, Jordan, Kuwait, Luxembourg, New Zealand, Oman, Qatar, Papua New Guinea, Saudi Arabia, Singapore, Switzerland, United Arab Emirates

B. Countries with Immigrants 6-9 per cent of total population:
Argentina, Barbados, Belgium, Congo-Brazzaville, Dominican Republic, Germany, Ghana, Malawi, Malaysia, Paraguay, Poland, Puerto Rico, Senegal, St. Kitts, Somalia, South Africa, Swaziland, Thailand, Togo, Trinidad and Tobago, United Kingdom, USA

C. Countries with immigrants 1-5 per cent of total population:
Austria, Bangladesh, Belize, Benin, Bolivia, Botswana, Burkina Faso, Burundi, Cameroon, Central African Republic, Comoros, Costa Rica, Denmark, Egypt, Fiji, India, Iran, Italy, Kenya, Mali, Mauritania, Netherlands, Norway, Sierra Leone, South Korea, Sudan, Tanzania, Tunisia, Venezuela, Zaire, Zambia, Zimbabwe

D. Countries with immigrants less than 1 per cent of total population:
Brazil, China, Chile, Colombia, Czechoslovakia, Ecuador, Finland, Guyana, Hungary, Japan, Indonesia, Iraq, Nigeria, Philippines, Spain, Turkey, Uganda, USSR, others

Sources: UN Population Division, *World Migrant Populations: The Foreign-Born*, New York: United Nations, 1990
US Department of State, Bureau for Refugee Programs, *World Refugee Report*, Washington, DC, September 1990.

IMMIGRANTS AS A PERCENTAGE OF RECEIVING COUNTRY POPULATIONS

Receiving countries with immigrants as 10 per cent or more of their total population are often small, oil-exporting states. Their indigenous populations lack the skills and numbers to undertake the massive investment projects which their revenues permit. Immigrants are usually legal and illegal migrant workers denied naturalization or the presence of dependants and subject to strict controls. The fear of being out-numbered or even swamped by foreigners dictates immigration policies. Recruiting of migrant workers is often from several countries to avoid the dominance of any one nationality. Citizenship and naturalization controls are also used in Luxembourg, Côte d'Ivoire, Israel, and Switzerland to maintain a predetermined social composition for the receiving country.

Characteristics of Immigrant Receiving Countries
Countries where immigrants are approximately 6-9 per cent of the total population are often accept a mixture of refugees, immigrants and migrant workers. Several of these countries such as Argentina, Dominican Republic and Trinidad and Tobago are also important generators of emigrants. Low-income, less educated immigrants from poorer neighbouring countries are replacing better educated emigrants moving to richer countries. Most of the receiving countries in this category are medium-sized populations with economies capable of absorbing more foreigners.

Capability to Absorb Immigrants
Receiving countries with immigrants constituting 1-5 percent of their population tend to be larger with more diversified economies. Immigrants increasingly find employment in urban services rather than in traditional farm labour. Immigration in these countries may result in ethnic and other tensions but its economic impact is marginal. Except for Pakistan and Somalia with their staggering burdens of refugees, most receiving countries in this category potentially can accept more immigrants.

The world's largest countries, China, India, Indonesia and ex-USSR, receive very few immigrants except as refugees. Illegal immigration is a factor in Japan, Nigeria, Spain and a few other countries but it remains less than 1 per cent of the total population. Countries in this category are unlikely receivers of further immigrants, except perhaps to provide first country asylum to refugees.

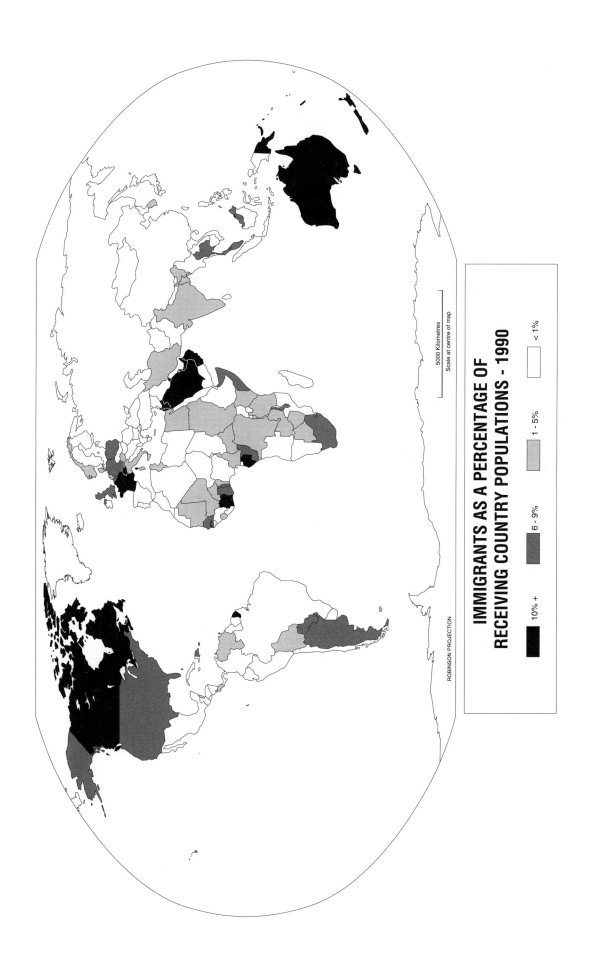

IMMIGRANTS AS A PERCENTAGE OF RECEIVING COUNTRY POPULATIONS - 1990

ROBINSON PROJECTION

5000 Kilometres
Scale at centre of map

10% +

6 - 9%

1 - 5%

< 1%

IMMIGRATION AND REFUGEE POLICIES

The chart indicates that these policies are in considerable flux. Eastern European countries are for the first time receiving refugees and asylum-seekers. Countries like Italy and Spain which have historically been exporters of migrants are becoming targets of opportunity. The European Community is attempting to adopt a uniform policy.

The most important constant is the limited number of countries (Canada, USA, Australia) which maintain open door immigration policies. Moreover the increasing needs for refugee resettlement are cutting into their global quotas.

Everywhere governments are reacting to the fear of being inundated by refugees from nearby strife by adopting policies of temporary asylum only (Malaysia, Greece, Egypt, etc.). The economic and social costs of maintaining refugees in temporary camps for indefinite periods until it is safe for them to return or a third country accepts them are escalating. More and more refugees, like the Palestinians, Cambodians and Laotians, have spent ten or more years in camps.

Ironically the countries most willing to resettle refugees (Norway, Sweden, USA, Canada) are also the principal donors to the UNHCR and to the International Organization for Migration (IOM) and the host of private organizations involved in donor relief. Whether or not donor or compassion fatigue is occurring it is imperative that nations such as Germany and Japan which restrict resettlement increase their financial support.

There seems to be little interaction between the international refugee organizations and domestic policies. Many developing countries have not signed the 1951 UN Convention and show little interest in their screening and other procedures for refugees conforming with UNHCR standards. The UNHCR has become a crisis-oriented relief agency with little ability to dialogue with member governments about their policies. Humane treatment for refugees, especially in temporary asylum, remains a distant hope. As governments distinguish between "economic migrants" and refugees the need for accepted standards and UNHCR monitoring is imperative.

IMMIGRATION AND REFUGEE POLICIES 1990

State	Immigration	Refugees/Asylum-seekers	
Southern Africa			
Botswana	closed door	first asylum	
Malawi	closed door	first asylum	
Mozambique	closed door		accepts repatriates
Namibia	closed door	immigration	repatriation of refugees
South Africa	formerly whites only	limited first asylum	accepts repatriates
Swaziland	closed door	first asylum	
Zambia	closed door	first asylum	
Zimbabwe	closed door	first asylum	some forced repatriation
Horn of Africa			
Djibouti	closed door	first asylum	
Ethiopia	closed door	first asylum	
Somalia	closed door	first asylum	
Sudan	closed door	first asylum	some integration
East Africa			
Kenya	closed door	first asylum	some forced repatriation
Tanzania	closed door	first asylum	some resettlement
Uganda	closed door	first asylum	repatriation
Central Africa			
Burundi	closed door	first asylum	repatriation
Cameroon	closed door	first asylum	
Central African Republic	closed door	first asylum	
Chad	closed door		accepts repatriates
Congo	closed door	first asylum	some resettlement
Rwanda	closed door	first asylum	
Zaîre	closed door	first asylum	some integration
West Africa			
Benin	closed door		accepts repatriates
Burkina Faso	closed door		integration
Côte d'Ivoire	limited immigration		integration
Gabon	closed door		integration
Gambia	closed door	first asylum	
Ghana	closed door		integration, UN Convention
Guinea	closed door	limited first asylum	
Guinea-Bissau	closed door	limited first asylum	
Liberia	limited immigration		accepts repatriation
Mali	closed door	limited first asylum	
Mauritania	closed door		expulsions/repatriations
Niger	closed door		repatriation of refugees
Nigeria	closed door		integration, expulsions
Senegal	closed door		expulsions/repatriations
Sierra Leone	closed door	first asylum	integration
Togo	closed door	limited first asylum	no integration
Asia/Pacific			
Australia	open door	asylum	resettlement, integration
Burma	closed door		
Cambodia	closed door		accepts some repatriates
China	closed door	no asylum	accepts some repatriates
Hong Kong	closed door	limited first asylum	some forced repatriation
Japan	closed door		opposed to resettlement

IMMIGRATION AND REFUGEE POLICIES 1990 continued

State	Immigration	Refugees/Asylum-seekers	
Laos	closed door		accepts some repatriates
Malaysia	closed door	limited first asylum	forced repatriation
New Zealand	limited/open door		accepts 800 refugees/year
Philippines	closed door	first asylum	
Singapore	limited/open door	limited first asylum	
South Korea	closed door	no asylum	
Taiwan	closed door		integration
Thailand	closed door	first asylum	limited settlement
Vietnam	open door		accepts some repatriates
Caribbean/Central America			
Bahamas	closed door	does not recognize asylum	
Belize	open door	first asylum	resettlement
Costa Rica	limited/open door	first asylum	some integration
Cuba	closed door	does not recognize asylum	
Dominican Republic	closed door		no integration
El Salvador	closed door		accepts some repatriates
Guatemala	closed door	first asylum	accepts some repatriates
Haiti	closed door		accepts some repatriates
Honduras	closed door	first asylum	
Mexico	closed door	first asylum	some integration
Nicaragua	closed door	first asylum	accepts some repatriates
Panama	limited/open door	no asylum	
Trinidad and Tobago	closed door	no asylum	
South America			
Argentina	limited/open door	first asylum	some resettlement
Bolivia	closed door	possible first asylum	
Brazil	limited/open door	limited first asylum	UN Convention
Chile	closed door		accepts repatriates
Colombia	closed door	possible first asylum	UN Convention
Ecuador	limited/open door		UN Convention, integration
Paraguay	limited/open door	possible asylum	
Peru	closed door		UN Convention
Suriname	closed door		accepts repatriates
Uruguay	closed door		accepts repatriates
Venezuela	limited/open door		integration
Near East, South Asia, and North Africa			
Algeria	closed door	first asylum for Sahrawi, Palestinians	
Bahrain	closed door	no asylum	legal migrant workers
Bangladesh	closed door		accepts some repatriates
Egypt	closed door	limited first asylum	
India	closed door	case by case policies	
Iraq	closed door	limited asylum	no settlement
Israel	limited/open door		resettlement
Jordan	limited to Palestinians		integration
Kuwait	closed door	no asylum	legal migrant workers
Morocco	closed door		limited integration
Nepal	closed door		integration of Tibetans
Pakistan	closed door	first asylum	
Saudi Arabia	closed door	no asylum	legal migrant workers
Sri Lanka	closed door		accepts some repatriates

IMMIGRATION AND REFUGEE POLICIES 1990 continued

State	Immigration	Refugees/Asylum-seekers	
Syria	closed door		limited integration
Tunisia	closed door	no asylum	no resettlement
Yemen	closed door	no asylum	no resettlement
Europe			
Austria	closed door	first asylum	limited settlement
Belgium	closed door	limited asylum	settlement
Bulgaria	closed door		expulsions (Ethnic Turks)
Cyprus	closed door	no asylum	
Czechoslovakia	closed door		policies being revised post 1989
Denmark	closed door	asylum	settlement, resettlement
Finland	closed door		refugee quota (Vietnamese), resettlement
France	closed door	asylum	resettlement, integration
Germany	open door for Ethnic Germans	asylum	
Greece	closed door	first asylum only	
Hungary	open door for Ethnic Hungarians	first country asylum	
Iceland	closed door		refugee quota (Vietnamese)
Ireland	closed door		refugee quota (Vietnamese)
Italy	closed door	temporary asylum only	
Luxembourg	closed door	limited asylum	legal migrant workers
Malta	closed door	no asylum	
Netherlands	closed door	asylum	resettlement, integration
Norway	closed door	asylum	resettlement (Vietnamese)
Poland	closed door	post-1989 policy being revised	
Portugal	closed door	temporary asylum only	
Romania	closed door	post-1989 policy not clear	
ex-Soviet Union	closed door	no asylum	
Spain	limited open door	limited asylum	
Sweden	closed door	asylum	refugee quota (1250/year), integration
Switzerland	closed door	asylum	settlement, integration
Turkey	open door for Ethnic Turks	limited temporary asylum	
United Kingdom	closed door	asylum	resettlement (Vietnamese)
Yugoslavia	closed door	limited temporary asylum	
North America			
Canada	open door	asylum	resettlement, integration
U.S.A.	open door	asylum	resettlement, integration

Notes:

Open Door refers to global, uniform pro-legal immigration policies.

Closed Door refers to policies severely restricting legal immigration.

Limited refers to policies favoring certain ethnic groups, e.g. Germany.

Integration refers to goal of full legal status for refugees.

Resettlement refers to acceptance of refugees from other countries.

Settlement refers to permanent asylum and state assistance.

Repatriates refers to acceptance of own country nationals for return.

First Country or Temporary Asylum refers to conditional refugee admission.

Asylum refers to temporary or permanent admission of asylum-seekers

Source: US Department of State, Bureau for Refugee Programs, *World Refugee Report,* September 1990, Washington, DC.

FREEDOM TO TRAVEL ABROAD/EMIGRATE 1991

Ratings:

1. High freedom to travel/emigrate. Easy access to passports, travel documents, foreign exchange; no restrictions on travel abroad by minorities, political opposition

2. Medium freedom to travel abroad/emigrate. Passports, travel documents and foreign exchange available but often costly and frequent delays; certain minorities and/or political opposition discouraged but not prevented from travel

3. Low freedom to travel abroad/emigrate. Severe restrictions on access to passports, travel documents and foreign exchange; certain minorities and/or political opposition denied travel; wives require husbands' consent to travel

4. Minimal right to travel abroad/emigrate. Passports, travel documents and foreign exchange granted as government favors to select few. Minorities and political opposition generally denied travel.

Country	Rating	Comments
Afghanistan	4	
Albania	4	Illegal emigration begins in 1990
Algeria	2	Wives need husbands' consent
Angola	4	
Argentina	2	Wives with children need husbands' consent
Australia	1	Freedom of movement with New Zealand
Austria	1	Rights respected
Bangladesh	2	Citizens of doubtful loyalty denied passports
Belgium	1	Rights respected
Benin	3	Special permission for travel outside West Africa
Bolivia	1	Rights respected
Botswana	1	Rights respected
Brazil	1	Rights respected
Bulgaria	4	Slight opening since 1989
Burkina Faso	1	Travel not restricted to neighbouring countries
Burma	4	Deports refugees
Burundi	4	
Cambodia	4	
Cameroon	2	Exit visas denied to political opponents
Canada	1	Rights respected
Central African Republic	4	
Chile	2	Improvement since 1989 return to democracy. Wife needs Husband's consent if children travel
China	4	Crack-down on travel since 1989
Colombia	1	Rights respected
Costa Rica	1	Rights respected
Côte d'Ivoire	2	Travel abroad is permitted
Cuba	4	Exit visa required; strict controls
Czechoslovakia	2	Travel abroad easier since 1989
Denmark	1	Rights respected
Dominican Republic	1	Rights respected
Ecuador	2	Exit permits depend on tax and military duties
Egypt	3	Restrictions on opponents; wives require husbands' consent
El Salvador	4	Massive illegal emigration
Ethiopia	4	Massive illegal emigration, refugees
Finland	1	Rights respected
France	1	Rights respected
Germany	1	Rights respected
Ghana	2	Passports denied to political opponents
Greece	1	Rights respected

FREEDOM TO TRAVEL ABROAD/EMIGRATE 1991 continued

Country	Rating	Comments
Guatemala	4	Mass illegal emigration
Guinea (Conakry)	4	
Haiti	3	Mass illegal emigration; exit permits corruptly administered
Honduras	2	
Hong Kong	1	Rights respected
Hungary	2	Travel easier since 1989; foreign exchange problem
India	2	Exchange control regulations limit travel
Indonesia	2	Exit permits required
Iran	4	Travel abroad strictly controlled
Iraq	4	Exit permits required; strict controls
Ireland	1	Rights respected. Free movement to England
Israel	1	Strict currency controls
Italy	1	Rights respected
Jamaica	1	Rights respected
Japan	1	Rights respected
Jordan	2	
Kenya	3	Passports of opposition withdrawn/denied
Korea, North	4	Only officials and special cases
Korea, South	2	Some travel denials to political opponents
Kuwait	3	Exit permits required; non-nationals expelled
Laos	4	Travel limited to selected officials
Lesotho	2	Passports require a "repatriation" deposit
Liberia	4	Exit visas and bribes
Libya	4	Required exit permits; strict controls
Madagascar	3	
Malawi	3	Travel unrestricted except for known political opponents
Malaysia	2	Most restrictions on travel to China lifted
Mali	3	
Mexico	1	Rights respected but mass illegal emigration
Morocco	3	No passports for political dissidents
Mozambique	4	Exit permits and passports for select few
Nepal	3	
Netherlands	1	Rights respected
New Zealand	1	Free movement to Australia
Nicaragua	3	Foreign exchange controls
Niger	3	Exit permit required
Nigeria	2	Corrupt bureaucracies for documents
Norway	1	Rights respected
Pakistan	3	Foreign exchange controls; many permits
Panama	2	Much corruption in obtaining documents
Papua New Guinea	1	Rights respected
Paraguay	2	Progress since 1989 coup
Peru	1	Rights respected
Philippines	1	Encourages emigration
Poland	2	Travel abroad easier since 1989
Portugal	1	Rights respected
Romania	4	Slight opening since 1989
Saudi Arabia	3	Exit permit and permission for women needed
Senegal	1	Rights respected
Sierra Leone	1	Rights respected
Singapore	1	Rights respected
Somalia	4	Mass illegal emigration
South Africa	3	Improvement since 1989 in granting passports
Spain	1	Rights respected
Sri Lanka	1	Emigration encouraged
Sudan	4	Mass illegal emigration

FREEDOM TO TRAVEL ABROAD/EMIGRATE 1991 continued

Country	Rating	Comments
Sweden	1	Rights respected
Switzerland	1	Rights respected
Syria	4	Exit permits required; strict controls
Taiwan	4	1984 law allows withdrawl of passports
Tanzania	4	Passports refused on currency grounds
Thailand	1	Surveillance for emigration of prostitutes
Togo	4	Passports seldom obtained
Trinidad and Tobago	1	Rights respected
Tunisia	2	Some political opponents denied passports
Turkey	3	Arbitrary denial of passports
Uganda	4	
United Kingdom	1	No legal right to passport
Uruguay	1	Rights respected since return to democracy
USA	1	Rights respected
USSR	4	Some opening since 1986 on travel, emigration
Venezuela	1	Rights respected
Vietnam	4	Orderly emigration and mass illegal emigration
West Bank/Gaza	4	Exit visa required for travel
Yemen	4	
Yugoslavia	2	Travel disrupted by 1991 civil war
Zaïre	4	Required exit visas and much corruption
Zambia	4	Passports of dissidents withheld
Zimbabwe	4	Passports of dissidents withdrawn

Source: Revised and updated to 1991 from Charles Humana, *World Human Rights Guide*, New York: Facts on File, 1986. See also the Glossary.

GLOBAL FREEDOM OF MOVEMENT

The idea that anyone should be free to travel, to live, to seek work, and to die anywhere on the planet has few advocates in a world of 5.5 billion inhabitants whose population continues to increase at 2 per cent annually. Governments cling to controls over immigration as the essence of sovereignty no matter how they profess the right to emigrate. This same right to emigrate has little meaning unless and until other countries freely and extensively permit immigration. However, freedom of movement does not feature in the United Nations or other declarations of human rights and has the support of no major governments or globe-girdling non-governmental organizations. International migration constitutes a privilege rather than a right, entirely subject to the disposition of receiving countries and governments.

Regional Freedom of Movement
This longstanding state of affairs is being altered incrementally on a regional rather than a global basis. Neighbouring countries with similar standards of living and political and cultural values are legislating freedom of movement including travel, residence, employment, and even in some instances voting rights to each others' citizens. This regional freedom of movement is embodied in international treaties and other formal intergovernmental agreements.   (See also Overseas Citizens, p. 148)

Other Regional Arrangements
The Scandinavian nations of Sweden, FInland, Norway, Denmark and Iceland were the first to legislate regional freedom of movement in the 1970s. The effects have been modest with limited numbers of FInnish workers migrating to Sweden for higher wages, as well as an increased interchange of students. However, there has been an increase in regional tourism and an end of visas and other immigration documents. The closeness of wage levels between the countries and the generally high levels of employment have kept people at home. Absolute numbers of foreign workers from outside the region (Yugoslavia, Turkey) outnumber fellow Scandinavians in each country.

Australia and New Zealand initiated bilateral and reciprocal freedom of movement in the 1920s. There has been a small, net exodus of New Zealanders drawn to the larger and more prosperous Australian economy. Again net immigration from outside the two countries is significantly greater than two-country free movement.

European Community Freedom of Movement
The twelve nation European Community (EC) at the end of 1992 will have for its citizens comprehensive freedom of movement including Spain and Portugal who joined the EC in 1986. Barriers and restrictions on the licensing of professionals, acceptance of technical credentials, and other restraints to movement are scheduled to be removed. In principle the EC will become the largest multinational free labour market in the world for its citizens, thus fulfilling the goals of the 1957 Treaty of Rome.

In practice freedom of movement within the EC has had limited impact. Culture, language, costs of relocation, and other variables have sharply limited job-taking across national borders. Some progress has been made on harmonization of retirement, social security and other benefits but significant national differences remain.

Guest Workers in the European Community
Prior to 1973 the EC relied primarily on migrant workers from Turkey, North Africa and elsewhere outside the EC. While Spanish workers migrated to Germany and Portuguese workers to France, and Italian workers to Switzerland and Germany these movements were nationally regulated. Any resumption of large-scale temporary migrant labour in the EC would probably be filled by workers from Eastern Europe rather than EC member states whose wage rates and employment levels are considerably higher.

Legal freedom of movement is not irrelevant, though, in the EC. It enables more than 25,000 persons from all member states to find employment with the Commission itself, for companies to move staff freely within the EC, for highly skilled specialists such as researchers to find work to match their skills, and of course for intra-EC travel to flourish without visas. Recently the EC Commission has established Project Erasmus to provide scholarships for EC citizens to study outside their home countries. Although it is unlikely that nationals from other EC states will come to constitute more than 5 per cent of the labour force of any EC member except for tiny Luxembourg, freedom of movement plays a valuable psychological role in the process of European unity.

Prospects for Regional Free Movement
What are the prospects of regional expansion of this concept? Austria and Sweden with standards of living comparable to Northern European states have applied for EC membership. So have Turkey, Cyprus, Morocco and other net emigration countries. Austria and Germany already have a *de facto* freedom of movement with no visas required for travel and relatively simple access respectively to residence and to work permits.

It is possible to envisage an EC expanded to include Austria, Sweden, Norway, FInland and Switzerland while embracing freedom of movement. Any form of association between the EC and Eastern Europe or Turkey, or North Africa is likely to exclude freedom of movement due to the enormous differences in standards of living and the demographic pressures to emigrate. Wherever the threat of massive, spontaneous emigration is perceived freedom of movement is regarded as too dangerous. Similarly Australia and New Zealand are unwilling to extend freedom of movement to all the South Pacific islands or to Southeast Asia.

Prospects in North America
The prospects are limited for converting *de facto* freedom of movement to *de jure* status. Canada and the USA continue to insist on immigration visas and work permits

but these are generally quickly granted for qualified applicants. The proposed Canada-Mexico-USA Free Trade Area explicitly excludes freedom of movement of persons, given Mexico's massive legal and illegal emigration to the USA. Thus it is likely that Canada and the USA will continue their easy access to each others' territory without further formal measures.

Prospects for South America

The Southern Cone of South America offers some potential for establishing *de facto* if not *de jure* freedom of movement. Already Argentina harbours millions of legal and illegal migrants from Uruguay, Paraguay and Bolivia. Brazilian colonists have moved into eastern Paraguay. The proposed Southern Cone Common Market for 1994 (Argentina, Brazil, Paraguay, Uruguay) does not call for freedom of movement of persons. Efforts to accelerate the industrialization of the region are likely to be based on existing growth poles such as São Paulo and Buenos Aires and to accelerate emigration from neighbouring countries. Disparities of income and living standards are considerable but not so great as to rule out any attempt at freedom of movement.

Prospects in Asia

There are slight prospects for eventual freedom of movement in Southeast Asia among the six ASEAN states (Brunei, Singapore, Thailand, Malaysia, Philippines and Indonesia). Recent sustained economic growth has resulted in large-scale illegal and legal migration within the region while also raising standards of living. Although controlled temporary migration is the current response, a political regional framework exists in which to consider alternatives.

Elsewhere in the world the chances of regional freedom of movement are slim to non-existent. Fears of unemployment, nationalism, multi-ethnic tensions and growing populations all preclude open door immigration policies, even on a reciprocal basis. Possible economic efficiencies from allowing human resources to move freely are feeble arguments in the face of deep-seated fears. Even where cultural affinites are strong between nations, as in Central America and the West Indies, political opposition to freedom of movement prevails. Reciprocity is insufficient to overcome each sides' fears of being swamped by unwanted immigrants.

Freedom to Travel

Travel is one of the most cherished aspects of international movement. Each of over 180 independent sovereign-states is free to determine under what conditions it will accept visitors from any other country, subject to no appeals. Citizens of certain countries such as Haiti and Rwanda must obtain visas for almost all countries they wish to visit. Citizens of Switzerland hold the worlds' record for the maximum number of countries which they may visit without a visa. Normally governments exempt visa requirements on a reciprocal basis but some countries seeking tourism drop visas for visitors from certain countries without reciprocity.

A world organized in terms of freedom of movement would be free of visas and other travel documents. Although in the 1990s only about 550 million persons, or less than 10 per cent of the worlds' population, exercised some degree of regional freedom of movement, a start had been made.

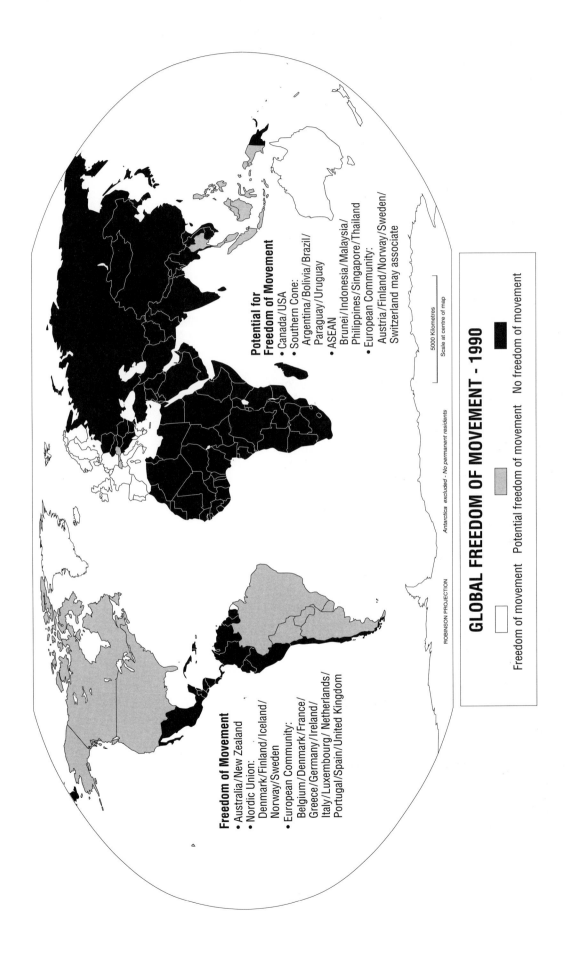

Freedom of Movement

- Australia/New Zealand
- Nordic Union:
  Denmark/Finland/Iceland/
  Norway/Sweden
- European Community:
  Belgium/Denmark/France/
  Greece/Germany/Ireland/
  Italy/Luxembourg/ Netherlands/
  Portugal/Spain/United Kingdom

**Potential for
Freedom of Movement**

- Canada/USA
- Southern Cone:
  Argentina/Bolivia/Brazil/
  Paraguay/Uruguay
- ASEAN
  Brunei/Indonesia/Malaysia/
  Philippines/Singapore/Thailand
- European Community:
  Austria/Finland/Norway/Sweden/
  Switzerland may associate

ROBINSON PROJECTION

Antarctica excluded - No permanent residents

Scale at centre of map

5000 Kilometres

GLOBAL FREEDOM OF MOVEMENT - 1990

Freedom of movement   Potential freedom of movement   No freedom of movement

WORLD LABOUR FORCE

The world labour force, global income per head and international migration are clearly related. Presumably were there a world open to movements of labour there would be massive migration toward higher income regions. According to economic theory an equilibrium of labour demand and supply would be reached through the most efficient allocation of resources.

Global Mobility of Labour

The reality is that financial services, investments, and even trade, move around the planet much more easily than do job-seekers. Extra-regional migration of all kinds is a small percentage of global labour movements. Most migration is of the country-next-door variety with the exception of the remarkable recruiting to the Arabian Peninsula.

Does it make more sense to move capital and technology to create jobs *in situ* or to move workers? During the nineteenth century the movement of workers to the sources of capital was hailed; now it is rejected except as a temporary expedient. Yet the disparities in income distribution and sizes of labour forces continue to produce demands to emigrate. Instead a variety of incentives have been created to induce manufacturing and services to go offshore where cheap labour is available.

Global Immobility of Labour

The European Community observes that "labour is largely immobile in a global sense, being unable to move between countries due to the severe restrictions most countries apply to foreign national immigrants. This even goes as far as inhibiting trade in certain service sectors which require temporary movements of personnel". What is striking is how much movement, legal and illegal, does go on in spite of these restrictions.

Equally remarkable is that China, India and the ex-Soviet Union, the three most populous countries in the world, barely take part in international migration. Japan is a marginal player. Movement is being driven by North America, Western Europe, the Middle East, Africa and Latin America. Global movements are from poor to rich but also from poor to less poor countries and regions. There is every indication that as labour forces grow more rapidly in some regions than others and income disparities widen, that the pressures that underlie international migration will become stronger.

Sources: European Community, *Social Europe*, Brussels: EC, 1992.
European Community, *Employment in Europe*, Brussels: EC, 1989.

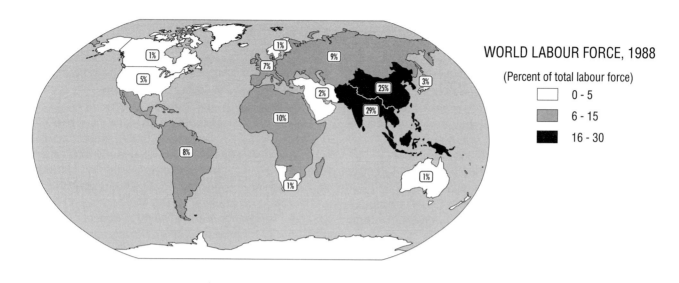

WORLD LABOUR FORCE, 1988

(Percent of total labour force)

- 0 - 5
- 6 - 15
- 16 - 30

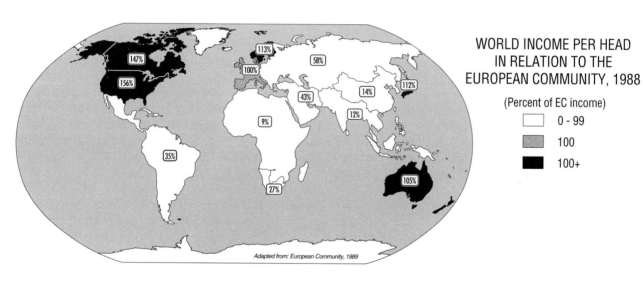

WORLD INCOME PER HEAD
IN RELATION TO THE
EUROPEAN COMMUNITY, 1988

(Percent of EC income)

- 0 - 99
- 100
- 100+

Adapted from: European Community, 1989

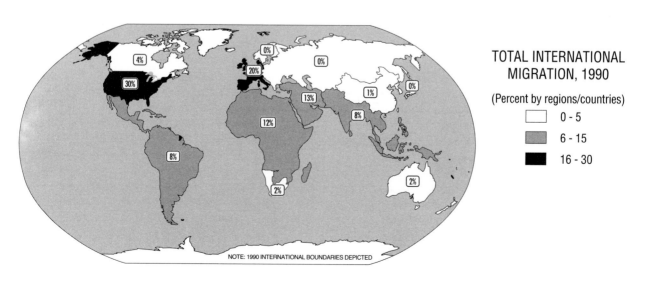

TOTAL INTERNATIONAL
MIGRATION, 1990

(Percent by regions/countries)

- 0 - 5
- 6 - 15
- 16 - 30

NOTE: 1990 INTERNATIONAL BOUNDARIES DEPICTED

INTERNATIONAL MIGRANT WORKERS:
COUNTRIES OF ORIGIN AND EMPLOYMENT 1990
(These estimates exclude immigrants and refugees while including legal and illegal workers)

Sending Countries
1. Algeria — France 400,000: Belgium
2. Austria — Germany 200,000
3. Bangladesh — Gulf States 250,000-300,000. Contract subject to repatriation
4. Burkina Faso — Agricultural labourers in Côte d'Ivoire and Ghana 900,000
5. Central African Republic — 200,000 Cameroon
6. Colombia — Venezuela 800,000; USA 400,000; Ecuador. Legal and illegal
7. Dominican Republic — USA 800,000. Legal and illegal. 50,000 Dominican workers in Puerto Rico
8. Egypt — 2.9 million Gulf, Saudi Arabia and Iraq prior to 1990. Contract workers, Libya
9. El Salvador — 800,000 in USA. Legal and illegal
10. Greece — Germany and other EC countries. Less than 100,000
11. Haiti — Dominican Republic 500,000; USA 600,000; French Guiana 20,000. Legal and illegal. Recruited to Dominican sugar estates, Bahamas, Canada 100,000
12. Jamaica — USA 400,000 includes seasonal workers recruited by US Department of Labor for harvests, Canada 125,000
13. India — Gulf States 815,000-1 million. Contract labor
14. Indonesia — Malaysia 350,000-500,000; Gulf 100,000. Contract labor
15. Italy — Germany, Switzerland 350,000. Generally contract labor
16. Jordan — Iraq, Saudi Arabia and Gulf 400,000 prior to 1990 war. Includes some Palestinians with Jordanian passports
17. Mali — Senegal, France 200,000
18. Mexico — USA 2.5 million. Legal and illegal.
19. Morocco — France, Belgium, Spain 400,000. Legal and illegal
20. New Zealand — Australia 100,000. Reciprocal freedom of movement
21. Papua New Guinea — Australia 100,000
22. Pakistan — Gulf States 850,000-1 million. Repatriated contract labor
23. Philippines — USA 900,000; Gulf 800,000; Malaysia 100,000; also Hong Kong, Japan, Singapore
24. Portugal — France 300,000. Earlier migrants return or become French citizens
25. Senegal — France 200,000
26. Spain — Germany 300,000. Net return since 1980
27. Sri Lanka — Gulf States 200,000-300,000. Contract and repatriation
28. Syria — Gulf States 200,000
29. Tunisia — 200,000, France; Italy, Libya 50,000
30. Turkey — Germany 600,000. Net return since 1973; Gulf States 100,000 on contract; other EC countries 300,000
31. Yugoslavia — Austria 120,000; Germany 800,000; Sweden 9,000

No recent estimates are available for Bolivia, Paraguay and Uruguay for migrant workers in Argentina

Other Sending Countries not shown on map: Central African Republic, China, Ecuador, Lesotho, Malaysia, Sudan, Swaziland, Yemen

Sources: Reginald Appleyard, ed. *International Migration Today, Volume I: Trends and Prospects.* Paris: UNESCO, 1988.
Charles Stahl, ed. *International Migration Today, Volume 2: Emerging Issues.* Paris: UNESCO, 1988.
International Institute for Strategic Studies. *The Military Balance 1990-1991.* London: International Institute for Strategic Studies, 1990.

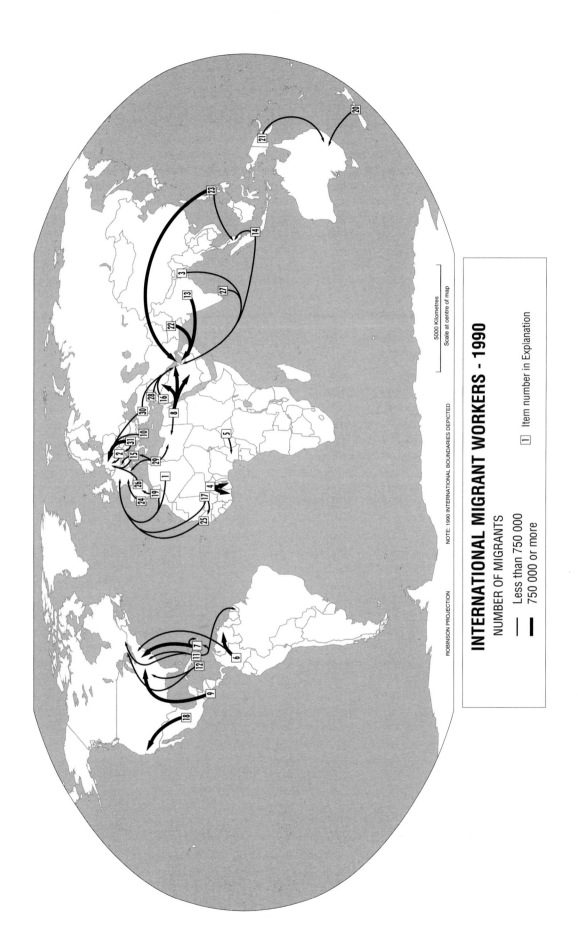

INTERNATIONAL MIGRANT WORKERS - 1990

NUMBER OF MIGRANTS

— Less than 750 000

▬ 750 000 or more

1 Item number in Explanation

5000 Kilometres

Scale at centre of map

ROBINSON PROJECTION   NOTE: 1990 INTERNATIONAL BOUNDARIES DEPICTED

INTERNATIONAL MIGRANT WORKERS

An international migrant worker is defined as someone residing outside his home country, legally or illegally, for purposes of employment, with the intention of returning home. All recruited workers subject to fixed-stay contracts and repatriation are included in this definition. The data available emphasize legal unskilled and semi-skilled workers, whether or not on contract. The intention to return may be vague and never implemented. However, this definition excludes those persons who have sought naturalization or legal amnesty in their new countries.

Estimates of Migrant Workers
This definition produces a crude estimate of 20 million legal and illegal international migrant workers in 1990 prior to the Gulf War. Less than 3 million were subject to formal recruitment contracts, used primarily in the Gulf. An astonishing 5 per cent came from states with populations less than one million: Barbados, Belize, Cape Verde, Cyprus, six independent Eastern Caribbean islands (Antigua, St. Lucia, St. Kitts, Grenada, Dominica and St. Vincent); Guyana, and the Comoros. Migrant workers accounted for one-third or more of the active labour force in these mini-states, and remittances often for the largest source of income.

Globally international migration for employment is focused on the Gulf States, North America and Western Europe. Japan, with the world's second largest economy, is a minor if growing destination. Eastern Europe and the ex-Soviet Union participate only marginally as sources of employment or migrant workers but this is likely to change. Migrant labour across national boundaries is beginning to play a significant role in the fast-growth economies of East Asia.

Plight of Illegal Workers
Reliable figures are not available but a distressingly high proportion of foreign workers are illegal in their countries of employment, especially the USA. Subject to deportation they are also (without protection) in terms of labour laws and basic rights. Australia, Canada, France, USA and other countries have experimented with amnesty programs to legalize some foreign workers. However, many lack the documents, the necessary length of residence, or the awareness of amnesty programs. The alternatives of temporary legal guestworker or illegality trap many persons in limited choices.

International Circular Migration
Prior to the twentieth century the term circular migration referred to immigrants who returned to their countries of origin. Some returned with savings to retire or to resume pre-immigration lives. Many more returned frustrated and disillusioned. Some returned deported by immigration authorities on health or other grounds. It has been estimated that perhaps one-fifth of all immigrants to the New World returned in the nineteenth century; even higher proportions of indentured labourers.

History of Circular Migration
Circular migration also touched the lives of other migrants. Chinese workers recruited for the mid-nineteenth century railroad construction in the USA were often repatriated. Slaves freed at sea or emancipated by purchase in the USA and Brazil were shipped to West Africa where some became the founders of Liberia and Sierra Leone. However, only a miniscule percentage of involuntary, indentured, convicts or slaves were able to return. Some indentured labourers from Europe to the Caribbean were able to re-emigrate to the American colonies after working out their terms.

Future of Circular Migration
Circular international migration has expanded and been transformed dramatically in the twentieth century. It is likely to take on new and even more striking directions in the twenty-first century. The essential change is that more and more people are finding ways to spend part of their lives in more than one society while retaining the right to return to their country of origin whether by birth or nationality. While governments insist on sovereign control over the granting of dual nationality which continues to be available only between a limited number of states, the opportunities to live and to work abroad have multiplied.

Definitions of Expatriates
There are several million 'expatriates' in the world; persons 'living in a foreign country'. The majority live abroad for years rather than lifetimes and re-visit their home countries. Few change their nationalities and many do not bother to register with their home embassies or consulates. The largest number of expatriates come from the USA with more than 900,000 estimated followed by Japan 600,000, the United Kingdom, France and Germany. Smaller countries such as Australia, the Netherlands, Sweden and Switzerland are also known for their large numbers of expatriates.

Expatriates come in a bewildering variety of types. There are no reliable global estimates of expatriates and only sketchy figures for individual nationalities or categories. Expatriates are concentrated in the principal cities of the world economy: New York, Tokyo, Paris, Rome, Frankfurt, Cairo, Bangkok, Singapore, Mexico City, Nairobi, etc. They are also found in the most remote areas working as missionaries, volunteers for non-profit organizations, and researchers.

Expatriate Categories

1. Managers and businessmen primarily employed by multi-national corporations. Americans, Japanese, British, Germans, French, Swiss, etc. Most return and are re-assigned.
2. Unskilled and semi-skilled workers. Legal or illegal temporary migrant workers. An unknown percentage do not return.
3. Technicians. Often on short-term assignments.
4. Professionals. Health workers, teachers, trans-

lators, artists, etc. Often employed by non-profit, non-governmental organizations. Includes volunteers from USA, Japan, Germany, Norway, Switzerland, France, etc. Primarily one or two year assignments subject to renewal or return.

5. Missionaries/clergy. Several hundred thousand Catholic, Evangelical and other clericals working for brief periods to lifetimes overseas.

6. Students/researchers. Globally more than one million. Discussed in Study Abroad Section.

7. Retirees. Growing numbers retired in communities or individually overseas. Canadians in the USA; Americans in Mexico (400,000); Costa Rica (40,000); British in Spain and Italy, proposals for Japanese retirement communities in Brazil.

8. Independents. Expatriates with their own sources of income, e.g. wealthy Arabs in Spain.

9. International organizations. Several hundred thousand career and contract employees of the UN system, non-governmental organizations such as Doctors Without Borders, etc.

10. Spouses, dependants, relatives.

Expatriates tend to cluster abroad by nationality in informal communities not unlike those of ethnic groups. For example, Paris with an estimated 80,000 residents from English-speaking countries in 1990 had five English language bookstores, two hospitals, several pharmacies, and one newspaper (Herald-Tribune).

As the world economy expands the demand for expatriates is certain to grow, especially in Eastern Europe and the ex-Soviet Union. The likelihood that large numbers of people will spend part of their working lives abroad will become a reality in regions like the European Community where freedom of movement is encouraged. The estimated 50,000 Japanese businessmen in New York City in 1990 represent the tip of the iceberg of a series of expatriate communities in all of the major capitals of the world. These communities will often reconstruct their schools, playing fields, restaurants, places of worship and other institutions. The effect is to diffuse and to globalize rather than to homogenize cultures and values.

Migrant Workers

This term has an enormous range of meanings. It refers to unskilled workers recruited through government to government channels for seasonal harvests (Jamaica-USA, Mexico-Canada, Haiti-Dominican Republic, etc.), to factory workers recruited on one to two year contracts (EC prior to 1973 and the oil and economic crises); to illegal workers who find service jobs in USA cities (El Salvador, Mexico-USA) and who return frequently to their countries of origin; and to industrial, service and agricultural workers in the Gulf States recruited on contracts. Historically, agricultural labour which has been recruited, also has stayed on (Fiji, Guyana, Trinidad and Tobago, Suriname, South Africa).

History of Migrant Workers

International migrant labour reached its apogee during the early 1970s at an estimated 20-25 million persons. The principal growth poles were West Germany with its *gastarbeiter* (guestworker) factory recruitment schemes from Turkey, Yugoslavia, Italy, Spain and other countries, as well as France, Belgium, the Netherlands and Sweden. Legal recruitment of migrant workers from outside the EC was terminated after 1973 although illegal immigration continues. Ironically between 1970 and 1990 East Germany, Czechoslovakia and the Soviet Union recruited workers in small numbers from Vietnam and Mozambique.

Currently, international migrant labour is concentrated in the six oil-exporting Gulf States where 30 to 60 per cent of the labour force is foreign-born. Professional, managerial, and technical workers continue to be drawn from North America and Europe with unskilled and semi-skilled labour in all sectors of the economy from Egypt, Jordan, the Palestinian diaspora, the Sudan, India, Pakistan, Sri Lanka, the Philippines, Bangladesh, Turkey and other countries. Migrant workers are often recruited without dependants, are overwhelmingly male except for female house servants, are relatively well-paid, and denied any opportunity for permanent residence or employment. In spite of complaints about dependence on foreign labour, reliance on migrant workers has become a way of life, interrupted only in Iraq by war and loss of foreign exchange.

Trends in International Migrant Labour

Elsewhere in the world international migrant labour lacks the magnitude and formal structure of the Gulf. Japan, facing a labour shortage, is said to have between 250,000 and 350,000 mostly illegal foreign workers; Malaysia depends on nearly one million Indonesians for its rubber and other harvests; South Africa has cut drastically its recruitment of foreign mine and agricultural workers to favour locals; the Côte d'Ivoire and Ghana rely on seasonal harvesters from Burkina Faso; about 800,000 Colombians are legally and illegally employed in Venezuela; several million Bolivians, Paraguayans and Uruguayans work in Argentina in spite of its stagnant economy; Mexicans and Central Americans determinedly enter the USA illegally to seek mostly urban service jobs; Haitians crowd into the Dominican Republic, the Bahamas, and as far as French Guiana looking for work, etc.

Migrant Labour Supply

The above and many other examples indicate an emerging pattern of international migrant labour. Wherever economic growth and investment creates a demand for unskilled labour there will be an international response if transport, remittable earnings and access are available. The opportunities to earn and to save, especially in convertible currencies, outweigh the real hardships of separation from families, harsh living and working conditions, and strangeness of cultures and languages. Whether in the crowded cities of North Africa or the villages of Pakistan there is no shortage of young adult males willing to work abroad, whether legally or illegally. Working conditions have improved since nineteenth century indentured labour but the lack of perceived opportunities at home has not.

Host Country Reactions
Host countries fear that migrant workers will not return home, thus engendering multi-ethnic social and other problems. The experience of EC countries indicates that many migrant workers will try to stay and to reunite their families, especially if home conditions have deteriorated. The Gulf States guarantee against migrant stays by recruiting from distant lands, including repatriation in contracts, and denying residence permits. Those seeking to stay have been predominantly Arabic-speakers from neighbouring countries such as Jordan, Yemen and Egypt as well as Palestinians.

Regulation of Migrant Labour
International labour migration is here to stay. Should it be nationally, regionally or internationally regulated? Should it be organized through formal recruitment schemes which provide for return, through multi-national companies fulfilling construction or other contracts (South Korea, Turkey), or through government to government channels? Should there be more schemes and incentives to encourage repatriation and reinvestment of savings earned abroad at home? What should be the role of women and dependants in migrant labour? Whether in Mexico or Yugoslavia women are increasingly leaving home to seek work and earnings abroad. The International Labour Organisation (ILO) is the principal advocate of protection and rights for international migrant workers. Its authority and competence need to be greatly extended if those who seek temporary work in another country are not to be further abused.

Swallows (Recycling Migrants)
There is a small if unknown number of international migrant workers who are able to go back and forth legally and regularly between jobs and countries. Known colloquially as 'swallows' whose returns to home nests they imitate, these individuals are often found in professional sports. For instance, there are nearly 500 baseball players from the Dominican Republic employed in the North American professional leagues. A smaller number of West Indians compete professionally in the English cricket leagues. European professional football is enhanced by increasing numbers of African and Latin American players. Many of these athletes compete during the professional season and then return home to another round of competition, training or adulation.

Swallow migrants can be found in other activities from tourism to entertainment. The service sector particularly lends itself to producing swallows. So does belonging to one of the well organized ethnic communities overseas which provide business opportunities between home country and one of adoption. Swallows are the fraternal cousins of 'snowbirds' who maintain a winter and a summer home; Canada and the Bahamas; Switzerland and Tunisia. Many but not all snowbirds are retirees; some are swallows with employment in two countries.

Overseas Citizens
About 6 million persons are the overseas citizens of metropolitan states, thus giving them the right to travel, reside, and work in two societies. This status exists for 3.6 million island Puerto Ricans, 300,000 USA citizens living in the US Virgin Islands, American Samoa and Guam; and the nearly two million French citizens of the Caribbean islands of Guadeloupe and Martinique, New Caledonia, French Polynesia in the Pacific, and the Indian Ocean island of Réunion. Other overseas citizens are the Azores and Madeira islanders of Portugal and Greenlanders of Denmark.

Wherever overseas citizenship exists it results in high rates of net emigration to the continental metropole (400,000 for France; 1.8 million for the USA). Given air fares and other re-location costs it also makes it possible for some persons to maintain two residences and employments. At a minimum it encourages and facilitates circular migration as another form of freedom of movement.

Military Migration
Soldiers have been stationed outside their home countries for purposes of war, conquest, occupation, deterrence, training, and other objectives. Most overseas tours are one to two years in bases carefully screened from contact with local populations. However, there are also hundreds of smaller military advisor groups and missions which have more extensive contacts with their local counterparts.

At the beginning of the 1980s there were approximately three million soldiers stationed abroad from a dozen countries, primarily the ex-Soviet Union and the USA. Extraordinarily by 1990 these numbers had dropped to two million due to several strategic withdrawals. These included Soviet troops in process of withdrawal from Cuba, Germany, Poland, Hungary and Czechoslovakia and withdrawn from Afghanistan; Cuban troops withdrawn from Angola; South African troops withdrawn from Angola and Namibia; and partial withdrawal of USA forces from Germany and the Philippines.

While national forces were being withdrawn or reduced the UN expanded its peace-keeping operations (Iraq, Nicaragua, Cambodia, Yugoslavia, etc.). A dozen or more countries (Colombia, Fiji, Finland, Canada, Austria, Spain, Sweden, Australia, Ireland, France, Netherlands, Italy, New Zealand, Uruguay) provided lightly-armed soldiers and observers to UN missions. The costs of keeping 10-12,000 UN forces in the field were borne by voluntary contributions to the UN (1990).

Future Military Deployment
The prospects for future stationing of forces abroad are confused. France seems determined to maintain a rapid deployment force of 5,000-7,000 at several points in Africa (Djibouti, Côte d'Ivoire, Gabon, etc.). This commitment is an important element in France's ongoing ties to

certain of its ex-colonies. The USA maintains important contingents in Japan, South Korea, and subject to negotiation in Singapore, as components of mutual security in the Pacific.

European Military Concerns

The withdrawal in process to ex-Soviet borders is changing the context of European security. The heart of the matter is whether foreign forces will continue with consent to be based in a unified Germany (USA, French, British, Dutch, Italian and Belgian forces). There are many options including the deployment of German forces elsewhere in Europe. The chances are that the North Atlantic Treaty Organization (NATO) and NATO forces in Germany will continue while alternate arrangements are considered.

While other minor military deployments abroad continue in the 1990s, e.g. 1500 British forces in Belize as protection against Guatemala, 10-12,000 USA forces in Panama, the age of massive forces abroad may be ending. An exception is Syria with 40,000 soldiers in Lebanon to provide political control over its neighbour. Advanced technologies and improved logistics may be reducing the value of keeping permanent forces abroad beyond the Cold War.

The Future of International Migration

International migration in the twenty-first century is likely to assume new directions. Rapidly demographically ageing affluent societies will need both to retire some elderly abroad and to import workers for service sectors. As freedom of movement extends within and perhaps between world regions, the possibilities of circular migration will improve. Working in a world economy more managers, professionals and technicians will be expected to have international experience. International migration of unskilled workers will become subject to international controls and regulations, intended both to inhibit immigration and to encourage remittances. The number of soldiers stationed abroad will stablilize at relatively low levels. Circular international migration will largely replace immigration as the predominant mode.

GLOBAL REMITTANCES

The transfer of funds by voluntary migrants to their home countries has characterized much international migration since its inception. Remittances have been used for personal consumption, to finance education of relatives left behind, to pay for the costs of migration, and to invest funds for other purposes.

Definition of Remittances

The World Bank defines net workers' remittances "as payments and receipts of income by migrants who are employed or expect to be employed for more than a year in their new economy, where they are considered residents." This definition excludes transfers from shorter or illegal stays. The World Bank also does not publish data on remittances to countries with populations less than one million. Several small states in the Eastern Caribbean, Cape Verde Islands, Sâo Tome, and the Comoros are highly dependent on remittances. The World Bank data also underestimate transfers that occur through informal and unrecorded channels.

Value of Global Remittances

Using the World Bank data the total value of remittances in the world economy has risen from $3,133 billion in 1970 to $30,401 billion in 1988. Although remittances continue to be less than five per cent of total world trade they represent a rapidly growing sector. The data suggest that it is becoming easier to move labour internationally with remittances as an incentive than it is to move goods and services.

Impact of Remittances

The effects of remittances on receiving societies remains highly controversial. Caribbean islands such as St. Kitts and Nevis now receive a majority of their income from remittances with the elderly and young left behind while adults leave to work. Remittances in Turkey and Yugoslavia have been used to create new investments and small businesses but this has not happened elsewhere. Generally, remittances are used for personal consumption, often for import of consumer durables.

The list of countries exporting workers and receiving remittances girdles the globe. It includes countries as relatively prosperous as New Zealand and Italy and some of the poorest countries in the world. Remittances have become vital sources of foreign exchange to many countries from Egypt to Mexico. Yet income from remittances is highly vulnerable, as demonstrated in the 1990-1991 Gulf War when over 1 million migrant workers were repatriated.

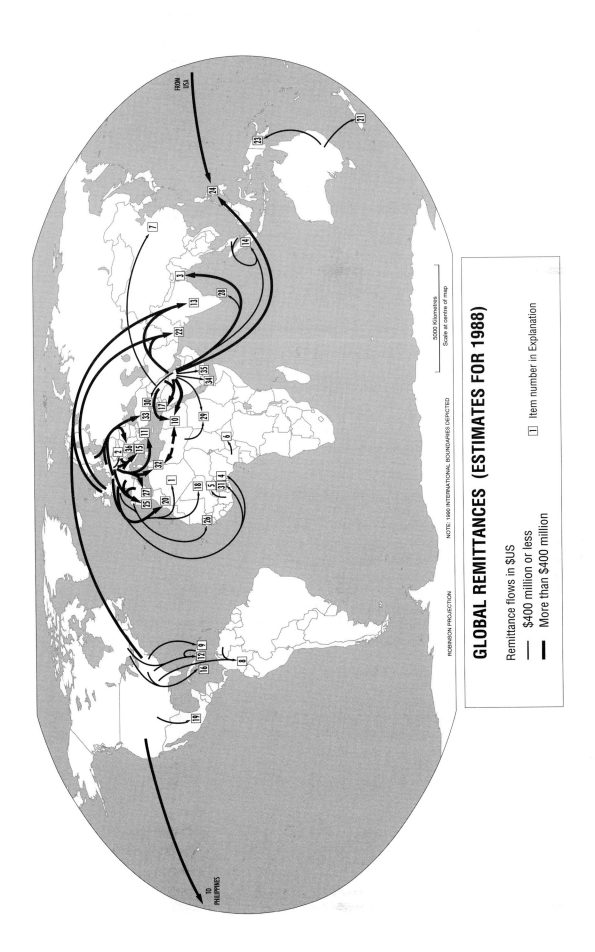

GLOBAL REMITTANCES (ESTIMATES FOR 1988)

ROBINSON PROJECTION

NOTE: 1990 INTERNATIONAL BOUNDARIES DEPICTED

5000 Kilometres
Scale at centre of map

Remittance flows in $US

— $400 million or less

— More than $400 million

1 Item number in Explanation

FROM USA

TO PHILIPPINES

GLOBAL REMITTANCES
Explanation
(Estimates for 1988)
US Dollars

Remittance Receiving Countries

1. Algeria — $279 million from France, Belgium
2. Austria — $284 million from Germany
3. Bangladesh — $737 million from Gulf States and Saudi Arabia
4. Benin — $87 million from France, francophone Africa
5. Burkina Faso — $215 million from Ivory Coast
6. Central African Republic — $29 million from Cameroon
7. China — $129 million from Iraq
8. Colombia — $384 million from USA., Venzuela
9. Dominican Republic — $328 million from USA.
10. Egypt — $3,386 billion from Gulf, Iraq, Saudi Arabia, Libya
11. Greece — $1,675 billion from Germany, Switzerland
12. Haiti — $64 million from the Dominican Republic, USA.
13. India — $2,850 billion from Gulf, United Kingdom, USA.
14. Indonesia — $99 million from Gulf, Malaysia, Singapore
15. Italy — $1,229 billion from Switzerland, Austria, Germany
16. Jamaica — $65 million from USA.
17. Jordan — $813 million from Gulf, Saudi Arabia, Iraq
18. Mali — $41 million from France
19. Mexico — $264 million from USA.
20. Morocco — $1,289 billion from France, Belgium
21. New Zealand — $312 million from Australia
22. Pakistan — $2,018 billion from Gulf, Saudi Arabia, United Kingdom
23. Papua New Guinea — $42 million from Australia
24. Philippines — $388 million from Gulf, Saudi Arabia, USA
25. Portugal — $3,381 billion from Germany, France, Spain
26. Senegal — $78 million from France, Spain
27. Spain — $1,413 billion from Germany, Luxembourg, Switzerland
28. Sri Lanka — $357 million from Gulf, Saudi Arabia, Iraq
29. Sudan — $300 million from Gulf, Saudi Arabia, Libya
30. Syria — $210 million from Gulf
31. Togo — $13 million from France
32. Tunisia — $539 million from France, Libya
33. Turkey — $1,755 billion from Germany, Sweden, Belgium
34. Yemen (Arab Republic) — $190 million from Gulf, Saudi Arabia
35. Yemen (People's Democratic Republic) — $259 million from Gulf, Saudi Arabia
36. Yugoslavia — $4,893 billion from Germany, Austria, Sweden

Note: Figures are officially recorded transfers which underestimate other transactions. Remittances received by small countries are often unrecorded, e.g. Cape Verde, Comoros, Bahamas, Antigua.

Source: World Bank, World Development Report 1990, Table 18. Washington, DC: World Bank, 1990

GLOBAL BRAIN-DRAIN

The voluntary or involuntary movement of persons with specialized qualifications and skills goes back several thousand years. Historically it has been one of the most important means of transferring technology. Diaspora minorities such as Armenians and Jews used their skills as physicians, scholars, astronomers, financiers and linguists to move between or within empires. Craftsmen with engineering, military fortifications, printing and other skills were highly sought across national and imperial boundaries.

The modern "brain-drain" reflects earlier migrations but with a new context. The movements are asymmetrical rather than reciprocal and overwhelmingly from developing to developed countries. Many of those involved in these migrations have studied abroad for advanced degrees and failed to return home or return only to re-emigrate. In some instances the migrants are deliberately recruited or induced to stay overseas.

What is also new is the persistent international concern over the outflow. The European scientists who fled Nazi Germany in the 1930s enormously enriched the intellectual life of the USA., Canada, and other countries which hosted them. Their contributions to the development of the atomic bomb and other innovations emphasized the loss to countries which had allowed them to leave. Most of these emigrés remained abroad after World War II, making their most important scientific contributions in their new lands.

The objections to the emigration of high-level manpower are several. There is the cost to the sending society of their education at home and sometimes for overseas study. There is the opportunity cost of their lost talent, incalculable but significant. There are the psychological effects on a society of some of its most talented members leaving, usually permanently. There are concerns of national pride, of domestic scientific and technological capabilities, of malaise among those who stay behind, of the setbacks to local universities and research centres, and other considerations.

Those who argue that brain-drain disadvantages are exaggerated use several arguments. The most important is the opportunity to talented people to better realize their potential, to increase not only their earnings but their outputs. The most specialized the skills the less likely that they can be fully exercised at home, even in small, rich countries such as Denmark or Switzerland. Emigrants provide remittances, prestige, role models, and do contribute positively to home countries.

The debate continues in the absence of agreed definitions. Some use narrow range definitions limited to scientists, engineers, physicians and a few other professions. The broadest definitions encompass nurses, pharmacists, lab technicians and other often scarce subprofessionals in many countries.

There is also a qualitative dimension to the debate. India may be educating in excess of its needs in various fields. However, if its best physicists, biochemists and neurosurgeons emigrate then the losses are not so easily replaced.

The UN has calculated that between 1950 and 1975 international migration of high-level manpower totalled between 300,000 and 400,000. India was the main sender but several smaller countries, reputed for their educational standards, also participated disproportionately (Ghana, Sri Lanka, Argentina, Chile). It was estimated that the USA. absorbed 120,000, the United Kingdom 84,000, and Canada 82,000. These figures are mostly for permanent immigrants with a few resettled refugees and contract workers.

Since the mid-1970s the brain-drain has altered in several respects. The UN adopted the term the "reverse transfer of technology" to reduce confrontation. The Gulf States and Saudi Arabia have become major importers of highly qualified manpower on often renewable contracts. Egypt, Nigeria, the Sudan, Somalia, and other countries have experienced massive outflows, partly at the expense of their own health care services.

There has also been a rapid increase in brain-drains between developing countries, generally on contract rather than as immigrants. The rapid expansion of universities and proliferation of graduates has raised supply in some countries while others are still unable to meet their needs from their own people. South-South movements include Argentine and Chilean scientists and engineers to Venezuela, Haitians to francophone Africa, Egyptians to North Africa, and Indians and Pakistanis to many countries. Some observers consider that the so-called brain-drain problem has become one of "maldistribution of resources" or "reverse transfer of technology." International organizations such as the UN agencies have employed many "South" professionals. However, nationally there is generally a tendency to hire professionals from within the region on limited contracts to be replaced eventually by trained nationals.

Meanwhile the brain-drain towards the developed world has not abated. During 1990 one-fifth of all the science and engineering doctorates awarded in the USA went to foreigners. Many of these persons will stay given the acute shortages of Americans in critical fields such as engineering education and mathematics. The United Kingdom imports professionals from India, Pakistan, Nigeria and other countries to offset partly its own brain-drain to Canada and the USA. Japan is unique among western countries in not benefiting from an important inflow.

Moreover the brain-drain is spreading globally. The opening of emigration opportunities in Eastern Europe and the ex-Soviet Union is producing an outflow in search of better wages, working conditions and challenges. Yugoslavia reported in 1990 that it had more academics outside than within the country. Twenty per cent of the 250 members of the Soviet Academy of Science were abroad on long-term contracts in 1990, and one-third of the Bulgarian Institute of Biology. Cut-off from mainstream science for decades, lacking equipment, many of the top ex-Soviet and Eastern European scientists are

GLOBAL BRAIN-DRAIN
Explanation

Sending Countries

1. Haiti, West Indies to USA., Canada
2. Brazil to USA., Western Europe, Canada
3. Argentina to USA., Western Europe, Canada
4. Sub-Saharan Africa to Western Europe (70,000), USA. and Canada (10,000)
5. Algeria, Morocco, Tunisia to France, Belgium, others
6. Sudan and Somalia to Gulf States, Saudi Arabia
7. Eastern Europe, ex-Soviet Union to Western Europe, North America, Israel
8. Pakistan, Bangladesh to USA, Canada, Gulf States, others
9. India to USA, Canada, Gulf States, United Kingdom, Australia
10. China to USA., Australia, others
11. Philippines to USA, Gulf States

Receiving Countries

12. Canada: 125,000 from 1960-1986 (estimated)
13. United Kingdom: 84,000 from 1950-1975 (estimated)
14. USA.: 700,000 from 1960-1986 (estimated)

Others: Australia, France, Germany, etc. (not shown on map)

Note

The UN has compiled an extensive list of occupations considered to be skilled and/or professional. National data on immigrants is relied on for education/occupation.

Sources: D.F. Heisel, "International Migration", in J.A. Ross, ed. *Encyclopedia of Population*, pp.366-73, Vol. I, New York: Macmillan, 1982.
 S.S. Russell, K. Jacobsen, and W.D. Stanley, *International Migration and Development in Sub-Saharan Africa*, Vol. I. Overview, World Bank Discussion Papers, Washington, DC: World Bank, 1990.
UN Conference on Trade and Development, "Trends and Current Situation in Reverse Transfer of Technology", Geneva: UNCTAD, 13 July 1987.

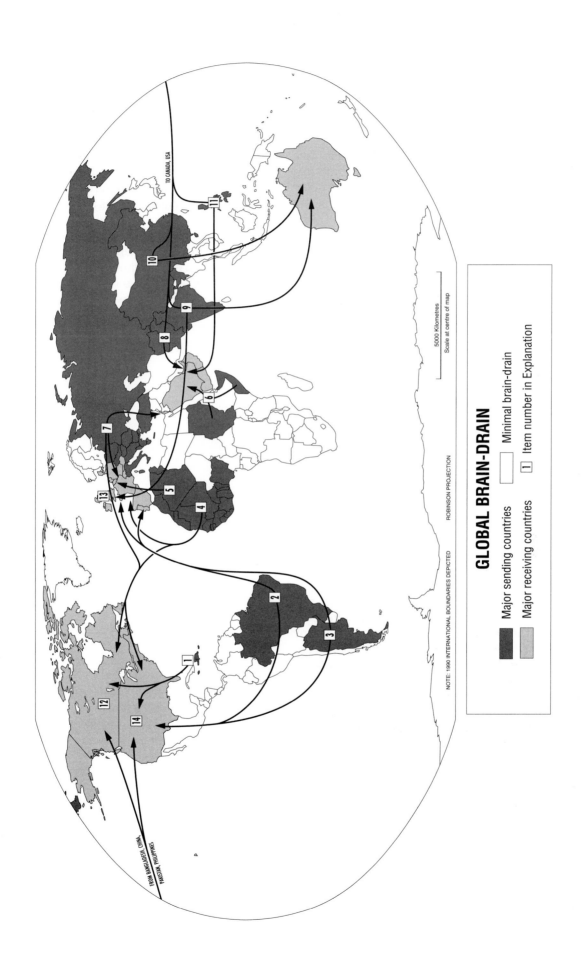

GLOBAL BRAIN-DRAIN

Major sending countries   Minimal brain-drain

Major receiving countries   Item number in Explanation

NOTE: 1990 INTERNATIONAL BOUNDARIES DEPICTED   ROBINSON PROJECTION

5000 Kilometres

Scale at centre of map

TO CANADA, USA

FROM BANGLADESH, CHINA, PAKISTAN, PHILIPPINES

likely to lead a brain-drain to the west.

The Latin American brain-drain continues to be directed towards the USA, with smaller flows to Spain and within the region. The Maghreb exports high-level mainpower to France; India and Pakistan to many countries but principally to the USA. The rapidly growing economies of Southeast Asia are experiencing minimal brain-drains due to the opportunities available at home.

Sub-Saharan Africa is experiencing the most acute brain-drain. Between 1984 and 1987 estimates of the numbers of high-level Africans abroad increased from about 40,000 to 80,000. The total numbers abroad were estimated at 70,000 in 1987 in the 12 European Community countries, and another 10,000 Nigerians and others in the USA. UNCTAD asserts that about 30 per cent of the total high-level manpower stock of sub-Saharan Africa has emigrated, many permanently.

The effects of this outflow on sending countries has been devastating. Somalia and the Sudan have many of their health care professionals in the Gulf. Zambia is unable to fill half its physicians' posts due to emigration to higher-wage countries. War-torn Mozambique, one of the poorest countries in the world, spends $180 million a year to hire 3,000 foreigners while its students stay abroad. While there is some intra-African movement of high-level manpower it is not covering the losses abroad.

What, if anything, should be done about the brain-drain? Some believe that supply and demand will achieve equilibrium if South-South movements are encouraged. Several international organizations do provide assistance to those seeking to return. (International Organization for Migration). The absolute numbers involved are in the hundreds of persons.

Certainly there are sending countries persistently educating more high-level manpower than their economies can fully absorb. These include Algeria, Morocco, Tunisia, Egypt, Ghana, Nigeria, Benin, Senegal, Iraq, India, Pakistan, Sri Lanka, Israel, Argentina, Brazil, Haiti, Chile and the West Indies. Most of Eastern Europe and the ex-Soviet Union will join this list if they allow freedom to emigrate. Can this surplus manpower be utilized by chronic deficit countries if suitable arrangements are made? The potential for expansion exists, mostly on short-term contracts. The reality though is that much of the surplus manpower is interested in emigrating to North America, Western Europe, or the high-paying positions in the Gulf. It is unlikely that South-South migrations can restructure the brain-drain.

Sending governments have relied on four kinds of policies to curb the brain-drain. Regulations have restricted study abroad and financially punished students who fail to return. These measures have generally not worked while causing considerable bitterness. Some governments have "delinked" local education from overseas norms; another source of bitterness and non-compliance. Incentive policies involving tax benefits and other measures have been used with limited success to encourage return. The most successful efforts have been those of South Korea and Taiwan. Engineers and others abroad have been lured back with the promise of credits

and other aid to start export companies. Also effective in Egypt, Sri Lanka and a few other countries have been schemes to invite back emigrants to take part in short-term projects with local people.

Receiving countries have rejected proposals to pay financial compensation to the brain-drain senders. Instead they have allocated modest resources towards cooperative research with developing country scientists. Some restrictions have also been enacted to discourage developing country students from trying to become immigrants. Faced though with important shortages of high-level manpower and declining numbers of their own students in certain fields, receiving countries have increased their immigration quotas for professional categories.

The brain-drain is a miniscule proportion of total international migration. It represents for a privileged few the opportunity to bargain their talents for access to a new land. It is a hyper-sensitive issue which can neither be satisfactorily resolved nor swept under the carpet.

GLOBAL STUDY ABROAD

The origins of study abroad go back 2500 years to the practise of Greek city-states sending young men to Athens or Sparta for education and training. Its latest manifestations include the opening of an American University in Bulgaria and campuses in the USA of Japanese universities.

Benefits of Study Abroad

Study abroad is widely considered to benefit sending countries through the transfers of languages, cross-cultural experiences, and technologies. Host societies and institutions benefit from cultural broadening, expenditures of international students, and knowledge of other countries. Study abroad is generally regarded as mutually beneficial. The principal disadvantage to the sending society is considered to be the "brain-drain" from students who fail to return or mal-adaptation of those who do. The adaptation problems of the "been to" who has studied overseas are a frequent theme in African literature as in Cheikh Hamadou Kane's novel *Ambiguous Adventure* (New York: Doubleday, 1968).

Study Abroad History

Historically, study abroad has played a vital role in very different societies. The Roman Empire invited students from the provinces to Rome to instill loyalty and to promote learning. The expansion of Islam was furthered by the establishment of Koranic schools and universities (*medrasas*) which attracted students from many countries. European universities like the Sorbonne, Oxford, Cambridge, Padua and others relied on Latin as the language of instruction for centuries and were thus able to attract students from all over Europe.

Study abroad also contributed decisively to the opening up of China and Japan to western influence. Between 1880 and 1940 thousands of Chinese and Japanese students were sent to Europe and to North America. Many of the returnees played leading roles as change-agents in medicine, engineering, diplomacy, the arts, science, business and other fields.

Study Abroad Statistics

Currently a crudely estimated one million post-secondary students are formally enrolled in universities or technical schools outside their country of permanent residence. National data on study abroad are not consistent since some countries count and others do not foreign military in training, internships, and other forms of non-academic study. Although the total number of students involved in study abroad is less than 1 per cent of all world university students, the absolute numbers have been growing rapidly for more than two decades.

Almost all study abroad takes place subject to the control of host country educational authorities. The United Nations University offers international graduate and post-doctoral programs at several sites but is primarily a research institution. The European University in Florence and the European College in Bruges offer graduate level courses. The supranational University of the West Indies with campuses in three countries (Barbados, Jamaica, Trinidad and Tobago) is the only undergraduate institution of its kind in the world. Once supranational universities like the former University of East Africa, and the American University of Beirut now have students drawn primarily from a single country.

Study Abroad Trends

The international flows of students have four principal patterns. These are:

1. Graduate and undergraduate students from Africa, Asia, the Middle East and Latin America to the USA, Canada, Western Europe, the ex-Soviet Union, and Japan
2. USA and Canadian students to Western Europe
3. Western European students enrolled elsewhere than their home countries in Western Europe
4. Japanese students in North America or Western Europe.

Other flows of students exist but in numbers generally less than 5,000 per year, e.g. African students to China and to India, ex-Soviet Union and Eastern European students to Western Europe and North America, North American and Western European students to Africa, Asia, Latin America, Middle East and Japan.

Courses of study are also distinct. Developing country students abroad are concentrated in engineering, agriculture, the sciences and business; reflecting in part available scholarships. More than two-thirds are studying at the post-graduate level as governments insist that first degrees be taken at home. Developed country students overseas are much more likely to be found in the arts, humanities, languages and social sciences with a substantial number relying in part on private funds. Many come on one or two semester special study abroad programs often co-sponsored by sending and receiving institutions.

Student Exchange Patterns

International flows of students reflect and reinforce dominant patterns in international politics and economics. Few developing countries except for Egypt and Mexico attract students from other countries. However, Japanese universities which offer instruction in English are attracting Asian students. Small countries with generous scholarship programs such as the Netherlands, New Zealand and Sweden have become magnets for developing country students. Since 1989 there has been a pronounced increase in ex-Soviet Union and Eastern European two-way student exchanges but the absolute numbers involved remains very low. Globally demand from developing countries, especially at the graduate and post-doctoral level, far exceeds the availability of places in the developed world. Meanwhile pre-1989 scholarships for foreign students in the ex-Soviet Union, China, and Eastern Europe have been eliminated or drastically cut back. Cuba still hosts an estimated 21,000 mostly African students, many at the secondary level.

GLOBAL STUDY ABROAD
Explanation
(Estimates for 1986)

The principal receiving countries are: (1986 estimates)

1. USA	349,610 from China, Malaysia, South Korea, India, Canada, others
2. France	126,762 from Morocco, Algeria, Tunisia, sub-Saharan Africa, others
3. Germany	76,918 from Turkey, Iran, Greece, USA, Austria, others
4. United Kingdom	53,438 from Hong Kong, Malaysia, USA, Nigeria, others
5. Canada	27,210 from USA, Malaysia, China, United Kingdom, others
6. Japan	22,154 from China, Taiwan, South Korea, others
7. Belgium	20,045 from Morocco, Zaïre, Italy, Netherlands, others
8. Australia	16,734 from Hong Kong, Indonesia, others

Other receiving countries include Brazil (Portuguese-speaking Africa), Mexico (Central America), Egypt (Middle East/Africa), India (Africa), Cuba (Angola), China (Africa), ex-Soviet Union (Africa, Middle East, Asia), New Zealand (Asia/Pacific), Sweden (Africa, Middle East, Asia), Italy (Africa, Middle East), Spain (Latin America), Netherlands (Caribbean, Africa, Asia, Middle East), Austria, Switzerland.

The principal sending countries are: (1986 estimates)

9. China	53,378
10. Malaysia	38,980
11. Iran	37,054
12. Greece	34,267
13. Morocco	29,683
14. South Korea	25,987
15. Jordan	24,410
16. Hong Kong	24,293
17. Germany	23,114
18. USA	20,614
19. India	20,398
20. Japan	17,296
21. Canada	17,205
22. Italy	17,004
23. Nigeria	16,549

Source: K. Okamoto, *Foreign Students in OECD Countries,* Tokyo: unpublished, 1990.
Institute of International Education, *Annual Open Doors Report on Foreign Students in the USA,* New York: Institute of International Education, 1990.

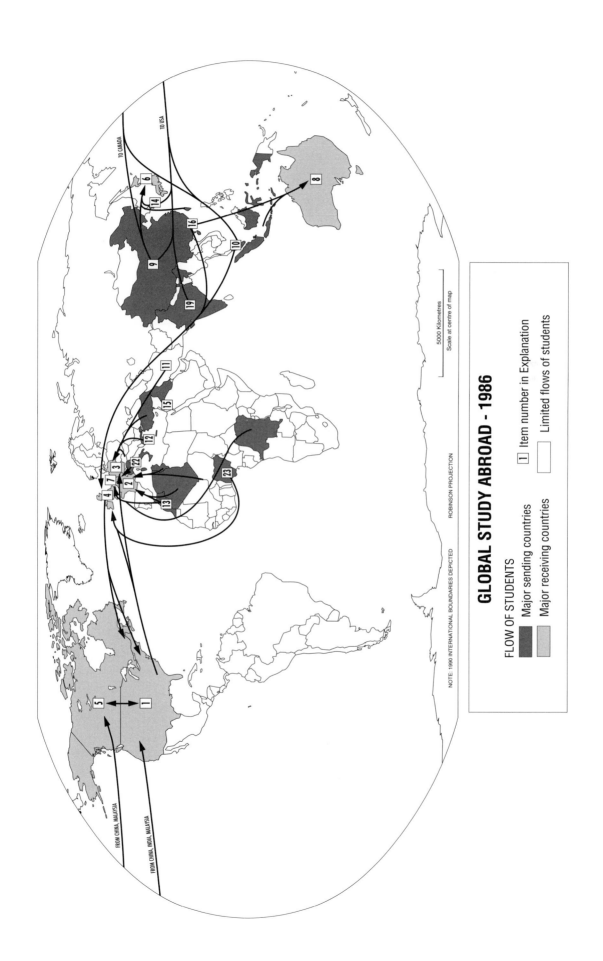

GLOBAL STUDY ABROAD - 1986

FLOW OF STUDENTS

Major sending countries

Major receiving countries

☐ Item number in Explanation

☐ Limited flows of students

5000 Kilometres

Scale at centre of map

NOTE: 1990 INTERNATIONAL BOUNDARIES DEPICTED   ROBINSON PROJECTION

Study Abroad Costs

There are no global estimates of the annual costs of study abroad. However, a very rough estimate would be about $3 billion. Governments cover much of these costs through scholarships, tuition remissions and loans. Most host governments, though, impose strict limitations on paid employment by foreign students. Non-profit foundations, company grants, especially for training courses, and private family funds are also important.

There is little evidence that study abroad represents a significant burden for receiving or sending societies. Foreign student enrolment represents less than 5 per cent of total university enrolment in most receiving countries (higher in Belgium, France, Austria and Switzerland); rarely more than 10 per cent of total enrolment in a single academic institution. A few poor countries with low populations and weak post-secondary institutions may be sending more students abroad than they are educating at home at university level (The Gambia, Maldives, etc.). However, most of the costs are being provided by donors while the costs of establishing a full home university remain high.

Study Abroad - Who Benefits?

The returns to individuals of studying abroad are much harder to quantify. A disproportionate number of persons who have studied abroad subsequently achieve career leadership roles, from President John F.Kennedy to artists like Rufino Tamayo of Mexico. The causation is not clear and may not consist of more than the cross-cultural and broadening effects of travel.

INTERNATIONAL MIGRATION: ZONES OF CONFLICT

Historically voluntary and involuntary international migration has been closely associated with state-organized coercion and violence. British, Dutch, Portuguese and Spanish colonists and settlers relied on state support to conquer indigenous peoples and to procure slaves and indentured labour. Japanese state-sponsored colonists in the twentieth century in Manchuria, Korea and Taiwan acted similarly. Settler colonies tended to have conflict built-in as a primary mode of maintaining the domination of immigrant communities, e.g. Algeria, Kenya, Rhodesia, (Zimbabwe) and South Africa.

Historic Emigration and Conflicts
Mass emigration, especially from Europe in the nineteenth century, probably served to reduce social tensions stemming from land shortages, lack of social mobility, and demographic pressures. Emigration as a historic 'escape valve' for discontent, and potential social unrest has characterized much voluntary migration.

Return migration has also played a significant role in twentieth century decolonization. France repatriated 2.5 million persons at the end of the Algerian War; Portugal absorbed nearly 500,000 people from its ex-colonies, and the Netherlands about 350,000 after the independence of Indonesia and then Suriname. These costly and painful repatriations transformed once settler colonies into post-independence multi-ethnic societies with most Europeans removed. Decolonization has not yet been followed by a large-scale exodus of European settlers in Kenya, Namibia, Zimbabwe or South Africa.

Changing International migration
The post-independence period since the 1960s has seen profound changes in international migration. Conflicts which generate mass refugee movements, e.g. Vietnam, Iraq, and Horn of Africa, have been primarily due to ethnic power struggles within or between newly independent countries. Pressures for spontaneous voluntary migration have been from developing to developed countries, although since the establishment of freedom to emigrate in 1989, Eastern Europe has added its weight.

Pressures to emigrate voluntarily combine demographic, socio-economic and transport factors with the assistance and contacts provided by ethnic networks abroad and government policies. These pressures continue to be regional in direction although a global character is emerging. Certain sending countries such as Lebanon and the Philippines are providing emigrants to four or more world regions.

Emigration Demands vs. Host Supply
The pressures to emigrate substantially exceed the willingness of host countries to accept either refugees or immigrants. One outcome is increasing illegal immigration. These pressures are primarily directed at the USA and Canada from Mexico, the Caribbean, Central America and Asia. Japan is subject to growing pressure from legal and illegal immigration originating in China and East Asia, as is Australia and New Zealand. Western Europe, especially Germany and Austria, is experiencing new waves of immigrants from Eastern Europe and the ex-Soviet Union. Meanwhile, North African and Turkish pressures to emigrate continue to be directed principally at Germany, France, Spain and Italy.

Gulf States Migration
The six oil-exporting Gulf States (Saudi Arabia, Kuwait, Oman, Bahrain, Qatar and the United Arab Emirates) recruit temporary migrant labour from Egypt, Yemen, Jordan, the Sudan, the Palestinian Diaspora, and much of the Islamic World and beyond. Prior to the 1990-91 Gulf War, the Gulf States and Iraq contracted 2.5 million foreign workers annually; a small fraction of those potentially available. It is probable that in the twenty-first century, with population increase in predominantly young societies, that the pressures and demands for emigration will grow; whatever the response of actual and potential receiving societies.

Types of Conflict
International migration can be a source of conflict within societies and between societies. The causal relationships are multiple and do not necessarily apply universally. International migration is often one of several factors that contribute to engendering conflict rather than the controlling factor. The map, code, and list of factors that follows provide empirical examples of how international migration has been involved in conflicts.

A. Wars
International migration can precipitate a war by threatening to change the balance of power between rival groups. The 'Green March' in 1976 of Moroccan settlers into the former Spanish colony of Western Sahara prompted the Polisario movement to initiate a guerrilla war for independence. The build-up of Salvadorean illegal migrants in Honduras and their repatriation was a significant factor in the 1968 El Salvador-Honduras war. The 1977 Ethiopia-Somalia war was catalyzed by a conflict over the territory of Ogaden and its nomadic population.

B. Historical Legacy
Most of the world's multi-ethnic and multi-racial societies were founded as a result of international migration from Fiji and Guyana to the USA and Canada. This legacy in terms of national myths, stereotypes and institutions continues.

C. Conflict Management of Multi-Ethnic Societies
Recent immigration has given a multi-ethnic character to societies such as France, Germany, the United Kingdom, and even Italy and Spain. The permanent presence of multiple immigrant communities presents problems for employment, language policies, housing, education and other domestic issues.

INTERNATIONAL MIGRATION: ZONES OF CONFLICT
Explanation

1. Afghanistan — Millions of refugees in Iran and Pakistan from 1979 war. Internal displaced persons

2. Albania — Spontaneous emigration in 1990-91 to Greece and Italy after prolonged denial of freedom to emigrate

3. Algeria — Pressure to emigrate to France and to Western Europe. Similar to pressure in Morocco and Tunisia. Concerns over treatment of North African minorities in Western Europe

4. Australia — Immigration policy a domestic issue. Pressures to admit more immigrants from East Asia

5. Bulgaria — Treatment of 1 million Turkish minority. 300,000 repatriated to Turkey in 1989

6. China — Pressures to allow emigration, especially of dissidents. Settlement of Tibet with Chinese population

7. Colombia — Concern over treatment of Colombians in Venezuela

8. Cuba — Spontaneous emigration to the USA (1979); denial of freedom to emigrate vs. pressures to leave

9. Cyprus — 80,000 Turkish settlers after 1979 partition and 200,000 displaced Greek Cypriots

10. Dominican Republic — Treatment of recruited and illegal Haitian migrant workers. Also Haitians in Bahamas

11. El Salvador — Refugees and illegal migrants in Honduras

12. Ethiopia — Refugees in Djibouti, Sudan, and displaced in country

13. France — Management of multi-racial, multi-ethnic immigrants. Immigration policy a domestic issue; decisions on asylum requests

14. Gabon — Riots and repatriation of migrant workers, mostly from the Cameroon

15. Germany — Pressures to emigrate from Eastern Europe; immigration a domestic policy issue; management of multi-ethnic immigrants, e.g. Turks, Poles

16. Gulf States — Repatriation of foreign workers 1990; management of migrant worker labor forces; immigration conflicts with sending states, e.g. Saudi Arabia and Yemen workers' expulsion 1990

17. Indonesia — Legal and illegal workers to Malaysia; sends settlers to occupy Timor, ex-Portuguese colony

18. Iraq — Post Gulf War refugees to Iran and Turkey; internal displaced persons

19. Japan — Pressures to emigrate from East Asia, growing labor shortage, and anti-immigration policies

20. Liberia — Refugees from civil war in Côte d'Ivoire, Sierra Leone, internal displaced persons

21. Libya — Expulsions of Egyptian and Tunisian migrant workers

22. Mexico — Large-scale, spontaneous illegal emigration to USA

23. Mozambique — Refugees from civil war in Malawi, Zimbabwe, others

24. Netherlands — Management of multi-ethnic immigration from Suriname, Moluccas, Morocco, Turkey, etc.

25. Nigeria — Expulsion of migrant workers from Ghana, Nigeria, Cameroon, etc.

26. Romania — Hungarian minority estimated 2 million. Some expulsions

27. Rwanda — Invasion in 1990 by refugees based in Uganda

28. Senegal — Riots and mutual repatriation, 1990, of Senegalese living in Mauritania and Mauritanians in Senegal

29. South Africa — Reductions in force and repatriations of migrant workers from Lesotho, Botswana, Swaziland, Mozambique

30. ex-Soviet Union — External and internal pressures to establish freedom to emigrate. Treatment of minorities in new states

31. United Kingdom — Management of multi-ethnic, multi-racial society; strict immigration policy since 1963

32. US Virgin Islands — Legal and illegal immigration from the Eastern Caribbean changes demographic balance

33. Vietnam — Refugees in Thailand, Malaysia, Hong Kong, USA, France, Canada, Australia; pressures to emigrate. Cambodian and Laotian refugees in Thailand, etc.

34. Yugoslavia — The disintegration of the Federal Republic and the ensuing civil war brought the worst refugee and displaced persons crisis in Europe since the end of World War II.

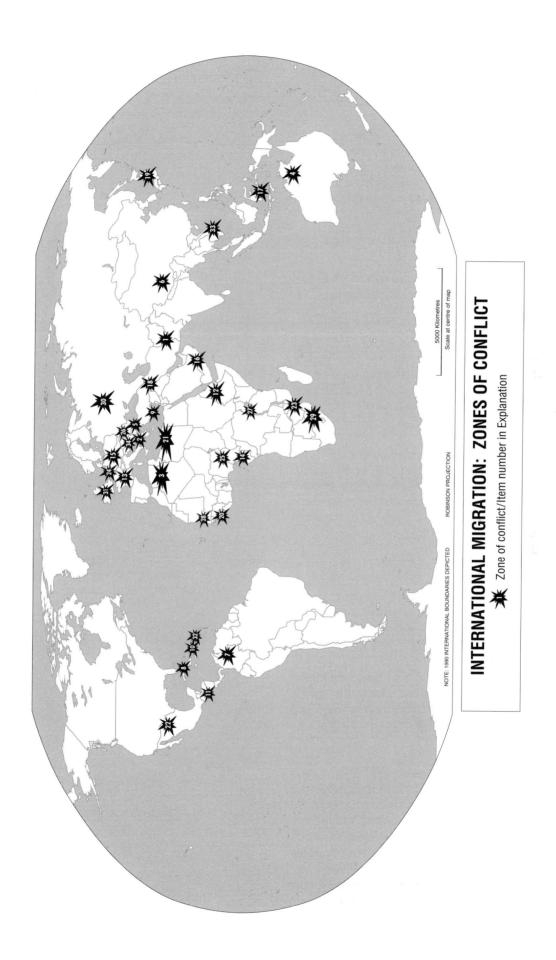

NOTE: 1990 INTERNATIONAL BOUNDARIES DEPICTED   ROBINSON PROJECTION

5000 Kilometres

Scale at centre of map

INTERNATIONAL MIGRATION: ZONES OF CONFLICT

✹ Zone of conflict/Item number in Explanation

D. Treatment of Immigrant Minorities

This is both a domestic and an international issue, especially where migrant workers are involved. Since 1980 millions of migrant workers have been expelled from Nigeria, Libya, Saudi Arabia, South Africa and other countries in spite of the protests of their home governments.

E. Refugee Conflicts

Refugees are a threat both to their host countries and to their homelands. They also represent economic burdens, an inability to locate third countries for resettlement, and sensitive issues of asylum. Conflicts have included the 1990 invasion of Rwanda by refugees based in Uganda, and the inability of Malaysia to find resettlement for Vietnamese refugees.

F. Immigration Policies

These are often domestic issues as in the USA, as well as conflicts between sending and receiving countries.

G. Movement of People

Used as a diplomatic instrument at the end of World War I between Greece and Turkey, and in the 1947 partition of India, the deliberate movement of ethnic groups is now in disfavor. However, it proved effective in the decolonization of Algeria, and Portugal's African colonies.

H. Freedom of Movement

The international community, spurred by the USA, has brought pressure on the ex-Soviet Union and China to legalize at least limited freedom to emigrate, especially for dissidents. Meanwhile, freedom of movement within a federal state contributed to the break-up of the West Indian Federation (1961) and to the current disintegration of Yugoslavia (1992).

I. Frontiers

Spontaneous migrations from several countries to low population density, remote frontier areas are both an historic and a contemporary problem, e.g. the Amazon.

J. Regime Legitimacy

Spontaneous voluntary emigrations or demands for the same can threaten the legitimacy and control of a regime, e.g. exodus of Cubans in 1979, Albanians in 1990, and East Germany and the Berlin Wall.

K. North-South Conflicts

International migration has not been a priority issue on the North-South Agenda. It has appeared primarily in the form of demands to limit and/or to provide compensation for the brain-drain. Other manifestations include demands for conventions to protect foreign migrant workers and to channel some portion of earnings back to home countries and governments. Voluntary immigration, especially in the form of migrant-worker agreements, may emerge as an important twenty-first century North-South issue.

REFERENCE
SOURCES

GLOSSARY

Assimilation Total acceptance of immigrants by a host society and their absorption into that society. Also known as *Melting pot* to refer to merging of ethnic identities into a homogeneous or assimilated entity.

Asylum/Asylum-seeker The protection given by one country to refugees from another. *First-country asylum* refers to a country granting a refugee first or temporary asylum. *Third country asylum.* Country granting permanent asylum to a refugee transferring or resettling from a first country of asylum. *B Status Humanitarian Asylum.* Used in Scandinavian countries to grant a form of temporary asylum.

Boat -people Haitians, Vietnamese, or others relying on ocean voyages in small boats to emigrate. Often denied asylum.

Brain-drain Emigration of highly qualified persons. Also known as *reverse transfer of technology and transfer of talent.*

Brain-exchange refers to transfers of qualified persons between developed and developing countries on a permanent or temporary basis. *Brain-overflow* Countries which educate or train surplus persons in specialized fields thus encouraging emigration.

Carrier-sanctions Fines or other sanctions inflicted on airlines or other transport firms for knowingly carrying international passengers lacking visas or other documentation.

Circulation Circuits of movements by individuals and small groups between points of origin and destination. Other terms used are *return, circular, wage-labour, seasonal mobility, sojourner, transhumant, and commuting* or *swallow* migration.

Citizenship/Naturalization Legally granted status as members of a particular nationality. Obtained through birth and registration or through a procedure of naturalization prescribed by national authorities.

Comparative advantage Theory of international trade and migration based on demand and supply factors. Also known as push-pull factors explaining international migration.

Conjuncture-buffer Use of temporary, replaceable pools of international migrant labour in times of economic expansion and recession. See also *industrial reserve army.*

Coolie Derogatory term used to refer to indentured labour from China and India, e.g. railway workers in nineteenth century USA.

Creole Term used in Spanish to refer to persons born in colonial America. Currently used to denote syncretized immigrant languages such as Haitian Creole, Papamiento in Curacao.

Diaspora From the Greek. Any scattering of people with a common origin, background, belief.

Durable solution Permanent settlement of refugees whether through repatriation to homeland, resettlement in a third country, or settlement in first country of asylum. Term used by UN High Commissioner for Refugees.

Early warning Attempts and methods to detect a possible refugee exodus and to take appropriate measures.

Emigration Leaving one country or region to settle in another.

Environmental refugees Persons displaced by natural disasters such as drought, deforestation, or other environmental degradation.

Escape from violence Proposal to broaden the official definition of refugee to include structural and economic violence and any person escaping life-threatening violence.

Ethnic, national, racial quotas Criteria sometimes used in national immigration policies, e.g. Germany and ethnic Germans.

Expatriate/Expatriates To leave the homeland and to establish temporary residence in another country/persons who do so. Also known as *professional transients.*

Expulsions Forced removal of legal and undocumented foreigners as carried out by Ghana, Nigeria and other governments.

Extended voluntary departure Asylum-seekers granted permission to extend their departure temporarily while on parole. Used in USA for El Salvadorean and other asylum-seekers. See also *B-Status Humanitarian Asylum,* and *Temporary Protected Status.*

External frontier convention Single visa European Community objective to establish by 1992 for its 12 member states a uniform procedure and single visa for entry.

Family reunification Highest preference in many countries for legal immigration of divided spouses, siblings, other family members.

Feet-people Term used for emigrants from Central America headed north by foot and bus to Mexico and the USA.

Flows/Stocks Annual flows between countries of different kinds of migrants. Total stocks of foreign-born persons living in a country, usually recorded during a census. Flow data is obtained from immigration, emigration and other records; stock information from census data, registrations, etc.

Forced migration/Involuntary migration Refers to refugees, or other persons compelled to migrate by massive coercion. May also refer to internally displaced persons resulting from political violence or natural disasters.

Freedom of movement/Free migrations Legal right to emigrate, to travel, to seek work and to establish residence in certain other countries. Embodied in the European Community, Nordic Council, and Australia-New Zealand Agreements.

Heimkehrillusion German for belief among immigrants that some day they will return to their home countries permanently although few actually do return or make plans to do so.

Hispanics Used in the USA for census and other purposes to designate persons born in or descended from Spanish-speaking countries in the western hemisphere, e.g. Cuban-American, Mexican-Americans, Puerto Ricans. Also known as Latinos.

ICARA International Conference of African Refugees. Held in 1981 and 1984 under UN auspices to raise funds and to coordinate refugee aid and development projects.

ILO Internationanal Labour Organisation. UN agency based in Geneva which regulates some international labour migration.

Industrial reserve army Use of immigrant, mostly unskilled labour to counteract developed country economic cycles, and to reduce wages and trade union activities.

Immigration To come into a country to settle there.

Immigration preferences Refers to criteria used to select immigrants by host countries, e.g. family reunification, skills, etc.

Permanent immigration Immigrants who settle, often becoming naturalized citizens.

Integration Policies to provide immigrants with equal status to citizens without relinquishing previous ethnic or other identities.

Internal displaced persons Victims of political violence and/or natural disasters who seek refugee status within their own country. Often these persons lack access to another host country.

International spatial division of labour Location of facilities and assignment of staff by multinational corporations.

Melting pot See assimilation.

Migrant workers Persons seeking employment for temporary periods in other country; sometimes recruited. Known also as guestworkers from the German gastarbeiter, as contract workers, temporary workers, and braceros from the Spanish term for unskilled workers.

Mojados Spanish for wetbacks, persons who illegally enter the USA by crossing the Rio Grande River.

Multi-ethnic; Multi-racial Societies consisting of persons from different ethnic and/or racial groups organized into distinct communities usually resulting from immigration. Also known as plural societies.

Naturalization Procedure whereby foreign-born can acquire the nationality and citizenship of another country.

NGOs Non-governmental organisation. Many such as the International Committee of the Red Cross and OXFAM work with refugees.

Non-refoulement From the French. The 1951 UN Convention on Refugees commits contracting states to not expel or return a refugee whose life or freedom would be threatened due to race, religion, membership of a social group or political opinion. This convention does not protect persons denied asylum who are regularly deported.

Orderly departure Procedures used to resettle refugees from a first country of asylum to a third country of permanent resettlement e.g. Vietnamese from the Philippines to the USA. May also refer to a fixed departure schedule for legal emigrants.

Overseas Chinese, Overseas Indians Refers to globally dispersed diaspora communities of the world's two most populated nations. Overseas Chinese are concentrated in Southeast Asia; Overseas Indians in Fiji, Sri Lanka, Malaysia, Guyana, Mauritius and Trinidad and Tobago. Greece, Italy, Ireland, Poland, Portugal, Spain and Cyprus are other countries with large overseas communities.

Outliers Countries with a high proportion of residents who are foreign-born, usually 10 per cent or more of total population as in Bahrain, Oman and other Gulf States.

Overstayers Persons who enter a country legally on tourist or other temporary visas or documents and then stay beyond the allowed time period.

Patrials Persons who seek to immigrate legally on the basis of ancestral descent from a country, e.g. United Kingdom immigration laws.

Plural societies Societies composed of different ethnic and racial groups often as a result of immigration. Term is also used to designate societies with competitive political forces and organized groups.

Professional transients Persons whose careers and employment takes them to several countries, e.g. staff of multinational corporations who are re-assigned, technical assistance experts, etc.

Push-pull See *Comparative advantage*. Regarded by some as the variables that explain international voluntary migration.

Refugees Persons with a well-founded fear of persecution on return to their country of origin according to the 1951 UN Convention and the 1967 Protocol. Within a country known as displaced persons.

Refugee Policy Group/Refugee Studies Programme Washington, DC and Oxford University respectivly based research centres examining national and international refugee policies.

Refugee-warriors Armed guerilla forces who live in or close to refugee camps, e.g. Afghans in Pakistan, Cambodians in Thailand. The Organisation of African Unity Convention on Refugees forbids the use of camps for "subversive purposes" but is not operational.

Remittances Money sent from abroad, generally by migrant workers or other international migrants. Remittances are sent through formal and informal channels and were conservatively estimated at over $30 billion globally in 1988.

Repatriation Sending a person or group of persons back to their country of birth or origin. Often refers to return of refugees to their homelands. May be forced or voluntary. See also non-refoulement.

Resettlement The transfer of refugees from a first country of asylum to a third country of permanent resettlement, e.g. Vietnamese from Thailand to Australia.

Return migration Immigrants, migrant workers, or other persons who voluntarily return to their country of origin.

Safe haven Various types of temporary asylum subject to restrictions, e.g. Temporary Protected Status in the USA. Safe haven asylums may or may not allow persons to seek employment, housing, welfare benefits, etc.

Seasonal migration Migrant workers recruited for agricultural harvests or other seasonal employment. These workers may be undocumented, recruited on temporary and restricted labour permits, and/or some other basis.

Sojurner Generic term for various kinds of temporary migrants, often adult males, expected to refturn.

Strandee Persons who have become stranded outside their home country, sometimes due to political events such as coups, e.g. Chinese students abroad after the 1989 events in Beijing. Strandees may seek various forms of temporary asylum.

Stateless persons Individuals who have been denied or had removed national identity documents. After World War I the League of Nations created special passports for such persons. Current practise is for them to seek asylum and/or refugee status. Known in French as *les apatrides*.

Temporary Protected Status (TPS) Legal status used in the USA to designate asylum-seekers allowed to seek employment while waiting adjudication of their asylum requests. See also *Asylum*.

Transients/Professional transients Temporary emigration of high-level manpower, sometimes from country to country. Includes managers, engineers, senior health workers, researchers and others. See also *Expatriates*.

Two-fold integration Concept that immigrants and their offspring will retain homeland identities and be integrated within host countries. Example is Germany where immigrant children are taught German and Turkish.

United Nations Border Relief Operation. Established in the 1980s for humanitarian programs on the Cambodian border.

Undocumented aliens Persons whose status does not meet the legal conditions for immigration of the host country. Also known as *illegal aliens, illegals, irregular migrants*, and similar terms in other languages. The terminology used to designate this group of persons has become highly sensitive with undocumented serving as a neutral term.

UNHCR United Nations High Commissioner for Refugees. Based in Geneva with responsibilities for assisting refugees globally. Budget from voluntary contributions by governments. The UNHCR works closely with various NGOs in the administration of refugee camps.

Unrecognized refugees/Economic migrants Terms used to refer to Haitian and Vietnamese boat-people and to others rejected by governments as refugees on the grounds that their primary motives for migration are economic. UNHCR at times screens the decisions by national immigration officials to determine whether applicant motives are primarily economic.

UNRWA United Nations Relief and Works Agency. Established after the 1948 Arab-Israeli War, this Agency has exclusive responsibility for the Palestinian refugees in Jordan, Syria, the West Bank, Gaza and elsewhere. It remains separate from the UNHCR which has responsibility for all other refugees.

Voluntary/Involuntary migration The distinction between refugees and internal displaced persons, and all other types of international migration. Historically slavery is considered to be involuntary while indentured labour for designated periods of time is regarded as voluntary. All forms of convict, bankruptcy, and debt migration as in Australian history, are classified as involuntary.

ANNOTATED BIBLIOGRAPHY

There are thousands of publications on international migration with the numbers rapidly expanding. We offer a brief annotated bibliography of the leading journals, documents, and titles in the field. The purpose is to enable users to identify quickly the most important and useful sources.

Valuable Journals

There are many periodicals that carry material related to international migration, a highly interdisciplinary topic. However, several academic journals are exclusively dedicated to international migration offering essential research and reference sources.

Immigrants and Minorities, Frank Cass, Gainsborough House, 11 Gainsborough Road, London E11 1RS, UK. British quarterly which focuses on immigrant minorities in Western societies.

International Migration Review, Quarterly published by the Center for Migration Studies, Staten Island, NY 10034, USA. The leading journal in the field contains current research articles, book reviews, documents and bibliographies.

International Migration, International Organization for Migration, P.O. Box 71, Geneva, Switzerland. Intergovernmental quarterly journal of documents, conference reports, and articles.

Journal of Refugee Studies, Refugee Studies Programme, Queen Elizabeth House, University of Oxford, OX1 3LA, UK. Definitive quarterly journal on all aspects of refugee issues.

Revue Européenne des Migrations Internationales, University of Poitiers, France 86022. Published bi-annually by the Geography Department since 1984 with special issues on Antilleans in Europe, Immigration in the Americas, etc.

Other useful publications include the *Journal of International Refugee Law, Migration World, Estudios Migratorios, Studi Migrazione, Population and Development*.

Important Document Sources

UN Population Division, New York. World Population Trends, Reports, World Foreign-Born Populations, World Migration Studies.

UN High Commissioner for Refugees (UNHCR), Geneva, Refugee Abstracts, Refugee Documentation Centre, Annual UNHCR Reports, World Refugee Maps.

UN Conference on Trade and Development (UNCTAD), Geneva Conference Resolutions and Reports on Reverse Transfer of Technology.

US Bureau of the Census, World Population Trends, US Population Reports on Foreign Born Populations in the US, Suitland, MD, USA.

US Immigration and Naturalization Service (INS), Washington, DC) Annual Reports on legal and illegal immigration to the USA.

US Committee for Refugees, Washington, DC. Annual survey of world refugees by a non-profit organization.

Bureau for Refugee Programs, US Department of State, Washington, DC. Annual official report to Congress of world refugee situation.

Council of Europe, Strasbourg, France. Resolutions, conference reports and studies of asylum and other issues in Europe.

European Community, Brussels. Reports on employment and immigration-related issues among the member states.

Organisation for Economic Cooperation and Development (OECD), Paris with Washington, DC publications office. Quarterly reports by member states of immigration policies and trends. Conferences and policy studies of immigration issues.

UNESCO (United Nations Educational, Scientific, and Cultural Organization), Paris. Published studies of conferences on regional and global aspects of international migration.

Australia, Canada, the Netherlands, Sweden and other countries publish extensive official documents on immigration.

Leading Books

The selection emphasizes titles with a conceptual and global or regional interest. It does not include books which focus on the international migration experience of single countries.

Alonso, William, ed. *Population in an Interacting World*, Cambridge: Harvard, 1987. An informative collection of essays on demographic migration history, migrant workers, and other subjects.

Appleyard, Reginald, ed. *International Migration Today*, Vol, I Paris: UNESCO, 1988. Informative contributions on global and regional trends and prospects.

————— ed. *The Impact of International Migration on Developing Countries*, Paris: OECD, 1985. Essays which analyze economic, social and political impact on developing countries.

Bailyn, Bernard, Voyagers to the West, New York: Knopf, 1981. Superb study of the eighteenth century British emigration to North America.

Böhning, W.R., *Studies in International Migration*, New York: St. Martin's, 1984. Critical analysis of guestworker experiences.

Caves, George, *Le Tourisme International*, Paris: Hatier, 1989. Outstanding brief introduction to international tourism by a leading French geographer.

CNRS, *Les Migrations Internationales de la Fin Du XVIII Siècle à Nos Jours,* Paris: CNRS, 1980. The definitive empirical study of global international migration from the end of the eighteenth century to the present by a team from the French National Council for Scientific Research.

Curtin, Philip D., *The Atlantic Slave Trade; A Census*, Madison: University of Wisconsin Press, 1969. This classic volume is the definitive quantitative study of the Atlantic Slave Trade.

—— *Cross-Cultural Trade in World History*, New York: Cambridge University Press, 1984. Absorbing study of merchant trading communities and their role in world history.

—— *Death by Migration: Europe's Encounter with the Tropical World in the Nineteenth Century,* New York: Cambridge University Press, 1989. Important study in historical demography of the effects of nineteenth century European-Tropics migrations.

Davies, Julian, compiler *Displaced Persons and refugee Studies,A Resource Guide*, London: Hans Zell Publisher, 1990. A highly useful guide to publications, research centres, bibliographies and organizations.

Díaz-Briquets, Sergio, *International Migration in Latin America*, New York: Center for Migration Studies, 1983. Useful survey of contemporary cross-border migration in the region.

Harrell-Bond, Barbara, *Imposing Aid,* London: Oxford University Press, 1985. Critical study of aid programmes for refugees.

Hawkins, Freda, Critical Years in *Immigration*, Canada and Australia, Montreal: McGill University Press, 1989. Effective comparison of recent immigration policies in Canada and Australia.

Horowitz, Donald L., *Ethnic Groups in Conflict*, Berkeley: University of California Press, 1985. Thoughtful global survey of ethnicity and ethnic conflicts.

Hourani, Albert, *A History of the Arab Peoples*, Cambridge, MA: Harvard Belknap Press, 1991. Masterful history of the Arab world with extensive discussion of Middle East migrations.

Jackson, J.A., *Migrations*, London: Cambridge University Press, 1984. Useful introduction to the sociology of migrations.

Kritz, M.M., Keely, C., Tomasi, S.M., eds, *Global Trends in Migration*, New York: Center for Migration Studies, 1981. An effective summary by various contributors of theory and research on international population movements in the early 1980s.

McEvedy, Colin, Jones, Richard, *Atlas of World Population History,* New York: Penguin, 1978. Skimpy on migration but useful as a demographic and geographic reference.

Môrner, Magnus, *Adventurers and Proletarians, The Story of Migrants in Latin America*, Pittsburgh: University of Pittsburgh Press, 1985. Spirited and comprehensive history from colonial times to the present, with emphasis on Europe to Latin America.

OECD, *The Future of Migration*, Paris: OECD, 1987. Compilation of views on immigration policies and problems with emphasis on Western Europe.

Piore, M.J., *Birds of Passage: Migrant Labour in Industrial Societies*, New York: Cambridge University Press, 1979. Bold attempt to use economic theory to explain international migration with emphasis on the USA.

Reinhard, H., Armengaud, A., Dupaquier, J., *Histoire Generale de la Population Mondiale*, Paris: CNED, 1968. An impressive reference volume of world population history by a team of French demographers. Extensive reference to migration.

Ross, J.A., ed. *Encyclopedia of Population,* 2 vols., New York: Macmillan, 1982. Includes an excellent essay on international migration by D. Heisel and useful definitions.

Simon, Rita, Bretell, C., eds, *International Migration, The Female Experience*, New Jersey: Rowman and Allanheld, 1986. Important collection of studies on women and migration in different countries.

Zollberg, Aristide R., Arguayo, S*ergio, Suhrke, Astri, Escape from Violence, Conflict and the Refugee Crisis in the Developing World,* New York: Oxford University Press, 1989. Thoughtful and informed discussion of historical and current roots of refugee crises globally.

BIBLIOGRAPHY

Abadan-Unat, N., *Bati Almanya'daki Turk iscileri ve sorunlari* [Turkish Workers in Germany and their Problems]. Ankara: State Planning Organization, 1964.

Abadan-Unat, N., 'Implications of Migration on Emancipation and Pseudoemancipation of Turkish Women', *International Migration Review* 2 (1977), pp.31-57.

Abadan-Unat, N., et al., eds. *Migration and Development: A Study of Effects of International Labor Migration on Bogazliyan District.* Ankara: Ajans-Turk', 1976.

Abbasi, N. and Irfan, M., Socio-economic Effects of International Migration on the Families left Behind. Paper presented at the Conference on Asian Labour Migration to the Middle East, 19-23 September 1983. Honolulu: East-West Population Institute, 1983.

Abella, Irving M., *None is too Many: Canada and the Jews of Europe, 1933-1948.* Toronto: Lester & Orpen Dennys, 1982.

Abella, M.I., 'Labour Migration from South and South East Asia: Some Policy Issues', *International Labour Review* 123 (1984), pp.491-506.

Abowd, John M., *The Internationalization of the US Labor Market.* Cambridge, MA: National Bureau of Economic Research, 1990.

Abrams, Elliot and Abrams, F., 'Immigration Policy: Who Gets In and Why?', *The Public Interest* 38 (1975), pp.3-29.

Abrams, Elliot, *Human Rights and the Refugee Crisis: June 2, 1982.* Washington, DC: US Department of State, Bureau of Public Affairs, Office of Public Communication, Editorial Division, 1982.

Abu-Lughod, J., 'Social Implications of Labour Migration in the Arab World', In: I. Ibrahim, ed. *Arab Resources: The Transformation of a Society*, pp.237-66. London: Croom Helm, 1983.

Abumere, S.I., 'Population Distribution Policies and Measures in Africa South of the Sahara: A Review', *Population and Development Review* 7, no.3 (1981).

Acuna Gonzalez, Beatriz, *Transmigración legal en la frontera Mexico-Estados Unidos.* Mexicali: Universidad Autonoma de Baja California, Instituto de Investigaciones Sociales, 1986.

Adamako-Sarfoh, J.L., 'The Effects of the Expulsion of Migrant Workers on Ghana's Economy, with Particular Reference to the Cocoa Industry', In: S. Amin, ed. *Modern Migrations in Western Africa.* London: Oxford University Press, 1974.

Addo, N.O., 'Employment and Labour Supply on Ghana's Cocoa Farms in the Pre- and Post-Alien Compliance Order', *Economic Bulletin of Ghana* 2 (1972).

Addo, N.O., 'Government-induced Transfers of Foreign Nationals', In: J.I. Clarke and L.A. Kosinski, eds. *Redistribution of Population in Africa.* London: Heinemann, 1982.

Addo, N.O., 'Immigration and Socio-demographic Change', In: J.C. Caldwell, ed. *Population Growth and Socio-economic Change in West Africa.* New York: The Population Council, 1975.

Adegbola, O., 'The Migrant as a Factor in Regional Development: The Case of Ghana Returnees in Western Nigeria', *Jimlar Muntane* 1, no.1 (1976).

Adelman, Howard, *Canada and the Indochinese Refugees.* Regina: L.A. Weigl Educational Associates, 1982.

Adepoju, A., 'Issues in the Study of Migration and Urbanization in Africa South of the Sahara', In: P.A. Morrison, ed. *Population Movements, Their Forms and Functions in Urbanization and Development.* Liège: International Union for the Scientific Study of Population/Ordina Editions, 1983.

Adepoju, A., Mass Population Movements in West Africa. Lagos, 1984. (Project report to Ford Foundation)

Adepoju, A., 'Migration and Development in Tropical Africa: Some Research Priorities', *African Affairs* 76 (1977), p.303.

Adepoju, A., 'Migration and Socio-economic Change in Africa', *International Social Science Journal* 31 (1979), pp.207-25.

Adepoju, A., 'The Dimension of the Refugee Problem in Africa', *African Affairs* 81 (1982), p.322.

Adepoju, A., 'Undocumented Migration in Africa: Trends and Policies', *International Migration* 12, no.2 (1983).

Adepoju, A., Urbanization and Migration in West Africa. University of Ife, 1975. (Unpublished Ms thesis)

Adler, S., *A Turkish Conundrum: Emigration, Politics and Development, 1961-1980*. ILO, World Employment Programme, International Migration for Employment Project, WEP 2-26/WP 52, 1981.

African Bibliographic Center, *African Refugees: A Guide to Contemporary Information Sources*. Washington, DC, 1982.

Agnew, John, *The United States in the World Economy: A Regional Geography*. New York: Cambridge University Press, 1987.

Agnihotri, Rama Kant, *Crisis of Identity: The Sikhs in England*. New Delhi: Bahri Publications, 1987.

Aguayo, Sergio, *Central Americans in Mexico and the United States: Unilateral, Bilateral, and Regional Perspectives*. Washington, DC: Hemispheric Migration Project, Center for Immigration Policy and Refugee Assistance, Georgetown University Press, 1988.

Aguayo, Sergio, *El exodo centroamericano: consecuencias de un conflicto*. Mexico, DF: Secretaría de Educación Publica, 1985.

Aguiar, Cesar, A., *El impacto de las migraciones internacionales en el mercado de empleo del pais de origen, el caso uruguayo*. Montevideo: CIEDUR, 1983.

Aguiar, Cesar A., *Uruguay, pais de emigración*. Montevideo: Ediciones de la Banda Oriental, 1982.

Ahlburh, Dennis A., *The North East Passage: A Study of Pacific Islander Migration to American Samoa and the United States*. Canberra: National Centre for Development Studies, Research School of Pacific Studies, the Australian National University, 1990.

Ahooja-Patel, K., 'Regulations Governing the Employment of Non-nationals in West Africa', In: S. Amin, ed. *Modern Migrations in Western Africa*. London: Oxford University Press, 1974.

Aiboni, Sam, *Protection of Refugees in Africa*. Uppsala: Swedish Institute of International Law, 1978.

Aiken, Rebecca Bruff, *Montreal Chinese property ownership and occupational change, 1881-1981*. New York: AMS Press, 1989.

AIM (Agency for Industrial Mission), *That They Might Have Hope*. Johannesburg: AIM, 1984.

Ainslie, R., *Masters and Serfs: Farm Labour in South Africa*. London: International Defence and Aid Fund, 1973.

Aitchison, Jean, *International Thesaurus of Refugee Terminology*. Dordrecht & Boston: M. Nijhoff Publishers, 1989.

Akbari, Ather H., 'The Benefits of Immigrants to Canada: Evidence on Tax and Public Services', *Canadian Public Policy* 15 (December 1989).

Aker, A., *Isci gocu* [Migration of Workers]. Istanbul: Sander Publications, 1972.

Alam, Fazlul, *Salience of Homeland: Societal Polarization within the Bangladeshi Population in Britain*. Coventry: Centre for Research in Ethnic Relations, University of Warwick, 1988.

Alberts, J., *Migración hacia áreas metropolitanas de América Latina: un estudio comparativo*. Santiago: CELADE, 1977.

Albrecht, Richard, *Exil-Forschung: Studien zur deutschsprachigen Emigration nach 1933*. Frankfurt: P. Lang, 1988.

Alegre, H., 'La colonización en el Paraguay: el eje este', *Revista Paraguaya de Sociología* 14 (1977), pp.135-55.

Allen, Calvin H., 'The Indian Merchant Community of Masqat', *Bulletin of the School of Oriental and African Studies* 45 (1981), pp.39-43.

Allen, S., 'Perhaps a Seventh Person?', *Women's Studies Quarterly International* 3 (1980).

Allen, S., et al., *Work, Race, Immigration*. Bradford: University of Bradford, 1977.

Alpers, Edward A., *Ivory and Slaves in the East Central Africa: Changing Patterns of International Trade in the Late 19th Century*. London: Heinemann, 1975.

Altamirano, Teofilo, *Los que se fueron: peruanos en Estados Unidos*. Lima: Pontificia Universidad Catolica del Peru, Fondo Editorial, 1990.

Altman, Ida, *Emigrants and Society: Extremadura and America in the Sixteenth Century*. Berkeley: University of California Press, 1989.

Alvarez, J.H., *Return Migration to Puerto Rico*. Berkeley: University of California Press, 1967. (Population Monograph Series 1)

Alvarez, Rolando Estevez, *Azucar e Inmigración 1900-1940*. Havana: Editorial Ciencias Sociales, 1988.

Amar, M. and Milza, P., *L'immigration en France au XX siècle*. Paris: Armand Colin, 1990.

Ambrosy, Anna, *New Lease of Life: Hungarian Immigrants in Victoria: Assimilation in Australia.* Adelaide: Dezsery Ethnic Publications, 1984.

Amersfoort, J.M.M., *Immigration and the Formation of Minority Groups: The Dutch Experience, 1945-1975.* Translated by Robert Lyng. Cambridge & New York: Cambridge University Press, 1982.

Amin, S., ed. *Modern Migrations in Western Africa.* London: Oxford University Press, 1974.

Amin, S., *Unequal Development: An Essay on the Social Formations of Peripheral Capitalism.* New York: Monthly Review Press, 1976.

Amselle, J.L., ed. *Les migrations africaines: réseaux et processus migratoires.* Paris: Francois Maspéro, 1976.

Anderson, A.B. and Frideres, J.S., *Ethnicity in Canada: Theoretical Perspectives.* Toronto: Butterworths, 1981.

Anderson, G.M. and Christie, L.T., 'Networks: The Impetus for New Research Initiatives', *Research in Race and Ethnic Relations* 3 (1982), pp.207-25.

Anderson, Virginia DeJohn, *New England's Generation: The Great Migration and the Formation of Society and Culture in the Seventeenth Century.* Cambridge: Cambridge University Press, 1991.

Andrew, T.W., Trans-Tasman Migration 1945-79. Hamilton: University of Waikato. (MSocSc thesis)

Andrews, George Reid, *Blacks and Whites in São Paulo Brazil 1888-1988.* Madison: University of Wisconsin Press, 1991.

ANIF (Asociacíon Nacional de Instituciones Financieras), *No a Venezuela.* Bogotá: Editorial Carrera Septima, 1981.

Anker, Deborah E., *The Law of Asylum in the United States: A Manual for Practitioners and Adjudicators.* Washington, DC: American Immigration Lawyers Association, 1989.

Anon, 'Latin American Refugees in Argentina', *Migration News* 4 (1977).

Appleyard, R.T., *British Emigration to Australia.* London: Weidenfeld & Nicolson, 1964.

Appleyard, R.T., 'Cooperative Research Project on Problems of Assessing Causes and Impacts of International Migration. A New Approach to Cooperative Research in the Population Field', *International Migration in the Third World* 4 (1981), Paris: CICRED.

Appleyard, R.T., *Immigration: Policy and Progress.* Sydney: Australian Institute of Political Science, 1970. (Monograph 7)

Appleyard, R.T., 'International Migration in the ESCAP Region,' In: United Nations, Economic and Social Commission for Asia and the Pacific, *Selected Papers. Third Asian and Pacific Population Conference,* Colombo, September 1982. pp.212-23. New York: United Nations, 1984.

Appleyard, R. T., *International Migration Today.* Vol. 1. Edited by R. Appleyard: *International Migration in Asia and the Pacific.* Paris: UNESCO, 1988. pp.89-167.

Appleyard, R.T., 'Issues of Socio-cultural Adaptation and Conflict', In: M.E. Poole et al., eds. *Australia in Transition, Culture and Life Possibilities.* Sydney: Harcourt Brace Jovanovich, 1985.

Appleyard, R.T., 'Major International Population Movements and Policies: An Historical Review', *International Population Conference, Mexico* 1 (1977), International Union for the Scientific Study of Population.

Appleyard, R.T., Migrants as Agents of Social Change. International Union for the Scientific Study of Population. Workshop on the Consequences of International Migration, Canberra, 1984.

Appleyard, R.T., *Proceedings of the Perth Conference.* Background Paper on Causes and Impacts of International Migration upon Third World Development. Paris: CICRED, 1981.

Appleyard, R.T., ed. *The Impact of International Migration on Developing Countries.* Paris: OECD, 1989.

Appleyard, R.T. and Amera, A., 'The Education of Greek Migrant Children in Australia: A Parent View', *International Migration* 16 (1978), pp.105-21.

Appleyard, R.T. and Manford, T., *The Beginning: European Discovery and Early Settlement of Swan River, Western Australia.* Nedlands: University of Western Australia Press, 1979.

Arasaratnum, S., *Indians in Malaysia and Singapore.* London: Oxford University Press, 1970.

Arbelaez, C., 'El éxodo de colombianos en el período 1963-73', *Boletín Mensual de Estadística* (May 1977), pp.7-43.

Arcinas, Fe R., *The Odyssey of the Filipino Migrant Workers to the Gulf Region.* Diliman & Quezon City: Department of Sociology, College of Social Sciences and Philosophy, University of the Philippines, 1986.

Ardaya, G., Inserción ocupacional de los migrantes bolivianos en la Argentina. FLACSO, 1978. (Unpublished thesis)

Argentina. Ministry of Labour, El comportamiento del empleo en el sector industrial-periodo. Buenos Aires: Ministry of Labour, 1981. (Internal document)

Arizpe L., *Campesinado y migración*. Mexico, DF: Secretaría de Educación Publica, 1985.

Arizpe, L., *Migración, etnicismo y cambio económico: un estudio sobre migrantes campesinos a la ciudad de México.* Mexico City: El Colegio de Mexico, 1978.

Arizpe, L., 'Relay Migration and the Survival of the Peasant Household', In: J. Balán, ed. *Why People Move: Comparative Perspectives on the Dynamics of Internal Migration.* Paris: UNESCO, 1981.

Arizpe, L., *The Rural Exodus in Mexico and Mexican Migration to the United States.* College Park: Center for Philosophy and Public Policy, University of Maryland, 1981.

Arnold, F. and Shah, N.M., 'Asian Labour Migration to the Middle East', *International Migration Review* 18 (1984), pp.294-318.

Arroteia, Jorge Carvalho, *A emigracão portuguesa: suas origens e distribuicão.* Lisboa: Instituto de Cultura e Lingua Portuguesa, Ministerio de Educacão, 1983.

Arrupe, Pedro, *The Refugee Crisis in Africa: Opportunity and Challenge for the Church: A Survey Undertaken for the VI SECAM General Assembly.* Yaounde, Cameroon, Rome, June 28-July 6, 1981.

Arthur, W. Brian, *US Immigration Policy, Immigrants' Ages and US Population Size.* Washington, DC: Urban Institute, 1987.

As-Sabah, 'In an Official French Report: The Future Cannot be Imagined Without the Immigrants', *As-Sabah* (Beirut, 28 September 1983, Arabic text)

As Sharq al Wasat, 'The Lifespan of Saudi Oil Reserves: 148 Years, Possibly More', *As Sharq Al Wasat* (Riyadh, 22 September 1983).

Ascher, Carol and Alladice, D., eds. *Refugees in the United States: A Bibliography of ERIC documents.* New York: ERIC Clearinghouse on Urban Education, Institute for Urban and Minority Education, Teachers College/ Columbia University Press, 1982.

Ascher, Carol, *The Social and Psychological Adjustment of Southeast Asian Refugees.* New York: ERIC Clearinghouse on Urban Education, Institute for Urban and Minority Education, Teachers College/Columbia University Press, 1984.

Ashabranner, Brent K., *Into a Strange Land: Unaccompanied Refugee Youth in America.* New York: Dodd, Mead, 1987.

Ashabranner, Brent K., *The New Americans: Changing Patterns in US Immigration.* New York: Dodd, Mead, 1983.

Ashdown, Peter, *Caribbean History in Maps: Trinidad and Jamaica.* London: Heinemann, 1988.

Ashe, Var Hong, *From Phnom Penh to Paradise: Escape from Cambodia.* London: Hodder and Stoughton, 1988.

Ashmun, Lawrence F., ed. *Resettlement of Indochinese Refugees in the United States: A Selective and Annotated Bibliography.* Dekalb: Northern Illinois Centre for South East Asian Studies, Illinois University, 1983.

Ashraf, S.A., et al., eds. Labor Migration from Bangladesh to the Middle East. Washington, DC: World Bank, 1981. (Staff working paper 454)

Astudillo Romero, Jaime, *Huayrapamushcas en USA: Flujos migratorios de la region centro-sur del Ecuador a los Estados Unidos.* Quito: Editorial El Conejo, 1990.

Austey, Roger, *The Atlantic Slave Trade and the British Navy 1700-1810.* London: Heinemann, 1975.

Australia, Committee to Advise on Australia's Immigration Policies, *Immigration, a Commitment to Australia: Legislation.* Canberra: Australian Government Public Service, 1988.

Austria, Nationalrat, *Aufgaben und Probleme bei der Betreuung von Flüchtlingen in Österreich.* Vienna: Österreichische Staatsdruckerei, 1982.

Avedon, John F., *In Exile from the Land of Snows.* New York: Knopf, 1984.

Avila, F.B., *Immigration in Latin America.* Washington, DC: Pan American Union, 1964.

Avni, Haim, *Argentina and the Jews: A History of Jewish Immigration.* Translated by Gila Brand. Tuscaloosa: University of Alabama Press, 1991.

Avni, Haim, *Mexico: Immigration and Refuge.* Washington, DC: Woodrow Wilson International Center for Scholars, 1989.

Azzam, H. and Shaib, D., The Women Left Behind - A Study of the Wives of Lebanese Migrant Workers in the Oil-rich Countries of the Region. Beirut: ILO Regional Office, World Employment Programme, 1980. (Working paper 3)

Bach, Robert L., *America's Labor Market in the 1990s: What Role Should Immigration Play?* Washington, DC: Immigration Policy Project of the Carnegie Endowment for International Peace, 1990.

Bach, Robert L., *Labor Force Participation and Employment of Southeast Asian Refugees in the United States.* Washington, DC: US Department of Health and Human Services, Office of Refugee Resettlement, 1984.

Bach, Robert L., *Western Hemispheric Immigration to the United States: A Review of Selected Research Trends.* Washington, DC: Georgetown University Press, Center for Immigration Policy and Refugee Assistance, 1985.

Bachofner, H., *Verfassungstreue und Verfassungsbruch: Dargestellt am Problem der Überfremdung und Übervolkerung der Schweiz: Eine Mahnschrift zum Hundertjährigen Bestehen der Bundesverfassung von 1874.* Zurich: Selbstverlag, 1974.

Bade, Klaus J., Vom Auswanderungsland zum Einwanderungsland?: Deutschland 1990-1980. Berlin: Colloquium, 1983.

Baez Evertsz, Franc, *Braceros haitianos en la Republica Dominicana.* Santo Domingo: Instituto Dominicano de Investigaciones Sociales, 1986.

Baez Evertsz, Franc, *La emigración de dominicanos a Estados Unidos: Determinantes socio-economicos y consecuencias.* Santo Domingo: Fundación Friedrich Ebert, 1985.

Bagana, E., et al., *Treff- und Informationart für Frauen aus der Türkei und Möglichkeiten der Sozial- und Gemeinswesenarbeit.* West Berlin: Berlin Verlag, 1982.

Bailyn, Bernard, *Voyagers to the West.* New York: Knopf, 1986.

Baines, Dudley, *Migration in a Mature Economy: Emigration and Internal Migration in England and Wales, 1861-1900.* New York: Cambridge University Press, 1985.

Baker, Reginald P. and North, David S., *The 1975 Refugees: Their First Five Years in America.* Washington, DC: New Transcentury Foundation, 1984.

Baker, Ron, ed. *The Psychological Problems of Refugees.* London: BRC and ECRE, 1983.

Balán, J. and Dandler, J., Migration and the Onset of Fertility Decline: A Study in Bolivia and Argentina. Research proposal presented to the Population Council, 1982.

Balán, J., 'Clases sociales en un municipio rural no indígena en México', *Revista Mexicana de Sociología* 32, no.5 (1970).

Balán, J., et al., *El hombre en una sociedad en desarrollo: movilidad geográfica y social en Monterrey.* Mexico City: Fondo de Cultura Económica, 1973.

Balán, J., *International Migration in the Southern Cone.* Washington, DC: Georgetown University Press, Center for Immigration Policy and Refugee Assistance, 1989.

Balán, J., et al., *Men in a Developing Society: Geographic and Social Mobility in Monterrey.* Austin: University of Texas Press, 1984.

Balán, J., Migraciones temporarias y mercado de trabajo rural en America Latina: Una revisión del problema y de la información disponible. Geneva: ILO, 1981. (Working paper 48)

Balán, J., ed. *Why People Move: Comparative Perspectives on the Dynamics of Internal Migration.* Paris: UNESCO, 1981.

Balaran, Paul, *Refugees and Migrants: Problems and Program Responses: A Look at the Causes and Consequences of Today's Major International Population Flows, and at the Ford Foundation's New Programs to Address the Problems.* New York: The Foundation, 1983.

Ballard, J., 'Four Equatorial States', In: G.M. Carter, ed. *National Unity and Regionalism in Eight African States.* Ithaca: Cornell University Press, 1966.

Balmore, Diana, *Hispanic Immigrants in the Construction Industry: New York City, 1960-1982.* New York: Center for Latin American and Caribbean Studies, New York University, 1983. (Occasional paper 38)

Bardill, J., Southall, R. and Perrings, C., The State and Labour Migration in the South African Political Economy, with Particular Reference to Gold Mining. Geneva: ILO, World Employment Programme, 1977. (Research working paper, mimeo)

Bariani, Didier, *Les immigrés, pour ou contre la France?* Paris: France-Empire, 1985.

Barry, Deborah, *Diagnostico nacional de Nicaragua sobre refugiados, repatridaos y población desplazada, 1988.* Managua, Nicaragua: Coordinadora Regional de Investigaciones Economicas y Sociales, 1989.

Basavarajappa, K. and Verma, R., *Asian Immigrants in Canada: A Decade of Experience.* May 1984. (Mimeo)

Bau, Ignatius, *This Ground is Holy: Church Sanctuary and Central American Refugees.* New York: Paulist Press, 1985.

Baucic, I., Some Economic Consequences of Yugoslav External Migrations. Paper presented at the Colloque sur les Travailleurs Immigrés en Europe Occidentale, Paris, 5-7 June 1974.

Bauer, Yehuda, *Out of the Ashes: The Impact of American Jews on Post-Holocaust European Jewry.* Oxford: Pergamon Press, 1989.

Baumgartner-Karabak, A. and Landesberger, G., *Die Verkauften Braüte.* Reinbek bei Hamburg: Rowholt, 1978.

Beach, Hugh, *A New Wave on a Northern Shore: The Indochinese Refugees in Sweden.* Norrköping, Sweden: Statens invandrarverk, Arbetsmarknadsstyrelsen, 1982.

Beaglehole, Ann, *A Small Price to Pay: Refugees from Hitler to New Zealand, 1936-46.* Wellington: Allen & Unwin, New Zealand Department of Internal Affairs, Historical Branch, 1988.

Bean, Frank D., *Opening and Closing the Doors: Evaluating Immigration Reform and Control.* Santa Monica, CA: Rand, 1989.

Beauftragte der Bundesregierung Für Ausländerfragen, *Bericht zur Ausländerpolitik.* Bonn: Beauftragte der Bundesregierung für Ausländerfragen, 1985.

Beck, E.M., Horan, P.M. and Tolbert II, C.M., 'Stratification in a Dual Economy: A Sectoral Model of Earnings Determination', *American Sociological Review* 43 (1978), pp.704-20.

Becker, Elizabeth, *When the War is Over, The Voices of the Cambodian Revolution.* New York: Simon and Schuster, 1985.

Bedford, R., 'Social Aspects of Population Change in Small Island Countries of the ESCAP/SPC Region', In: ESCAP, *Report and Working Papers of the ESCAP/SPC Conference Seminar on Small Island Countries of the ESCAP/SPC Region,* Noumea, 15-19 February 1982.

Bednarz, I., *Einstellungen von Arbeiterjugendlichen zur Bildung und Ausbildung.* Munich: 1978.

Beijer, G.J., 'Modern Patterns of International Migratory Movements', In: J.A. Jackson, ed. *Migration.* Cambridge: Cambridge University Press, 1969.

Bellati, C., 'Bolivianos en las fincas y viñedos de la provincia de Mendoza', *Los migrantes de países limítrofes.* Buenos Aires: Oficina Sectorial de Desarrollo de Recursos Humanos, 1973.

Bellwood, P., *The Polynesians: Prehistory of an Island People.* London: Thames and Hudson, 1978.

Ben-Porath, Yossef S., *Issues in the Psycho-social Adjustment of Refugees.* Minnesota: Technical Assistance Center, 1987.

Benamrane, Djilali, *L'emigration algérienne en France: passe, present, et devenir.* Alger: Société Nationale d'Edition et de Diffusion, 1983.

Benard, Cheryl, 'Politics and the Refugee Experience', *Political Science Quarterly* 101 (1986).

Bentley, Judith, *Refugees: Search for a Haven.* New York: J. Messner, 1986.

Benton, Barbara, *Ellis Island.* New York: Facts on File, 1987.

Benton, G., Two Revolutions: Political and Economic Development in Saudi Arabia under the Saudi Family. Exeter University, 1979. (Unpublished conference paper)

Berar-Awad, A., *Towards Self-reliance: A Programme of Action for Refugees in Eastern and Central Sudan.* Geneva: ILO, UNHCR, 1984.

Berger, S. and Piore, M.J., *Dualism and Discontinuity in Industrial Societies.* Cambridge: Cambridge University Press, 1980.

Berghahn, Marion, *Continental Britons: German-Jewish Refugees from Nazi Germany.* Oxford: Berg Publishers, 1988.

Berghahn, Marion, *German-Jewish Refugees in England: The Ambiguities of Assimilation.* London: Macmillan Press, 1984.

Berninghaus, Siegfried, *International Migration under Incomplete Information: A Microeconomic Approach.* Berlin & New York: Springer-Verlag, 1991.

Bertoncello, Rodolfo, *Los argentinos en el exterior.* Buenos Aires, Argentina: Centro de Estudios de Población, United Nations Research Institute for Social Development, 1985.

Beshers, J.M. and Sassen-Koob, Saskia, Micro Social Ecology and Social Distance: Residential Patterns of Six Immigrant Groups in Queens, New York City, 1970-1980. New York: Department of Sociology, Queens College, CUNY, 1982. (Unpublished Ms thesis)

Bethell, Leslie, *The Abolition of the Brazilian Slave Trade: Britain, Brazil, and the Slave Trade Question, 1807-1869*. Cambridge: Cambridge University Press,1970.

Bettati, Mario, *L'asile politique en question: un statut pour les refugies*. Paris: Presses Universitaires de France, 1985.

Betts, Katharine, *Ideology and Immigration: Australia 1976 to 1987*. Carlton: Melbourne University Press, 1988.

Bhattacharyya, Gayatri, *Refugee Rehabilitation and its Impact on Tripura's Economy*. New Delhi: Omsons Publications, 1988.

Bingemer, K., Meistermann-Seeger, E. and Neubert, E., eds. *Leben als Gastarbeiter: Beglückte and Misblückte Integration*. Cologne: Westdeutscher Verlag, 1970.

Birercin, M., 'Dis ulkelere isgucu sevkinin sosyal ve ekonomik hayatimizdaki etkileri [Effects of Labor Migration on Social and Economic Life of the Country]', *Sosyal Syaset Konferanslarn* (1966), pp.199-204. Istanbul: IUIF Publications.

Birks, J.S. and Rimmer, J.A., *Developing Education Systems in the Oil States of Arabia: Conflicts of Purpose and Focus*. Durham University Centre for Middle Eastern and Islamic Studies, 1984. (Occasional paper 21)

Birks, J.S. and Sinclair, C.A., *Arab Manpower: The Crisis of Development*. London: Croom Helm, 1980.

Birks, J.S. and Sinclair, C.A., *International Migration and Development in the Arab Region*. Geneva: ILO, 1980.

Birks, J.S. and Sinclair, C.A., *Nature and Process of Labour Importing: The Arabian Gulf States of Kuwait, Bahrain, Qatar and the UAE*. Geneva: ILO, World Employment Programme, 1978. (Working paper 30)

Birks, J.S. and Sinclair, C.A., The Kingdom of Saudi Arabia and the Libyan Arab Jamahiriyah: The Key Countries of Employment. Geneva: ILO, World Employment Programme, 1979. (Working paper 39)

Birks, J.S. and Sinclair, C.A., The Socio-economic Determinants of Intra-regional Migration. Paper presented to the Conference on International Migration in the Arab World, Nicosia, 11-16 May 1981.

Birrell, Robert, 'A New Era in Australian Migration Policy', *International Migration Review* (New York) 18 (Spring 1984), pp.65-84.

Birrell, Robert, *An Issue of People Population and Australian Society*. Melbourne: Longman Cheshire, 1987.

Blackburn, R. and Mann, M., *The Working Class and the Labour Market*. London: Macmillan, 1979.

Boeder, R., 'The Effects of Labour Emigration on Rural Life in Malawi', *Rural African* 20 (1973).

Bogamolov, O.T., Interdependence, Structural Change and Conflicts in the World Economy. Solicited paper presented to the Seventh World Congress of the International Economic Association, Madrid, 5-9 September 1983.

Bogan, M., La migración internacional en Costa Rica. Heredia: Instituto de Estudios Sociales en Población, Universidad Nacional, 1980. (Working paper 23)

Bogen, Elizabeth, *Immigration in New York*. New York: Praeger, 1987.

Bonacich, Edna and Cheng, Lucie, *Labor Immigration Under Capitalism: Asian Workers in the United States Before World War II*. Los Angeles: University of California Press, 1984.

Bonacich, Edna and Hirata, L.C., International Labor Migration: A Theoretical Orientation. Paper presented at the Conference on New Directions on Immigration and Ethnicity Research. Durham: Duke University, May 1981.

Bonavia, G., Focus on Canadian Immigration. Ottawa, 1977. (Mimeo)

Bonnerjea, L., *Shaming the World: The Needs of Women Refugees*. London: WUS, 1985.

Bookbinder, Bernie, *City of the World: New York and its People*. New York: Abrams, 1989.

Boone, Margaret S., *Capital Cubans: Refugee Adaptation in Washington, DC*. New York: AMS Press, 1989.

Borjas, George J., *Ethnic Capital and Intergenerational Mobility*. Cambridge, MA: National Bureau of Economic Research, 1991.

Borjas, George J., *International Differences in the Labor Market Performance of Immigrants*. Kalamazoo: W.E. Upjohn Institute for Employment Research, 1988.

Borjas, George J., *National Origin and the Skills of Immigrants in the Postwar Period*. Cambridge, MA: National Bureau of Economic Research, 1991.

Borjas, George J., *On the Labor Market Effects of Immigration and Trade*. Cambridge, MA: National Bureau of Economic Research, 1991.

Borjas, George J., *The Economic Consequences of Immigration*. Madison: University of Wisconsin Press, 1986.

Boserup, E., *Women's Role in Economic Development*. New York: St. Martin's Press, 1970.

Boshyk, Yuri and Balan, Boris, eds. *Political Refugees and 'Displaced Persons': 1945-54. A Selected Bibliography with Special Reference to the Ukrainians.* Edmonton: Canadian Institute of Ukrainian Studies, University of Alberta, 1982.

Boswell, T.D., Rivero, M. and Diaz, M., eds. *Bibliography for the Mariel-Cuban Diaspora*. Gainesville: Centre for Latin American Studies, University of Florida, 1988.

Bouvier, Leon F., *Many Hands, Few Jobs: Population, Unemployment and Emigration in Mexico and the Caribbean*. Washington, DC: Center for Immigration Studies, 1986.

Boxer, Charles R., *Portuguese Society in the Tropics*. Madison: University of Wisconsin Press, 1965.

Boyd, M., 'At a Disadvantage: The Occupational Attainments of Foreign Born Women in Canada', *International Migration Review* 18 (1984), pp.1091-119.

Boyd, M., 'The American Emigrant in Canada: Trends and Consequences', *International Migration Review* 15 (1981), pp.650-70.

Boyd, M. and Taylor, C., Temporary Workers in Canada: Expanding Research Horizon. May 1985. (Mimeo)

Boye-Miller, M., 'Language Training for Immigrant Workers in Sweden', *International Labour Review* 108 (1973), pp.505-15.

Böhning, W.R., *Black Migration to South Africa: What are the Issues?* Geneva: ILO, World Employment Programme, 1977. (Research paper 10)

Böhning, W.R., Guest Worker Employment, with Special Reference to the Federal Republic of Germany, France, and Switzerland - Lessons for the United States? College Park: Center for Philosophy and Public Policy, University of Maryland, 1980.

Böhning, W.R., International Migration: Implications for Development and Policies. Paper prepared for the Expert Group on Population Distribution, Migration and Development, Hammamet, Tunisia, March 1983. (Mimeo)

Böhning, W.R., 'International Migration and the Western World: Past, Present, Future', *International Migration* 16 (1979), pp.1-23.

Böhning, W.R., 'International Migration in Western Europe: Reflections on the Past Five Years', *International Labour Review* 118 (1979), pp.401-14.

Böhning, W.R., *Mediterranean Workers in Western Europe: Effects on Home Countries and Countries of Employment*. Geneva: ILO, World Employment Programme, 1975. (Research working paper)

Böhning, W.R., *Studies in International Migration*. New York: St. Martin's Press, 1984.

Böhning, W.R., *The Economic Effects of the Employment of Foreign Workers: With Special Reference to the Labour-markets of Western Europe's Post-industrial Countries*. Paris: OECD, 1973.

BPER, *Africa and Its Refugees. Africa Refugee Day.* Addis Ababa: The Bureau for the Placement and Education of African Refugees, 1975.

Braham, P., *Migration and Settlement in Britain*. Milton Keynes: Open University Press, 1982.

Braham, P. and Rhodes, E., *Ethnic Employment and Employment*. Milton Keynes: Open University Press, 1977.

Braham, P., Rhodes, E. and Pearn, M., eds. *Discrimination and Disadvantage in Employment*. London: Harper and Row, 1982.

Bramwell, Anna, ed. *Refugees in the Age of Total War: Twentieth-century Case Studies of Refugees in Europe and the Middle East*. London: Unwin Hyman, 1987.

Brana-Shute, Rosemary, *A Bibliography of Caribbean Migration and Caribbean Immigrant Communities*. Gainesville: University of Florida Press, 1983.

Braun, R., *Sozio-Kulturelle Probleme der Eingliederung italienischer Arbeits-Kräfte in der Schweiz*. Erlenbach/Zurich: Rentsch, 1970.

Breitman, Richard, *American Refugee Policy and European Jewry, 1933-1945*. Bloomington: Indiana University Press, 1987.

Brennan, Tom, *Uprooted Angolans: From Crisis to Catastrophe*. Washington, DC: US Committee for Refugees, 1987.

Breton, F., 'Working and Living Conditions of Migrant Workers in South America', *International Labour Review* 114 (1976), pp.339-54.

Breton, R., Reitz, J. and Valentine, V., *Cultural Boundaries and the Cohesion of Canada*. Montreal: Institute for Research on Public Policy, 1981.

Breytenbach, W.J., *Migratory Labour Arrangements in Southern Africa*. Pretoria: Africa Institute, 1972.

Brooks, Hugh C. and El-Ayouty, Yassin, eds. *Refugees South of the Sahara: An African Dilemma*. Westport, CT: Negro Universities Press, 1970.

Briggs, V.M., *Foreign Labor Programs as an Alternative to Illegal Immigration into the United States: A Dissenting View*. College Park: Center for Philosophy and Public Policy, University of Maryland, 1980.

Briggs, V.M., 'Nonimmigrant Labor Policy: Future Trend or Aberration?', In: D.G. Papademetriou and M.Miller, eds. *The Unavoidable Issue: United States Immigration Policy in the 1980s*. Philadelphia: Institute for the Study of Human Issues, 1983.

Broomberger, N., *Mining Employment in Southern Africa 1946-2000*. Geneva: ILO, World Employment Programme, . (Research working paper)

Brown, William A., *Indochinese Refugees and Relations with Thailand*. Washington, DC: US Department of State, Bureau of Public Affairs, Office of Public Communication, Editorial Division, 1988.

Browning, H.L. and Singelmann, J., 'The Transformation of the US Labor Force: The Interaction of Industry and Occupation', *Politics and Society* 8 (1978), pp.481-509.

Bulcha, Mekuria, *Flight and Integration: Causes of Mass Exodus from Ethiopia and Problems of Integration in the Sudan*. Uppsala: Scandinavian Institute of African Studies, 1988.

Bullivant, B., *The Pluralist Dilemma in Education*. London: George Allen & Unwin, 1981.

Bullivant, B.M., *Race, Ethnicity and Curriculum*. Melbourne: Macmillan, 1981.

Bundesanstalt für Arbeit, *Ausländische Arbeitnehmer 1971*. Nuremberg: Bundestanstalt für Arbeit, 1972.

Bundesanstalt für Arbeit, *Repräsentativ-Untersuchung 1972*. Nuremberg: Bundesanstalt für Arbeit, 1973.

Bundesminister für Bildung und Wissenschaft, *Berufsbildungsbericht 1981*. Bonn, Bundesminister für Bildung und Wissenschaft, 1981.

Buric, O., 'Modernization of the Family and Inconsistency of Its Structure: A Model for Family Transformation Research', *International Journal of Sociology of the Family* 1 (1971), pp.1-16.

Burke, B.M., *The Outlook for Labour Growth and Employment in Lesotho 1980-2000*. Maseru: World Bank/UNDP, 1981.

Bustamante, J., 'Undocumented Migration from Mexico: Research Report', *International Migration Review* 11 (1977), pp.149-77.

Bustamante, J. and Martínez, G.G., 'Undocumented Immigration from Mexico: Beyond Borders but Within Systems', *Journal of International Affairs* 33 (1979).

Butcher, J.M., Egli, E.A., Shiota, N.K. and Ben-Porath, Y.S., *Psychological Interventions with Refugees*. Minnesota: Technical Assistance Group, 1988.

Butcher, B. and Trent, H., 'Some Aspects of the Department of Labour's Research into Migration', *Proceedings of the New Zealand Demographic Society Fifth Annual Conference*. Wellington: New Zealand Demographic Society, 1979.

Cabezas Moro, O., *Emigración española a Iberoamérica: evolución histórica y características sociológicas*. Paper prepared for the Reunión sobre Migraciones Latinas y Formación de la Nación Latinoamericana. Caracas: Simón Bolívar University, 1980.

Cable, V., *Whither Kenyan Emigrants*. London: The Fabian Society, 1969.

Cagan, Steve, *This Promised Land, El Salvador: The Refugee Community of Colomoncagua and their Return to Morazan*. New Brunswick: Rutgers University Press, 1991.

Caldwell, J.C., *African Rural-Urban Migration: The Movement to Ghana's Towns*. Canberra: Australian National University Press, 1969.

Caldwell, John, ed. *Population Growth and Socio-economic Change in West Africa*. London: Macmillan, 1975.

Caldwell, John, 'The Enslavement of Africans: A Demographic Model', *Canadian Journal of African Studies* 16 (1982), p.17-30.

Caldwell, J.C., *The Sahelian Drought and its Demographic Consequences*. Washington, DC: OLCP, 1975. (Paper 8)

Camarda, Renato, *Traslado forzado: refugiados salvadoreños en Honduras*. Tegucigalpa: Centro de Documentación de Honduras, 1987.

Campbell, E.K., A Note on the Role of Migrant Labour in Liberia. Monrovia: University of Liberia, Demographic Unit, 1981. (Unpublished working paper)

Campbell, Gwyn R., 'Madagascar in the Slave Trade 1810-1895', *Journal of African History* 22 (1981), p.203-227.

Canada, Employment and Immigration Canada (EIC), *Annual Report to Parliament on Immigration Levels.* Ottawa: Employment and Immigration Canada, 1975-83.

Canada, EIC, *Background Paper on Future Immigration Levels: A Companion Report to the Annual Report to Parliament on Future Immigration Levels.* Ottawa: EIC, 1 November 1983.

Canada, EIC, *Immigration Statistics - Canada.* Ottawa: EIC, 1965-83.

Canada, EIC, *Indochinese Refugees: The Canadian Response, 1979 and 1980.* Ottawa: EIC, 1982.

Canada, Manpower and Immigration, *Highlights from the Green Paper on Immigration and Population.* Ottawa: Information Canada, 1979.

Canada, Ministry of Supply and Services, *Review of Literature on Migrant Mental Health.* Ottawa: Ministry of Supply and Services, 1988.

Canada, *Report of Special Joint Committee of the Senate and the House of Commons on Immigration Policy.* Ottawa: Information Canada, 1983.

Canak, W. and Schmitter, B., Uneven Development, Labor Migration and State Policy: Theoretical and Methodological Issues. Paper presented at the Conference on New Directions on Immigration and Ethnicity Research. Duke University, May 1981.

Caplan, Nathan S., *The Boat People and Achievement in America: A Study of Economic and Educational Success.* Ann Arbor: University of Michigan Press, 1989.

Caporaso, J., 'Dependence, Dependency, and Power in the Global System: A Structural and Behavioral Analysis', *International Organization* 32 (1978), pp.13-43.

Caporaso, J., Introduction to a special issue on 'Dependence and Dependency in the Global System', *International Organization* 32 (1978), pp.1-12.

Cardona, R., et al., *Emigración de colombianos a Venezuela.* Bogotá: CCRP, 1979.

Cardona, Ramiro and Rubinano, Sara, eds. *El éxodo de Colombianos.* Bogotá: Corporación Centro Regional de Población y Colciencias/Ediciones Tercer Mundo, 1980.

Cardoso, F.H., *Dependency and Development in Latin America.* Translated by M.M. Urquidi. Berkeley: University of California Press, 1979.

Carron, J.M., *Factores condicionantes de las migraciones internacionales intra-regionales en el cono sur de America Latina.* Santiago: PROELCE, 1976. (FLASCO-CELADE)

Carron, J.M., 'Shifting Patterns in Migration from Bordering Countries to Argentina: 1914-1970', *International Migration Review* 13 (1979), pp.475-87.

Castellón, Raúl Hernández, *La Revolución Demografica en Cuba.* Havana: Editorial Ciencias Sociales, 1988.

Castells, M., 'Immigrant Workers and Class Struggles in Advanced Capitalism: The Western European Experience', *Politics and Society* 5 (1975), pp.55-66.

Castle, S. and Kosack, G., *Immigrant Workers and Class Structure in Western Europe.* London: Oxford University Press, 1973.

Castle, S. and Kosack, G., *Language Use in Canada.* Ottawa: Statistics Canada/Supply and Services Canada, 1980.

Castro, M.G., *Mary and Eve's Social Reproduction in the Big Apple: Colombian Voices.* New York: Center for Latin American and Caribbean Studies, New York University. (Occasional paper 35)

Castro, Mary, 'Women in Migration: Colombian Voices in the Big Apple', *Latinamericanist* 18, no.2 (March 1983).

Caves, G., *Le tourisme international: mirage ou strategie d'avenir.* Paris: Hatier, 1989.

CCSDPT, *CCSDPT Handbook: Refugee Services in Thailand.* Bangkok: Committee for Co-ordination of Services in Thailand, 1988.

CDR (Committee for the Defense of Refugees), *Selected and Annotated Bibliography on Refugee Children.* Geneva: CDR, UNHCR and Refugees Policy Group, 1989.

CDR, *Selected and Annotated Bibliography on Refugee Women*, 2nd ed. Geneva: CDR, UNHCR, and Refugee Policy Group, 1989.

CELADE (Latin American Demographic Studies Center), Migración de mano de obra no calificada entre países latinoamericanos. Santiago: CELADE, 1981. (Series A 169, mimeo)

CELADE, 'Principal país de destino de la emigración de cada país de América Latina', *Boletín Demográfico* 10 (1977).

CENIET, *Análisis de algunos resultados de la primera encuesta a trabajadores no documentados devueltos de los Estados Unidos.* Mexico City: CENIET, 1980.

CENIET, Los trabajadores mexicanos en Estados Unidos: primeros resultados de la Encuesta Nacional de Emigración. December 1978-January 1979. (Mimeo)

Center for Continuing Study of the California Economy, *Projections of Hispanic Population for the United States, 1990 and 2000*. Palo Alto: CCSCE, 1982.

Center for Cuban Studies, *Cuba Update*. New York, quarterly.

Center for the Study of Human Rights at Columbia University, ed. *Human Rights: A Topical Bibliography*. New York. Boulder: Westview Press, 1983.

Chakravarti, N.R., *The Indian Minority in Burma: The Rise and Decline of an Immigrant Community*. London: Oxford University Press, 1971.

Chaliand, Gérard , ed. *People Without a Country: the Kurds and Kurdistan*. London: Zed Press, 1980.

Chaliand, Gérard and Rageau, Jean-Pierre, *Strategic Atlas. A Comparative Geopolitics of the World's Powers*. New York: Harper and Row, 1983.

Chan, Kwok B. and Indra, Doreen, *Uprooting, Loss and Adaptation: the Resettlement of Indochinese Refugees in Canada*. Ottawa: Canadian Public Health Association, 1987.

Chandavarkar, A.G., 'Use of Migrants' Remittances in Labour-exporting Countries', *Finance and Development* (June 1980).

Chandler, David L., *Health and Slavery in Colonial Colombia*. New York: Arno, 1981.

Chaney, Elsa, *Colombian Migration to the United States*. Vol. 2. Washington, DC: Smithsonian Institution, Interdisciplinary Communications Program, 1976. (Occasional monograph series 5)

Chaney, E.M. and Lewis, M.W., *Women, Migration, and the Decline of Small Holder Agriculture*. Washington, DC: Office of Women in Development, AID, 1980.

Chantavanich, Supand and Reynolds, E. Bruce, eds. *Indochinese Refugees: Asylum and Resettlement*. Bangkok: Chulalongkorn University, 1988.

Chaparro, Fernando and Arias Osorio, Eduardo, *La emigración de profesionales y técnicos colombianos y latinoamericanos, 1960-1970*. Bogotá: Colciencias, 1970.

Charon, Milly, ed. *Between Two Worlds: The Canadian Immigration Experience*. Dunvegan: Quadrant Editions.

Chen, Jack, *The Chinese of America*. New York: Harper and Row, 1980.

Ching-hwang, Yen, *A Social History of the Chinese in Singapore and Malaya 1800-1911*. Singapore: Oxford University Press, 1986.

Chiswick, B., *An Analysis of the Economic Progress and Impact of Immigrants*. Paper prepared for the Employment and Training Administration, US Department of Labor, 1980.

Choucri, N., *Asians in the Arab World: Labor Migration and Public Policy*. Cambridge, MA: Cairo University/ Massachusetts Institute of Technology, 1983.

Christensen, H., *Afghan Refugees in Pakistan: from Emergency towards Self-reliance: a Report on the Food Relief Situation and Related Socio-economic Aspects*. Geneva: UNRISD, 1984.

Christensen, H., comp. 'Bibliography of Documentation on Refugees in Africa South of the Sahara,' *Refugee Abstracts* 1, no. 3 (1982), pp. 72-87. Geneva: UNCHR, 1982.

Christensen, H., *History and Field Study of a Burundian Settlement in Tanzania*. Geneva: UNRISD, 1985.

Christensen, H. and Scott, W., *Survey of the Social and Economic Conditions of Afghan Refugees in Pakistan*. Geneva: UNRISD, 1990.

Ciencia y Tecnologia para Guatemala, *Crisis en Centro America y refugiados guatemaltecos en México*. México DF: 1985.

CIMADE, *Africa's Refugee Crisis: What's to be done?* Translated by Michael John. London: Zed Books, 1986.

Cipolla, Carlo M., *Guns, Sails, and Empires: Technological Innovation and the Early Phases of European Expansion, 1400-1700*. Harmondsworth: Penguin, 1983.

Clarence-Smith, Gervase, 'The Portuguese Contribution to the Cuban Slave and Coolie Trades in the 19th century', *Slavery and Abolition* 5, no.1 (1984), p.25-33.

Clarence-Smith, Gervase, *The Third Portuguese Empire 1825-1925*. Manchester: Manchester University Press, 1985.

Clark, H., *The Politics of the Common Market*. Englewood Cliffs: Prentice-Hall, 1967.

Clarke, D., *Contract Workers and Underdevelopment in Rhodesia*. Gwelo: Mambo Press, 1974.

Clarke, D., Foreign Migrant Labour in Southern Africa; Studies on Accumulation in the Labour Reserves, Demand Determinants and Supply Relationships. Geneva: ILO, World Employment Programme, 1977. (Research working paper, mimeo)

Clay, J. and Holcomb, B.K., Politics and the Ethiopian Famine 1984-1985. Cambridge, MA: Cultural Survival, Inc., 1986.

CNRS (National Council of Scientific Research), Les migrations internationales de la fin du XVIII siecle a nos jours. Paris: CNRS, 1980.

Coard, B., How a West Indian Child is Made Educationally Subnormal. London: New Beacon, 1971.

Cobbe, J., 'Emigration and Development in Southern Africa, with Special Reference to Lesotho', International Migration Review 16, no.4 (1982).

Cohen, Robin, The New Helots: Migrants in the International Division of Labour. Aldershot: Gower, 1987.

Cohen, S.M. and Sassen-Koob, Saskia, Survey of Six Immigrant Groups in Queens, New York City. New York: Queens College, CUNY, 1982.

Colclough, C., 'Some Aspects of Labour Use in Southern Africa: Problems and Policies', Bulletin of the Institute of Development Studies 11, no.4 (1980).

Coles, G.J.L., Problems Arising from Large Numbers of Asylum Seekers: A Study of Protection Aspects. Geneva: International Institute of Humanitarian Law, 1981.

Colombia, Ministerio de Trabajo y Seguridad Social (SENALDE), Migraciones laborales, 20-volume series, relevant titles:
1. El desarrollo de la política de migraciones laborales in Colombia, by Lelio Marmora.
2. Las migraciones laborales en la frontera de Colombia con Panamá, by Ponciano Torales.
3. Primer seminario latinoamericano sobre políticas de migraciones laborales.
4. Migración de trabajadores colombianos al Ecuador, by Renzo Pi Hugarte.
6. Organización del sistema de estadísticas continuas migratorias internacionales, by Peter Jones.
8. Inserción laboral de migrantes indocumentados, by Luis Mansila; Mercados de trabajo y salarios diferenciales en zona fronteriza, by Maria F. Velosa.
10. Mercados de trabajo y migración en ciudades fronterizas, by Inés Gomes, Jacques Hierbel, Hector Oviedo and Carlos Pardo.

11. La migración de trabajadores colombianos a Venezuela: la relación ingreso-consumo como uno de los factores de expulsión, by Gabriel Murillo Castaño.
12. Sistemas de seguridad social y migración colombo-venezelona, by Jestis R. Marquez and Alberto Mayansky.
13. Evaluación del programa de retorno de profesionales y técnicos.
14. Mercados de trabajo y éxodo de competencias, by Ponciano Torales.
17. Legislación migratoria de Colombia y acuerdos bilaterales y subregionales sobre la materia.
Bogotá: SENALDE, 1980 to present.

Commission of the European Communities, Comparative Survey of Conditions and Procedures for Admission of Third Country Workers for Employment in the Member States. Brussels, Directorate-General, Employment and Social Affairs, 1980. (v/510/1/78-EN)

Commission of the European Communities, Employment in Europe. Brussels: European Community, 1989.

Conde, J., Migration in West Africa: Some Considerations. Paris: OECD, 1979.

Conde, J., Study of Illegal Immigrants Through a Socio-economic Survey of Malian, Mauritanian and Senegalese Migrants Resident in France. ICM Sixth Seminar on Adaptation and Integration of Immigrants: Undocumented Migrants or Migrants in an Irregular Situation, Geneva, n.d. (Background paper)

Conde, Julien, 'The Future of International Migration', International Migration in the Arab World (1982), Beirut: United Nations Economic Commission for Western Asia.

Conde, J. and Zachariah, K.C., International Migration in West Africa - Demographic and Economic Aspects. Conference on Economic and Demographic Change: Issues for the 1980s. Helsinki, 1978. Liège: IUSSP, 1978.

Connell, J., Migration in the South Pacific: An Overview. Paper presented to the SPC/ILO Conference on Migration, Employment and Development in the South Pacific, Noumea, February 1982.

Conrad, Robert Edgar, Children of God's Fire: A Documentary History of Black Slavery in Brazil. Princeton: Princeton University Press, 1983.

Conrad, Robert Edgar, World of Sorrow: The African Slave Trade to Brazil. Baton Rouge: Louisiana State University Press, 1986.

Conroy, M.E., et al., *Migration as the Consequence of the Old International Economic Order: Sources and Policy Implications of Recent Changes in Real-wage Incentives for Migration from Mexico to the United States*. Austin: The University of Texas, 1980. (Texas Population Research Center Papers series 2)

Corley, T., *A History of the Burmah Oil Company*. London: Heinemann, 1983.

Cornelius, W., *Mexican Migration to the US: Causes, Consequences, and US Responses*. Cambridge, MA: Center for International Studies, Migration and Development Group, Massachusetts Institute of Technology, 1977. (Monograph c/78-9)

Cornelius, W.A., 'The Reagan Administration's Proposals for a New United States Immigration Policy: An Assessment of Potential Effects', *International Migration Review* 15 (1981), 769-78.

Cornelius, W. and Montoya, R. A., eds. *America's New Immigration Law: Origins, Rationales, and Potential Consequences*. La Jolla: Center for US-Mexican Studies, University of California, San Diego, 1983.

Coser, Lewis A., *Refugee Scholars in America: Their Impact and Their Experiences*. New Haven: Yale University Press, 1984.

Cossali, Paul, *Stateless in Gaza*. London: Zed Books, 1986.

Coudert, Vincent, *Refuge, refugies: des guatemalteques sur terre mexicaine*. Paris: L'Harmattan, 1987.

Council of Europe, Committee of Ministers, Protection of Persons Satisfying the Criteria in the Geneva Convention who are not Formally Recognised as Refugees: Recommendation R(84)1 Adopted by the Committee of Ministers of the Council of Europe. Strasbourg: The Council, 1984.

Council of Europe, Committee on Migration, Refugees and Demography, Situation of the Palestine Refugees: Report. Strasbourg: The Council, 1989.

Council of Europe, Committee on the Legal Aspects of Territorial Asylum and Refugees, The Harmonisation of National Procedures Relating to Asylum: Recommendation R (81)16: and Explanatory Memorandum. Strasbourg: The Council, 1982.

Crewdson, J., 'Plan on Immigration', *New York Times* (31 July 1981), p.A12.

Criddle, Joan D., *To Destroy You is no Loss: The Odyssey of a Cambodian Family*. New York: Anchor Books, 1989.

Crisp, Jeff, *Voluntary Repatriation Programmes for African Refugees: A Critical Examination*. Oxford: Refugees Studies Programme, Queen Elizabeth House, British Refugee Council, 1984.

Cross, G., The Structure of Labor Immigration in France Between the Wars. Madison: University of Wisconsin, 1977. (Unpublished dissertation)

Cruz, Carmen Inés and Castaño, Juanita, 'Colombian Migration to the United States, Part 1, Interdisciplinary Communications Program, The Dynamics of Migration', *International Migration* 11 (1976). (Occasional monograph series 5)

CSUCA/PCCS, *Estructura demográfica y migraciones internas en Centroamérica*. San José: Editorial Universitaria Centroamericana, 1978.

Curtin, Philip D., ed. *Africa Remembered: Narratives by West Africans from the Era of the Slave Trade*. Madison: University of Wisconsin Press , 1967.

Curtin, Philip D., *Cross Cultural Trade in World History*. New York: Cambridge University Press, 1984.

Curtin, Philip D., *The Atlantic Slave Trade: A Census*. Madison: University of Wisconsin Press, 1969.

Curtin, Philip D., *The Rise and Fall of the Plantation Complex*. New York: Cambridge University Press, 1990.

Dandler, J., *Household Diversification and Labour Processes: Some Anthropological Perspectives on Andean Peasantry*. Paper presented to the SSRC Conference on Demographic Research in Latin America, Mexico City, 23-27 August 1982. (Mimeo)

Daniles, Roger, *Asian America: Chinese and Japanese in the United States since 1850*. Seattle: University of Washington Press, 1989.

Dasgupta, B., 'Rural-Urban Migration and Rural Development', In: J. Balán, ed. *Why People Move: Comparative Perspectives on the Dynamics of Internal Migration*. Paris: UNESCO, 1981.

Davis, K., 'Emerging Issues in International Migration', *International Population Conference, Manila* 2 (1981), Liège: International Union for the Scientific Study of Population.

Davis, K., 'Future Migration into Latin America', *Milbank Memorial Fund Quarterly* 25 (1947), pp.44-62.

Davis, K., 'International Inequality and Migration in the Middle East and North Africa: An Analysis of Trends and Issues', *Population Bulletin of ECWA* 21 (December 1981).

Davis, K., 'The Migration of Human Populations', *Scientific American* 231, no.3 (1974), pp.93-100.

Davis, K., *The Population of India and Pakistan.* Princeton: Princeton University Press, 1951.]

Davis, Marilyn P., *Mexican Voices/American Dreams: An Oral History of Mexican Immigration to the United States.* New York: Holt, 1990.

Davison, R.B., *Black British.* London: Institute of Race Relations/Oxford University Press, 1966.

Davison, R.B., *West Indian Migrants.* London: Institute of Race Relations/Oxford University Press, 1962.

Deakin, N., *Colour, Citizenship and British Society.* London: Panther Books, 1970.

De Martínez, María Mercedes, 'Crisis en Venezuela: impacto sobre Colombia', *Revista Estrategia* (Bogotá), 1983.

De Vletter, F., ed. *Labour Migration and Agricultural Development in Southern Africa.* Rome: FAO, 1982.

De Vletter, F., et al., 'Labour Migration in Swaziland', In: W.R. Böhning, ed. *Black Migration to South Africa: A Selection of Policy-oriented Research.* Geneva: ILO, 1981.

De Vletter, F., 'Recent Trends and Prospects of Black Migration to South Africa', *International Migration for Employment* (1985), p.7. Geneva: ILO. (WIG Working paper 20)

De Vries, J. and Vallee, F.G., *Language Use in Canada.* Ottawa: Statistics Canada/Supply and Services Canada, 1980.

De Waal, Alexander, *Famine That Kills.* Oxford: Clarendon Press, 1989.

DeLey, M., French Immigration Policy Since May 1981. Champaign-Urbana: University of Illinois, 1983. (Mimeo)

Demery, L., Asian Labor Migration to the Middle East: An Empirical Assessment. Paper prepared for the Conference on Asian Labor Migration to the Middle East, 19-23 September 1983. Honolulu: East-West Population Institute, 1983.

Demuth, C., *'Sus': A Report on the Vagrancy Act of 1824.* London: The Runnymede Trust, 1976.

Denich, B., 'Urbanization and Women's Role in Yugoslavia', *Anthropological Quarterly* 49 (1976), pp.11-19.

Deschamps, Hubert, *Histoire de la traite des noirs de l'antiquité à nos jours.* Paris: Presses Universitaires, 1971.

Descloitres, R., *The Foreign Worker: Adaptation to Industrial Work and Urban Life.* Paris: OECD, 1967.

DeWenden, W.C., *Les immigrés dans la cité.* Paris: Ministère de Travail/La Documentation Française, 1978.

Diallo, I., Border Migrations: A Survey of the Senegambian Rural Areas, Dakar. Dakar: IDEP, 1972. (Mimeo)

Diaz-Santana, A., 'The Role of Haitian Braceros in Dominican Sugar Production', *Latin American Perspectives* 3 (1976), pp.120-32.

Diaz-Briquets, S., *International Migration within Latin America and the Caribbean. An Overview.* New York: Center for Migration Studies, 1983.

Diaz-Briquets, S., *International Migration within Latin America: A Review of the Available Evidence.* Washington, DC: Population Reference Bureau, 1980.

Diaz-Briquets, S. and Weintraub, S., *Determinants of Emigration from Mexico, Central America, and the Caribbean.* Boulder: Westview Press, 1991.

Dib, George, International Migration: The Law and Practice. Solicited paper presented at the Seventh World Congress of the International Economic Association, Madrid, 5-9 September 1983.

Dib, George, 'Laws and Decrees and Their Application: Their Influence on Migration in the Arab World: Towards a Regional Covenant', *International Migration in the Arab World* 2 (1982).

Dickson, G.L., 'The Relationship Between Immigration and External Balance', *Australian Economic Review* (2nd quarter 1975), pp.10-16.

Diez-Canedo, J., Migration, Return and Development in Mexico. Cambridge, MA: Massachusetts Institute of Technology, 1979. (Unpublished PhD thesis)

Diller, Janelle M., *In Search of Asylum: Vietnamese Boat People in Hong Kong.* Washington, DC: Indochinese Resource Action Center, 1988.

DNP (National Department of Planning), *Dinámica demográfica y proyecciones de población del país, territorios nacionales, el Distrito Especial de Bogotá, los departamentos y las 30 principales ciudades.* Bogotá: DNP Social Development Unit, 1982.

Doeringer, P.B. and Piore, M.J., 'Unemployment and the 'Dual Labor Market' ', *The Public Interest* 38 (Winter 1975), pp.67-79.

Dohse, K., *Ausländische Arbeiter und bürgerlicher Staat-Genese und Funktion von staatlichem Ausländerrecht.* Königstein: Hain, 1981.

Dommen, Arthur, *Laos, Keystone of Indochina.* Boulder: Westview, 1985.

Dorais, L-J., Chan, K.B. and Indra, D., *Indochinese Communities in Canada.* Ottawa: Canadian Asian Studies Association, 1988.

Dorais, L-J., Pilon-Le, L. and Nguyen, Huy, *Exile in a Cold Land: a Vietnamese Community in Canada.* New Haven,: Yale University Centre for International and Area Studies, 1987.

Doran, H.M., Swaziland Labour Migration - Some Implications for a National Development Strategy. Geneva: ILO, World Employment Programme, 1977. (Research working paper, mimeo)

Downing, Bruce T. and Olney, Douglas P., *The Hmong in the West.* Minneapolis: University of Minnesota Press, 1982.

Dowty, Alan, *Closed Borders: The Contemporary Assault on Freedom of Movement.* New Haven: Yale University Press, 1987.

Duany, Jorge, *Los Dominicanos en Puerto Rico: Migración en la semi-periferia.* Río Piedras: Ediciones Huracán, 1990.

Duffy, J., *Portugal in Africa.* Cambridge, MA: Harvard University Press, 1962.

Dummett, A., *Citizenship and Nationality.* London: The Runnymede Trust, 1976.

Durham, W.H., *Scarcity and Survival in Central America - Ecological Origins of the Soccer War.* Stanford: Stanford University Press, 1979.

Duvall, R., 'Dependence and Dependencia Theory: Notes toward Precision of Concept and Argument', *International Organization* 32 (1978), pp.51-78.

Easterlin, R.A., *Population, Labor Force, and Long Swings in Economic Growth: The American Experience.* New York: National Bureau of Economic Research, 1968.

ECA (Economic Commission for Africa), *International Migration, Population Trends and Their Implications for Africa.* Addis Ababa: ECA, 1981. (African Population Studies series 4)

Eckart, C. and Jaerisch, U.G., et al., *Frauenarbeit in Familie und Fabrik.* Frankfurt & New York: Campus, 1979.

Eckert, J.B., 'The Employment Challenge Facing Lesotho', *Development Studies Southern Africa* 2 (1983).

Economist, 'World Travel and Tourism: A Survey', *The Economist* London (March 23, 1991), pp.58-68.

ECOWAS, *Treaty of the Economic Community of West African States (ECOWAS).* Lagos: 1975.

Edwards, V., *The West Indian Language Issue in British Schools.* London: Routledge & Kegan Paul, 1979.

EEC (European Economic Community), *Journal Officiel des Communautés Européenes. Various.* Brussels: EEC, 1980 to present.

EEC , *Treaties Establishing the European Communities.* Luxembourg: EEC, 1973.

Egero, B., 'Migration and Under-development: A General Discussion with Examples from Africa and Tanzania', In: V. Stolle-Heiskanen, ed. *Population and Underdevelopment.* Helsinki: Institute of Development Studies, University of Helsinki, 1977.

Egero, B., *Colonization and Migration: A Summary of Border-crossing Movements in Tanzania before 1967.* Uppsala: Scandinavian Institute of African Studies, 1979. (Research report 52)

Ehrlich, P.R., Bilderback, L. and Ehrlich, A.H., *The Golden Door: International Migration, Mexico and the United States.* New York: Ballantine Books, 1979.

EIU (Economist Intelligence Unit), *Studies on Immigration from the Commonwealth.* London: Basic Statistics, 1961.

Ekstrand, L.H., 'Home Language Teaching for Immigrant Pupils in Sweden', *International Migration Review* 14 (1980), pp.409-27.

Elizaga, J.C., *Migraciones a las áreas metropolitanas de América Latina.* Santiago: CELADE, 1971.

Elkan, W., 'Labour Migration from Botswana, Lesotho and Swaziland', *Economic Development and Cultural Change* 28 (1980), pp.583-96.

Elkan, W., 'Labour Migration from Botswana, Lesotho and Swaziland', In: W.M.J. Van Binsbergena and H.A. Meilink, eds. *Migration and the Transformation of Modern Africa Society.* Leiden: African Perspectives, 1978.

Elson, A. and Pearson, B., 'Discussion', *IDS Bulletin*, (April 1979), p.20. (Special issue on the continuing subordination of women in the development process)

Eltis, David, 'Free and Coerced Transatlantic Migrations: Some Comparisons', *American Historical Review* 88 (1983), p.251-280.

Emmanuel, A., *Unequal Exchange: A Study of the Imperialism of Trade*. London: New Left Books, 1972.

Emmer, P.C., ed. *Colonialism and Migration; Indentured Labour Before and After Slavery*. Dordrecht: Martinus Nijhoff, 1986.

Entzinger, H., *Return Migration from West European to Mediterranean Countries*. Geneva: ILO, International Migration for Employment Project, 1978. (Research working paper)

Epstein, L, 'Some Economic Effects of Immigration: A General Equilibrium Analysis', *Canadian Journal of Economics* 7 (1974), pp.174-90.

Equal Economic Opportunity Commission, *Job Patterns for Minorities and Women in Private Industry, 1980*. Vol. 2. Washington DC: US Government Printing Office, 1983.

Erickson, C., *American Industry and the European Immigrant, 1790-1950*. New York: Russell & Russell, 1957.

Erickson, C., *Emigration from Europe 1815-1914*. London: Adam & Charles Black, 1976.

Erickson, C.E. and Harris, Michael, 'Even in a Recession There Are 100 Winners', California Business (September 1982), pp.81-93.

Erikson, E.G., Melander, G. and Nobel, P., *Analysing Account of the Conference on the African Refugee Problem (Arusha, May 1979)*. Uppsala: Scandinavian Institute of African Studies, 1981.

ESCAP (Economic and Social Commission for Asia and the Pacific), *Demographic Trends and Policies in ESCAP Countries*. Bangkok: United Nations, 1979.

ESCAP, *Report and Working Papers of the ESCAP/SPC Conference Seminar on Small Island Countries of the ESCAP/SPC Region*, Noumea, New Caledonia, 15-19 February 1982.

Esser, E., *Ausländerinnen in der Bundesrepublik. Eine Soziologische Analyse des Eingliederungsverhaltens ausländischer Frauen*. Frankfurt/Main: Fischer, 1982.

Exter, T.G., Rural Community Structure and Migration: A Comparative Analysis of Acatic and Acatlan de Juarez in Jalisco. Ithaca: Cornell University, 1976. (Unpublished thesis)

Fagan, Brian M., *The Journey from Eden, The Peopling of Our World*. London: Thames and Hudson, 1990.

Falchi, G., 'Le régime définitif de la libre circulation et límmigration des pays tiers,' *Droit Social* 2 (1971), pp.17-28.

Farah, T., Al-Salem, F. and Al-Salem, M., 'Alienation and Expatriate Labour in Kuwait', *Journal of South Asian and Middle Eastern Studies* 4 (1980), pp.3-40.

Farmer, E.L., et al., eds. *Comparative History of Civilizations in Asia*. Reading, MA: Addison-Wesley, 1977.

Farmer, R.S.J., 'International Migration', In: R.J.W. Neville and C.J. O'Neill, eds. *The Population of New Zealand. Inter-disciplinary Perspectives*. Auckland, 1979.

Farmer, R.S.J., New Zealand's External Migration Changes in the 1970s. Contributed paper to the International Population Conference, International Union for the Scientific Study of Population, Manila, 1981.

Farmer, R.S.J., The New Zealand Experience. Paper presented at the IUSSP Workshop on Consequences of International Migration. Canberra, July 1984. (Mimeo)

Farmer, R.S.J. and Andrew, T.W., 'Trans-Tasman Migration: A New Zealand Viewpoint', In: I. Pool, ed. *Trans-Tasman Migration*. Hamilton, 1980.

Farnos Morejon, A. and Catasus Cervera, S., 'Las migraciones internacionales', *La población de Cuba*. Havana: OEDEM, 1976. (CICRED series)

Fawcett, J.T., Arnold, F. and Minocha, U., Asian Immigration to the United States: Flows and Processes. Paper prepared for the Conference on Asia-Pacific Immigration to the United States, 20-25 September 1984. Honolulu, East-West Population Institute. (Mimeo)

Fawcett, James T., Carino, Benjamin V. and Arnold, Fred, Asia-Pacific Immigration to the United States: A Conference Report. Honolulu: East-West Population Institute, East-West Center, 1985.

Fellberg, U.C. and Neumann, K.H., et al., 'Typische Konstellationen der Beschäftigung Ausländischer Arbeitnehmer. Ergebnisse einer Cluster-Analyse von Betrieben des Verarbeitenden Geweryes', *Mittbeilungen aus der Arbeitsmarkt und Berufsforschung* 13 (1980), pp.272-92.

Fergany, N., ed. *Foreign Labour in the Arab Gulf States*. Beirut: Centre for Arab Unity Studies, 1983. (Arabic text)

Fergany, N., The Affluent Years Are Over: Emigration and Development in the Yemen Arab Republic. Geneva: ILO, World Employment Programme, 1980. (Working paper 50)

Fernández Robaina, Tomás, *El negro en Cuba 1902-1958*. Havana: Editorial de Ciencias Sociales, 1990.

Ferreira Levy, M., 'Les migrations internationales et la population bresilienne de 1872 à 1972', *La Population de Brasil* (CICRED, 1975).

Ferris, Elizabeth, *Central American Refugees and the Politics of Protection*. New York: Praeger, 1987.

Ferris, Elizabeth, ed. *Refugees and World Politics*. New York: Praeger, 1985.

Field, Simon, *Resettling Refugees: The Lessons of Research*. London: HMSO, 1985.

Findley, S., *Planning for Internal Migration: A Review of Issues and Policies in Developing Countries*. Washington, DC: Bureau of the Census, 1977.

First, R., 'Struktura autoriteta u seoskim domacinstvima', *Sociologija Sela* 7 (1969), pp.53-60.

First-Dilic, R., 'Struktura moci u porodici zapposlene zene', *Sociologija Sela* 15 (1973), pp.79-102.

Fisher, Humphrey J. and Fisher, Allan G.B., *Slavery and Muslim Society in Africa: The Institution in Saharan and Sudanic Africa and the Trans-Saharan Trade*. Garden City: Doubleday, 1971.

Flores, J.T., *Migration and its Impact on Employment and Development. Country Statement: Guam*. Paper presented to the SPC/ILO Conference on Migration, Employment and Development in the South Pacific. Noumea, February 1982.

Florida International University, *Annotated Bibliography on Cubans in the United States: 1960-1976*. Miami, 1977.

Foerster, R.F., *The Italian Emigration of our Times*. New York: Russell & Russell, 1919. (Reprint, Cambridge, MA: Harvard University Press, 1968)

Fogel, Robert and Engerman, Stanley, *Time on the Cross: The Economics of American Negro Slavery*. New York: Little-Brown, 1970.

Foner, N., *Jamaica Farewell*. London: Routledge & Kegan Paul, 1979.

Fontgalland, Santhiapillai Guy de, *Tamils Displaced, Sri Lankans in Exile*. Madras: The Ceylon Refugees and Repatriates Organization, 1987.

Foot, P., *Immigration and Race in British Politics*. Harmondsworth: Penguin Books, 1966.

Forbes, Susan, *Adaptation and Integration of Recent Refugees to the United States*. Washington, DC: RPG, 1985.

Fraginals, Manuel Moreno, Pons, Frank Moya and Engerman, Stanley L., *Between Slavery and Free Labor: The Spanish Speaking Caribbean in the Nineteenth Century*. Baltimore: Johns Hopkins University Press, 1990.

Francis, O.C., 'The Characteristics of Emigrants Just Prior to Changes in British Commonwealth Immigration Policies', *Caribbean in Transition*. Puerto Rico: Institute of Caribbean Affairs, 1965.

Frank, A.G., 'The Development of Underdevelopment', *Monthly Review Press* 18 (1966), pp.17-31.

Frankel, Robert, ed. *Resettlement of Indochinese Refugees in the US: A selected Bibliography*. Washington, DC: Indochinese Refugees Action Center, ORR, Department of Health and Human Services, 1980.

Franz, F., 'Aufenthaltsrechtliche Stellung der ausländischen Arbeiter', In: T. Ansay and V. Gessner, eds. *Gastarbeiter in Gesellschaft und Recht*, pp.31-56. Munich: Beck, 1974.

Freeman, G.P., *Immigrant Labor and Racial Conflict in Industrialized Societies*. Princeton: Princeton University Press, 1979.

Freiburg Ethnographic Studies, *Asiatische Flüchtlinge in der Schweiz: Fragen zur Integration*. Freiburg, Switzerland: Universitätsverlag, 1984.

Friedland, Joan and Rodriguez y Rodriguez, Jesus, *Seeking Safe Ground: The Legal Status of Central American Refugees in Mexico*. San Diego: Mexico-US Law Institute, 1987.

Fuss, Felicia, comp. *Displaced Persons: A Selected Bibliography, 1939-47*. New York: Russell Sage Foundation, 1948.

Gail, A., ed. *Les réfugies en Afrique: Bibliographie Commentée* [Refugees in Africa: Annotated Bibliography]. Abidjan: INADES Documentation, Institut Africaine pour le Développement Economique, 1986.

Galbraith, J.K., *The Nature of Mass Poverty*. Cambridge, MA: Harvard University Press, 1979.

Galeano, L.A., 'Dos alternativas históricas del campesinado paraguayo, migración y colonización (1970-1950). *Revista Paraguaya de Sociología* 15 (1978), pp.115-42.

Gallagher, Dennis, ed. 'Refugees: Issues and Directions', *International Migration Review* 20 (Summer 1986), New York: CMS, 1986.

Galtung, J., 'A Structural Theory of Imperialism', *Journal of Peace Research* 8 (1971), pp.81-117.

Gans, H.J., *The Urban Villagers*. New York: Free Press, 1962.

Garcia y Griego, M., *El volumen de la migración de mexicanos no documentados a los Estados Unidos*. Mexico City: CENIET, 1979.

García Castro, Mary, *Migración laboral femenina en Colombia*. Bogotá: SENALDE, 1981. (Migraciones laborales 16)

Gardiner Harvey, C., *The Japanese and Peru, 1873-1973*. Albuquerque: University of New Mexico Press, 1975.

Garraty, John A. and Gay, Peter, eds. *The Columbia History of the World*. New York: Harper and Row, 1985.

Garrison, V. and Weiss, C.I., 'Dominican Family Networks and United States Immigration Policy: A Case Study', *International Migration Review* 13, no.2 (1979).

Gasarasi, G.P., The Life of a Refugee Settlement: The Case of Muyenzi in Ngara District, Tanzania. University of Dar es Salaam, 1976. (Mimeo)

Gauhar, A., ed. 'The Politics of Exile', *Third World Quarterly* vol. 9, London: Third World Foundation, 1987.

Gay, J.S., 'Basotho Women Migrants: A Case Study', *Southern Africa: The Political Economy of Inequality, IDS Bulletin* 11, no.2 (University of Sussex, 1980).

Geertz, C., *Agricultural Involution*. Berkeley: University of California Press, 1963.

Gemery, Henry A. and Hogendorn, Jan S., eds. *The Uncommon Market: Essays in the Economic History of the Atlantic Slave Trade*. New York: Academic Press, 1979.

Genizi, Haim, *American Apathy: The Plight of Christian Refugees from Nazism*. Jerusalem: Bar-Ilan Press, 1983.

Gerstenmaier, J. and Hamburger, F., 'Bildungswünsche ausländischer Arbeiterkinder-Ergebnisse einer Befragung von Eltern und Kindern', *Soziale Welt* 25 (1974), pp.278-93.

Ghai, Y. and Ghai, D., *The Asian Minorities of East and Central Africa*. London: Minority Rights Group, 1971.

Ghansah, D.K., 'The Volume and Structure of International Migration in Africa', *IUSSP Conference London* (1969).

Gibson, K.D., *International Migration: A Development Option in the South Pacific?* Paper presented to the SPC/ILO Conference on Migration, Employment and Development in the South Pacific. Noumea, February 1982.

Gieselberger, S., *Schwarzbuch: Ausländische Arbeiter*. Frankfurt/Main: Fischer Verlag, 1972.

Gilani, I.S., *Citizens, Slaves, Guest Workers*. Islamabad: Institute of Policy Studies, 1985.

Gilani, I.S., Khan, F. and Munawar, I., *Labor Migration from Pakistan to the Middle East*. Washington, DC: World Bank, 1981.

Gilani, I.S., Overseas Pakistanis: An Overview about the Volume of Migration and its Socio-economic impact on the Home Communities. Paper presented at the Conference on Asian Labor Migration to the Middle East, 19-23 September 1983. Honolulu: East-West Population Institute, 1983.

Gilani, I.S., *Overseas Pakistanis: Profile, Problems, Plans and Proposals*. Pakistan Institute of Public Opinion, 1983. (Migration report 3)

Gilani, I.S., *Returnee Migrants: A Case Study of Pakistani Workers Returning from Overseas*. Pakistan Institute of Public Opinion, 1983. (Migration report 2)

Gilani, Ijaz, *A Strategy for the Overseas Pakistanis: Summary of Findings and Policy Implications of the Research Project on Overseas Pakistanis*. Islamabad: Pakistan Institute of Development Economics, 1983. (Migration report 7)

Gilani, Ijaz, *A Technical Note on the Research Project on Overseas Pakistanis*. Islamabad: Pakistan Institute of Public Opinion, 1983. (Migration report 6)

Gilani, Ijaz, *High Migration Districts: Statistical Profile of Five Districts with High Overseas Migration*. Islamabad: Pakistan Institute of Public Opinion, 1983. (Migration report 4)

Gilani, Ijaz, et al., *Labour Migration from Pakistan to the Middle East and Its Impact on the Domestic Economy*. Islamabad: Pakistan Institute of Development Economics, 1981. (Research report series 126, 127, 128)

Gilani, Ijaz, *Left Behind or Left Out: A Study of the Left Behind Families of Overseas Pakistanis*. Islamabad: Pakistan Institute of Public Opinion, 1983. (Migration report 1)

Gilani, Ijaz, *The Affluent Village: A Study of Five Villages with High Overseas Migration*. Islamabad: Pakistan Institute of Public Opinion, 1983. (Migration report 5)

Gilbert, M., *Atlas of Russian History*. New York: Dorset, 1985.

Gillespie, F. and Browning, J., 'The Effect of Emigration upon Socio-economic Structure: The Case of Paraguay', *International Migration Review* 13 (1979), pp.502-18.

Gitmez, A. and Wilpert, C., Social Networks Among Turkish Migrants in Germany: The Berlin Case - There Are Just No Plain Turks. Paper presented at the Seminar on Formal and Informal Networks and Associations Among Immigrants in Europe. Florence, September 1983.

Gitmez, A.S., Die Rückwanderung der Gastarbeiter. Ankara: METU, 1980. (Research Report)

Gitmez, A.S., Return Migration of Turkish Workers: Effects and Implications. Ankara: METU, 1977. (Research report)

Gitmez, A.S., Yurtdisindan donen iscilerin yeniden uyumlari [Reintegration of Returning Migrants]. Ankara: METU, 1981. (Research report)

Glaser, W., *The Brain Drain: Emigration and Return*. Oxford: Pergamon Press, 1978.

Glaser, W. and Habers, G.G., 'The Migration and Return of Professionals', *International Migration Review* 8 (Summer 1974), pp.227-44.

Glass, R., *Newcomers*. London: Allen & Unwin/Centre for Urban Studies, 1960.

Glick, Clarence E., *Sojurners and Settlers*. Honolulu: University of Hawaii Press, 1980.

Godfrey, N. and Walton, G., eds. *Supplementary Feeding Programmes in Refugee Populations: A Review and Selected Annotated Bibliography*. London: Refugee Health Group, London School of Hygiene and Tropical Medicine, 1986.

Gokdere, U.Y., *Yabanci ulkelere isgucu akimi ve Turk ekonomisi uzerindeki etkileri* [Labor Migration and Its Effects on Turkish Economy]. Ankara: Is Bankasi Publications, 1978.

Golden, R. and McConnell, M., *Sanctuary: the New Underground Railroad*. Maryknoll, NY: Orbis Books, 1986.

Goldlust, J. and Richmond, A.H., 'A Multivariate Model of Immigrant Adaptation', *International Migration Review* 8 (1974), pp.193-225.

Goldlust, J. and Richmond, A.H., 'Cognitive and Linguistic Acculturation of Immigrants in Toronto: A Multivariate Analysis', *Ethnic Studies* 2 (1978), pp.2-17.

Golini, A. and Gesano, G., 'Regional Migration in the Process of Italian Economic Development from 1881 to the Present', In: J. Balán, ed. *Why People Move: Comparative Perspectives on the Dynamics of Internal Migration*. Paris: UNESCO, 1981.

Gonzales-Rothvoss and Gil, Julio, *La emigración española a Iberoamérica*. Madrid, 1979.

Goodwin-Gill, Guy, *The Refugee in International Law*. Oxford: Clarendon Press, 1983.

Gordenker, Leon, *Refugees in International Politics*. London: Croom Helm, 1987.

Gordon, E., 'Analysis of the Impact of Labour Migration on the Lives of Women in Lesotho', *Journal of Development Studies* (London) 17 (1981).

Gordon, E., 'Easing the Plight of Migrant Workers' Families in Lesotho', In: W.R. Böhning, ed. *Black Migration to South Africa*. Geneva: ILO, 1981.

Gorman, R.F., *Coping with Africa's Refugee Burden: A Time for Solutions*. Dordrecht: Martinus Nijhoff, 1987.

Gould, W.T.S., ed. 'International Migration in Tropical Africa: A Bibliographical Review', *International Migration Review* 8, no.3 (1974).

Gould, W.T.S., 'Refugees in Tropical Africa', *International Migration Review* 8, no.3 (1974). (Special edition on international migration in tropical Africa)

Gould, W.T.S. and Prothero, R.M., 'Government Policies Affecting International Migration in Africa', In: R.K. Udo et al., eds. *Population Education Source Book for Sub-Saharan Africa*. London: Heinemann, 1979.

Gómez Jiménez, Alcides and Díaz Mesa, Luz Marina, *La moderna esclavitud. Los indocumentados en Venezuela*. Bogotá: Fines, Editorial La Oveja Negra, 1983.

Grahl-Madsen, Atle, *Territorial Asylum*. Stockholm: Almqvist and Wiksell, 1980.

Grahl-Madsen, Atle, *The Status of Refugees in International Law*. Leiden: A.W. Sijthoff, 1966.

Granotier, B., *Les travailleurs immigrés en France*. Paris: Maspero, 1976.

Grasmuci, Sherri and Pessar, Patricia R., *Between Two Islands. Dominican International Migration*. Berkeley: University of California Press, 1991.

Green, A.G., *Immigration and the Postwar Canadian Economy*. Toronto: Macmillan, 1976.

Greenfield, H.I., *Manpower and the Growth of Producer Services*. New York: Columbia University Press, 1966.

Greenstreet, M., 'Labour Conditions in the Gold Coast during the 1930s with Particular Reference to Migrant Labour and the Mines', *Economic Bulletin of Ghana* 2 (1972).

Gregory, D.D., *La odisea Andaluza: Una emigración intereuropea*. Madrid: Editorial Tecnos, 1978.

Gregory, J.W. and Piche, V., 'African Migration and Peripheral Capitalism', In: W.M.J. van Vinsbergen and H.A. Meilink, eds. *Migration and the Transformation of Modern African Society*. Leiden: African Perspectives, 1981.

Gregory, R.C., *India and East Africa: A History of Race Relations within the British Empire, 1890-1939*. Oxford: Clarendon Press, 1971.

Gulati, I.S. and Mody, A., Remittances of Indian Migrants to the Middle East: An Assessment with Special Reference to Migrants from Kerala State. Centre for Development Studies, 1983. (Working paper 182)

Gulati, L., Impacts of Male Migration to the Middle East on the Family: Some Evidence from Kerala. Paper presented at the Conference on Asian Labor Migration to the Middle East, 19-23 September 1983. Honolulu: East-West Population Institute, 1983.

Gurak, D., Dominicans and Colombians in New York City. Research in Progress. New York: Fordham University Hispanic Research Center, 1982. (Various interim reports)

Gurak, D.T. and Kritz, M.M., 'Dominican and Colombian Women in New York City: Household Structure and Employment Patterns', *Migration Today* 10, nos. 3 & 4 (1983).

Gutierrez, M., Jamail, M. and Stolp, C., eds. *Sourcebook on Central American Refugee Policy: A Bibliography*. Austin: Central American Refugee Policy Research Project, Lyndon Baines Johnson School of Public Affairs, University of Texas, 1985.

Gwan, E.A., 'Types, Processes, and Policy Implications of Various Migrations in Western Cameroon', *The Dynamics of Migration: Internal Migration and Migration and Fertility*. Washington, DC: Smithsonian Institution, 1976. (Occasional monograph series 5, no. 1)

Harley, J.B. and Woodward, David, eds. *The History of Cartography*. Chicago: University of Chicago Press, 1988.

Haberman, Clyde, 'The Kurds: In Flight Once Again', *New York Times Sunday Magazine* (May 5, 1991), pp.32-37, 52-54.

Habermas, J., *Legitimation Crisis*. Translated by Thomas A. McCarthy. Boston: Beacon Press, 1975.

Hagmann, H., *Les travailleurs étrangers, chance et tourment de la Suisse*. Lausanne: Payot, 1966.

Haines, D., Rutherford, D. and Thomas, P., 'Family and Community among Vietnamese Refugees', *International Migration Review* 15 (1981), pp.310-19.

Haines, D. and Yinh, A., eds. *Refugee Resettlement in the US: An Annotated Bibliography on the Adjustment of Cuba, Soviet and South-east Asian Refugees*. Washington, DC: ORR for Dept. of Health and Human Services, 1981.

Hakovirta, H. and Nordbergh, D., eds. *Third World Conflicts and Refugeeism: Dimensions, Dynamics and Trends of the World Refugee Problem*. Helsinki: Finnish Society of Science and Letters, n.d.

Hall, S., et al., *Policing the Crisis*. London: Macmillan, 1978.

Halladay, E., *The Emergent Continent: Africa in the 19th Century*. London: Ernest Benn, 1972.

Halliday, F., 'The Gulf Between Two Revolutions: 1958-75', In: T. Niblick, ed. *Social and Economic Development in the Arab Gulf*, pp.210-38. London: Croom Helm, 1980.

Hamilton, T., 'Swiss Reject Bid to Reduce Aliens', *New York Times* (8 June 1970), p.11.

Hammar, T., *The First Immigrant Election*. Stockholm: Commission on Immigration Research, 1977.

Hammer, P.C., ed. *Colonialism and Migration: Indentured Labour Before and After Slavery*. Dordrecht: Martinus Nijhoff, 1986.

Hamond, R.E. and Hendricks, G.L., comp. *South East Asian Refugee Youth: An Annotated Bibliography*. Minneapolis: South East Asian Refugee Studies, Center for Urban and Regional Affairs, University of Minnesota, 1988.

Hamrell, Sven, ed. *Refugee Problems in Africa*. Uppsala: Scandinavian Institute of African Studies, 1967.

Hannum, H., *The Right to Leave and Return in International Law and Practice*. Dordrecht: Martinus Nijhoff, 1987.

Hansen, Art and Oliver-Smith, A., eds. *Involuntary Migration and Resettlement: The Problems and Responses of Dislocated People*. Boulder: Westview Press, 1982.

Harney, David W., ed. *Refugees as Immigrants: Cambodians, Laotians, and Vietnamese in America*. Totowa: Rowman and Littlefield, 1988.

Harrell-Bond, Barbara and Honahan, Laila, eds. 'The Sociology of Involuntary Migration', *Current Sociology* 36 (Summer 1982).

Harrison, B. and Sum, A., 'The Theory of 'Dual' or Segmented Labor Markets', *Journal of Development Economics* 5 (1979), pp.215-31.

Hartung, Gerald and Patterson, David, eds. *Disease in African History*. Durham: Duke University Press, 1978.

Harvey, M.E., 'Interregional Migration in Eastern Africa', In: R.M. Prothero and L.A. Kosinski, eds. *People on the Move*. London: Methuen, 1975.

Hawkins, F., *Canada and Immigration: Public Policy and Public Concern*. Montreal: McGill-Queen's University Press, 1972.

Hawkins, F., 'Canadian Immigration: A New Land and a New Approach to Management', *International Migration Review* 11 (1977), pp.77-94.

Hawkins, F., 'Canadian Immigration Policy and Management', *International Migration Review* 8 (1974), pp.141-54.

Hawkins, F., *Critical Years in Immigration, Australia and Canada*. Toronto: McGill University Press, 1989.

Hawkins, F., 'Immigration Law and Management in the Major Receiving Countries Outside of the Arab Region', *International Migration in the Arab World* (1982), Beirut: United Nations Economic Commission for Western Asia.

Hawkins, F., 'Multiculturalism in Two Countries: The Canadian and Australian Experience', *Journal of Canadian Studies* 17 (1982), pp.64-80.

Hayase, T., 'Overseas Chinese in Southeast Asia', *The Oriental Economist* (Tokyo) 33 (1965), pp.580-4.

Headrick, Daniel R., *The Invisible Weapon: Telecommunications and International Politics 1851-1945*. New York: Oxford University Press, 1991.

Headrick, D.R., *The Tools of Empire: Technology and European Imperialism in the Nineteenth Century*. New York: Oxford University Press, 1981.

Hecker, U. and Schmidt-Hackenberg, D., *Bildungs und Beschäftigungssituation ausländischer Jugendlicher in der Bundesrepublik Deutschland. Teil I: Grunddaten der Befragund* 30. West Berlin: Bundesinstitut für Berufsbildung, 1980.

Heinl, Robert Debs, Jr. and Heinl, Nancy Gordon, *Written in Blood: The Story of the Haitian People 1492-1971*. Boston: Houghton Mifflin, 1978.

Heisel, D.F., 'International Migration', In: *Encyclopedia of Population*. Vol. 1. Edited by J.A. Ross. New York: Macmillan, 1982.

Heisel, D.F., 'Theories of International Migration', *International Migration in the Arab World*. Beirut: United Nations Economic Commission for Western Asia, 1982.

Helweg, A.W., 'Emigrants Remittances: Their Nature and Impact on a Punjabi Village', *New Community* 10, no.3 (1983).

Hendricks, Glenn L., *The Dominican Diaspora*. New York: Teachers College Press, 1974.

Hendricks, Glenn L., Downing, Bruce T. and Deinard, Amos, eds. *The Hmong in Transition*. Staten Island: Center for Migration Studies, 1986.

Hepple, R., *Race, Jobs and the Law in Britain*. Harmondsworth: Penguin Books, 1968.

Hiemenz, U. and Schatz, K.W., *Transfer of Employment Opportunities as an Alternative to the International Migration of Workers: The Case of the Federal Republic of Germany*. Geneva: ILO, World Employment Programme, 1976. (Research working paper)

Higham, J., *Strangers in the Land: Patterns of American Nativism, 1860-1925*. New York: Atheneum, 1969.

Hilton, A., *The Kingdom of Kongo*. London: Oxford University Press, 1983.

Hinawaeola, M., The Case of Papua New Guinea. Paper presented to the Third Asian and Pacific Population Conference, Colombo. (Mimeo)

Hinderink, J. and Tempelman, G.J., 'Rural Change and Types of Migration in Northern Ivory Coast', In: W.M.J. van Vinsbergen and H.A. Meilink, eds. *Migration and the Transformation of Modern African Society*. Leiden: African Perspectives, 1978.

Hirschman, A.O., *The Strategy of Economic Development*. New Haven: Yale University Press, 1958.

Hirschman, Albert, *Exit, Voice and Loyalty*. Cambridge, MA: Harvard University Press, 1970.

Hirschon, Renén, *Heirs of the Greek Catastrophe: The Social Life of Asia Minor Refugees in Piraeus.* Oxford: Oxford University Press, 1989.

Hobson, J.A., *Imperialism.* Ann Arbor: University of Michigan Press, 1971.

Hoepfner, K.H. and Huber, M., Regulating International Migration in the Interest of the Developing Countries. With Particular Reference to Mediterranean Countries. Geneva, ILO, World Employment Programme, International Migration for Employment Project, 1978. (WEP 2-26 working paper 21)

Hoffman-Nowotny, Hans-Joachim, *Migration: Ein Beitrag zu einer soziologischen Erklärung.* Stuttgart: Enke, 1970.

Hoffman-Nowotny, Hans-Joachim, 'Sociological and Demographic Aspects of the Changing Status of Migrant Women in Europe', *Zeitschrift für Bevolkerungswissenchaft* 2 (1977), pp.3-22.

Hoffmann-Nowotny, Hans-Joachim, *Soziologie des Fremdarbeitersystem: Eine theoretische und empirische Analyse am Beispiel der Schweiz.* Stuttgart: Enke Verlag, 1973.

Hoffman-Nowotny, Hans-Joachim and Hondrich, Karl-Otto, *Auslander in der Bundesrepublik Deutschland und in der Schweiz: Segregation und Integration: Eine vergleichende Untersuchung.* Frankfurt/Main: Campus Verlag, 1982.

Hoffmann-Nowotny, Hans-Joachim and Killias, M., 'Switzerland', In: R.E. Krane, ed. *International Labor Migration in Europe*, pp.45-62. New York: Praeger, 1979.

Holborn, Louise W., *Refugees: A Problem of Our Time.* Metuchen, NJ: Scarecrow Press, 1975.

Holborn, Louise W., *The International Refugee Organization: Its History and Work 1946-1952.* Oxford: Oxford University Press, 1956.

Holtgrugge, H., *Türkische Familien in der Bundesrepublik. Erziehungsvorstellungen und familiale Rollen und Autoritätsstruktur.* Duisburg: Verlag der Sozialwissenschaftlichen Kooperative, 1975.

Home Office, Control of Immigration Statistics. London: HMSO, 1967-79.

Honekopp, E. and Ullman, H., 'The Status of Immigrant Workers in the Federal Republic of Germany', In: E.J. Thomas, ed. *Immigrant Workers in Europe and the Question of their Legal Status.* 1982. (Mimeo)

Hooper, A. and Huntsman, J., 'A Demographic History of the Tokelau Islands', *Journal of Polynesian History* 82, no.4 (1973).

Horwich, I., *Immigration and Labor.* New York: Putnam, 1912.

Hourani, A., *A History of the Arab People.* Cambridge, MA: Harvard Belknap Press, 1991.

Hourani, A., *Syria and Lebanon.* Oxford: Oxford University Press, 1968.

Hourani, A. and Shahady, I., eds. *The Lebanese and the World, A Century of Emigration.* New York: St. Martin's Press, 1991.

Howe, K.R., *Where the Waves Fall: A New South Sea Islands History from First Settlement to Colonial Rule.* Sydney: George Allen & Unwin, 1984.

Howlett, D., 'Economic Aspects of Population Change and Development in the Small Island Countries of the ESCAP/SPC Region', In: ESCAP, *Report and Working Papers of the ESCAP/SPC Conference Seminar on Small Island Countries of the ESCAP/SPC Region,* Noumea, 15-19 February 1982.

Hucker, J., 'The New Immigration in Canada: Impact and Management', In: R. Bryce-Laporte, ed. *Sourcebook on the New Immigration.* pp.203-11. New Brunswick: Transaction, 1980.

Hughes, R., *The Fatal Shore, The Epic of Australia's Founding.* New York: Knopf, 1986.

Hugo, C.J., 'New Conceptual Approaches to Migration in the Context of Urbanization: A Discussion based on Indonesian Experience', In: P.A. Morrison, ed. *Population Movements: Their Forms and Functions in Urbanization and Development.* Liège: Ordina, 1981.

Hugo, G.J., 'Implications of the Imbalance in Age and Sex Composition of Sub-areas as a Consequence of Migration', *International Population Conference* 2 (1981), Manila: International Union for the Scientific Study of Population.

Human, Louis, ed. *The International Bill of Rights.* New York: Columbia University Press, 1981.

Human Rights Internet Reporter, 'Africa: Human Rights Directory and Bibliography', *Human Rights Internet Reporter* 4 (1988/9).

Humana, Charles, *World Human Rights Guide.* New York: Facts on File, 1986.

Hveem, H., 'The Global Dominance System: Notes on a Theory of Global Political Economy', *Journal of Peace Research* 10 (1973), pp.319-40.

Ibrahim, S.E., *The New Arab Social Order: A Study of the Impact of Oil Wealth.* Boulder: Westview Press, 1982.

ICM (Intergovernmental Committee for Migration), Worldwide Situation and Problems of Undocumented Migration; and the Role of Planned Migration of Qualified Personnel from Developed to Developing Countries. Paper prepared for the Expert Group on Population Distribution, Migration and Development, Hammamet, Tunisia, March 1983. (Mimeo)

ICRC (International Committee of the Red Cross) and Henry Dunant Institute, *Bibliography of International Humanitarian Law Applicable in Armed Conflicts.* 2nd ed. Geneva, 1987.

IIDH (Instituto Interamericano de Derechos Humanos), *Refugiados: Boletin Documental 1.* San Jose, Costa Rica: IIDH, 1989.

ILGWU (International Ladies Garment Workers Union), *The Chinatown Garment Industry Study.* New York: Local 23-25 and the New York Skirt and Sportswear Association, 1983. (Prepared by Abeles, Swartz, Hackel & Silverblatt, Inc.)

Iliffe, L., 'Estimated Fertility Rates of Asian and West Indian Immigrant Women in Britain', *Journal of Biosocial Science* 10 (1978), pp.189-97.

ILO (International Labour Organisation), *Employment, Status and Conditions of Non-national Workers in Africa.* Geneva: ILO, 1971.

ILO, *International Labour Organisation Migration Laws and Treaties.* Vol. 1. Geneva: ILO, 1928.

ILO, *International Migration, 1945-57.* Geneva: ILO, 1959.

ILO, *Migrant Workers. Summary of Reports on Conventions Nos. 97 and 143 and Recommendations Nos. 86 and 151.* Part 1 and 2. Geneva: ILO, 1980.

ILO, Seminario regional tripartito sobre la situación de los trabajadores immigrantes en Sud-América. Buenos Aires: ILO: 1974. (Working paper 1/2)

ILO, 'The Implications of Contract Migration to West Asia', *Selected Papers, Third Asian and Pacific Population Conference.* Colombo, September 1982, pp.238-50. New York: United Nations, 1984.

ILO, *Tripartite Regional Seminar on the Situation of Migrant Workers in West Africa.* Geneva: ILO, 1975.

Independent Commission on International Humanitarian Issues, *Refugees: Dynamics of Displacement.* London: Zed Books, 1986.

Indochinese Center of Material Development and Training, ed. *Annotated Bibliography of Indochinese Materials.* Arlington Heights: Bilingual Education Service Center (BESC), 1979.

Indochinese Material Center, US Office of Education, *Bibliography on Indochinese Education Materials.* Kansas City, MO, 1979.

Indra, Doreen, ed. *South East Asian Refugee Settlement in Canada: A Research Bibliography.* Ottawa: Carleton University Canadian Asian Studies Association, 1984.

Inkori, Joseph E., ed. *Forced Migration: The Impact of the Export Slave Trade in African Societies.* London: Hutchinson, 1981.

Inman, S.G., 'Refugee Settlements in Latin America', *Annals of the American Academy of Political and Social Sciences* (1939), pp.183-93.

Institute of International Education, *Open Doors: Survey of International Students in the US.* New York: IIE, 1991.

Institute on Pluralism and Group Identity, *The Ethnocultural Factor in Mental Health: A Literature Review and Bibliography.* New York: Institute on Pluralism and Group Identity, American Jewish Committee, 1977.

International Council of Voluntary Agencies, *Assistance to African Refugees by Voluntary Organizations.* Geneva, 1984.

International Defence and Aid Fund, *South Africa 'Resettlement': the New Violence to Africans.* London: Christian Action, 1969.

International Institute for Strategic Studies, *The Military Balance 1990-1991.* London: International Institute for Strategic Studies, 1990.

International Refugee Integration Resource Centre, *International Bibliography of Refugee Literature.* Geneva, 1985.

Iqbal, M. and Khan, M.F., *Economic Implications of the Return Flow of Immigrants from the Middle East: A Preliminary Study.* Pakistan Institute of Development Economics, 1981. (Research report series 132)

Irwin, Graham W., ed. *Africans Abroad: A Documentary Survey of the Black Diaspora in Asia, Latin America, and the Caribbean.* New York: , 1977.

Isaac, J., *Economics of Migration.* New York: Oxford University Press, 1947.

Isajiw, W.W., *Ethnic Identity Retention*. Toronto: Centre for Urban and Community Studies, University of Toronto, 1981. (Research paper 125)

Isajiw, W.W. and Makabe, T., *Socialization as a Factor in Ethnic Identity Retention*. Toronto: Centre for Urban and Community Studies, University of Toronto, 1982. (Research paper 134)

Jackson, John Archer, *The Irish in Britain*. London: Routledge & Kegan Paul, 1976.

Jaeger, G., 'Refugee Asylum: Policy and Legislative Developments', *International Migration Review* 15 (1981), pp.53-4.

Jain, R.K., *South Indians on the Plantation Frontier in Malaya*. New Haven: Yale University Press, 1969.

James, D.D. and Evans, J.S., 'Conditions of Employment and Income Distribution in Mexico as Incentives for Mexican Migration to the United States', *International Migration Review* 13, no.1 (1979).

Jarrar, Najeh and Seddon, David, eds. 'Palestinian Economy and Society, and Palestinian Refugees: A Preliminary Bibliography', *Current Sociology* 36 (1988), pp.115-153.

Jayasuriaya, L., 'Multiculturalism: Fact, Policy and Rhetoric', In: M.E. Poole, et al., eds. *Australia in Transition, Culture and Life Possibilities*, pp.23-34. Sydney: Harcourt Brace Jovanovich, 1985.

Jelin, E., Labour Migration and Female Labour Force in Latin America. Paper prepared for the Conference on Women and Development, Wellesley College, 2-6 June 1976.

Jenness, R.A., 'Canadian Migration and Immigration Patterns and Government Policy', *International Migration Review* 8 (1974), pp.5-22.

Jenschke, B., Arbeit und Beruf - Chancen und Grenzen der Eingliederung von Ausländern in Berlin, West Berlin, 1982. (Mimeo)

Jiménez, Gonzalo, *Colombianos en Venezuela: los que nunca volvieron*. Bogotá: Editorial Pluma, 1980.

Johnson, K.F. and Williams, M.W., *Illegal Aliens in the Western Hemisphere: Political and Economic Factors*. New York: Praeger, 1981.

Joly, Daniéle, ed. *Refugees In Britain: An Annotated Bibliography (9)*. Warwick: Centre for Research in Ethnic Relations, 1988.

Jones, K. and Smith, A., *The Economic Impact of Commonwealth Immigration*. London: Cambridge University Press, 1970.

Jones, P.C., La migración internacional de El Salvador, 1950-2000. San Salvador: El Salvador, Ministerio de Planificación y Coordinación del Desarrollo Económico y Social, Unidad de Población y Recursos Humanos, 1976. (Mimeo)

Jones, P.N., 'The Distribution and Diffusion of the Coloured Population in England and Wales, 1961-71', *Transactions of the Institute of British Geographers* 3 and 4 (1978).

Jones, Peter, *Organización y puesta en marcha del sistema de estadísticas continuas migratorias internacionales*. Bogotá: SENALDE, 1980. (Migraciones laborales 6)

Joreskog, K.G. and Wold, H., The ML and PLS Techniques for Modeling with Latent Variables: Comparative Aspects. Paper presented at the Conference on Systems Under Indirect Observation (Causality/Structure/Prediction), Centre de Rencontres, Cartigny, University of Geneva. Geneva, October 1979.

Jupp, James, ed. *The Australian People: An Encyclopedia of the Nation, its People, and their Origins*. North Ryde, NSW, Australia: Angus & Robertson Publishers, 1988.

Kabwegyere, T., 'Asian Question in Uganda', *East African Journal* 9 (1972), pp.10-13.

Kalbach, W.E., *Ethnic Residential Segregation and its Significance for the Individual in an Urban Setting*. Toronto: Centre for Urban and Community Studies, University of Toronto, 1981. (Research paper 124)

Kalbach, W.E., 'Growth and Distribution of Canada's Ethnic Populations, 1871-1971', In: L. Driedger, ed. *The Canadian Ethnic Mosaic*, pp.82-104. Toronto: McClelland & Stewart, 1978.

Kalbach, W.E., *The Impact of Immigration on Canada's Population*. Ottawa: Dominion Bureau of Statistics, 1970.

Kallen, E. and Kelner, M., *Ethnicity, Opportunity and Successful Entrepreneurship in Canada*. Toronto: Institute for Behavioral Research, York University, 1983.

Kallen, H.M., *Culture and Democracy in the United States*. New York: Arno Press, 1970.

Kane-Berman, J., *Contract Labour in South West Africa*. Johannesburg: South African Institute of Race Relations, 1972.

Kay, Diana, *Chileans in Exile: Private Struggles, Public Lives*. London: Macmillan, 1987.

Kay, G., 'South-Central Africa: European Settlements and Economic Development', In: R.M. Prothero, ed. *A Geography of Tropical Africa*. London: Routledge & Kegan Paul, 1969.

Kayser, B., *Cyclically Determined Homeward Flows of Migrant Workers*. Paris: OECD, 1972.

Kayser, B., *Manpower Movements and Labour Markets*. Paris: OECD, 1971.

Keegan, John, and Wheatcroft, Andrew, *Zones of Conflict: An Atlas of Future Wars*. New York: Simon and Schuster, 1986.

Keely, C., *Asian Worker Migration to the Middle East*. New York: The Population Council, 1980. (Centre for Policy Studies working paper)

Keely, C., 'Counting the Uncountable Estimate of Undocumented Aliens in the United States', *Population and Development Review* 3 (1977), pp.473-81.

Keely, C., *Global Refugee Policy: The Case for a Development-oriented Strategy*. New York: The Population Council, 1981.

Keely, C., 'The Development of United States Immigration Policy since 1965', *Journal of International Affairs* 33, no.2 (1979).

Keely, C., *US Immigration: A Policy Analysis*. New York: The Population Council, 1979.

Keely, C. and Kraly, E.P., 'Recent Net Immigration to the US: Its Impact on Population Growth and Native Fertility', *Demography*, 15 (1978), pp.267-83.

Keller, Stephen L., *Uprooting and Social Change: The Role of Refugees in Development*. Delhi: Manohar, 1975.

Kennedy, E.M., 'Refugee Act of 1980', *International Migration Review* 15 (1981), pp.141-56.

Kennedy, J.C., 'Refugees in Africa: The Continuing Challenge', *World Refugee Survey 1982*. New York: United States Committee for Refugees, 1982.

Kent, Randolph, *The Anatomy of Disaster Relief: The International Network in Action*. London: Pinter Publishers, 1987.

Khafagy, F., 'Socio-economic Impact of Emigration from a Gaza Village', In: A. Richards and P.L. Martin, eds. *Migration, Mechanization and Agricultural Labour Markets in Egypt*, pp.135-58. Boulder: Westview Press, 1984.

Khoury, N.A., 'The Politics of Intra-regional Migration in the Arab World', *Journal of South Asian and Middle Eastern Studies* 6 (1982), pp.3-20.

Kibreab, G., *Reflections on the African Refugee Problem*. Uppsala: Scandinavian Institute of African Studies, 1983. (Research report 67)

Kibreab, Gaim, *African Refugees: Reflections on the African Refugee Problem*. Trenton: Red Sea Press, 1985.

Kibreab, Gaim, *Refugees and Development in Africa: The Case of Eritrea*. Trenton: Red Sea Press, 1987.

Kilson, Martin L., 'Whither Integration?', *Economic Impact* 17 (1977), pp.21-6.

Kilson, Martin L. and Rotberg, Robert I., eds. *The African Diaspora: Interpretive Essays*. London: Oxford University Press, 1976.

Kim, S., Contract Migration in the Republic of Korea. Geneva: ILO, International Migration for Employment Project, 1982. (Working paper 4)

Kindelberger, C.P., *Europe's Post-war Growth: The Role of Labor Supply*. Cambridge, MA: Harvard University Press, 1967.

King, Russell, ed. *Return Migration and Regional Economic Problems*. London: Croom Helm, 1986.

Kiple, Kenneth F., *Blacks in Colonial Cuba 1774-1899*. Gainesville: University of Florida Press, 1976.

Kiple, Kenneth F., *The Caribbean Slave: A Biological History*. New York: Cambridge University Press, 1984.

Kiribati, Country Statement. SPC/ILO Conference on Migration, Employment and Development in the South Pacific. Noumea, 1982. (Mimeo)

Kirwan, F.X., 'Impact of Labour Migration on the Jordanian Economy', *International Migration Review* 15 (1981), pp.671-95.

Kjurciev, Alexandar, Contribution of Workers' Remittances to Development. Solicited paper presented to Seventh World Congress of the International Economic Association, Madrid, 5-9 September 1983.

Klee, E., *Gastarbeiter: Analysen und Berichte*. Frankfurt/Main: Suhrkamp, 1972.

Klein, Herbert S., *Slavery in the Americas: A Comparative Study of Virginia and Cuba*. Chicago: University of Chicago Press, 1967.

Klein, Herbert S., *The Middle Passage: Comparative Studies in the Atlantic Slave Trade*. Princeton: Princeton University Press, 1978.

Knight, D., *Refugees: Africa's Challenge*. London: Christian Aid, 1978.

Knight, Franklin W., *The Caribbean, The Genesis of a Fragmented Nationalism*. New York: Oxford University Press, 1990.

Knight, Franklin W. and Palmer, Colin A., eds. *The Modern Caribbean*. Chapel Hill: University of North Carolina Press, 1989.

Knowles, L.C.A., *Economic Development of the British Overseas Empire*. London: Routledge & Kegan Paul, 1936.

Knudsen, John, *Boat People in Transit*. Bergen: Migration Project, University of Bergen, n.d.

Knudsen, John, *Vietnamese Survivors: Processes Involved in Refugee Coping and Adaptation*. Bergen: Migration Project, University of Bergen, 1988.

Koelstra, R. and Simon, G., 'France', In: R.E. Krane, ed. *International Labor Migration in Europe*, pp.133-44. New York: Praeger, 1979.

Korale, R.B.M., Migration for Employment to the Middle East: Its Demographic and Socio-economic Effects on Sri Lanka. Paper presented at the Conference on Asian Labor Migration to the Middle East, 19-23 September 1983. Honolulu: East-West Population Institute, 1983.

Korner, H., Return Migration: From Federal Republic of Germany. First European Conference on International Migration, ISA Seminar, Rome, 11-14 November. (Mimeo)

Kosack, G., 'Migrant Women: The Move to Western Europe - A Step Towards Emancipation', *Race and Class*, 17 (1976), pp.27-33.

Kosinski, L.A. and Clarke, J.I., 'African Population Redistribution Trends, Patterns and Policies', In: J.I. Clarke and L.A. Kosinski, eds. *Redistribution of Population in Africa*. London: Heinemann, 1982.

Kowet, D.K., *Land, Labour Migration and Politics in Southern Africa: Botswana, Lesotho and Swaziland*. Uppsala: Scandinavian Institute of African Studies, 1978.

Krallert-Sattler, G., ed. *Kommentierte Bibliographie zum Flüchtlings- und Vertriebenenproblem in der Bundesrepublik Deutschland, in Österreich und in der Schweiz*. Vienna: William Braumüller, 1989.

Krell, Eitinger and R., eds. *Psychological and Medical Effects of Concentration Camps and Related Persecutions on Survivors of the Holocaust*. Vancouver: University of British Columbia Press, 1985.

Kritz, M.M., 'The Impact of International Migration on Venezuelan Demographic and Social Structure', *International Migration Review* 9 (1975), pp.513-43.

Kritz, Mary, ed. *Migraciones internacionales en las Américas*. Vol. 1, No. 1. Caracas: Centro de Estudios de Pastoral y Asistencia Migratoria (CEPAM), 1980.

Kritz, Mary, Socio-economic Issues Arising from Immigration in Receiving Countries. Solicited paper presented at the Seventh World Congress of the International Economic Association, Madrid, 5-8 September 1983.

Kritz, M.M. and Gurald, D.T., 'International Migration Trends in Latin America: Research and Data Survey', *International Migration Review* 13 (1979), pp.407-27.

Kritz, M.M., Keely, C.B. and Tomasi, S.M., *Global Trends in Migration*. New York: Center for Migration Studies, 1981.

Kubat, D., ed. *The Politics of Migration Policies*. New York: Centre for Migration Studies, 1979.

Kudat, A., et al., *International and External Migration Effects on the Experience of Foreign Workers in Europe*. West Berlin: Wissenschaftszentrum Berlin, 1976.

Kudat, A., 'Pilot Study of Return Migration', *Migration and Development Information Bulletin* 3 (1977), pp.22-6.

Kudat, A., *Stability and Change in the Turkish Family at Home and Abroad*. West Berlin: Wissenschaftszentrum Berlin, 1975.

Kudat, A. and Wilpert, C., et al., *International Labour Migration: A Description of the Preliminary Findings of the West Berlin Migrant Worker Survey*. West Berlin: Wissenschaftszentrum Berlin, 1974.

Kuepper, W.G., Lackey, G.L. and Swinnerton, E.N., *Ugandan Asians in Great Britain: Forced Migration and Social Absorption*. London: Croom Helm, 1975.

Kuhlman, T., Ibrahim, S. and Kok, W., *Refugees and Regional Development: Final Report of the Research Project: Eritreans in Kassala*. Khartoum, 1987.

Kumekpor, T. and Looky, S.I., 'External Migration in Togo', In: S. Amin, ed. *Modern Migrations in Western Africa*. London: Oxford University Press/International African Institute, 1974.

Kunz, E.F., *The Intruders: Refugee Doctors in Australia*. Canberra: Australian National University Press, 1975.

Kunz, Egon F., *Displaced Persons: Calwell's New Australians*. Sydney: Australian National University Press, 1988.

Kuper-d'Alessandro, A., *Los movimientos migratorios. El caso de las inmigraciones en Venezuela*. Valencia: Universidad de Carabobo, 1982.

Lambert, T., *Crime, Police and Race Relations*. London: Oxford University Press, 1970.

Lanphier, G.M., 'Canada's Response to Refugees', *International Migration Review* 15 (1981), pp.113-30.

Lattes, A., *Acerca de los patrones recientes de movilidad territorial de la población en el mundo*. Buenos Aires: CENEP, 1983. (Cuaderno de CENEP 27)

Lawless, Richard and Monahan, Laila, eds. *War and Refugees: The Western Sahara Conflict*. London: Pinter Publishers, 1987.

Lebon, A. and Falchi, G., 'New Developments in Intra-European Migration since 1974', *International Migration Review* 14 (1980), pp.539-79.

Lebon, A., 'Feminisation de la main-d'oeuvre étrangère', *Hommes et migrations* 963 (February 1979), pp.27-33.

Lee, E., 'A Theory of Migration', *Demography* 3 (1966), pp.47-57.

Leiserson, W.M., *Adjusting Immigrant and Industry*. New York: Harper and Row, 1924.

Lenin, V.I., *Imperialism, The Highest Stage of Capitalism*. New York: International Publishers, 1969.

Leoetti, I. and Levi, F., *Femmes et immigrées*. Paris: La Documentation Française, 1979.

Lesotho, Kingdom of, *Third Five Year Development Plan, 1981/84-1984/85*. Maseru: Central Planning and Development Office, 1980.

Letcher, J., 'The Political Refugee in Buenos Aires: A Few Psycho-social Perspectives', *Migration News* (1977).

Levi, F., 'Modeles et pratiques en changement', *Ethnologie française* 7, no.3 (1977).

Levine, Barry B., ed. *The Caribbean Exodus*. New York: Praeger, 1987.

Levy, B.S. and Sussett, D.C., *Years of Horror, Days of Hope: Responding to the Cambodian Refugee Crisis*. New York: Associate Faculty Press, 1987.

Lewis, John P., Promoting Positive North-South Interdependence and Adjustment in the Medium Term, in a Context of Nation-state Politics. Solicited paper presented to the Seventh World Congress of the International Economic Association, Madrid, 5-9 September 1983.

Ley, K., *Frauen in der Emigration: Eine soziologische Untersuchung der Lebens-und Arbeitssituation italienischer Frauen in der Schweiz*. Frauenfeld: Huber Verlag, 1979.

Library of Congress, European Affairs Division, *Displaced Persons Analytical Bibliography*. Washington, DC: US Government Printing House, 1950.

Lifu, K.G., Country Statement - Papua New Guinea. Paper presented to the SPC/ILO Conference on Migration, Employment and Development, Noumea, 1982. (Mimeo)

Light, Ivan, *Ethnic Enterprise in America: Business and Welfare Among Chinese, Japanese, and Blacks*. Berkeley: University of California Press, 1972.

Lim, L.L., Labour Shortages in the Malaysian Rural Agricultural Sector: A Search for Explanations and Solutions. Seminar paper read to the Department of Economics, Australian National University. Canberra: ANU, 1982.

Lim, Linda Y. and Gosling, Peter L.A., eds. *The Chinese in Southeast Asia*. 2 vols. Singapore: Maruzen Asia, 1983.

Lippmen, L. and Diaz-Briquets, S., 'Latin America and Caribbean Migration: A Regional View', *Intercam* (July 1981).

Livingstone, I., *Rural Development, Employment and Incomes in Kenya*. Addis Ababa: ILO/JASPA, 1981.

Loescher, G. and Monahan, L., eds. *Refugees and International Relations*. Oxford: Oxford University Press, 1989.

Loescher, G. and Scanlan, J., *Calculated Kindness: Refugees and America's Half Open Door 1945-Present*. New York: Free Press, 1986.

Lomes, G.B., *Census 1971: The Coloured Population of Great Britain*. London: The Runnymede Trust, 1974.

Lorimer, J.G., *Gazetteer of the Persian Gulf, Oman and Central Arabia*. Calcutta: Government of India, 1908-15.

Lovejoy, Paul E., 'The Volume of the Atlantic Slave Trade: A Synthesis', *Journal of African History* 22 (1982), p.479-502.

Lovejoy, Paul, *Transformation in Slavery: A History of Slavery in Africa*. New York: Cambridge University Press, 1983.

Low, A.R.C., Migration and Agricultural Development in Swaziland: A Micro-economic Analysis. Geneva: ILO, World Employment Programme, 1977. (Research working paper, mimeo)

Lucas, D. and Waddell-Wood, P., 'Population Policies of the Small Island Countries of the ESCAP/SPC Region', In: ESCAP, *Report and Working Papers of the ESCAP/SPC Conference Seminar of Small Island Countries of the ESCAP/SPC Region*, Noumea, 15-19 February 1982.

Lutz, V., 'Some Structural Aspects of the Southern Problem: The Complementary of 'Emigration' and Industrialisation', *Quarterly Review* (1961), Rome: Banca Nazionale del Lavaro.

Lytle, E.E., ed. *Palestinian Refugees: A selected Bibliography*. Bloomington: Indiana University, 1976.

Mabogunje, A.L., *Regional Mobility and Resource Development in West Africa*. Montreal: McGill-Queen's University Press, 1972.

Mabogunje, A.L., Research Priorities for Population Redistribution Politics in Africa South of the Sahara. Paper prepared for the Third IRG Workshop on Research Priorities for Population Policy. Nairobi, 6-8 September, 1978.

Macalister-Smith, Peter, *International Humanitarian Assistance: Disaster Relief Action in International Law and Organization*. Dordrecht: Martinus Nijhoff, 1985.

MacDonald, I., *Race Relations: The New Law*. London: Butterworth, 1972.

Macheret, A., *L'immigration étrangère en Suisse à l'heure de l'integration européenne*. Geneva: George & Cie, 1969.

Machlup, F., *The Production and Distribution of Knowledge in the United States*. Princeton: Princeton University Press, 1962.

Mackie, J.A.C., ed. *The Chinese in Indonesia*. Singapore: Heinemann, 1976.

Madhaven, M.C., 'Indian Emigrants: Numbers, Characteristics, and Economic Impact', *Population and Development Review* 11 (1985), pp.457-81.

Mafeje, A., The Fallacy of 'Dual Economies' Revisited - A Case for East, Central and South Africa. The Hague: Institute of Social Studies, 1973.

Maillat, D., *Les effets économiques de l'emploi des travailleurs étrangère: le cas de la Suisse*. Paris, OECD, 1973.

Maillat, D., 'The Economic Effects of Migrants: The Case of Switzerland', In: W.R. Böhning and D. Maillat, eds. *The Effects of the Employment of Foreign Workers,* pp.111-49. Paris: OECD, 1974.

Maillat, D., Jeanrenaud, C. and Widmer, J.P., *Transfert d'emplois vers les pays qui disposent d'un surplus de main-d'oeuvre comme alternative aux migrations internationales: le cas de la Suisse*. Geneva: ILO, World Employment Programme, 1976. (Research working paper)

Majava, A., 'The Scandinavian Countries', In: D. Kubat, ed. *The Politics of Migration Policies*, pp.163-92. New York: Center for Migration Studies, 1979.

Malloy, James A. and Gamarra, Eduardo A., eds. *Latin America and Caribbean Contemporary Record*. Vol.8. New York: Holmes and Meier, 1989.

Mamdani, M., *From Citizen to Refugee: Uganda Asians Come to Britain*. London: Pinter Publishers, 1973.

Mangat, J.S., *A History of the Asians in East Africa*. Oxford: Clarendon Press, 1964.

Manning, Diana, ed. *Disaster Technology: An Annotated Bibliography*. Oxford: Pergamon Press, 1976.

Mansila, Luis, Inserción laboral de migrantes indocumentados. Bogotá: SENALDE, 1980. (Migraciones laborales 18)

Mantero, F., *Manual Labour in São Tomé and Principe*. New York: Negro University Press, 1969.

Manz, Beatriz, *Refugees of a Hidden War: The Aftermath of Counter-Insurgency in Guatemala*. Albany, NY: State University of New York Press, 1988.

Markakis, J., *National and Class Conflict in the Horn of Africa*. Cambridge: Cambridge University Press, 1987.

Marmora, L., 'Labour Migration Policy in Colombia', *International Migration Review* 13 (1979), pp.440-54.

Marmora, Lelio, *El desarrollo de la politica de migraciones laborales en Colombia*. Bogotá: SENALDE, 1980.

Marnham, P., *Nomads of the Sahel.* Rev. ed. London: Minority Rights Group, 1979. (Report 33)

Marrus, Michael R., *The Unwanted: European Refugees in the Twentieth Century.* Oxford: Oxford University Press, 1985.

Marshall Islands, Republic of the, Country Statement. Third Asian and Pacific Population Conference. Colombo, September 1982. (Mimeo)

Marshall, A., 'Immigrant Workers in the Buenos Aires Labour Market', *International Migration Review* 13 (1979), pp.488-518.

Marshall, A., 'Labour Markets and Wage Growth: The Case of Argentina', *Cambridge Journal of Economics* (March 1980), pp.37-60.

Marshall, A., 'Structural Trends in International Labor Migration: The Southern Cone of Latin America', In: M.M. Kritz, et al., eds. *Global Trends in Migration.* New York: Center for Migration Studies, 1981.

Marshall, A., *The Import of Labour: The Case of the Netherlands.* Rotterdam: University Press, 1973.

Marshall, Adriana, *Immigration in a Surplus-worker Labor Market: The Case of New York.* New York: Center for Latin American and Caribbean Studies, New York University Press, 1983. (Occasional paper 39)

Marshall, A. and Orlansky, D., Cross-national Migration to Excess-supply Labor Markets: The Southern Cone of Latin America. Tenth World Congress of Sociology, Mexico City, August 1983.

Marston, John, ed. *Annotated Bibliography of Cambodian Refugees.* Ed. by John Marston. 2 vols. Minneapolis Center of Urban and Regional Affairs, 1987, p.121. (South East Asian Refugee Studies occasional paper 5)

Martin, David A., ed. *The New Asylum Seekers: Refugee Law in the 1980s.* Dordrecht: Martinus Nijhoff, 1989.

Martin, J.I., *Refugee Settlers: A Study of Displaced Persons in Australia.* Canberra: Australian National University Press, 1965.

Martin, J.I., *The Migrant Presence.* Sydney: George Allen & Unwin, 1978. (Studies in Society 2)

Martin, P., 'Germany's Guestworkers', *Challenge* (July/August 1981).

Martin, P., *Guestworker Programs: Lessons from Europe.* Report prepared for the Joint Economic Committee, US Congress. Washington, DC, June 1979.

Martin, Philip L., 'Labor Migration in Asia', *International Migration Review* 25 (Spring 1991), pp.176-193.

Martine, G., 'Recent Colonization experiences in Brazil: Expectations versus Reality', In: J. Balán, ed. *Why People Move: Comparative Perspectives on the Dynamics of Internal Migration.* Paris: UNESCO, 1981.

Marx, K. and Engels, F., 'Forced Emigration', *On Ireland and the Irish Question: A Collection of Writings.* London: Lawrence & Wishart, 1971.

Mascie-Taylor, C.G.N. and Lasker, G.W., eds. *Biological Aspects of Human Migration.* New York: Cambridge University Press, 1988.

Masud-Pilato, Felix Roberto, *With Open Arms: Cuban Migration to the US.* Totowa: Rowman & Littlefield, 1988.

Maxwell, Kenneth R., *Conflict and Conspiracies: Portugal and Brazil, 1750-1808.* New York: Cambridge University Press, 1973.

May, R.J., ed. *Between Two Nations: The Indonesia-Papua New Guinea Border and West Papuan Nationalism.* Bathurst: Robert Brown, 1986.

Mayer, K., 'Migration, Cultural Tensions, and Foreign Relations: Switzerland', *Journal of Conflict Resolution* 11 (1967).

McCarthy, K. and Ronfeldt, D., 'Immigration as an Intrusive Global Flow: A New Perspective', In: M.M. Kritz, ed. *US Immigration and Refugee Policy: Global and Domestic Issues*, pp.381-99. Lexington, MA: D.C. Heath, 1982.

McDowall, M., Basotho Labour in South Africa Mines: An Empirical Study, 1973. (Mimeo)

McDowell, David, *The Kurds.* London: Minority Rights Group, 1989.

McEvedy, C. and Jones, R., *Atlas of World Population History.* New York: Penguin, 1979.

McNeill, William, H., *Plagues and Peoples.* Garden City: Doubleday, 1976.

Meagher, A.J., The Introduction of Chinese Laborers to Latin America: The 'Coolie Trade', 1847-1874. Davis: University of California, 1975. (PhD thesis)

Mehrlander, U., 'Career Aspirations of Native and Foreign Born: Federal Republic of Germany', *International Migration Review* 15 (1981), pp.522-28.

Mehrlander, U., 'Federal Republic of Germany', In: D. Kubat, ed. *The Politics of Migration Policies*, pp.145-62. New York: Center for Migration Studies, 1979.

Mehrlander, U., *Situation der Ausländischen Arbeitnehmer und ihrer Familien: Angehörigister für Arbeit und Sozialordnung.* Bonn, 1981.

Mehrlander, U., et al., *Situation der Ausländischen Arbeitnehmer und ihrer Familienangehörigen in der Bundesrepublik Deutschland. Repräsentativ - Untersuchung 1980.* Bonn: Bundesminister für Arbeit und Sozialordnung, 1981.

Melander, Göran and Nobel, Peter, eds. *African Refugees and the Law.* Uppsala: Scandinavian Institute of African Studies, 1978.

Melander, Göran, *Refugees in Orbit.* Geneva: International University Exchange Fund, 1978.

Melander, Göran, *Refugees in Somalia.* Uppsala: Scandinavian Institute of African Studies, 1980. (Research report 56)

Miers, Suzanne, *Britain and the Ending of the Slave Trade.* New York: Africana, 1975.

Migot, Michel, ed. *Kampuchean, Laotian and Vietnamese Refugees in Australia, New Zealand, Canada, the United States, France and the United Kingdom: A Bibliography.* Paris: Centre National de la Recherche Scientifique, Asie du Sud-Est Continentale, and Oxford: Refugee Studies Programme, Queen Elizabeth House, Oxford University, 1988.

Miles, R. and Phizacklea, A., eds. *Racism and Political Action in Britain.* London: Routledge & Kegan Paul, 1979.

Miller, Joseph C., 'Mortality in the Atlantic Slave Trade: Statistical Evidence on Causality', *Journal of Interdisciplinary History* 11 (1981), p.385-434.

Miller, Joseph C., *Way of Death: Merchant Capitalism and the Angolan Slave Trade, 1730-1830.* Madison: University of Wisconsin Press, 1988.

Miller, Judith, 'Displaced in the Gulf War', *New York Times Sunday Magazine* (June 16, 1991), p.20-24.

Miller, Kerby A., *Emigrants and Exiles: Ireland and the Irish Exodus to North America.* New York: Oxford University Press, 1985.

Miller, M., 'Reluctant Partnership: Foreign Workers in Franco-Algerian Relations', *Journal of International Affairs* 33 (1979), pp.219-38.

Miller, M.J., 'The Political Impact of Foreign Labor: A Reevaluation of the Western European Experience', *International Migration Review* 16 (1982).

Miller, M. and Papademetriou, D.G., 'Immigration Reform: The US and Western Europe Compared', In: D.G. Papademetriou and M. Miller, eds. *The Unavoidable Issue. United States Immigration Policy in the 1980s.* pp.271-98. Philadelphia: Institute for the Study of Human Issues, 1983.

Miller, M. and Yeres, D., A Massive Temporary Worker Programme for the US: Solution or Mirage. Geneva: ILO, World Employment Programme, International Migration for Employment Project, November 1979. (WEP 2-26 working paper 44)

Minet, G., 'Spectators or Participants? Immigrants and Industrial Relations in Western Europe', *International Labor Review* 117 (January/February 1978), pp.21-36.

Mintz, Sidney W. and Price, Sally, eds. *Caribbean Contours.* Baltimore: Johns Hopkins University Press, 1985.

Miro, C.A. and Potter, J.E., *Population Policy: Research Priorities in the Developing World.* London: Frances Pinter, 1980.

Miserez, Diana, ed. *Refugees: The Trauma of Exile. The Humanitarian Role of the Red Cross and Red Crescent.* Dordrecht: Martinus Nijhoff, 1988.

Mitchell, J.C., 'Wage Labour and African Population Movements in Central Africa', In: K.M. Barbour and R.M. Prothero, eds. *Essays on African Population.* London: Routledge & Kegan Paul, 1961.

Mlay, W., Migration: An Analysis of the 1978 Census. Dar es Salaam, 1983. (Mimeo)

Monstead, M. and Waiji, P., *Demographic Analysis of East Africa: A Sociological Interpretation.* Uppsala: Scandinavian Institute of African Studies, 1978.

Moore, R. and Wallace, T., *Slamming the Door.* London: Martin Robertson, 1975.

Morales Vergara, J., Panorama de la inmigración internacional entre países latinoamericanos. Santiago: CELADE, 1974. (Series A 121, mimeo)

Morales, Rebecca, 'Undocumented Workers in a Changing Automobile Industry: Case Studies in Wheels, Headers and Batteries', *Proceeding of the Conference on Contemporary Production: Capital Mobility and Labor Migration.* San Diego: Center for US-Mexican Studies, University of California Press, 1983.

Morgan, Scott and Colson, Elizabeth, eds. *People in Upheaval.* Staten Island: Center for Migration Studies, 1987.

Morokvasic, M., 'Birds of Passage Are Also Women', *International Migration Review* 18 (1984), pp.886-907. (Special issue on women in migration)

Morokvasic, M., 'Emigration of Women and Some Subsequent Social Transformations with Special Reference to Yugoslav Women', *OECD, CD/AG*, 74 (1974), pp.825-6.

Morokvasic, M., *Jugoslawische Frauen im Ausland*. Frankfurt/Main: Stroemfeld/Roter Stern, 1986.

Morokvasic, M., 'Sexuality and Procreation', In: K. Young, et al., eds. *Of Marriage and the Market; Women's Subordination in International Perspective*. London: CSE Books, 1981.

Morokvasic, M., 'Why Do Women Migrate? Toward an Understanding of Sex Selectivity in the Migratory Movements of Labour', *Studi Emigrazione* 70 (1983), pp.123-42.

Morokvasic, M., 'Women in Migration: Beyond the Reductionist Outlook', In: A. Phizacklea, ed. *The One Way Ticket: Migration and Female Labour*, pp.13-31. London: Routledge & Kegan Paul, 1983.

Morokvasic, M., *Yugoslav Women in France, Germany, and Sweden*. Paris: Centre National de la Recherche Scientifique, 1980.

Morris, Benny, *The Birth of the Palestinian Refugee Problem, 1947-1949*. Cambridge: Cambridge University Press, 1987.

Morris, H.S., *The Indians in Uganda*. Chicago: University of Chicago Press, 1968.

Moulier, Y. and Tapinos, G., 'France', In: D. Kubat, ed. *The Politics of Migration Policies*, pp.127-44. New York: Center for Migration Studies, 1979.

Mörner, M., Adventures and Proletarians, *The Story of Migrants in Latin America*. Pittsburgh: University of Pittsburgh Press, 1985.

Mörner, Magnus, *Race Mixture in the History of Latin America*. Boston: Houghton Mifflin, 1967.

Mulvaney, D.J., *The Prehistory of Australia*. Melbourne: Penguin, 1975.

Muñoz de Castillo, Cecilia, *El niño trabajador migrante en Colombia*. Bogotá: SENALDE, 1981. (Migraciones laborales 18)

Murillo, C.G., Colombian Labor Migration to Venezuela. Caracas, 1980. (Mimeo)

Murillo, C.G., 'La migración de trabajadores colombianos a Venezuela: la relación ingreso-consumo como uno de los factores de expulsión', Migraciones laborales (Bogotá, 1979).

Murillo Castaño, Gabriel, *La migración de trabajadores colombianos a Venezuela: la relación ingreso-consumo como uno de los factores de expulsión*. Bogotá: SENALDE, 1981. (Migraciones laborales 11)

Murillo Castaño, Gabriel, Los trabajadores migrantes en las Américas: consideraciones políticas en un estudio comparado de la migración entre Colombia y Venezuela y entre México y Estados Unidos. Preliminary version of a paper presented to the Session on International Migration in South America: Sociological Theory and Social Practice, at the Tenth World Congress of Sociology, Mexico City, 16-21 August 1982.

Murillo Castaño, Gabriel, *Migrant workers in the Americas: A Comparative Study of Migration between Colombia and Venezuela and between Mexico and the United States*. San Diego: Center for US-Mexican Studies, University of California, 1983. (Monograph series 15)

Murillo Castaño, Gabriel and Rothlisberger, Dora, *La migración laboral internacional en la periferia: su incidencia en la alteración de los mercados de trabajo y en la expansión del sector informal urbano de Colombia*. Bogotá: Editorial Guadalupe, 1986.

Murray, C., 'From Granary to Labour Reserve: An Economic History of Lesotho', *South African Labour Bulletin* 6, no.4 (1980).

Murray, Colin, *Families Divided: The Impact of Migrant Labour in Lesotho*. Cambridge: Cambridge University Press, 1981.

Myburgh, C.A.L., 'Migration in Relationship to the Economic Development of Rhodesia, Zambia and Malawi', *World Population Conference, Belgrade*. New York: United Nations, 1965.

Myntti, C., 'Yemeni Workers Abroad: The Impact on Women', *MERIP* 124 (June 1984), pp.11-16.

Nash, Alan E., ed. *Human Rights and the Protection of Refugees under International Law*. South Halifax, Canada: Institute for Research on Public Policy, 1988.

Nash, June and Fernandez-Kelly, M.P., eds. *Women, Men and the International Division of Labor*. New York: SUNY Press, 1983.

Neiva, A.H., 'International Migrations affecting Latin America', *The Milbank Memorial Fund Quarterly* 43 (1965), pp.119-43.

Neumann, U., *Erziehung ausländischer Kinder. Erziehungs und Bildungsvorstellungen in Türkischen Arbeiterfamilien.* Düsseldorf: Schwann, 1980.

Neuwirth, G. and Clark, L., 'Indochinese Refugees in Canada: Sponsorship and Adjustment', *International Migration Review* 15 (1981), pp.131-40.

Neville, R.J.W., 'Trends and Sources', In: R.J.W. Neville and C.J. O'Neill, eds. *The Population of New Zealand. Inter-disciplinary Perspectives.* Auckland, 1979.

New Caledonia, Country Statement. Paper presented to the ILO/SPC Conference on Migration, Employment and Development in the South Pacific, Noumea, 1982. (Mimeo)

New York State Department of Labor, *Occupational Employment Statistics: Finance, Insurance and Real Estate, New York State, May-June 1978.* New York: New York State Department of Labor, 1979.

New York State Department of Labor, *Occupational Employment Statistics: Services, New York State, April-June 1978.* New York: New York State Department of Labor, 1980.

New York State Department of Labor, *Report to the Governor and the Legislature on the Garment Manufacturing Industry and Industrial Homework.* New York: New York State Department of Labor, 1982.

New York State Department of Labor, *Study of State-federal Employment Standards for Industrial Homeworkers in New York City.* New York: New York State Department of Labor, 1982.

New Zealand, Country Statement. Third Asian and Pacific Population Conference, Colombo, September 1982. (Mimeo)

New Zealand, Department of Statistics, *Handbook 1981.* Wellington: Population Section, Department of Statistics, 1981.

New Zealand, Immigration Division, Department of Labour, *Immigration and New Zealand. A Statement of Current Immigration Policy*, 6 October 1978. (Supplement on permanent entry for overseas investors and entrepreneurs)

New Zealand, Permanent Entry Policy. Wellington: Department of Statistics. (Mimeo)

Newland, K., *International Migration: The Search for Work.* Washington, DC: Worldwatch Institute, 1979. (Worldwatch paper 33)

Nichols, Bruce, *The Uneasy Alliance: Religion, Refugee Work and US Foreign Policy.* Oxford: Oxford University Press, 1988.

Nightingale, J., *Migrant Household Economic Behavior.* Canberra: Australian National University Press, 1978.

Nikolinakos, M., 'Notes towards a General Theory of Migration in Late Capitalism', *Race and Class* 7 (1975), pp.5-16.

Nikolinakos, M., *Politische Ökonomie der Gastarbeiterfrage: Migration und Kapitalismus.* Hamburg: Robchet, 1973.

Noonan, R. and Wold, H., 'NIPALS Path Modeling with Latent Variables: Analyzing School Survey Data Using Nonlinear Iterative Partial Least Squares', *Scandinavian Journal of Educational Research* 21 (1977), pp.33-61.

Norman, N.R., Economic Consequences of Alternative Types of International Migration on Receiving Countries: The Australian Experience. Canberra, International Union for the Scientific Study of Population Workshop on the Consequences of International Migration, 1984.

Norman, N.R. and Meikle, K.F., *The Economic Effects of Immigration on Australia.* Vol. 1. Melbourne: CEDA, 1985.

North, D.S., 'Non-immigrant Workers: Visiting Labor Force Participants', *Monthly Labor Review* 103 (1980), pp.26-30.

North, D. and LeBel, A., *Manpower and Immigration Policies in the United States.* Washington, DC: National Commission for Manpower Policy, 1978.

Nott, Roger, 'The Civil Right We are Not Ready For: The Right of Free Movement of People on the Face of the Earth', *Ethics* 81 (1971), p.219-226.

Nzula, P. and Nzula, N., *Forced Labour in Colonial Africa.* London: Zed Press, 1979.

Oberg, K., 'Treatment of Immigrant Workers in Sweden', *International Labour Review* 110 (1974), pp.1-16.

Ockwell, R., ed. *Assisting in Emergencies: A Resource Handbook for UNICEF Field Staff.* Geneva & New York: UNICEF, 1986.

OECD (Organization for Economic Cooperation and Development), *Les enfants des migrants et l'emploi.* Paris: OECD, 1983.

OECD, Migration, *The Demographic Aspects.* Paris: OECD, 1991.

OECD, *The Future of Migration.* Paris: OECD, 1987.

OECD/SOPEMI (Directorate for Social Affairs, Manpower and Education), *Continuous Reporting System on Migration*. Paris: OECD, 1973-82.

OFIAMT, *Le problème de la main-d'oeuvre étrangère*. Bern, Switzerland: OFIAMT, 1964.

ONM (Oficina Nacional de la Mujer), *Condiciones de vida y de trabajo de la familia migrante con especial referencia al rol de la mujer*. Buenos Aires: ONM, 1973.

OSDRH (Oficina Sectorial de Desarrollo de Recursos Humanos), *La inmigración desde países limítrofes hacia la Argentina: Análisis estadístico*. Buenos Aires: OSDRH, 1973.

Ohadike, P.O., 'African Immigration and Immigrants in Zambia: A Study of Patterns and Characteristics', In: P. Cantrelle, ed. *Population in African Development*. Liège: Oridna Edition, 1975.

Ohadike, P.O., 'Immigrants and Development in Zambia', *International Migration Review* 8 (1974).

Ohadike, P.O., 'Migrants in the Copper Mines of Zambia', In: S.H. Ominde and C.N. Ejiohu, eds. *Population Growth and Economic Development in Africa*. London: Heinemann, 1972.

Ohadike, P.O. and Tesfaghiorghis, H., *The Population of Zambia*. Paris: CICRED, 1974.

Okamoto, K., *Foreign Students in OECD Countries*. Tokyo: unpublished, 1990.

Oliver, R., *History of East Africa*. Oxford: Clarendon Press, 1963.

Oliver, W.H. and Williams, B.R., eds. *The Oxford History of New Zealand*. Wellington: Oxford University Press, 1981.

Olney, Douglas P., ed. *Bibliography of the Hmong Miao of South East Asia and the Hmong Refugees in the United States*. Minneapolis: South East Asian Studies Project, Center for Urban and Regional Affairs, University of Minnesota, 1983, p.57. (SARS occasional paper 1)

Olney, L., 'Refugees Seen as 'A Threat to the West'', *The West Australian* (22 August 1983).

Onwuka, R.I., 'ECOWAS Protocol on the Free Movement of Persons: A Threat to Nigerian Security?', *African Affairs* 81 (1982), p.323.

Open University, *Third World Atlas*. Philadelphia: Milton Keynes, Open University Press, 1983.

Oppong, C., *Marriage Among a Matrilineal Elite*. Cambridge: Cambridge University Press, 1974.

Orsatti, A., *Las migraciones internacionales en Argentina*. Buenos Aires: CIDES, 1982. (Mimeo)

Osborne, M., 'Indochina's Refugees', *International Affairs*. January 1980.

Owen, R., *Migrant Labour in the Gulf*. London: Minority Rights Group, 1985.

Ozkan, Y., The Legal Status of Foreign Workers in the Federal Republic of Germany. West Berlin: Freie Universität, 1973. (Mimeo)

Paine, S., *Exporting Workers*. Cambridge: Cambridge University Press, 1974.

Palmer, H., *Immigration and the Rise of Multiculturalism*. Toronto: Copp Clark, 1975.

Pan, Lynn, *Sons of the Yellow Emperor: A History of the Chinese Diaspora*. Boston: Little Brown, 1990.

Pang, Eng Fong and Lim, Linda, 'Foreign Labour and Economic Development in Singapore', *International Migration Review* 16 (1982), pp.548-75.

Papademetriou, D.G., 'A Retrospective Look at Mediterranean Labor Migration to Europe', In: C.F. Pinkele and A. Pollis, eds. *The Contemporary Mediterranean World*, pp.237-56. New York: Praeger, 1983.

Papademetriou, D.G., 'Dilemmas in International Migration: A Global Perspective', *Government and Policy* 2 (1984), pp.383-98.

Papademetriou, D.G., 'Emigration and Return in the Mediterranean Littoral', *Comparative Politics* October 1985.

Papademetriou, D.G., 'European Labor Migration: Consequences for the Countries of Workers Origin', *International Studies Quarterly* 22 (1978), pp.377-408.

Papademetriou, D.G., 'Immigration Reform, American Style', *International Migration* 22 (1984), pp.265-79.

Papademetriou, D.G., *New Immigrants to Brooklyn and Queens: Policy Implications Especially with Regard to Housing*. New York: Center for Migration Studies, 1983.

Papademetriou, D.G., 'Rethinking International Migration: A Review and Critique', *Comparative Political Studies* 15 (1983), pp.469-98.

Papademetriou, D.G., 'The Economics of Immigration', *The Immigration Dilemma: America Closes its Doors*. Special Issue of *Rights, Magazine of the National Emergency Civil Liberties Committee* (June-August 1982), pp.12-15.

Papademetriou, D.G., *Undocumented Migration in the New York Metropolitan Area*. New York: Centre for Migration Studies, 1985.

Papademetriou, D.G., 'US Immigration Policy at the Crossroads', In: D.C. Piper and R. Tercheck, eds. *Foreign Policy as Public Policy*. Washington, DC: American Enterprise Institute, 1983.

Papademetriou, D.G. and DiMarzio, N., Profiling Unapprehended Undocumented Aliens in the New York Metropolitan Area: An Exploratory Study. New York: Center for Migration Studies, 1982. (Interim report)

Papademetriou, D.G. and Hopple, G., 'Casual Modelling in International Migration Research: A Methodological Prolegomenon', *Quality and Quantity* 16 (1982), pp.369-402.

Papademetriou, D.G., and Martin, P.L., eds. *The Unsettled Relationship: Labor Migration and Economic Development*. New York: Greenwood, 1991.

Papademetriou, D.G., Martin, P. and Miller, M., 'US Immigration Policy: The Guestworker Option Revisited', *International Migration* 21 (1983), pp.39-55.

Papademetriou, D.G. and Miller, M., *The Unavoidable Issue: United States Immigration Policy in the 1980s*. Philadelphia: Institute for the Study of Human Issues, 1983.

Papademetriou, D.G. and Miller, M., 'US Immigration Policy: International Context, Theoretical Parameters, and Research Priorities', In: D.G. Papademetriou and M. Miller, eds. *The Unavoidable Issue: United States Immigration Policy in the 1980s*, pp.1-141. Philadelphia, Pa.: Institute for the Study of Human Issues, 1983.

Parai, L., 'Canada's Immigration Policy, 1962-74', *International Migration Review* 9 (1975), pp.449-78.

Patterson, Orlando, *Slavery and Social Death: A Comparative Study*. Cambridge, MA: Harvard University Press, 1982.

Patterson, S., 'Climates of European Migration', *New Community* 1 (1971), pp.2-21.

Patterson, S., *Dark Strangers*. Harmondsworth: Penguin Books, 1965.

Peach, G.C., *West Indian Migration to Britain*. London: Institute of Race Relations/Oxford University Press, 1968.

Pear, R., 'White House Asks a Law to Bar Jobs for Illegal Aliens', *New York Times* (31 July 1981), p.A1.

Peil, M., 'Ghana's Aliens', *International Migration Review* 8, no.3 (1974).

Pellegrini, V. and de Paula Olive, F., 'La inmigración ilegal paraguaya, una minoría condenada?', *Revista del Centro de Investigación y Acción Social* (Buenos Aires) 19 (1970), pp.5-23.

Pelletier, Stephen, *The Kurds, An Unstable Element on the Gulf*. Boulder: Westview Press, 1984.

Pennisi, G., *Development, Manpower and Migration in the Red Sea Region: The Case for Co-operation*. Hamburg: Deutsches Orient-Institut, 1981.

Pesic-Golubovic, Z., 'A Theoretical-hypothetical Framework for Research on Changes in Family Structure', *Sociologija Sela* 3 (1966), pp.237-57.

Pessar, P.R., The Role of Households in International Migration. Paper presented at the Conference on New Directions on Immigration and Ethnicity Research. Durham: Duke University Press, May, 1981.

Pessar, Patricia, *When Borders Don't Divide: Labor Migration and Refugee Movements in the Americas*. Staten Island Center for Migration Studies, 1988.

Peterson, W., *Population*. 2nd ed. London: Macmillan, 1969.

Petras, Elizabeth, *Jamaica Labor Migration: White Capital and Black Labor 1850-1930*. Boulder: Westview Press, 1988.

Petruccelli, J.L., 'Consequences of Uruguayan Immigration: Research Note', *International Migration Review* 13 (1979).

Petruccelli, J.L. and Fortuna, J.C., *La dinámica migratoria del Uruguay del último siglo, 1875-1975*. Montevideo: Centro de Informaciones y Estudios del Uruguay, 1976. (CIESU 22)

Philips, William D., Jr. *Slavery from Roman Times to the Early Transatlantic Trade*. Minneapolis: University of Minnesota Press, 1985.

Phizaklea, A. and Miles, R., *Labour and Racism*. London: Routledge & Kegan Paul, 1980.

Picouet, M., 'Use and Possibilities of Sample Surveys for the Measurement of International Migration in Africa', In: G. Tapinos, ed. *International Migration. Proceedings of a Seminar on Demographic Research in Relation to International Migration, Buenos Aires*. Paris: CICRED, 1974.

Pidoux de Drachemberg, L., 'Inmigración y colonización en el Paraguay', *Revista Paraguaya de Sociología* 12 (1975), pp.65-123.

Pietri, Anne Lise and Pietri, René, *Empleo y migración en la Región de Patzcuaro*. Mexico City: Instituto Nacional Indigenista, 1976.

Pinsker, Sanford and Jack Fischel, eds. *America and the Holocaust*. Greenwood, FL: Penkevill Publishing Co., 1984.

Piore, M.J., *Birds of Passage: Migrant Labor and Industrial Societies*. Cambridge: Cambridge University Press, 1979.

Pirie, P., 'The Demographic Situation in the Pacific Islands and the Maldives', In: ESCAP, *Report and Working Papers of the ESCAP/SPC Conference Seminar on Small Island Countries of the ESCAP/SPC Region,* Noumea, 15-19 February 1982.

Platzky, Laurine and Walker, Cherryl, *The Surplus People: Forced Removals in South Africa*. Braamfontein: Ravan Press, 1985.

Plender, Richard, ed., *International Migration Law*. 2nd ed. Dordrecht: Martinus Nijhoff, 1988.

Poitras, G., *International Migration to the United States from Costa Rica and El Salvador*. San Antonio: Border Research Institute, Trinity University, 1980.

Poitras, G., *Return Migration from the United States to Costa Rica and El Salvador*. San Antonio: Border Research Institute, Trinity University, 1980.

Pool, D.I., *The Maori Population of New Zealand, 1769-1971*. Auckland: Auckland University Press/Oxford University Press, 1977.

Pool, I., 'Population Problems of the Small-island Countries of the ESCAP Region', In: United Nations-ESCAP, *Selected Papers, Third Asian and Pacific Population Conference,* Colombo, September 1982. New York: United Nations, 1984.

Poole, M.E., 'Australian Multicultural Policy: Future Prospects', In: M.E. Poole, et al., eds. *Australia in Transition*. Sydney: Harcourt Brace Jovanovich, 1985.

Pooley, Colin G. and White, Ian D., eds. *Migrants, Emigrants and Immigrants - A Social History of Migration*. London: Routledge & Kegan Paul, 1991.

Portes, A., *Migraciones y sector informal, algunos aspectos de su articulación. Politicas de migraciones laborales internacionales en la periferia: el caso latinoamericano*. Bogotá: Editorial Garrera, 1982.

Portes, A., 'Modes of Structural Incorporation and Present Theories of Labor Immigration', In: M.M. Kritz, et al., eds. *Global Trends in Migration*. New York: Center for Migration Studies, 1981.

Portes, A., 'On the Sociology of National Development: Theories and Issues', *American Journal of Sociology* 82 (1976), pp.55-85.

Portes, A., 'Toward a Structural Analysis of Illegal (Undocumented) Immigration', *International Migration Review* 12 (1978), pp.469-85.

Portes, A. and Bach, R.L., *Dual Labor Markets and Immigration: A Test of Competing Theories of Income Inequality*. Durham: Center for International Studies, Duke University Comparative Studies of Immigration and Ethnicity, 1979. (Occasional papers series)

Portes, A. and Bach, R.L., *Latin Journey: Cuban and Mexican Immigrants in the United States*. Berkeley: University of California Press, 1984.

Portes, A. and Guarnizo, L., Tropical Capitalists: US Bound Immigration and Small Enterprise Development in the Dominican Republic. Washington, DC: Working Papers, Commission for the Study of International Migration and Cooperative Economic Development, 1988.

Portes, A. and Walton, J., *Labor, Class and the International System*. New York: Academic Press, 1981.

Poston, Jr., Dudley, and Ye, Mei-Yu, 'The Distribution of Overseas Chinese in the Contemporary World', *International Migration Review* 211 (Fall 1990), pp.480-508.

Poulsen, M.F. and Johnston, R.J., 'Patterns of Maori Migration', In: R.J. Johnston, ed. *Urbanisation in New Zealand*. Wellington: Reed Education, 1973.

Power, J., *Migrant Workers in Western Europe and the United States*. Oxford: Pergamon Press, 1979.

Power, J., 'The Great Debate on Illegal Immigration - Europe and the USA Compared,' *Journal of International Affairs* 33 (1979), pp.239-48.

Price, C., 'Trans-Tasman Migration: An Australian Viewpoint', In: I. Pool, ed. Trans-Tasman Migration. Hamilton: University of Waikato, 1980. (Mimeo)

Prothero, R.M., 'Migration in Tropical Africa', In: J.C. Caldwell and C.O. Okonjo, eds. *The Population of Tropical Africa*. London: Longman, 1968.

Pryce, K., *Endless Pressure*. Harmondsworth: Penguin, 1979.

Pryor, R.J., The Interrelationship between Internal and International Migration, with Some Evidence from Australia. Solicited paper presented to the Conference on Economic and Demographic Change: Issues for the 1980s. Liège: International Union for the Scientific Study of Population, 1978.

Pyne, P., 'Demography', In: C.A. Price, ed. *Australian Immigration, A Bibliography and Digest*. Supplement. Canberra: Australian National University, 1981.

Rack, Philip, *Race, Culture and Mental Disorder*. London: Tavistock, 1982.

Rallu, J.-L., 'Les Wallisiens à Wallis et Futuna et en Nouvelle-Calédonie', *Population* 37, no.1 (1982).

Refugee Studies Programme, University of Oxford, 'The West Bank and Gaza Strip', *Journal of Refugee Studies* 2 (1989), Oxford: Oxford University Press, 1989.

Regierungspräsident Köln, 'Ausländische Schüler und Lehrer an deutschen Schulen in der Stadt Köln', Schriftenreihe des Regierungspräsidenten Köln series 13 (1974).

Reichert, J.S. and Massey, D.S., 'History and Trends in United States-bound Migration from a Mexican Town', *International Migration Review* 14 (1980), pp.475-91.

Reichert, J.S. and Massey, D.S., 'Patterns of United States Migration from a Mexican Sending Community: A Comparison of Legal and Illegal Migrants', *International Migration Review* 13 (1979), pp.599-623.

Reiman, H. and Reiman, H., 'Federal Republic of Germany', In: R.E. Krane, ed. *International Labor Migration in Europe*, pp.63-87. New York: Praeger, 1979.

Reinans, S., *Immigrants in Sweden*. Strasbourg: Council of Europe, 1971.

Reinhard, M., Armengaud, A. and Dupaquier, J., *Histoire générale de la population mondiale*. 3rd ed. Paris: CNED, 1968.

Reiterer, M., *Protection of Refugees by their State of Asylum*. Vienna: AWR, 1984.

Reitz, J.G., *The Survival of Ethnic Groups*. Toronto: McGraw Hill-Ryerson, 1980.

Renner, E., *Erziehungs und Sozialisationsbeinigungen Türkischer Kinder. Ein Vergleich zwischen Deutschland und der Türkei*. Neuburgweier: Schindele, 1975.

Resource Consultants, Inc., *Bibliography of ESL/Bilingual and Employment/Vocational Materials for indochinese*. McLean, VI, 1980.

Ressler, E.M., Boothby, N. and Steinbeck, D.J., *Unaccompanied Children: Care and Placement in Wars, Natural Disasters and Refugee Movements*. Oxford: Oxford University Press, 1987.

Reubens, E.P., *Interpreting Migration: Current Models and a New Integration*. Research Program in Inter-American Affairs, Center for Latin American and Caribbean Studies, New York University Press, 1981. (Occasional paper 29)

Rex, J. and Moore, R., *Race, Community and Conflict*. London: Institute of Race Relations/Oxford University Press, 1967.

Rex, J. and Tomlinson, S., *Colonial Immigrants in a British City: A Class Analysis*. London: Routledge & Kegan Paul, 1979.

Reynell, Josephine, *Political Pawns: Refugees on the Thai-Kampuchean Border*. Oxford: Refugee Studies Programme, University of Oxford, 1989.

Reynolds, Edward, *Stand the Storm, A History of the Atlantic Slave Trade*. New York: Alison and Busby, 1985.

Rhoda, R., Rural Development and Urban Migration: Can We Keep Them Down on the Farm? 1981. (Mimeo)

Ricca, Sergio, *International Migration in Africa, Legal and Administrative Aspects*. Geneva: ILO, 1989.

Richards, A. and Martin, J., 'The Laissez-faire Approach to International Labour Migration: The Case of the Middle East', *Economic Development and Cultural Change* 31 (1983), pp.455-74.

Richardson, A., *British Immigrants and Australia: A Psycho-social Inquiry*. Canberra: Australian National University Press, 1974.

Richmond, A.H., 'Canadian Immigration: Recent Developments and Future Prospects', In: L. Driedger, ed. *The Canadian Ethnic Mosaic*, pp.105-23. Toronto: McClelland & Stewart, 1978.

Richmond, A.H., *Aspects of the Absorption of Immigrants*. Ottawa: Manpower and Immigration Canada, 1974.

Richmond, A.H., *Ethnic Variation in Family Income and Poverty in Canada*. York University: Institute for Behavioral Research, 1979. (Publication 87-0)

Richmond, A.H., *Comparative Studies in the Economic Adaptation of Immigrants in Canada*. Toronto: Institute for Behavioral Research, York University, 1981.

Richmond, A.H., 'Immigrant Adaptation in a Post Industrial Society', In: M.M. Kritz, C.B. Keely and S.M. Tomasi, eds. *Global Trends in Migration: Theory and Research on International Population Movements*. New York: Center for Migration Studies, 1981.

Richmond, A.H., 'Income Inequality in Canada: Ethnic Generational Aspects', *Canadian Studies in Population* 5 (1978), pp.25-36.

Richmond, A.H., 'The Green Paper: Reflections on the Canadian Immigration and Population Study', *Canadian Ethnic Studies* 7 (1975), pp.5-21.

Richmond, A.H. and Goldlust, J., *Family and Social Integration of Immigrants in Toronto*. Toronto: Institute for Behavioral Research, York University Press, 1977.

Richmond, A.H. and Kalbach, W.E., *Factors in the Adjustment of Immigrants and their Descendants*. Ottawa: Statistics Canada, 1980.

Richmond, A.H. and Verma, R.P., 'The Economic Adaptation of Immigrants: A New Theoretical Perspective', *International Migration Review* 23 (1978), pp.3-38.

Richmond, A.H. and Zubrzycki, J., 'Occupational Status in Australia and Canada: A Comparative Study of the Native and Foreign Born', *Comparative Social Research* 4 (1981), pp.91-110.

Riesner, R., 'National Regulation of the Movement of Workers in the European Community', *American Journal of Comparative Law* (1964), pp.360-84.

Rippy, J., 'The Japanese in Latin America', *Inter-American Economic Affairs* 3 (1949), pp.50-65.

Rist, R., *Guestworkers in Germany: The Prospects for Pluralism*. New York: Praeger, 1978.

Ritner, P., *The Death of Africa*. New York: Macmillan, 1960.

Rittstieg, H., 'Gesellschaftliche und politische Perspektive des Ausländerrechts', In: T. Ansay and V. Gessner, eds. *Gastarbeiter in Gesellschaft und Recht*, pp.56-79. Munich: Beck, 1974.

Rivarola, D.M., 'Aspectos de la migración paraguaya', *Revista Paraguaya de Sociología* 4 (1967), pp.40-88.

Rivera-Batiz, F.L., A Demand-Pull Model of Labor Migration. Bloomington: Indiana University, Department of Economics, 1980. (Discussion papers 80-2)

Robbins, R., 'Myth and Realities of International Migration into Latin America', *Annals of the American Academy of Political and Social Sciences* 316 (1958), pp.102-10.

Roberts, B.R., 'Migration and Industrializing Economies: A Comparative Perspective', In: J. Balán, ed. *Why People Move: Comparative Perspectives on the Dynamics of Internal Migration*. Paris: UNESCO, 1981.

Roberts, G. and Mills, D., 'Study of External Migration Affecting Jamaica', *Social and Economic Studies* 7, no.2 (Supplement, 1958)

Roberts, K.D., et al., Agrarian Structure and Labor Migration in Rural Mexico: The Case of Circular Migration of Undocumented Workers to the United States. Austin: Institute of Latin American Studies, 1980. (Mimeo)

Roberts, K.D., et al., The Mexican Migration Numbers Game: An Analysis of the Lesko Estimate of Undocumented Migration from Mexico to the United States. Austin: Bureau of Business Research, 1978. (Mimeo)

Robertson, Claire C. and Klein, Martin, eds. *Women and Slavery in Africa*. Madison: University of Wisconsin Press, 1983.

Rogers, R., 'Incentives to Return: Patterns of Policies and Migrants' Responses', In: M.K. Kritz, C.B. Keely and S.M. Tomasi, eds. *Global Trends in Migration: Theory and Research on International Population Movements*. New York: Center for Migration Studies, 1981.

Rogers, R., *The Process of International Migrants' Integration into Host Societies: A Hypothesis and Comments*. Cambridge, MA: Center for International Studies, Massachusetts Institute of Technology, 1978.

Rogge, J.R., ed. *Refugee Materials Center Bibliography*. Kansas City MO: Refugee Materials Center, US Dept of Education, 1982.

Rogge, J.R., 'Refugee Migration and Resettlement', In: J.I. Clarke and L.A. Kosinski, eds. *Redistribution of Population in Africa*. London: Heinemann, 1982.

Rogge, J.R., ed. *Refugees: A Third World Dilemma*. Totowa: Rowman and Littlefield, 1987.

Rogge, J.R., ed. *Too Many, Too Long: Sudan's Twenty-year Refugee Dilemma*. Totowa: Rowman and Littlefield, 1985.

Rose, E.G., et al., *Colour and Citizenship: A Report on British Race Relations*. London: Institute of Race Relations/Oxford University Press, 1969.

Rosen-Prinz, B.D. and Prinz, F.A., Migrant Labour and Rural Homesteads: An Investigation into the Sociological Dimensions of the Migrant Labour System in Swaziland. Geneva: ILO, World Employment Programme, 1978. (Research working paper, mimeo)

Rout, Leslie B., Jr., *The African Experience in Spanish America: 1502 to the Present*. New York: Cambridge University Press, 1976.

Runnymede Trust, Radical Statistics Race Group, *Britain's Black Population*. London: Heinemann, 1980.

Runnymede Trust, *Review of the Race Relations Act 1976*. London: The Runnymede Trust, 1979.

Runnymede Trust, *The Coloured Population of Great Britain*. London: The Runnymede Trust, 1974.

Russell, Sharon Stanton, Jacobsen, Karan and Stanley, William Deane, International Migration and Development in Sub-Saharan Africa. 2 vols. Washington, DC: World Bank, 1990. (Discussion paper 102)

Sachar, Howard M. *Diaspora: An Inquiry into the Contemporary Jewish World*. New York: Harper and Row, 1985.

Safa, Helen, 'Women, Production and Reproduction in Industrial Capitalism: A Comparison of Brazilian and US Factory Workers', In: J. Nash and M.P. Fernandez-Kelly, eds. *Women, Men and the International Division of Labor*. New York: SUNY Press, 1983.

Sage, W.W. and Henchy, J.A.N., comp. *Laos. A Bibliography*. Singapore: Institute of South East Asian Studies, 1986, p.254. (Library bulletin 16).

Saha, P., *Emigration of Indian Labour 1834-1900*. Delhi: People's Publishing House, 1970.

Saifullah-Khan, V., 'Some Comments on the Question of the 'Second Generation'', *On Immigration Children and Youth in Norway*. Oslo: Ministry of Local Government and Labour, 1981.

Saket, B., ed. *Worker Migration Abroad: Socio-economic Implications for Households in Jordan*. Amman: RSS, 1984.

Samman, M.L., *Les étrangers au recensement de 1975*. Paris: La Documentation Française, 1976.

Sanchez-Albornoz, N., *La población de América Latina*. Madrid: Alianza Universidad, 1973.

Sanchez-Albornoz, Nicolás, *The Population of Latin America*. Berkeley: University of California Press, 1974.

Sanderson, Steven E., ed. *The Americas in the New International Division of Labor*. New York: Holmes & Meier, 1985.

Sandhu, K.S., Indians in *Malaya: Some Aspects of their Immigration and Settlement, 1786-1957*. London: Cambridge University Press, 1969.

Sandler, Richard and Jones, Thomas C., *Medical Care of Refugees*. Oxford: Oxford University Press, 1987.

Sassen-Koob, Sakia, 'Economic Growth and Immigration to Venezuela', *International Migration Review* 13 (1979), pp.455-74.

Sassen-Koob, Sakia, *Exporting Capital and Importing New York Labor: The Role of Caribbean Basic Migration in New York City*. New York: Center for Latin American and Caribbean Studies, New York University Press, 1981. (Occasional paper 28)

Sassen-Koob, Sakia, 'Formal and Informal Associations: Colombians and Dominicans in New York City', *International Migration Review* 13 (1979), pp.314-31.

Sassen-Koob, Sakia, 'The New Labor Demand in Global Cities', In: M.P. Smith, ed. *Cities in Transformation*. Beverly Hills: Sage, 1984.

Scarman, Lord (Chairman), *The Brixton Disorders, April 10-12, 1981: Enquiry Report*. London: HMSO, 1981. (Cmnd. 8427)

Schapera, I., *Migrant Labour and Tribal Life: A Study of Conditions in the Bechuanaland Protectorate*. London: Oxford University Press, 1947.

Schauer, Arnold, *Ireland and the American Emigration 1850-1900*. Minneapolis: University of Minnesota Press, 1958.

Schildder, G., *Australia Unveiled: The Share of the Dutch Navigators in the Discovery of Australia*. Amsterdam: Theatrum Orbis Terrarum, 1976.

Schiller, G., 'Channelling Migration: A Review of Policy with Special Reference to the Federal Republic of Germany', *International Labour Review* 3 (1975), pp.335-55.

Schmitter, B.E., 'Immigrants and Associations: Their Role in the Socio-political Process of Immigrant Workers Integration in West Germany and Switzerland', *International Migration Review* 14 (1980), pp.179-92.

Schober, K., 'Zur Ausbildungs und Arbeitsmarktsituation ausländischer Jugendlicher in der Bundesrepublik Deutschland - Gegenwärtige Lage und känstige Perspektiven', *Mittbeilungen aus der Arbeitsmarkt und Berufsforschung*, 1 (1981), pp.11-21.

Schwartz, Stuart B., *Sugar Plantations in the Formation of Brazilian Society*. New York: Cambridge University Press, 1985.

SCIRP (Select Commission on Immigration and Refugee Policy), *US Immigration Policy and the National Interest. The Final Report and Recommendations of the Select Commission on Immigration and Refugee Policy to the Congress and the President of the United States*. 1 March 1981.

Scott, M.F., *Peasant Farmers, Masons and Maids: Migration and Family Structure in Tlaxcala.* Santa Barbara: University of California Press, 1977.

Seccombe, I.J., 'Immigrant Workers in an Emigrant Economy: An Examination of Replacement Migration in the Middle East', *International Migration Review* 24 (1986).

Seccombe, I.J., International Labour Migration and Skill Scarcity: The Hashemite Kingdom of Jordan. Geneva: ILO, International Migration for Employment Project, 1984. (Working paper 14)

Seccombe, I.J., *International Labour Migration in the Middle East: An Introductory Bibliography.* Durham University, Centre for Middle Eastern and Islamic Studies, 1984. (Occasional paper 24)

Seccombe, I.J. and Lawless, R.I., 'Some New Trends in Mediterranean Labour Migration - The Middle East Connection', *International Migration Review* 23 (1985), pp.123-48.

Selwyn, P., Industrial Development in Peripheral Small Countries. Brighton: IDS, 1973. (Discussion paper 14)

Senator für Schulwesen, Jugend und Sport, *Das Schuljahr 1981/82 in Zahlen.* West Berlin: Senator für Schulwesen, Jugend und Sport, 1982.

Serageldin, I., et al., *Manpower and International Labour Migration in the Middle East and North Africa.* London: Oxford University Press, 1983.

Servicio Social Internacional, Año Internacional del Niño. UNICEF, *Los movimentos migratorios y los niños.* Caracas: First Regional Seminar, 1980.

Sestito, R., *The Policies of Multiculturalism.* Sydney: Centre for Independent Studies, 1982.

Shadid, W.A., 'The Integration of Muslim Minorities in the Netherlands', *International Migration Review* 16 (1991), pp.355-74.

Sharma, Prakash C., ed. *Refugee Migration: A Selected International Research Bibliography.* Monticello: Council of Planning Librarians, 1975. (Exchange bibliography, no.801)

Sharp, P., 'Why Continue Immigration?', In: Australian Institute of Political Science, *How Many Australians?* Sydney: Angus & Robertson, 1971.

Shaw, R.P., *Mobilizing Human Resources in the Arab World.* London: Routledge & Kegan Paul, 1983.

Shawcross, William, *The Quality of Mercy: Cambodia, Holocaust and Modern Conscience.* New York: Simon and Schuster, 1984.

Sherbiny, N.A., 'Expatriate Labour Flows to the Arab Oil-producing Countries in the 1980s', *Middle East Journal* 38 (1984), pp.643-67.

Sheridan, Richard B., *Doctors and Slaves: A Medical and Demographic History of Slavery in the British West Indies 1680-1834.* New York: Cambridge University Press, 1985.

Siddiqui, A.M.A.H., Economic and Non-economic Impact of Migration from Bangladesh. An Overview. Paper presented at the Conference on Asian Labor Migration to the Middle East, 19-23 September 1983. Honolulu: East-West Population Institute, 1983.

Sierra, G., de, Migrantes uruguayos hacia la Argentina. Paper presented at the sixth meeting of the Task Force on Migration of the Commission of Population and Development of CLACSO, Mexico City, 1977. (Mimeo)

Simon, Rita James and Brettell, Caroline B., *International Migration. The Female Experience.* Totowa: Rowman and Littlefield, 1986.

Simmonds, Stephanie and Gabaudan, Michael, eds. *Refugee Camp Health Care: Selected Annotated References.* London: The Ross Institute, 1983.

Simmonds, Stephanie and Ryding, Diana, eds. *Refugee Mental Health: A Bibliography.* London: Refugee Health Group, London School of Hygiene and Tropical Medicine, 1986.

Singer, P., International Migration and Development. São Paulo: CEBRAP, n.d. (Mimeo)

Singh, B., Internal and International Migration: The Case of Fiji. Country Statement - Fiji. Paper presented to the SPC/ILO Conference on Migration, Employment and Development in the South Pacific, Noumea, 1982. (Mimeo)

Sjaastad, L.A., 'The Costs and Returns of Human Migration', *Journal of Political Economy* 70 (October 1962), pp.80-93.

Skopol, T., 'Wallerstein's World Capitalist System: A Theoretical and Historical Critique', *American Journal of Sociology* 82 (1977), pp. 1075-90.

Smart, J.E., Worker Circulation between Asia and the Middle East: The Structural Intersection of Labour Markets. Paper presented at the IUSSP Workshop on the Consequences of International Migration, Canberra, 1984.

Smith, A.D., *The Ethnic Revival in the Modern World.* London: Cambridge University Press, 1981.

Smith, D.J., *Racial Disadvantage in Employment.* London: Political and Economic Planning, 1974.

Smith, D.J., *The Facts of Racial Disadvantage: A National Survey*. London: Political and Economic Planning, 1976.

Smith, J. Christian, comp. *The Hmong: An Annotated Bibliography 1983-87*. Minneapolis: Centre for Urban and Regional Affairs, University of Minnesota, 1988. (Occasional paper 7)

Smith, Raymond T., *Kinship and Class in the West Indies*. New York: Cambridge University Press, 1988.

Smolicz, J.J., *Culture and Education in a Plural Society*. Sydney: Curriculum Development Centre, 1979.

Smyser, W.R., *Refugees: Extended Exile*. New York: Praeger, 1987.

Society for Research on Women in New Zealand, *Immigrant Women*. Christchurch: SRWNZ, 1979.

Solberg, C., 'Germans and Italians in Latin America: Recent Immigration Research', *Latin American Research Review* 11 (1976), pp.133-7.

Somoza, J.L., Emigration from Bolivia. Santiago: CELADE, 1981. (Mimeo)

Somoza, J.L., Estimación de la emigración de Colombia a partir de información sobre residencia de hijos sobrevivientes recogida en una encuesta. Santiago: CELADE, 1979. (Mimeo)

Somoza, J.L., Indirect Estimates of Emigration. Santiago: CELADE, 1979. (Mimeo)

Songpraset, P. and Chongwatana, N., eds. *Thailand: A First Asylum Country for Indochinese Refugees*. Bangkok: Institute of Asian Studies, Chulalongkorn University, 1989.

Songre, A., 'Mass Emigration from Upper Volta: The Facts and Implications', *International Labour Review* 108 (1973), pp.209-25.

SOPEMI (Continuous reporting system on migration). Paris: OECD, Manpower and Social Affairs Directorate, 1973-82.

SOPEMI, 'Federal Republic of Germany', *Continuous Reporting System on Migration*, Paris: OECD, 1982.

SOPEMI, *Report*, Paris: OECD, 1978.

Soysa, G.D.G.P., External Migration of Labour from Sri Lanka. Paper prepared for the ILO (ARPLA) Symposium on Overseas Recruitment Procedures, Islamabad, May 1981.

SPC (South Pacific Commission), *South Pacific Communities: A Statistical Summary*. Noumea: SPC, 1980.

SPC-ILO (South Pacific Commission-International Labour Organisation), Report of Meeting. Regional Conference on Migration, Employment and Development in the South Pacific, Noumea, 22-26 February 1982. (Mimeo)

Speare, A., Jr., 'The Relevance of Models of Internal Migration for the Study of International Migration', In: G. Tapinos, ed. *International Migration*. Paris: CICRED, 1974. (Proceedings of a seminar on demographic research in relation to international migration)

SPO (State Planning Organization), *Development Plans*. Ankara: DPT Publications, 1962, 1967, 1973, 1979.

Stahl, C.W., Contract Labour Migration and Economic Development with Special Reference to Indonesia, Malaysia, the Philippines and Thailand. Paper prepared for the Conference on Asian Labor Migration to the Middle East, 19-23 September 1983. Honolulu: East-West Population Institute, 1983.

Stahl, C.W., Contract Labour Migration from the Philippines: Trends and Issues. Paper presented to the Conference on International Migration in the Arab World, Nicosia, 11-16 May 1981.

Stahl, C.W., *International Labour Migration and International Development*. Geneva: ILO, 1982.

Stahl, C.W., *International Labour Migration and the ASEAN Economies*. Geneva: ILO, International Migration for Employment Project, 1984. (Working paper 13)

Stahl, Charles, ed. *International Migration Today: Emerging Issues*. Vol.2. Paris: UNESCO, 1988.

Stahl, C.W., 'Labor Emigration and Economic Development', *International Migration Review* 16 (1982), pp.869-99.

Stahl, C.W., 'Migrant Labour Supplies, Past, Present and Future: with Special Reference to the Gold-mining Industry', In: W.R. Böhning, ed. *Black Migration to South Africa*. Geneva: ILO, 1981.

Stahl, C.W., 'Recent Changes in the Demand for Foreign African Labour in South Africa and Future Prospects', In: F. de Vletter, ed. *Labour Migration and Agricultural Development in Southern Africa*. Rome: FAO, 1982.

Stahl, C.W. and Böhning, W.R., 'Reducing Dependence on Migration in Southern Africa', In: W.R. Böhning, ed. *Black Migration to South Africa*. Geneva: ILO, 1981.

Stark, O., 'Income Distribution Fertility Decisions and the Shadow Wage Rate: Implications of a New Approach to Rural-to-Urban Migration in Less Developed Countries', *Economic and Demographic Change: Issues for the 1980s*. Vol. 2. Liège: IUSSP, 1980.

Stark, O., Economic and Demographic Interactions in Agricultural Development: The Case of Rural-to-Urban Migration. Tel Aviv: Tel Aviv University, 1978. (Research reports 2 and 78)

Statistisches Bundesamt, *Statistisches Jahrbuch der Bundesrepublik Deutschland 1983*. Wiesbaden: Statistisches Bundesamt, 1984.

Statistisches Bundesamt, *Statistisches Jahrbuch für die Bundesrepublik Deutschland*. Wiesbaden: Statistisches Bundesamt, 1973-82.

Statistisches Landesamt Berlin, *Statistisches Jahrbuch 1973*. West Berlin: Statistiches Landesamt Berlin, 1974.

Stegmann, H. and Kraft, H., 'Ausländische Jugendliche in Ausbildung und Beruf', *Mitteilungen aus der Arbeitsmarkt und Berufsforschung* 2 (1983), pp.131-36.

Stegmann, H. and Kraft, H., Beschäftiztenstatistik, Ib4-4204 Sozialversicherung beschäftigte im Bundesgebiet, am 31. Dezember 1984. Nuremberg: Bundesanstalt für Arbeit, 1985.

Stegmann, H. and Kraft, H., 'Sozialversicherungspflichtig beschäftigte Arbeitnehmer', *Amtliche Nachrichten der Bundesanstalt für Arbeit*, Nuremberg, 1981, 1984.

Stein, B.N. and Tomasi, S.M., eds. 'Refugees Today', *International Migration Review* 15 (1981). (Special double issue)

Stein, Barry, comp. 'Refugee Research Bibliography', *International Migration Review* 15 (1981), pp. 331-393.

Steinberg, S., *The Ethnic Myth: Race, Ethnicity, and Class in America*. New York: Atheneum, 1981.

Stoller, A., ed. *New Faces: Immigration and Family Life in Australia*. Melbourne: F.W. Cheshire, 1966.

Strand, Paul J. and Jones, Woodrow, *Indochinese Refugees in America*. Durham: Duke University Press, 1985.

Streeten, Paul, Interdependence: A North-South Perspective. Solicited paper presented to the Seventh World Congress of the International Economic Association, Madrid, 5-9 September 1983.

Stuart-Fox, Stuart, *Laos, Politics, Economics, and Society*. Boulder: Lynne Rienner, 1986.

Sudarkasa, N., 'Commercial Migration in West Africa with Special Reference to the Yoruba in Ghana', African Urban Notes series B, no. 1 (1974/75).

Surplus Peoples Project Reports, *Forced Removals in South Africa*. Cape Town: The Surplus People Project, 1983.

Sussman, Gerald and Lent, John A., *Transnational Communications Wiring the Third World*. London: Sage, 1991.

Swamy, G., International Migrant Workers' Remittances: Issues and Prospects. Washington, DC: World Bank, 1981. (Staff working paper 481)

Swanson, J.C., *Emigration and Economic Development: The Case of the YAR*. Boulder: Westview Press, 1979.

Sweden, *Invandrarutredningen 3: Invandrarna och Minoriteterna*. Stockholm: Huvudbetankande av Invandrarutredningen, 1974.

Swindell, K., 'Family Farms and Migrant Labour: The Strange Farmers in the Gambia', *Canadian Journal of African Studies* 12, no.1 (1978).

Switzerland, *Rapport du Conseil Fédéral*. Bern, 1969.

Szapocznik, José, Cohen, Raquel and Hernandez, Roberto, E., *Coping with Adolescent Refugees: The Mariel Boatlift*. New York: Praeger, 1985.

Tabbarah, R., 'International Migration: Issues and Policies', *Migration Today* (August 1978), pp.14-19. (Uppsala)

Tabbarah, R., 'Population, Human Resources and Development in the Arab World', *UNECWA Population Bulletin* 20 (1981), pp.5-38.

Tabbarah, Riad, 'Arab Development and the Lebanese Human Resources', *Al Mustaqbal Al Arabi* 5 (Beirut: January 1983, Arabic text)

Tabbarah, Riad, 'Changing Patterns in International Migration and Their Demo-economic Implications', (Organizer's statement) *International Population Conference, Manila* 4 (1981), Liège: International Union for the Scientific Study of Population.

Tabbarah, Riad, Contemporary Issues of International Migration. Organizer's statement, Seventh World Congress of the International Economic Association, Madrid, 5-9 September 1983.

Tabbarah, Riad, 'International Migration and National Population Policies', *International Population Conference, Mexico* 4 (1977), Liège: International Union for the Scientific Study of Population.

Tabbarah, Riad, 'Population, Human Resources and Development in the Arab World', *Population and Development in the Middle East* (1982), Beirut: International Union for the Scientific Study of Population.

Tabbarah, R., Mamish, M. and Gamayel, Y., 'Population Research and Research Gaps in the Arab Countries', *Population Bulletin of the Economic Commission for Western Asia* no.15 (December 1978).

Tajibnapis, P., ed. *Selected Bibliography: Refugees and Refugee Migrations*. New York: Church World Services, 1980.

Tangatatutai, A., Country Statement - Cook Islands. Paper presented to the ILO/SPC Conference on Migration, Employment and Development in the South Pacific, Noumea, 1982. (Mimeo)

Tapinos, G., 'European Migration Patterns: Economic Linkages and Policy Experiences', In: Mary M. Kritz, ed. *US Immigration and Refugee Policy*. Lexington, MA: Lexington Books, 1982.

Tapinos, G., et al., Possibilités de transfert d'emplois vers les pays d'émigration en tant qu'alternative aux migrations internationales des travailleurs: Le cas français, I, II, III. Geneva: ILO, World Employment Programme, International Migration for Employment Project, 1978.

Tapinos, G., The Economic Effects of Intra-regional Migration. Conference on International Migration in the Arab World, Economic Commission for Western Asia, Nicosia, Cyprus, 1981.

Tate, S., Country Statement - Western Samoa. Paper presented to the SPC/ILO Conference on Migration, Employment and Development in the South Pacific, Noumea, 1982. (Mimeo)

Taylor, E., 'Egyptian Migration and Peasant Wives', *MERIP* 124 (June 1984), pp.3-10.

Taylor, M., *Caught Between: A Review of Research into the Education of Pupils of West Indian Origin*. London: National Foundation for Education Research, 1981.

Theolleyre, Jean-Marc, 'La lutte contre l'immigration clandestine', *Le Monde* (14 September 1983).

Therborn, G., 'Migration and Western Europe: The Old World Turning New', *Science* 237 (September 4, 1987), pp.1183-1188.

Thernstrom, S., ed. *Encyclopaedia of American Ethnic Groups*. Cambridge, MA: Harvard Belknap Press, 1981.

Thomas, B., 'Economic Factors in International Migration', In: L. Tabah, ed. *Population Growth and Economic Development in the Third World*. Liège: IUSSP, 1974.

Thomas, B., 'International Migration', In: P. Hauser and O.D. Duncan, eds. *The Study of Population*. Chicago: University of Chicago Press, 1959.

Thomas, B., International *Migration and Economic Development. A Trend Report and Bibliography*. Paris: UNESCO, 1961.

Thomas, E.J., 'The Status of Immigrant Workers in France', In: E.J. Thomas, ed. Immigrant Workers in Europe and the Question of Their Legal Status, 1982, pp. 51-106. (Mimeo)

Thompson, Robert Farris, *Flash of the Spirit*. New York: Vintage, 1984.

Tinker, H., *A New System of Slavery: The Export of Indian Labour Overseas, 1830-1920*. London: Oxford University Press, 1974.

Todaro, M.P., *Internal Migration in Developing Countries: A Review of Theory, Evidence, Methodology, and Research Priorities*. Geneva: ILO, 1976.

Tokelau, Discussant's Notes, Session on Small-island Countries, Third Asian and Pacific Population Conference, Colombo, 1982.

Tomasi, S.M., 'Socio-political Participation of Migrants in the Receiving Countries', In: M.M. Kritz, C.B. Keely and S.M. Tomasi, eds. *Global Trends in Migration: Theory and Research on International Population Movements*. New York: Center for Migration Studies, 1981.

Torales, Ponciano, *Las inmigraciones laborales en la frontera de Colombia con Panama*. Bogotá: SENALDE, 1980. (Migraciones laborales 2)

Torrado, S., 'International Migration Policies in Latin America', *International Migration Review* 13 (1979), pp.428-39.

Tranauer, Gabrielle, ed. *Gypsies and the Holocaust: A Bibliography and Introduction Essay*. Montreal: Institute for Genocide Studies, Centre Interuniversitaire d'Etudes Européenes, 1989.

Trebous, M., *Migration and Development: The Case of Algeria*. Paris: OECD, 1970.

Trlin, A.D., 'Race, Ethnicity and Society', In: R.J.W. Neville and C.J. O'Neill, eds. *The Population of New Zealand. Inter-disciplinary Perspectives*. Auckland, 1979.

Trommer, L and Kohler, H., *Ausländer in der Bundesrepublik Deutschland. Dokumentation und Analyse amtlicher Statistiken*. Munich: Deutsches Jugendinstitut, 1981.

Tuna, O. and Ekin, N., *Turkiye'den F. Almanya'ya isgucu akimi ve meseleleri* [Labour Flow to the Federal Republic of Germany and its Problems]. Vols. 1 and 2. Istanbul: IUIF Publications, 1966.

Tuna, O., *Yurda donen iscilerin intibak sorunlari* [Readaptation of Returning Workers]. Ankara: SPO, 1967. (Research report)

Udo, R.K., 'Rural Migrations and the Problem of Agricultural Labour in Western Tropical Africa', In: B.S. Hoyle, ed. *Spatial Aspects of Development*. New York: Wiley, 1974.

Udui, F.E., Country Statement - Republic of Palau. Paper presented to the SPC/ILO Conference on Migration, Employment and Development in the South Pacific, Noumea, February 1982. (Mimeo)

Ugalde, A., Bean, F.D. and Cardenas, G., 'International Migration from the Dominican Republic: Findings from a National Survey', *International Migration Review* 13 (1979), pp.235-54.

UNDP (United Nations Development Program), *Human Development Report 1991*. New York: Oxford University Press, 1991.

UNESCO (United Nations Educational, Scientific and Cultural Organization), *The African Slave Trade from the Fifteenth to the Nineteenth Century*, Paris: UNESCO, 1979.

Unger, K., *Ausländerpolitik in der Bundesrepublik Deutschland*. Saarbrücken: Breitenbach, 1980.

UNHCR (United Nations High Commissioner for Refugees), *Collection of International Instruments Concerning Refugees*. Geneva: UNHCR, 1979.

UNHCR, *Conclusions on the International Protection of Refugees adopted by the Executive Committee on International Protection of Refugees of the UNHCR Programme*. Geneva: UNHCR, 1980.

UNHCR, *Refugees* (UNHCR Magazine), 1981.

UNHCR, *Refugees in Africa*. Geneva: Office of the United Nations High Commissioner for Refugees, 1966.

United Kingdom, Central Office of Information, *West Indies towards Victory*. London: HMSO, 1975.

United Kingdom, Central Statistical Office, *Social Trends*. London: HMSO, 1970.

United Kingdom, Central Statistical Office, *Social Trends*. London: HMSO, 1983.

United Kingdom, Colonial Office, Annual Report for Jamaica, 1946. London: HMSO, 1949.

United Kingdom, Department of Employment, *The Role of Migrants in the Labour Market*. London: HMSO, 1977.

United Kingdom, Department of the Environment, *Dwelling and Household Survey*. London: HMSO, 1978.

United Kingdom, OPCS (Office of Population Census Surveys), *International Migration, 1974*. London: HMSO, 1977.

United Kingdom, OPCS (Office of Population Census Surveys), *International Migration, 1976*. London: HMSO, 1979.

United Kingdom, OPCS (Office of Population Census Surveys), *Population Trends*. London: HMSO. (Quarterly Bulletin)

United Nations, Conference on Trade and Development (UNCTAD), *Trends and Current Situation in Reverse Transfer of Technology*. Geneva: UNCTAD, 13 July 1987.

United Nations, Department of International, Economic and Social Affairs, *International Migration Policies and Programmes: A World Survey*. New York: United Nations, 1982. (Population studies 80)

United Nations, Department of International, Economic and Social Affairs, *The Prospects of World Urbanization*. New York: United Nations, 1988.

United Nations, Department of International, Economic and Social Affairs, Statistical Office, *Consolidated Statistics of all International Arrivals and Departures: A Technical Report*. New York: United Nations, 1985.

United Nations-ESCAP, 'Comparative Study on Migration....', Vol. VI: Migration, Urbanization. SPC/ILO, 1982, Report of Meeting.

United Nations-ESCAP, *Expert Group Meeting on International Migration in Asia and the Pacific. Manila, 6-12 November 1984*. Bangkok: United Nations, 1985. (Asian Population Studies series 61)

United Nations-ESCAP, Report of Policy Workshop on International Migration in Asia and the Pacific, 15-21 October 1986.

United Nations-ESCAP, Report of the Expert Group Meeting on Remittances from International Labour Migration. Bangkok, 2-4 September 1985, p.11. (Mimeo)

United Nations, International Migration: Levels and Trends. Paper prepared for the Expert Group on Population Distribution, Migration and Development, Hammamet, Tunisia, March 1983. (Mimeo)

United Nations, Population Division, Department of Economic and Social Affairs, International Migration Policies and Programmes: The View Since Bucharest. Paper prepared for the Expert Group on Population Distribution, Migration and Development, Hammamet, Tunisia, March 1983. (Mimeo)

United Nations, Population Division, *Population Policy Digest: Indicators, Perceptions and Policies.* New York: United Nations, Economic Commission for Africa, 1981. (ESA/P/WP/74)

United Nations, Population Division, *World Migrant Populations: The Foreign-born,* New York: United Nations, 1989.

United Nations, *The Refugee Situation in Africa: Needs, Assistance, Measures Proposed.* International Conference on Assistance to Refugees in Africa. Geneva: United Nations, 1981.

United Nations, *Trends and Characteristics of International Migration since 1950.* New York: United Nations, 1974.

United Nations, *World Population Trends and Policies 1979.* New York: United Nations, 1980. (Monitoring report vol. 1)

United Nations, *World Population Trends and Policies, 1989 Monitoring Report.* New York: United Nations, 1990.

United States, Bureau of Public Affairs, Department of State, *Afghan Refugees in Pakistan.* Washington, DC, 1982.

United States, Bureau of Public Affairs, Department of State, *African Refugees.* Washington, DC, 1982.

United States, Bureau of Public Affairs, Department of State, *African Refugees.* Washington, DC, 1985.

United States, Bureau of Public Affairs, Department of State, *African Refugees.* Washington, DC, 1989.

United States, Bureau of the Census, *The Hispanic Population in the United States.* Series P-20, No.449. Washington, DC, 1990.

United States, Bureau of the Census, *We, the Asian and Pacific Islander Americans.* Washington, DC, 1990.

United States Catholic Conference, *Resource Bibliography: A Compilation of Resources and Program Materials.* Washington, DC: US Catholic Conference, Migration and Refugees Services, 1988.

United States, Commission on Civil Rights, *The Tarnished Golden Door: Civil Rights Issues in Immigration.* Washington, DC, September 1980.

United States, Committee for Refugees, *Cambodians in Thailand: People on the Edge.* Washington, DC, 1985.

United States, Committee for Refugees, *World Refugee Survey, 1991.* Washington, DC, 1991.

United States Comptroller General, *Prospects Dim for Effectively Enforcing Immigration Laws.* Report to the Congress of the United States. Washington, DC: General Accounting Office, 5 November 1980.

United States Congress, Afghanistan: Peace and Repatriation? Staff report prepared for the use of the Subcommittee on Immigration and Refugee Affairs on the Committee on the Judiciary, United States Senate, One Hundredth Congress. Washington, DC: Congressional Sales Office, US Government Printing Office, 1988.

United States Congress, House of Representatives, Committee on Foreign Affairs, Report of the Commission for the Study of International Migration and Cooperative Economic Development: *Hearing Before the Committee on Foreign Affairs, House of Representatives, One Hundred First Congress, Second Session, July 24, 1990.* Washington, DC: Congressional Sales Office, US Government Printing Office, 1990.

United States Congress, Immigration Reform and Control Act of 1982. Washington, DC: Ninety-seventh Congress, Second Session, 27 May 1982.

United States Congressional Research Service, *Temporary Workers Programs: Background and Issues.* Washington, DC: US Government Printing Office, 1980.

United States, Department of Agriculture, *Foreign Agriculture 1990-91.* Washington, DC, 1991.

United States, Department of Justice, Immigration and Naturalization Service, *1979 Statistical Yearbook.* Washington, DC: Department of Justice, 1980.

United States, Department of Justice, Labor and State, *Interagency Task Force on Immigration Policy: Staff Report.* Washington, DC: Department of Justice, Labor and State, 1979.

United States, Department of State, Bureau for Refugee Programs, *World Refugee Report*. Washington, DC, September 1990.

United States, Department of State, Bureau of Public Affairs, *Atlas of United States Foreign Relations*. Washington, DC, June 1983.

United States, General Accounting Office, *Illegal Aliens: Estimating their Impact on the US*. Washington, DC: 14 March 1980. (PAD-80-22)

United States, General Accounting Office, *Information on the Enforcement of Laws Regarding Employment of Aliens in Selected Countries*. Washington, DC: 1982. (GAO/GGD-82-86)

United States, INS (Immigration and Naturalization Service), *Annual Report*. Washington, DC: US Government Printing Office, 1978.

United States, INS, *Fact Book*. Washington, DC, 1990.

United States, INS, Tabulation of Immigrants Admitted by Country of Birth. Washington, DC: INS, 1981. (Unpublished)

Urrea Giraldo, Fernando, *Life Strategies and the Labor Market: Colombians in New York City in the 1970s*. New York: Center for Latin American Studies, New York University, 1982. (Occasional paper 36)

Usher, D., 'Public Property and the Effects of Migration upon Other Residents of the Migrants' Countries of Origin and Destination', *Journal of Political Economy* 85 (1977), pp.1001-20.

Van de Walle, F., 'Migration and Fertility in Ticino', *Population Studies* 29 (1975).

Vansina, Jan, *Paths in the Rainforests: Toward a History of Political Tradition in Equatorial Africa*. Madison: University of Wisconsin Press, 1990.

Verger, Pierre, *Trade Relations Between the Bight of Benin and Bahia from the Seventeenth to the Nineteenth Century*. Ibadan: Ibadan University Press, 1976.

Vernez, Georges, and Ronfeldt, David, 'The Current Situation in Mexican Immigration', *Science* (8 March 1991), pp.1189-1193.

Verstappen, B., ed. *Human Rights Reports: An Annotated Bibliography of Fact-finding Missions*. Oxford: Hans Zell Publishers (for the Netherlands Institute of Human Rights), 1987.

Vickery, Michael, *Kampuchean Politics, Economics and Society*. Boulder: Lynne Rienner, 1986.

Villamizar, R., 'Propuesta de estudio y análisis de migraciones de trabajadores entre Colombia y Venezuela', Migraciones laborales 3 (Bogotá, 1979).

Viviani, Nancy, *The Long Journey: Vietnamese Migration and Settlement in Australia*. Victoria: Melbourne University Press, 1984.

Von Bethlenfalvy, Peterson, ed. *Problems Arising from Migratory Movements of Refugees, Migrants and Ethnic Minorities*. Stuttgart: Doc-Lap-Centre, European Programme to Combat Poverty, 1987.

Wachter, M., 'Primary and Secondary Labor Markets: A Critique of the Dual Approach', *Brookings Institution Papers on Economic Activity* 3 (1974), pp.637-80.

Wainerman, C. and Recchini de Lattes, Z., *El trabajo femenino en el banquillo de los acusados*. Mexico City: The Population Council, 1981.

Waldinger, Roger, *Through the Eye of the Needle: Immigrants and Enterprise in New York's Garment Trades*. New York: New York University Press, 1986.

Wallerstein, Immanuel, *The Modern World System*. 2 vols. New York: Academic Press, 1974, 1980.

Walsh, A.C., *Some Questions of the Effects of Migration in the Pacific Islands*. Paper presented to the Conference on Consequences of Migration in Asia and the Pacific, Honolulu, 1981.

Watson, J.L., ed. *Between Two Cultures: Migrants and Minorities in Britain*. Oxford: Basil Blackwell, 1977.

Webster, D., 'Migrant Labour, Social Formations and the Proletarianization of the Chope of Southern Mozambique', In: W.M.J. van Binsbergen and H.A. Meilink, eds. *Migration and the Transformation of Modern African Society*. Leiden: African Perspectives, 1978.

Wedel, J., 'Social Security and Economic Integration, I: Freedom of Movement and the Social Protection of the Migrants', *International Labour Review* 102 (1970), pp.459-77.

Wedel, J., 'Sweden', In: R.E. Krane, ed. *International Labor Migration in Europe*, pp.19-44. New York: Praeger, 1979.

Weiner, M., 'International Migration and Development: Indians in the Persian Gulf', *Population and Development Review* 9 (1982), pp.1-36.

Weinstein, Brian, and Segal, Aaron, *Haiti The Failure of Politics*. New York: Praeger, 1992.

Weis, P., *Nationality and Statelessness in International Law*. Dordrecht: Kluwer, 1979.

Weische-Alexa, P., *Sozial-kulturelle Probleme Junger Türkinnen in der Bundesrepublik Deutschland.* Cologne: 1978.

Weital, D., Population Issues of the Federated States of Micronesia. Paper prepared for the Third Asian and Pacific Population Conference, Colombo, September 1982. (Mimeo)

Wells, Louis, Jr., *Third World Multinationals, The Rise of Foreign Investment in Developing Countries.* Cambridge, MA: Massachusetts Institute of Technology Press, 1983.

Werth, M. and Yalcintas, N., *Transferability of the Turkish Model of Return Migration and Self-help Organizations to Other Mediterranean Countries.* Geneva: ILO, International Migration for Employment Project, 1978. (Research working paper)

Whiteford, M.B., 'Women, Migration and Social Change: A Colombian Case Study', *International Migration Review* 12 (1978), pp.236-47.

Wiesner, Louis A., *Victims and Survivors: Displaced Persons and Other War Victims in Vietnam, 1954-1975.* Westport: Greenwood, 1988.

Williams, C.L., ed. *Annotated Bibliography on Refugee Mental Health.* Washington, DC: US Dept. of Health and Human Services, 1987.

Williams, Carolyn L., comp. *An Annotated Bibliography on Refugee Mental Health.* Rockville: US Department of Health and Human Services, Public Health Service, Alcohol, Drug Abuse, and Mental Health Administration, National Institute of Mental Health, 1987.

Williams, Carolyn and Westermayer, Joseph, eds. *Refugee Mental Health in Resettlement Countries.* Washington, DC: Hemisphere Publishing Corporation, 1986.

Williams, J.C., 'Lesotho: Economic Implications of Migrant Labour', *South African Journal of Economics* 39, no.2 (1971).

Wilpert, C., 'Acculturation in Urban Areas: Labour Migration and the Settlement of Turks in Berlin', In: D. Frick, et al., eds. *Urban Settings*, West Berlin: de Gruyter, 1986.

Wilpert, C., 'Bedeutung von Sozialer und Kultureller Identität für ausländische Frauen und Mädchen', In: U. Welzel, ed. *Situation der Ausländerin*, pp.84-101, Munich: Minerva, 1981.

Wilpert, C., *Die Zukunft der zweiten Generation-Erwartungen und Verhaltensmöglichkeiten ausländischer Kinder.* Königstein: Hain, 1980.

Wilpert, C., 'International Migration and Ethnic Minorities: New Fields for Post-war Sociology in the Federal Republic of Germany', *Current Sociology* 32 (1984), pp.305-52.

Wilpert, C., 'Minorities' Influence on the Majority: Reactions of the Majority in Political, Institutional and Social Scientific Spheres', In: C. Fried, ed. *Minorities, Community and Identity*, pp.177-90. West Berlin: Springer, 1983.

Wilpert, C., 'Wanderung und Zukunftsorientierung von Migrantenfamilien', In: C. Wilpert and M. Morokvasic, eds. *Bedingungen und Folgen internationaler Migration*, West Berlin: Technische Universität Berlin, 1983.

Wilson Center, *The Americas at the Crosswords: Report of the Inter-American Dialogue.* Washington, DC: The Wilson Center, 1984.

Wilson, F., International Migration in Southern Africa. Geneva: ILO, World Employment Programme, 1976. (Research working paper, mimeo)

Wilson, F., *Migrant Labour.* Johannesburg: South African Council of Churches, 1972.

Wilson, J.P., Internal Migration in the Gillbert and Ellice Island Colony. University of Canterbury, 1979. (MSc thesis)

Wilson, K.L. and Portes, A., 'Immigrant Enclaves: An Analysis of the Labor Market Experience of Cubans in Miami', *American Journal of Sociology* 86 (September 1980), pp.295-319.

Wilson, M., Migration, Employment and Development in the South Pacific. Country Statement - Solomon Islands. Paper presented to the ILO/SPC Conference on Migration, Employment and Development in the South Pacific, Noumea, 1982. (Mimeo)

Winter, R.P., 'Refugees in Uganda and Rwanda: The Banyarwanda Tragedy', *World Refugee Survey* (25th Anniversary Issue). New York: US Committee for Refugees, 1983.

Wold, H., 'Soft Modeling: The Basic Design, and Some Extensions', In: K.G. Joreskog and H. Wold, eds. *Systems Under Indirect Observation: Causality-Structure-Prediction.* Amsterdam: North Holland, 1981.

Wolf, Eric R., *Europe and the People without History.* Berkeley: University of California Press, 1962.

Wolff, P., *Entwicklungspolitische Instrumente zur Rückkehrforderung und Reintegration Türkischer Arbeitnehme.* West Berlin: DIE, 1982.

Wood, C.H., Equilibrium versus Historical-structural Perspectives on Migration: A Dialogue of the Deaf. Paper presented at the Conference on New Directions on Immigration and Ethnicity Research. Durham: Duke University Press, 1981.

Woods, A., 'Computer Simulation and Migration Planning', In: W.R. Böhning, ed. *Black Migration to South Africa*. Geneva: ILO, 1981.

World Bank, *Final Report of Research Project on Manpower and International Labour Migration in the Middle East and North Africa*. Washington, DC: World Bank, 1981.

World Bank (IBRD), *Migration from Botswana, Lesotho and Swaziland*. Washington, DC: IBRD, 1978.

World Bank, *World Development Report, 1991*. New York: Oxford University Press, 1991.

Yahil, Len, *The Holocaust, The Fate of European Jewry 1932-1945*. New York: Oxford University Press, 1990.

Yans-McLaughlin, Virginia, ed. *Immigration Reconsidered: History, Sociology and Politics*. New York: Oxford University Press, 1990.

Yardeni, Myriam, *Le refugee protestant*. Paris: Presses Universitaires, 1985.

Yasa, I., *Yurda Do'nen Isciler ve Toplumsal Degisme*. Ankara: TIDAIE Publications, 1978.

Yesufu, T.M., 'Loss of Trained Personnel by Migration from Nigeria', In: U.G. Damachi and V.P. Diejomoah, eds. *Human Resources and African Development*. New York: Praeger, 1978.

Young, K., 'Formas de apropriación y la división sexual del trabajo', In: A. Kuhn and A. Wolpe, eds. *Feminism and Materialism: Women and Modes of Production*. London: Routledge & Kegan Paul, 1978.

Zachariah, K.C. and Conde, J., *Migration in West Africa: Demographic Aspects*. A Joint World Bank-OECD Study. London: Oxford University Press, 1981.

Zarjevski, Yefime, *A Future Preserved: International Assistance to Refugees*. Oxford: Pergamon Press, 1988.

Zolberg, A.R., 'International Migration in Political Perspective', In: M.M. Kritz, et al., eds. *Global Trends in Migration*. New York: Center for Migration Studies, 1981.

Zolberg, Aristide R., Suhrke, Astri and Aguayo, Sergio, *Escape from Violence: the Refugee Crises in the Developing World*. Oxford: Oxford University Press, 1989.

Zucker, Norman and Zucker, Naomi, *The Guarded Gate: the Reality of American Refugee Policy*. San Diego: Harcourt Brace Jovanovich, 1987.

INDEX

Note: Page numbers in **bold** refer to maps.